THE SHRINES OF THE 'ALIDS IN MEDIEVAL SYRIA

Edinburgh Studies in Islamic Art
Series Editor: Professor Robert Hillenbrand
Advisory Editors: Bernard O'Kane and Jonathan M. Bloom

Titles include:

Isfahan and its Palaces: Statecraft, Shi'ism and the Architecture of Conviviality in Early Modern Iran
Sussan Babaie

Text and Image in Medieval Persian Art
Sheila S. Blair

The Minaret
Jonathan M. Bloom

The 'Wonders of Creation': A Study of the Ilkhanid 'London Qazwini'
Stefano Carboni

Islamic Chinoiserie: The Art of Mongol Iran
Yuka Kadoi

The Shrines of the 'Alids in Medieval Syria: Sunnis, Shi'is and the Architecture of Coexistence
Stephennie Mulder

'Amirid Artistic and Cultural Patronage in Al-Andalus
Mariam Rosser Owen

China's Early Mosques
Nancy Steinhardt

www.euppublishing.com/series/esii

THE SHRINES
OF THE ʿALIDS
IN MEDIEVAL
SYRIA

SUNNIS, SHIʿIS AND THE
ARCHITECTURE OF COEXISTENCE

STEPHENNIE MULDER

EDINBURGH
University Press

In memory of Obaida Habbal (1987–2013)

Edinburgh University Press is one of the leading university presses
in the UK. We publish academic books and journals in our selected
subject areas across the humanities and social sciences, combining
cutting-edge scholarship with high editorial and production values to
produce academic works of lasting importance. For more information
visit our website: edinburghuniversitypress.com

Edinburgh University Press Ltd
The Tun – Holyrood Road
12 (2f) Jackson's Entry
Edinburgh EH8 8PJ

First published in hardback by Edinburgh University Press 2014

This paperback edition 2019

Typeset in 10/12 pt Trump Medieval by
Servis Filmsetting Ltd, Stockport, Cheshire,
and printed and bound in Great Britain by Severn

A CIP record for this book is available from the British Library

ISBN 978 0 7486 4579 4 (hardback)
ISBN 978 1 4744 4633 4 (paperback)

Published in association with al-Sabah Collection, Dar al-Athar
al-Islamiyyah, Kuwait.

Contents

List of Figures and Maps		vi
Series Editor's Foreword		xi
Acknowledgements		xii
INTRODUCTION	'A Road for All Muslims'	I
CHAPTER 1	A *Mashhad* at Balis	18
CHAPTER 2	Aleppo: An Experiment in Islamic Ecumenism	63
CHAPTER 3	Eclectic Ecumenism: The Cemetery of Bab al-Saghir in Damascus	114
CHAPTER 4	Perpetual Patronage: Four Damascene 'Alid Shrines	186
CHAPTER 5	A Landscape of Deeds: 'Alid Shrines and the Construction of Islamic Sacred Topography	247
CONCLUSION	A Time of Miracles	267
Bibliography		275
Illustration Acknowledgements		286
Index		288

Figures and Maps

Figures

1.1	Balis *mashhad*, main *miḥrāb*	18
1.2	Modern graves near Balis *mashhad*	19
1.3	Traces of stucco decoration at the base of the *miḥrāb*	20
1.4	View from prayer hall northward	20
1.5	View south across central room	21
1.6	Ruins of the city of Balis, seen from Lake Assad	23
1.7	Ruins of the Byzantine *praetorium*	23
1.8	View south along eastern city wall of Balis, from within the *praetorium*	23
1.9	Plan, Emar and Balis	25
1.10	SS Sergius and Bacchus	26
1.11	Plan of excavations in 1996 and 1998	26
1.12	Minaret at Balis	29
1.13	Plan, Qasr	31
1.14	Stucco panels from Balis, National Museum of Damascus	32
1.15	View of cliffs near the *mashhad*	33
1.16	South-east corner of prayer hall prior to Syrian-Princeton excavations	34
1.17	Damascus Museum stucco panels, central *miḥrāb*	36
1.18	Plan of *mashhad* as partially excavated in 2006	40
1.19	View showing collapsed exterior wall at south-east corner	42
1.20	*Miḥrāb* niche cut into south wall of prayer hall, south-east corner	43
1.21	East-central room, view towards south	43
1.22	Hallway on north side of east-central room	44
1.23	View east over east-central room	44
1.24	Latrines, view looking south-west	45
1.25	North-east corner of north-east room showing earlier wall structures below floor	45
1.26	Central area (courtyard) looking south	46
1.27	View down into cistern	47

1.28   View southward across central area   47
1.29   Main entrance, view towards south   48
1.30   Oven installation east of the main entrance   48
1.31   Pit feature   49
1.32   Reused basalt block in western face of doorway   50
1.33   Fallen squinches in rubble of doorway   51
1.34a and 1.34b Details of main *miḥrāb*   53
1.35   Stucco fragments from Balis *mashhad*   54
2.1   Mashhad al-Muhassin, view of entrance portal and
       east wall   69
2.2   Aleppo, Mashhad al-Muhassin (Mashhad al-Dikka),
       plan   69
2.3   Mashhad al-Muhassin, tomb chamber   70
2.4   Aleppo, Mashhad al-Muhassin, portal   71
2.5   Aleppo, Mashhad al-Muhassin, portal, elevation and
       section   72
2.6   View upward into stone *muqarnas* dome over entrance   76
2.7   Mashhad al-Muhassin, view from the west   77
2.8   Mashhad al-Muhassin, south wall of courtyard   77
2.9   Inscription of al-Malik al-Zahir   78
2.10   Mashhad al-Muhassin, view east from under main
       dome of prayer hall   78
2.11   Mashhad al-Muhassin, north wall of courtyard   79
2.12   Mashhad al-Muhassin, inscription of al-ʿAziz   79
2.13   Aleppo, Mashhad al-Husayn, east façade   83
2.14   Aleppo, Mashhad al-Husayn, plan   84
2.15   Mashhad al-Husayn, exterior courtyard   85
2.16   Mashhad al-Husayn, main portal giving entrance to
       shrine area   86
2.17   Mashhad al-Husayn, interior courtyard, view towards
       western *iwān*   88
2.18   Portal of al-Husayn, elevation and section drawing   91
2.19   Mashhad al-Husayn, foundation inscription   92
2.20   Mashhad al-Husayn, view into main portal   93
2.21   Mashhad al-Husayn, detail, right lateral face of portal
       bay   94
2.22 and 2.23 Mashhad al-Husayn, details, forward face of
       portal bay   94
2.24   Mashhad al-Husayn, detail, forward face of portal bay   95
2.25   Mashhad al-Husayn, view upward into *muqarnas* dome   96
2.26   View of the Caliph al-Nasir li-Din Allah's inscription
       on the gate of the *serdab* (cave) of the shrine of Imam
       al-Mahdi   104
3.1   Mausoleum of Bilal al-Habashi, north elevation   119
3.2   Mausoleum of Bilal al-Habashi, plan   120
3.3   Herzfeld's drawing of the Ayyubid arch that once
       formed the entrance to the tomb of Bilal al-Habashi   121

3.4   Inscriptions for Ibn ʿAqil and al-Shahrazuri in south-east
      corner of the mausoleum of Bilal al-Habashi   122
3.5   Inscription for al-Shahrazuri   123
3.6   Mausoleum of Bilal al-Habashi, inscription at foot of
      his grave   124
3.7   Inscription on lintel of west-facing entrance to
      mausoleum of Bilal al-Habashi   126
3.8   Inscription in the name of ʿUthman Agha, over the
      west-facing entrance to the mausoleum of Bilal
      al-Habashi   127
3.9   Western elevation of mausoleum of Sukayna and Umm
      Kulthum and mausoleum of the Qalandariyya   130
3.10 Plan, upper level, mausoleum of Sukayna and Umm
      Kulthum and mausoleum of the Qalandariyya   131
3.11 Hallway in crypt of Sukayna and Umm Kulthum, view
      from stairway, facing east   134
3.12 Plan, crypt of Sukayna and Umm Kulthum   134
3.13 Doorway to crypt of Sukayna, as seen from the
      hallway, facing north   134
3.14 View of multiple phases of buttressing, looking out
      door towards hallway from inside crypt of Sukayna   135
3.15 *Mihrāb* in crypt of Umm Kulthum   135
3.16 Cenotaph of Sukayna   137
3.17 South-eastern corner of mausoleum of the
      Qalandariyya   142
3.18 Entrance to mausoleum of the Qalandariyya, with
      entrance to Sukayna and Umm Kulthum on right   143
3.19 Entrance to mausoleum of the Qalandariyya, with
      Baybars' inscription on the lintel   144
3.20 Detail, inscription of Baybars   144
3.21 Mausoleum of Fatima al-Sughra   147
3.22 Mausoleum of Fatima al-Sughra, plan of upper level   147
3.23 Mausoleum of Fatima al-Sughra, plan of crypt level   148
3.24 East and south faces of stone sarcophagus in
      mausoleum of Fatima al-Sughra   149
3.25 Distant view from the north-west, Masjid Maqam
      Ruʾus al-Shuhadaʾ Karbalaʾ   151
3.26 Masjid Maqam Ruʾus al-Shuhadaʾ Karbalaʾ, plan   152
3.27 Ottoman mausoleum in first courtyard of Masjid
      Maqam Ruʾus al-Shuhadaʾ Karbalaʾ   153
3.28 Maqam Ruʾus al-Shuhadaʾ Karbalaʾ, view from first
      courtyard into second courtyard   154
3.29 Well in south-east corner of second courtyard   154
3.30 Stone upright in north-east corner of second
      courtyard   155
3.31 Basalt basin under cupola at the centre of second
      courtyard   155

3.32   Pilgrim tying fabric to a metal pipe inside the basalt
        basin   156
3.33   Inscription over entrance to Ottoman shrine in
        first courtyard, Masjid Maqam Ruʾus al-Shuhadaʾ
        Karbalaʾ   157
3.34   Mausoleum of ʿAbdallah b. Zayn al-ʿAbidin   158
3.35   Plan, mausoleum of ʿAbdallah b. Zayn al-ʿAbidin   159
3.36   Dome of mausoleum of ʿAbdallah b. Zayn al-ʿAbidin   160
3.37   Palm tree motif in the spandrels of the interior
        arches   161
3.38   Foundation inscription, mausoleum of ʿAbdallah b.
        Zayn al-ʿAbidin   161
3.39   Exterior, mausoleum of Aban ibn Ruqayya   163
3.40   Plan, mausoleum of Aban ibn Ruqayya   164
3.41   Aban ibn Ruqayya, Ottoman-era painted dome with
        inscriptions praising four Sunni caliphs   164
3.42   Inscriptions praising al-Hasan and al-Husayn   165
3.43   Cenotaph, mausoleum of Aban ibn Ruqayya   166
3.44   Stela, mausoleum of Aban ibn Ruqayya   166
3.45   Mausoleum of Asmaʾ, Maymuna and Hamida   168
3.46   Plan, upper level, mausoleum of Asmaʾ, Maymuna
        and Hamida   169
3.47   Plan, crypt level, mausoleum of Asmaʾ, Maymuna
        and Hamida   169
3.48   Blind arches in north wall of crypt of mausoleum of
        Asmaʾ, Maymuna and Hamida   170
3.49   Crypt, staircase with uneven wall masonry and blind
        window-like structure on top left   171
3.50   Mausoleum of ʿAbdallah ibn Jaʿfar al-Sadiq   172
3.51   Plan, mausoleum of ʿAbdallah ibn Jaʿfar al-Sadiq   173
3.52   Modern inscription over entrance to mausoleum of
        ʿAbdallah ibn Jaʿfar al-Sadiq   173
3.53   Mausoleum of Sayyida Fidda   174
3.54   Plan, mausoleum of Sayyida Fidda   175
3.55   Stone upright to the right of the door of mausoleum
        of Sayyida Fidda   176
3.56   Inscription over door of mausoleum of Sayyida Fidda   176
4.1   Damascus, neo-Safavid dome of Mashhad Sayyida
        Ruqayya   189
4.2   Outside the western wall of the shrine of Sayyida
        Ruqayya in the evening   190
4.3   Portal and neo-Safavid dome of Mashhad Sayyida
        Ruqayya, as seen from surrounding streets   191
4.4   Interior of Mashhad Sayyida Ruqayya, showing tomb
        enclosure and mirror-mosaic dome   192
4.5   Portico in the courtyard of the Umayyad mosque   202
4.6   Transept of the prayer hall, Umayyad mosque   202

4.7   Shiʿi flagellants during Muharram procession, entering
       the shrine of al-Husayn and Zayn al-ʿAbidin, Umayyad
       mosque   202
4.8   Inscription over entrance to the shrine of al-Husayn
       and Zayn al-ʿAbidin, Umayyad mosque   203
4.9   Prayer hall, shrine of al-Husayn and Zayn al-ʿAbidin,
       Umayyad mosque   204
4.10   Second prayer hall, shrine of al-Husayn and Zayn
       al-ʿAbidin, Umayyad mosque   204
4.11   Ottoman-era enclosure for Zayn al-ʿAbidin   205
4.12   Child placing head into niche where head of al-Husayn
       rested   205
4.13   Dome of Mashhad al-Husayn, Umayyad mosque   206
4.14   Main shrine area and enclosure marking the place
       where al-Husayn's head rested   206
4.15   Plan, Umayyad mosque, with detail of north-east
       corner   211
4.16   View of eastern side of Umayyad mosque   212
4.17   Dome of Mashhad al-Husayn, centre right below wall   213
4.18   Platform outside the Bab Jayrun, Umayyad mosque,
       view towards the north   214
4.19   Mashhad of Sayyida Zaynab, Rawiya (Qabr al-Sitt),
       Damascus   228
4.20   Shrine of Sayyida Zaynab in 1955   236

Maps

1   Medieval pilgrimage places   24
2   Plan of Aleppo   64
3   Plan of Damascus   115
4   Damascus, plan of cemetery of Bab al-Saghir   116
5   The route of the head of al-Husayn   256
6   ʿAlid shrines still extant in the eastern Mediterranean   262

Series Editor's Foreword

'Edinburgh Studies in Islamic Art' is a new venture that offers readers easy access to the most up-to-date research across the whole range of Islamic art. Building on the long and distinguished tradition of Edinburgh University Press in publishing books on the Islamic world, it is intended to be a forum for studies that, while closely focused, also open wide horizons. Books in the series will, for example, concentrate in an accessible way on the art of a single century, dynasty or geographical area; on the meaning of works of art; on a given medium in a restricted time frame; or on analyses of key works in their wider contexts. A balance will be maintained as far as possible between successive titles, so that various parts of the Islamic world and various media and approaches are represented.

Books in the series are academic monographs of intellectual distinction that mark a significant advance in the field. While they are naturally aimed at an advanced and graduate academic audience, a complementary target readership is the worldwide community of specialists in Islamic art – professionals who work in universities, research institutes, auction houses and museums – as well as that elusive character, the interested general reader.

Professor Robert Hillenbrand

Acknowledgements

This book about pilgrims' shrines was itself a pilgrimage of sorts: from the dust of an archaeological site in Syria, to the ivy-covered halls of a university in Philadelphia, back through to Syria on the path of medieval pilgrims' routes and from there, onward to Turkey and Egypt. In the end, it landed its author deep in the heart of Texas. In Philadelphia, at the University of Pennsylvania, I was a student of Professor Renata Holod. Her time was always mine for the asking, her energy near-legendary and her ability to transform my thinking – whether in conversations lasting many hours, or in a single, rousing line barked out in capital letters via email – have been a profound source of inspiration and a key force shaping my scholarship. My thinking was further formed and annealed over many years through gentlemanly, yet persistent challenges from Professor Oleg Grabar, with whom I first studied as an MA student. His passing left a hollow place in many hearts. The memory of his ideas and his words will forever serve as intermediary between the scholar I am, and the one I wish to become. I also owe a debt to Professor Thomas Leisten, who first brought me to Syria over ten years ago and convinced me that I'd be just the right person to catalogue his tens of thousands of potsherds from Balis, and who then opened up a world to me: that of Syria in the Ayyubid era. Here, I must thank him specifically for copies of plans and unpublished papers he generously shared. And finally, a thank you is reserved for Professor Robert Ousterhout. My thinking about the era of the Crusades in Syria, and in particular its remarkable architectural legacy, would be immensely poorer without his careful eye and liberality with both time and source material.

This research was funded by a generous fellowship from the Louis J. Kolb Foundation at the University of Pennsylvania Museum of Archaeology and Anthropology. My membership of this remarkable scholarly society allowed me the privilege to study and research full time and to fulfil multifarious aspects of my project unencumbered by financial hardship. Some years later, a Fulbright grant allowed me freedom to explore shrines in locations as central as Damascus and Cairo and as far-flung as eastern Turkey and north-eastern Syria.

Later, at the University of Texas, several grants, including the John
D. Murchison Fellowship in the Fine Arts from the Department
of Art and Art History and a College Research Fellowship from
the Department of Middle Eastern Studies, gave me the time and
leisure to transform the dissertation into a book. The book owes its
index, maps and photographs to the generosity of President William
Powers, who awarded me a University of Texas Co-op Subvention
grant.

A number of institutions and people in Syria were a tremendous
aid to the realisation of my project. These include the Department
of Islamic Waqfs, Damascus, the Ottoman Court Archives (*Markaz
al-wathāʾiq al-tarikhīyya*), the Institut Français d'Études Arabes de
Damas (French Institute), the National Museum of Damascus and
the Asad Library, Damascus. In my sojourns in these places I met
figures like the inimitable historian Dr Akram Hasan al-ʿUlabi, who
spent days poring over Ottoman legal documents with me, copying
long passages by hand and appearing each morning with a handful
of footnotes for me to chase down. The Syrian Deputy Minister of
Culture Dr ʿAbd al-Razzaq Moaz was always ready with a name,
a source to check or a wry comment on the state of American
academia. And though our acquaintance was brief, the overseer of
the ʿAlid shrines in the cemetery of Damascus, Mr Waʾel Murtada,
generously allowed me access to the shrines under his charge as well
as consenting to be interviewed about the history of the Murtada
family on more than one occasion. Lastly, I wish it were possible
to offer more than a collective thanks to the people of Syria, who,
whether in the cafés of Damascus or the mud brick villages of the
Jazira, have for over a decade have welcomed me into their homes
and their hearts and made my work in their country such a pleasure.
I dream, with them, of a better Syria.

A group of friends and colleagues offered support with sources, references and translations and I regret I must be so brief: they include
Professor Samer Ali, Professor Abraham Marcus and Dr Kristen
Brustad. In particular I thank Dr Yasser Tabbaa for giving me a copy
of his then-forthcoming article in *Artibus Asiae*, and archaeologist
David Lineberry for going above and beyond my call for a summary
of his excavation notes by providing complete photocopies of all
materials. Thoughts on translation and transliteration were provided
by my dear friend and colleague Yumna Masarwa, who will always
be normal. Further assistance was provided by Melanie Magidow.
Daniella Talmon-Heller has long been an inspiration as a scholar
and as a friend who seems to do it all, and over the years has granted
me a well of advice, sources, footnotes and copies of published and
forthcoming works without hesitation. I would never have been able
to complete my architectural drawings without the talents of Milena
Hijazi and Irina Rivero. To all of these I extend my gratitude.

Lastly, I am deeply grateful to many friends and family, too numerous to list, who have sometimes shared, sometimes been mystified by, my intellectual pursuits. Susanna McFadden, Glenn Peers, Julia Mickenberg, Emily Smith and my parents, Stephen and Faye Fullmer and Helen Mulder, are among them. Whether enthusiastically joining in my Gertrude Bell dreams or just plain baffled by why I want to muck around in the dust on the other side of the planet, they have been there for me, and I thank them. But for those who know me best, I must reserve my deepest thanks. Thank you, Dika, for truly seeing me, and in doing so, helping me to see myself. And thank you Naomi, Daniela and Alma, for being the best travelling companions a girl could ask for, and for reminding me of what, really, the point of it all is.

INTRODUCTION

'A Road for All Muslims'

IT WAS DAMASCUS, around the year AD 1238, and a bitter controversy had erupted between Sunnis and Shiʿis over the shrine of
a saintly figure – a certain Malika, said to be a descendant of the
Prophet Muhammad – located at the gate of Bab Jayrun. Apparently,
like many holy places in this period, the shrine had been 'rediscovered' by someone who had a vision in which he learned this was
the long-lost site of her grave.[1] In an outpouring of devotion, the
Shiʿi inhabitants of the city began enthusiastically to build a shrine
to commemorate the holy figure. The shrine quickly outgrew the
narrow space afforded by the passageway of the gate. Nevertheless,
a decision was made to block the gate and continue with construction. Not everyone was so enamoured of the plan, though. The
contemporary Sunni historian Abu Shama (d. 1268), for example,
was furious:

> (This gate was) a road, which was already too narrow for its
> traveller! (Now,) the narrowness and tightness has been multi-
> plied on those who come and go. May God multiply (instead)
> the punishment of (the Shiʿis) and enumerate the recompense
> of those who aid in (the shrine's) destruction and the removal of
> this hazard, following the Sunna of the Prophet in destroying the
> Masjid al-Dirar, erected by the infidels for his enemies![2]

This was indeed a harsh chastisement.[3] The Masjid al-Dirar was a
pseudo-mosque built by the Prophet's enemies to deceive the early
Muslims. The Prophet had ordered its destruction personally.[4] To
compare the shrine at the Bab Jayrun with the Masjid al-Dirar was
to utterly deny its legitimacy and to equate the actions of the Shiʿis
with those of the enemies of Islam. But despite such protestations,
the shrine persisted in one form or another for several centuries,
and even the Mamluk Sultan al-Ashraf Qaytbay's (r. 1468–96) direct
intervention could not deter attempts to eliminate it. Attempting
to resolve the dispute, which was apparently still ongoing by the
mid-sixteenth century, the Sunni historian Muhammad Ibn Tulun
(d. 1546) did not mince words:

The Shiʿis (al-ṭāʾifa al-rāfiḍa) and those ignoramuses who follow them, may God punish them many times over, allege it (is her burial place). That is one of the greatest lies. It is a road, for (all) Muslims! Nobody who possesses even a tiny bit of intelligence and faith doubts it. I replied . . . so that the truth may be known about that and so the words of every misguided and damned person (who comes along) is not adhered to . . .[5]

And yet, despite Ibn Tulun's outrage, the shrine, with its apparently specious origins, continued to be venerated for some time thereafter. That it was suggests that it was not only the city's small Shiʿi minority who supported its perpetuation, for Damascus was, and remains, a strongly Sunni city.

This study explores the unspoken subtext woven deeply within the supporting structure of the preceding story. Namely, it argues that throughout Islamic history, but particularly in the period between the eleventh and the thirteenth centuries in Syria, the shrines of the ʿAlids – the descendants of the Prophet Muhammad through his cousin and son-in-law ʿAli – repeatedly became objects of patronage by both Sunni and Shiʿi elites, and that this process created a newly unifying, and distinctly Islamic, sacred landscape. In each case, shrines that have been perceived or assumed to be primarily 'Shiʿi' spaces turn out to have been founded, or later reconfigured, by Sunni elite figures to be shared, pan-Islamic and inclusive. To that end, what is striking about the story of the shrine at Bab Jayrun is not the expectedness of such disputes among Sunnis and Shiʿis, but rather that it is a notably unusual story: in fact, it is a rare example of open controversy between Sunnis and Shiʿis regarding the burial place of a member of the ahl al-bayt, or Family of the Prophet. Although sectarian controversies around the shrines did occur – and some are hinted at by various indications of scepticism given by the medieval authors who list the shrines – the most salient attribute of the medieval Islamic cult of saints is not its controversial nature, but its remarkably ecumenical one. Furthermore, expressions of scepticism recorded by some medieval authors are probably reflective more of differences between the learned classes (ʿulamāʾ), who form the majority of the authors of our textual sources (and who would have been far more cautious in according authenticity to sites) – and ordinary people, who generally lacked the ability to verify their authenticity or were uninterested in doing so. Only infrequently do such controversies take on a sectarian character. And when they do, it is often tied to some other issue and only subsequently cast in sectarian terms: as was the case with the shrine at Bab Jayrun, which, like many other shrines that arose in this period, may perhaps have escaped controversy altogether had it not blocked a vital route through the city.[6] Indeed, expressions of caution about the authenticity of some locales in our sources are probably to be read as evidence of how beloved and heavily visited such sites were in actual practice, for if they were not, there would be no need for the learned to caution against their 'erroneous' visitation. In large part, shared reverence for the shrines of the ʿAlids seems to have been a point of commonality between medieval Muslims that has few parallels elsewhere in Islamic social and sectarian history.

This non-sectarian veneration of the ʿAlids was present from at least the ninth century,[7] but it became a major phenomenon at a time of great religious excitement in the Islamic lands: a period spanning the eleventh to thirteenth centuries AD and encompassing the dynasties of the Seljuks, Zangids, Ayyubids and Mamluks in Syria. 'Syria' is here conceived as the Islamic geographers conceived it: referred to by them as 'Bilad al-Sham', it included roughly the area from the Euphrates in the north and east to the Mediterranean in the west and the deserts that today mark the border with Jordan (or Saudi Arabia) in the south: the geographical area that is sometimes called the Levant. Thus, medieval al-Sham was a contiguous geographical entity that included the modern states of Syria, Lebanon, Palestine and Israel. For the sake of clarity and because the term is more well-known, this book uses 'Syria' instead of al-Sham, however the term is used with the caveat that it is the greater geographic designation that is meant.

Shrine visitation in this era was widely practised across all elements of medieval Islamic society, and the frequent performance of devotional activities was central to pious, religious and social interaction in the medieval Islamic lands.[8] Despite some sanctions against shrine visitation in the Mamluk era (which nevertheless appear to have been widely disregarded), there is no evidence that this was an issue of real concern in Seljuk and Ayyubid times.[9] Furthermore, this religious climate was one in which several streams of official and popular religious revivalism, reactionism and renewal converged: the Crusades motivated claims for the resacralisation of the land for Islam,[10] a movement for the revival of Sunnism (ihyāʾ al-sunna) begun under the Seljuks provoked an awareness of sectarian issues and a popular atmosphere of religious excitement that was the defining characteristic of the period, and the political claims of new, unstable and competing regimes in need of social and political legitimisation facilitated a commitment to pious architectural construction on the official level in Syria that was often elicited, mirrored and/or imitated by ordinary citizens. This was an era of great religious effervescence, in which hundreds of new religious buildings of all stripes were founded and endowed, and in which it was perfectly ordinary for large crowds to stay the night in mosques in anticipation of seeing a particularly beloved preacher.[11]

On the popular level, this excitement played a crucial role in the generation of a new landscape of sacred sites throughout Syria, for in these three centuries hundreds of new shrines were rediscovered, constructed and venerated. The broader geographic designation discussed above is important because it is precisely in this period, against the backdrop of these social and political events, that Syria's holiness was consciously and systematically inscribed upon the land, and that the boundaries of that landscape were defined. Along with the patronage of hundreds of new mosques, *madrasa*s and *khanqa*s (Sufi lodges) by the elite, the main engine for the generation of this landscape was the rediscovery and resanctification of sites of pilgrimage, in large part by ordinary people, and devoted to a truly astonishing number of holy figures. And accompanying their rediscovery was the invention or expansion of a literature to describe, categorise, hierarchise and commemorate the holy sites. That literature consisted of local chronicles, biographical dictionaries, historical topographies, pilgrimage guides and *fadāʾil* treatises (works on the merits of a locality), among others. Syria, land of the ancient monotheistic prophets, home of the sacred city of Jerusalem, had always been considered by Muslims to be a 'holy land' but, as recent research by Zayde Antrim has shown, this definition was not fixed, and it evolved over time and in response to the changing political mandate of the various ruling powers. According to Antrim,

> in the 6th/12th and 7th/13th centuries representations of the cities of Jerusalem and Damascus, and later Aleppo, proliferated. These city-centric representations gradually gave way to representations of Syria as a coherent region by the late 7th/13th century. In the first half of the 8th/14th century, however, representations of the Mamluk Empire as a revived Dar al-Islam, or 'Abode of Islam', within which the region of Syria was subsumed, began to dominate the discourse of place . . . These shifts in discourse paralleled the political history of the period.[12]

Thus, in the Zangid period, representations were city-centric; in the Nurid and Ayyubid period, they became somewhat broader for all Syria; and in the Mamluk period they included Syria, Egypt and the Jazira (Mesopotamia). Antrim's analysis focuses largely on the impetus for political legitimisation provided by this body of literature, but she also notes there were other factors that may have led ordinary people, as well, to throw themselves, their wealth and sometimes the work of their own hands into the building and establishment of this landscape. One of these, as noted above and examined in Chapter 5, may have been a newly urgent sense of the land as holy, brought about by the incursion of Crusader forces at the end of the eleventh century, which perhaps fuelled a desire to 'claim the land for Islam' – or perhaps simply generated a heightened awareness of, and sensitivity to, the holiness of the local geography.[13] Furthermore, the Crusades spelled the downfall of many formerly revered sites, as it was common practice to pillage the holy places of the Muslims and vice versa during the siege of a city, as happened, for example, to the shrines of al-Husayn and al-Muhassin in Aleppo.[14] Thus, the destruction of many shrines during this period led logically to their re-establishment and renewal, and this, too, may have generated an atmosphere of heightened devotion to such locales. In addition to spurring renovations, such acts of desecration may perhaps also have served as inspiration for the generation of new shrines. Similarly, as noted previously, the movement for the revivification of Sunnism, and also the growth and spread of Sufism, probably also contributed to a frame of mind in which the rediscovery of sites of pilgrimage was considered an appropriate and praiseworthy activity.

It is not the ambition of the present work to carefully catalogue the creation and establishment of the whole of this landscape with its many diverse shrines and holy places, for a series of studies over the past few decades have begun to tackle this project admirably.[15] Instead, the contribution I hope to make is twofold: first, to delineate the medieval history and architectural evolution of one subset of the buildings within that landscape: the shrines of the ʿAlids in Syria. These shrines, with their distinctly Islamic character and their broad appeal to Muslims across sectarian divisions, were some of the most intensively patronised and visited of all the sites employed in the generation of that medieval landscape. Nevertheless, it is only recently that the shrines of the ʿAlids have begun to attract scholarly attention, and many aspects of their histories, foundation and evolution are, as yet, unknown. Most sites have not received even the most basic study of their architectural and patronage histories. Thus, on the simplest level, there is a need for a comprehensive reconstruction of the medieval textual, architectural and archaeological histories of these shrines, and this has been an important goal of the research here.

An important secondary theme developed here is the question of how the patronage and survival of these shrines from the Seljuk to the Mamluk eras subverts, nuances and enriches many of the assumptions surrounding a dominant paradigm in Islamic historiography: that of the Sunni Revival. The Sunni Revival, a concept derived from the Arabic *iḥyāʾ al-sunna* (meaning 'revivification of the Sunna [tradition] of the Prophet Muhammad'), is a term often used to characterise the era from the eleventh to the thirteenth centuries, during which the Seljuk sultans and their ideological successors in Syria and Egypt, the Zangid and Ayyubids, actively sought to eliminate the Shiʿi dynasty of the Fatimids, who had ruled the Maghreb, Egypt, Syria and the Hijaz (the region including the holy cities of Mecca and Medina in Arabia) from the tenth to the late twelfth centuries. The Revival was also directed against the suzerainty of Twelver Shiʿi Buyid amirs over the Sunni ʿAbbasid caliph in Baghdad between the early tenth and the mid-eleventh centuries, and the perceived threat of more heterodox Shiʿi groups such as the

Zaydis and the Nusayris (collectively known in the sources as the *ghulāṭ*), who had grown in real or alleged strength in this period.[16] Indeed, the perceived influence of Shiʿism was so strong during the tenth century that it has famously been called the 'Shiʿi century', for in those days, it seemed as though the Islamic world might well tilt towards adoption of this now-minority sect.[17]

This did not happen, in part because of an ideological counter-trend that prevailed after the Sunni Seljuk viziers overthrew the Shiʿi dynasty of the Buyid amirs in 1055 and installed themselves as temporal rulers of the Islamic lands, under the spiritual sovereignty of the ʿAbbasid caliph. The Seljuks styled themselves overtly as the restorers of Sunnism, and as they extended political control over formerly Shiʿi lands, they and their successors the Zangids and Ayyubids also propagated *ihyāʾ al-sunna*, the reinvigoration of Sunnism. To this end, the Seljuks and their successors actively sponsored a renaissance in Sunni theology and jurisprudence that was disseminated and reinforced via their support and patronage of various Sunni institutions, in particular *madrasa*s, or schools for the teaching of Islamic law and theology. The Revival's sweetest moment of political victory was reserved for the Ayyubid Sultan Saladin, who overthrew the last Shiʿi Fatimid caliph in 1171. Some scholars have argued that for the arts, the implications of this movement may have been far-reaching: one recent work maintains that the Revival was 'the primary motivating force behind many of the cultural and artistic changes of the eleventh and twelfth centuries'.[18]

On the other hand, shrines, and commemorative architecture generally, have their own place in the historiography of Islamic lands. Indeed, much of the debate surrounding their initial appearance and, later, their proliferation in the medieval period has been tied to the assumption that in its earliest years Sunni Islam abjured the pre-Islamic practice of raising tombs over the graves of the dead, preferring a simple burial and the *taswiyat al-qubūr*, or 'levelling of the graves' to the ground.[19] Later, scholars have argued, it was only with the appearance of Shiʿi devotional practice, which in the eleventh century began to be sponsored, supported and propagated by the Shiʿi dynasty of the Fatimids, that shrine building and visitation re-emerged as a normative Islamic practice. According to this argument, the veneration of the dead was always suspect in Sunni circles, generally frowned upon by Islamic theologians and practised largely by those on the periphery of mainstream, 'orthodox' Sunnism, those perhaps denied access to the traditional means of religious participation: women, for example, or religious minorities such as the Shiʿis.

This research arose out of my initial puzzlement that the shrines of the ʿAlids did not seem to conform to any of these historiographical paradigms. First of all, it quickly became apparent that these 'Shiʿi' shrines had been built, maintained and perpetuated in large part by elite Sunnis. In fact, after carrying out a survey of some forty shrines following the itinerary of the medieval pilgrimage guide author ʿAli al-Harawi through Syria, Egypt, Turkey and Lebanon, it was clear that nearly all of them had, at some point in their evolution, benefited from the patronage of Sunnis, and some were entirely the result of Sunni intervention. Furthermore, as noted above, the peak of this flurry of shrine rediscovery, renewal and perpetuation occurred precisely in the period that was ostensibly most antagonistic to Shiʿi practice: the eleventh to thirteenth centuries, under the Seljuks and Ayyubids. Thus, they were clearly venerated, visited and sometimes patronised by both Shiʿis and Sunnis throughout their history, and it could hardly be said that they were exclusively 'Shiʿi' spaces in any unambiguous, clearly definable way. The 'Shiʿi-centric' theory of the development of shrine veneration has been challenged recently by several scholars, who have argued that reverence for the graves of holy figures was a feature of the earliest Islamic practitioners – both Sunni and Shiʿi – and that until the Mamluk period (in the thirteenth century), there was no real objection to the practice, to which a wide swath of Muslims was devoted across time, geography, and social and sectarian barriers. Moreover the practice remained an integral, even an essential, part of Islamic piety even after some challenges to it were raised in the thirteenth century.[20]

And yet, despite the apparently widespread practice of Sunni shrine veneration, there were clear differences between how Sunnis and Shiʿis approached devotional action and the emphasis it received in ritual and pious practice. For Shiʿis, the centrality of devotion to the Family of the Prophet meant that the shrines of the ʿAlids, and visitation of other holy sites, played an especially meaningful role within Shiʿi devotional life, and within Shiʿi piety more broadly. Thus, the patronage and propagation of the ʿAlid shrines had a far greater influence on the development of Shiʿi ritual and practice than it had on similar practices within Sunnism. While Sunnis revere sites devoted to the Prophet's family, and their visitation has traditionally been considered a meritorious activity, such visitation was only one aspect of a wide range of pious activities prescribed by Sunni piety. In contrast, for the Shiʿis, the performance of acts of visitation (ziyārāt) to the holy Family of the Prophet, and activities carried out in their vicinity such as repentance, requests for intervention (shafāʿa) or the renewal of vows to the Shiʿi Imams – all of whom are descendants of the Prophet – have an absolutely central role in religious and theological experience, without which much other spiritual activity is rendered hollow. This is because the Prophet's family played an essential role in the creation of the Shiʿi sense of self, dependent in large part on the generation over many centuries of a narrative of persecution and suffering under unjust rulers, a narrative initiated at the Battle of Karbalaʾ in Muharram 680, when hopes for the rightful succession to the Caliphate were dashed with the brutal murder and decapitation of ʿAli's son al-Husayn by the Sunni Umayyad caliph.

Ever after, reverence for the descendants of the Prophet and a desire for empathetic remembrance of their tragic fate have formed a fundamental aspect of Shiʿi identity and religious practice. Thus, while it could be said that both Sunnis and Shiʿis revere the *ahl al-bayt*, it cannot not also be said that reverence for the Prophet's family played an equal role in the religious ritual, history or self-imagination of the two sects.

A central concern, then, is how might we characterise these shrines as distinct architectural spaces created out of this complex, polyvalent and sometimes conflicting web of religious associations and piety? Here, I propose that in medieval Syria, ʿAlid devotional space was often reframed and experienced as shared, pan-Islamic and inclusive. At times this reconfiguration occurred for reasons of personal devotion or piety; at other times it was part of a political bid to gain influence over Shiʿi communities or part of a larger social policy of reconciliation between Sunnis and Shiʿis. These acts took place within an environment of intensive sanctification and renewal of the Islamic holy landscape, a trend that peaked between the eleventh and thirteenth centuries. This environment fostered the discovery of new shrines; a revived interest in shrine construction; and a newly ecumenical approach to the commemoration of holy figures, Sunni and Shiʿi alike. In the end, this Sunni investment in ʿAlid places of pilgrimage created a new type of polyvalent devotional space: space that meant multiple things to varied groups of devotees; space that served as nodes of interaction between factions often depicted in opposing terms. Thus, behind the political rhetoric of Sunni ascendancy, a complex and fluid interconfessional negotiation often took place. The history of these shrines allows for a more nuanced interpretation of the relationship between Sunnis and Shiʿis in the medieval period, and furthermore, the mapping of such sites reveals how material and devotional culture may often illuminate the disjuncture between official rhetoric and religious or social praxis.

Methodology

All of this interest and devotion naturally resulted in buildings with very complex architectural histories, and a major preoccupation of this study has been to develop a method of studying buildings that do not conform to the traditional template of medieval structures preserved largely intact.[21] Indeed, perhaps no form of architecture is more difficult to study than shrines. This is because they are truly living buildings: passionately beloved by devotees, visited unceasingly by pilgrims, their enormous popular appeal was constantly exploited through acts of patronage designed to express everything from the most high-minded piety to the basest of politics. In fact, shrines for such holy figures are arguably the most commonly built and rebuilt form of architecture in Islam. This pattern of continuous rebuilding presents a significant methodological problem. To meet this challenge, a wide variety of methodologies have been employed in this study, including textual investigation of the medieval Arabic sources, newly executed architectural studies and surveys, archaeological excavation, examination of epigraphy and the interpretation of inscriptions, analysis of the spatial relationships within and between buildings, and survey and mapping using GIS technology.

The fieldwork for this project was carried out in 2004 and 2005 in Syria, Egypt and south-eastern Turkey. The initial focus was to ascertain how many ʿAlid shrines mentioned by medieval authors were still extant, and in what condition they survived. It included an architectural survey of some forty shrines in Syria, Egypt and south-eastern Turkey, and produced measured architectural drawings of fourteen previously unrecorded mausolea, as well as documentary research in the Maktabat al-Assad (Assad Library) and the Markaz al-Wathaʾiq al-Tarikhiyya (Ottoman court archives) in Damascus. In addition, fieldwork included the archaeological investigation of an eleventh-century ʿAlid shrine at Balis carried out in 2005. Balis was a medieval city located on the Euphrates in northern Syria, and I have worked at the site for over a decade, with Thomas Leisten of Princeton University. Thus, primarily in response to the complexity of studying buildings that are in a constantly evolving state of being, the study embraces a variety of methods and sources to draw its conclusions, and intentionally blurs and crosses the boundaries of disciplines ranging from social history, art and architectural history, epigraphy and archaeology. In its final chapter, the study borrows from recent approaches in anthropology and the rapidly evolving field of archaeological ritual and landscape studies to move from the empirical and particular to the more general and conceptual, in order to say something meaningful about the place of Islamic landscape within a variety of late Antique and medieval landscape traditions.

Chapter outline

This study thus has two loosely defined parts, a larger and more empirical one (Chapters 1–4), focused both on the histories of individual ʿAlid shrines and on the implications of those histories for their contemporary social and sectarian context, and a more conceptual one (Chapter 5) that aims to derive broader meaning from the conclusions laid out in the first section. The more empirical part of the study catalogues, describes and traces the histories of the most important ʿAlid shrines and demonstrates the connection between architectural patronage and sectarian relations in the medieval period, while the more conceptual chapter takes these conclusions about the social history of medieval Islamic saint veneration and places them in the land: arguing for the shrines' role in the development of a new, and specifically Islamic, sacred landscape in the

eleventh to thirteenth centuries. As a result, this study aims for a
fine-grained textual, architectural and archaeological examination
of individual shrines, their materiality and their social and sectarian histories, and at the same time, places them within a broader
interpretive model whose purpose is to map and contextualise the
wider landscape of ʿAlid holy sites. In this, I follow the model of
recent scholarship that embraces the value of engaging both emic
and etic categories of interpretation, and enter into a dialogue about
historiography and methods of interpretation that has already begun
in the field of Islamic art.[22] In the final chapter, I bring an interpretive model that is in line with recent trends in archaeological and
landscape theory to bear on Islamic material culture. An approach
that simultaneously utilises these varied means and methods has
the advantage of allowing for the fullest possible picture of an
exceedingly complex and elusive phenomenon. Along the way, the
richness of these shrines' sectarian histories becomes apparent,
for the patronage and architecture of these ostensibly Shiʿi sites is
consistently revealed to have been a distinctly intersectarian social
practice, and one that enabled the Islamisation of a land long held
holy by believers of many faiths.

Chapter 1 begins with literally the most fine-grained of these
methodologies, archaeology: in the dirt of Balis, once a medium-
sized town on the river Euphrates in northern Syria. Balis was a town
that was occupied for millennia until its inhabitants fled, and never
returned, in advance of the Mongol incursion in the mid-thirteenth
century. This chapter explores an Islamic shrine excavated under
the direction of Thomas Leisten of Princeton University. The shrine
consists of a small, multi-room building with a prayer hall and a columned central space. High on a hill overlooking the city, it is among
the few extant examples of the many ʿAlid shrines that once existed
at Balis, the others having been lost in the 1970s when water rising
behind a dam on the Euphrates created the reservoir now called Lake
Assad, an event that inundated nearly the entire area of Balis. The
shrine was probably founded some time in the eleventh century, but
its archaeological record reveals that like the many other shrines
to be presented here, it was repeatedly renovated, enlarged and
expanded over the course of its 200-year history. In this sense, the
shrine at Balis can be seen as a model for many other sites in this
study, for the pattern of patronage it established is replicated at virtually all ʿAlid shrines. Indeed, although Balis was a majority Shiʿi
city in this epoch and the shrine would thus seem more likely to be
the outcome of Shiʿi patronage, this holy site, like so many others
we will survey here, was probably founded by a Sunni. The shrine at
Balis is thus a kind of microcosm for patterns of patronage and social
interaction at other sites within the wider landscape.

In Chapter 2, we move approximately 90km west of Balis, to the
great mercantile city of Aleppo. Aleppo, unlike Balis, was a major

regional capital, but it, too, was largely Shiʿi in the medieval period. Medieval authors report that even as late as the rule of the Ayyubid Sultan al-Malik al-Zahir (r. 1186–1216), the city had a substantial Shiʿi population, if not a majority. The two ʿAlid shrines examined in this chapter, the Mashhads al-Muhassin and al-Husayn, were initially founded by Shiʿis, but they were perpetuated and maintained in later years by some prominent Sunnis, among them Nur al-Din, founder of the Zangid dynasty, and Salah al-Din (Saladin), the Ayyubid sultan credited with the elimination of Shiʿism from the Islamic lands. How and why these Sunni rulers patronised these buildings reveals much about the complex interaction between accommodation and appropriation that is a little-known hallmark of the era of Sunni Revival and its alternately censorious and ecumenical attitude toward Shiʿism. Indeed, so appealing was this policy of accommodation or appropriation that the Sunni ʿAbbasid caliph himself, al-Nasir li-Din Allah (r. 1180–1225), also adopted it when he too made significant contributions to the upkeep of several Iraqi ʿAlid shrines.

In Chapter 3 we move southwards to Damascus, where the consistently Sunni orientation of the city created rather a different dynamic. But despite the city's Sunni allegiance, Damascus was nevertheless a critical site for the performance of Shiʿi devotional activity, for it housed the remains of many of the martyrs of the battle of Karbalaʾ, as well as shrines for the head of al-Husayn, and the fourth Shiʿi Imam Zayn al-ʿAbidin. They were brought to Damascus along with their female family members because at the time of the battle, the city was the capital of the Umayyad Caliphate. And yet, as the sources attest, these shrines were extremely popular among Sunnis as well. In fact, with one exception, their founding and preservation, as far as can be ascertained, is due almost entirely to the generosity of Sunni figures. Chapter 3 situates itself in the locale with the greatest concentration of ʿAlid shrines in Damascus: the cemetery of Bab al-Saghir, located at the south-west corner of the city wall and in use since early Islamic times. This chapter attempts to reconstruct systematically the architectural and patronage histories of some ten ʿAlid shrines located there. But here, a pattern of constant devotion and intervention, along with the antiquity of the locale, has taken its toll on our ability to visualise the original buildings. This is made more difficult by the fact that, aside from their inscriptions, these buildings had never previously been studied: no plans or elevations and only very few photographs had ever been made. With the aid of newly surveyed architectural drawings carried out for this project, however, and comparing the evidence provided by the Arabic sources, intact epigraphic evidence, and the spatial relationships between and within buildings, this chapter argues that these shrines' unusual plans reveal traces of – or in fact are themselves – the original buildings dating to the medieval period. In this way, Chapter 3 is similar to Chapter 1 in that it is archaeological in approach. But here, we have an exercise in archaeology without excavation: a methodological response to the unique set of problems and challenges posed by these ever-changing buildings.

If Chapter 3 explores the possibility of archaeology without a trowel, Chapter 4 takes that metaphor a step further: to the archaeology of texts. The four shrines examined in this chapter are by far the most heavily altered of all the shrines in this study: for in several cases, not a trace remains of their original structure or physical constitution. And yet, some of the shrines examined in this chapter, including Sayyida Ruqayya and Sayyida Zaynab, the Mashhad al-Husayn in the Umayyad mosque, and a lost shrine once devoted to ʿAli ibn Abi Talib, were, and still are, among the most popular and beloved in Damascus, attracting today well over a million visitors a year. The affection of the people for these shrines has led, in several cases, to their total transformation, and we are almost entirely reliant on the texts alone in our attempt to understand their histories. Thus, this chapter aims to reconstitute or re-imagine important nodes of ritual practice within the urban and suburban landscape of medieval Damascus. In large part, these re-imagined urban and suburban landscapes are a response to one of the central methodological questions of this book: how to study buildings that are continuously in flux.

Along with the fluidity of the shrines' physical presence in the landscape, a second theme of Chapter 4 is the concomitant flexibility of meaning that adheres to ʿAlid devotional structures. While sometimes highly charged with ideological significance, at other times they appear as neutral receptacles for generalised notions of piety, devoid of all particularity or sectarian meaning. This makes them uniquely suited as vehicles for a wide range of political or social messages, and patrons exploited this semiotic flexibility in a variety of ways. Related to this, another theme explored in Chapter 4 is these shrines' contribution to the generation and perpetuation of the urban and suburban landscape. Thus, we will examine the question of intramural vs extramural devotional and architectural practice. ʿAlid shrines are almost always associated with cities, and are rarely found in remote locales (as is often the case with more strictly Sunni-orientated shrines) yet, from the seventeen shrines presented in this study, only two are actually located inside the walls of a city.

Chapter 5 turns to more universal themes, moving outwards from this fine-grained examination of individual ʿAlid shrines to survey the broader sacred landscape they created, and proposing a new formulation for sacred topography in Islam. Chapter 5 is firmly rooted in the archaeological, art-historical and socio-historical approach of the four previous chapters, but it turns a more analytical eye on their conclusions, building on a recent body of scholarship in archaeology and other materially grounded fields that argues for, in the words of one researcher, 'the need for a distinction to be made between the use of the term "sacred" as a descriptor and its employment as an analytical concept'.[23] This chapter creates an analytical framework for examining the mechanisms that generated a new, and distinctly Muslim, sacred topography in the period between the eleventh and thirteenth centuries in Syria. It argues that, for most medieval Muslims, sacred history was intimately connected to place, and that they quite literally experienced sacred history, and thus learned what it meant to be Muslim, through the land, by means of *ziyāra* (visitation of shrines). This approach does not invalidate or disregard the role of narrative and textual sources of historical experience for elite members of a highly literate medieval Islamic society, but it proposes that despite this vast textual output, most ordinary Muslims related to sacred history primarily through ritual and material means, at sites like our ʿAlid shrines. It also proposes that the archaeology of ritual can provide insights into medieval Islamic sacred experience that more selective textual sources, written by and for elite members of society, are unable to provide.

Chapter 5 considers the medieval Islamic landscape as a 'landscape of deeds': a landscape that recorded actions in religio-historical time, both the actions of holy and saintly people, and the ritual actions of those who later revered them. Using models derived from recent scholarship in the archaeology of ritual that claim a close relationship between ritual practice and the generation of material traces, this chapter demonstrates that these actions were 'emplaced', meaning they both literally and figuratively used ritual action to create place, and that such places, in the aggregate, formed a new sacred landscape, holy to Islam. It was a landscape that was conversant with, and reliant on, previous polytheistic, Jewish and Christian traditions of holiness, but differentiated from them in its greater emphasis on action to create holiness in the land.

Chapter 5 also argues for the Crusades as an important impetus for why this Islamic landscape was created at this time. It builds on new scholarship from Crusader archaeology and architectural history that demonstrates a massive – and previously undocumented – Crusader building campaign, one that completely transformed the quantity and visibility of Christian sites in the Holy Land. Thus, although the heightened awareness of sectarianism outlined in Chapters 1–4 was an important internal impetus for the creation of this new Islamic sacred landscape, there was clearly also an external impetus, one that has largely been overlooked. The ʿAlid shrines, marking sites that were beloved by members of both sects, were a nearly universally agreed-upon mechanism for the creation of a landscape of Muslim sites that competed with Christian ones. Finally, Chapter 5 maps the foundational sacred route created by the movement of al-Husayn's head from Karbalaʾ to Cairo, and shows how it was a model for the subsequent creation of an ʿAlid sacred topography more broadly conceived.

The shrines of the ʿAlids raise a number of intriguing questions: namely, is there such a thing as sectarian architecture in Islam? If so, how does it manifest itself and what are its characteristics, iconography and/or semiotic content? How can we study these sites, constantly shifting and evolving over time? And, more broadly, what was their place within the range of other types of holy locales? These questions seem particularly relevant in light of recent studies in architectural history that argue for a sectarian architecture, whether of Sunnism or Shiʿism. Such claims, it will be shown, must elide the tangled patronage and devotional pasts of these buildings in order to place them in easy categories. For if one may find a single, defining characteristic that unites these buildings, it is their remarkably polyvalent flexibility of meaning: in other words, their ability to simultaneously mean different things to a remarkably varied and eclectic group of devotees. This theme of an expansive and inclusive flexibility of meaning will be the unifying thread on to which we shall hold as we explore these buildings and their role in generating a new Islamic sacred landscape in medieval Syria.

Notes

1. Shrines are nearly always 'rediscovered' in these narratives. The miraculous restoration of lost holiness was an essential mechanism by which new holy sites were generated and authenticated. For more on this aspect of shrine foundation, see Josef Meri, *The Cult of Saints Among Muslims and Jews in Medieval Syria* (Oxford: Oxford University Press, 2002), pp. 43–7.
2. As quoted in Ibn Tulun, *Qurrat al-ʿUyun fi Akhbar Bab Jayrun*, ed. S. al-Munajjid (Damascus: Matbuʿat al-Majmaʿ al-ʿIlmi al-ʿArabi bi-Dimashq, 1964), pp. 10–23. Portions of the text are translated by Meri, *Cult of Saints*, p. 45; the story is also explored in an interesting textual analysis by Aliaa El-Sandouby, 'The places of the Ahl al-Bayt in Bilad al-Sham: The making of a "shrine"', *ARAM Periodical* 19 (2007), 684, and noted by Daniella Talmon-Heller, 'Graves, relics and sanctuaries, the evolution of Syrian sacred topography', *ARAM Periodical* 19 (2007), 619; and *Islamic Piety in Medieval Syria: Mosques, Cemeteries and Sermons under the Zangids and Ayyubids (1146–1260)* (Leiden: Brill, 2007), p. 197. I thank Dr Talmon-Heller for kindly furnishing me with an offprint of her article.
3. See Qurʾan 14: 16–17 (Arberry's Translation), where a damned man is 'given to drink of oozing pus, which he gulps, and can scarce swallow, and death comes upon him from every side, yet he cannot die; and still beyond him is a harsh chastisement'.
4. Qurʾan 9: 107–10. Al-Tabari, *Taʾrikh al-Rusul wa-l-Muluk*, ed. M. J. de Goeje et al. (Leiden: Brill, 1879–1901), vol. 1, p. 1704.
5. Ibn Tulun, *Qurrat al-ʿUyun*, pp. 11–12; Meri, *Cult of Saints*, p. 45.
6. Louis Pouzet explores the complexity and contradiction of Sunni attitudes towards the Shiʿa in Damascus; see *Damas au VIIe–XIIIe siècle:*

vie et structures religieuses d'une métropole islamique (Beirut: Dar al-Machreq, 1988), esp. pp. 260–2.

7. Teresa Bernheimer, 'Shared sanctity: some notes on ahl al-bayt shrines in the early Talibid genealogies', *Studia Islamica* (forthcoming 2013); see also her *The ʿAlids: First Family of Islam* (Edinburgh: Edinburgh University Press, 2013).

8. Christopher Taylor, *In the Vicinity of the Righteous: Ziyara and the Veneration of Muslim Saints in Late Medieval Egypt* (Leiden: Brill, 1999).

9. Werner Diem and Marco Schöller have systematically addressed the question of the legal permissibility of *ziyāra*, in their *The Living and the Dead in Islam: Epitaphs in Context* (Wiesbaden: Otto Harrassowitz, 2004), pp. 169–293; see also Talmon-Heller, 'Graves, relics and sanctuaries', 611–18 and also her *Islamic Piety*, pp. 180–3. The permissibility of shrine visitation within Sunnism has been the subject of much scholarly debate in Islamic studies. For some prior discussions see Oleg Grabar, 'The earliest Islamic commemorative structures', *Ars Orientalis* 6 (1966), 7–46; Yusuf Raghib, 'Les premiers monuments funéraires de l'Islam', *Annales Islamologiques* 9 (1970), 21–36; Christopher Taylor, 'Reevaluating the Shiʿi role in the development of monumental Islamic funerary architecture: The case of Egypt', *Muqarnas* 9 (1992), 1–10; Thomas Leisten, *Architektur für Tote* (Berlin: D. Reimer, 1998); and most recently Leor Halevi, *Muhammad's Grave. Death Rites and the Making of Islamic Society* (New York: Columbia University Press, 2007).

10. Emanuel Sivan, 'Le caractère sacré de Jérusalem dans l'Islam aux XXIIe–XXIIIe siècles', *Studia Islamica* 27 (1967), 149–82; Yehoshuʿa Frenkel, 'Baybars and the sacred geography of *Bilad al-Sham*: A chapter in the Islamization of Syria's landscape', *Jerusalem Studies in Arabic and Islam* 25 (2001), 153–70; Talmon-Heller, 'Graves, relics and sanctuaries', 607 and 619, and *Islamic Piety*, pp. 206–7.

11. As they did to see the shaykh Shams al-Din Sibt Ibn al-Jawzi (d. 1256), who used to hold a preaching session every Saturday morning at a column in front of the Mashhad ʿAli Zayn al-ʿAbidin in the Umayyad mosque and where 'the people used to sleep in the mosque on Friday nights (in order to be able to hear him)'. Al-Nuʿaymi, *al-Daris fi Taʾrikh al-Madaris*, ed. Jaʿfar al-Husayni (Cairo: Maktabat al-Thaqafa al-Diniyya, 1988 [1948]), vol. 1, p. 478. For more on this climate of revivalism, see Talmon-Heller, 'Graves, relics and sanctuaries', pp. 619–20.

12. Zayde Antrim, 'Place and belonging in medieval Syria, 6th/12th to 8th/14th centuries'. PhD dissertation, Harvard University, 2004, 2–3. Forthcoming as *Routes and Realms: The Power of Place in the Early Islamic World* (New York: Oxford University Press, 2012).

13. An example of the claiming of an ʿAlid shrine on the site of a former Crusader church may be found in the work of the pilgrimage guide author ʿAli al-Harawi, *Kitab al-Isharat ila Maʿrifat al-Ziyarat*, ed. Janine Sourdel-Thomine (Damascus: Al-Majmaʿ al-ʿIlmi al-ʿArabi bi-Dimashq, 1953), pp. 22–3. French translation by Janine Sourdel-Thomine, *Guide des lieux de pèlerinage* (Damascus: Institut français de Damas, 1957), pp. 18–19; ed. and trans. by Josef Meri as *A Lonely Wayfarer's Guide to Pilgrimage* (Oxford: Oxford University Press, 2004), pp. 43–5. See also note 9 above.

14. See Chapter 2.

15. Christopher Taylor was among the first to focus on the spread of saint veneration in the Islamic world, and Josef Meri's considerable body of work on medieval shrine visitation and pilgrimage were path-breaking in this regard. I would especially single out Talmon-Heller's article 'Graves, relics and sanctuaries', 601–20, and her subsequent book, *Islamic Piety*, Chapter 6, where she accounts for the growing interest in the foundation of sites of pilgrimage in this period; see also El-Sandouby's article 'Places of ahl-al-bayt', where her remarkably comprehensive list of shrines gives one a true sense of how widespread they were. For a slightly earlier period, see Ian Straughn, 'Materializing Islam: An archaeology of landscape in early Islamic period Syria'. Unpublished PhD dissertation, University of Chicago, 2006.

16. For a clear and insightful summary of the 'Sunni Revival', see Yasser Tabbaa, *The Transformation of Islamic Art During the Sunni Revival* (Seattle, WA: University of Washington Press, 2001), Chapter 1. Its elements are familiar to most students of Islamic history, and the traditional viewpoint is summarized by George Makdisi, 'The Sunni Revival', in D. S. Richards, ed., *Islamic Civilization 950–1150* (Oxford: Oxford University Press, 1973), pp. 155–7. However, any notion of a strictly dichotomous and antagonistic Sunni–Shiʿi split has evolved considerably in recent decades. Already in the 1970s, Gary Leiser explored the nuanced sectarian negotiations of the Ayyubids in Cairo in his unpublished PhD dissertation, 'The restoration of Sunnism in Egypt: Madrasas and Mudarrisun, 495–647/1101–1249', University of Pennsylvania, 1976. A few years later, Erika Glassen argued that medieval Sunni–Shiʿi antagonism had been unduly emphasised by other authors, and that at least in the Seljuk era, a focus on political divisions between the Seljuk sultans and the Fatimid caliphs has elided the complex, fluid and often contradictory interactions of the religious policies of the rulers, the Sunni and Shiʿi schools of the religious sciences, the religiosity of ordinary Muslims and that of opposition movements. *Der mittlere Weg: Studien zur Religionspolitik und Religiosität der späteren Abbasiden-Zeit* (Wiesbaden: Steiner, 1981), pp. 3, 9–61. Others have argued that much Abbasid religious policy was directed not at eliminating Shiʿism but rather towards bringing 'moderate' Twelver Shiʿis into the realm of acceptable belief and practice, with any anti-Shiʿi polemic aimed primarily against the *ghulāt*, for example Michael Chamberlain and Jonathan Berkey, who have argued for the rethinking of a static characterisation of the Revival and have explored the ways the formulation is being reframed in recent scholarship; see Michael Chamberlain, 'The Crusader era and the Ayyubid dynasty', in Carl Petry, ed., *The Cambridge History of Egypt* (Cambridge: Cambridge University Press, 1998), vol. 1, p. 232; and Jonathan Berkey, *The Formation of Islam: Religion and Society in the Near East, 600–1800* (New York: Cambridge University Press, 2003), pp. 189–202. Some implications of Sunni revival in Egypt, particularly its emphasis on intra-Sunni purification over anti-Shiʿi polemic, were explored in Stephennie Mulder, 'The mausoleum of Imam al-Shafʿi', *Muqarnas* 23 (2006), 15–46.

17. Marshall G. S. Hodgson, *The Venture of Islam* (Chicago, IL: University of Chicago Press, 1974), vol. 2, pp. 36–9; Moojan Momen, *An Introduction to Shiʿi Islam* (New Haven, CT: Yale University Press, 1987), p. 82.

18. Tabbaa, *Transformation*, p. 8.

19. See note 9 above. For a more in-depth discussion of the historiography of this notion, see Stephennie Mulder, 'Shrines in the central Islamic lands', in Richard A. Etlin, ed., *The Cambridge World History of Religious Architecture* (New York and Cambridge: Cambridge University Press, forthcoming 2014). See also Thomas Leisten, 'Between orthodoxy and exegesis, some aspects of attitudes in the Shari'a toward funerary architecture', *Muqarnas* 7 (1990), 12. Leisten's article provides a succinct summary of debates in the secondary scholarship around commemorative architecture in Islam.

20. In addition to the references in note 9 above, May Farhat makes a similar argument; see her 'Islamic piety and dynastic legitimacy: The case of the shrine of Ali al-Rida in Mashhad (10th–17th century)'. Unpublished PhD dissertation, Harvard University, 2002.

21. Although many medieval buildings we tend to think of as having been 'preserved' are of course modern restorations.

22. Finbarr B. Flood, *Objects of Translation: Material Culture and Medieval 'Hindu-Muslim' Encounter* (Princeton, NJ: Princeton University Press, 2009), p. 14. For a recent summary of debates about methodology and historiography within the field, see the special issue 'Islamic art historiography', ed. Moya Carey and Margaret S. Graves, *Journal of Art Historiography* 6 (June 2012).

23. Ian Straughn, 'An aptitude for sacred space', in Cecelia Feldman Weiss and Claudia Moser, eds, *Locating the Sacred: Theoretical Approaches to the Emplacement of Religion*, Joukowsky Institute Press series, no. 3 (Oxford: Oxbow Books, forthcoming 2014). My sincere thanks to Cecelia Feldman Weiss for sharing an advance copy of several articles from this volume.

CHAPTER ONE

A *Mashhad* at Balis

On a desolate and dusty hilltop overlooking the Euphrates in northern Syria, a small green flag snaps and flutters under the sun (Fig. 1.1). Its pole, planted deep into the masonry of a ruinous pile of crumbling brick located 2km south of the now half-submerged medieval city of Balis, stretches almost to breaking with each gust of the hot wind. Seeming at first to mark just another nameless ruin of the sort that are scattered millennia-deep across Syria, the tattered marker suggests that this mound of crumbling masonry, which otherwise appears lost to the depredations of time, is still very much alive in both memory and devotion. People from the local agricultural villages raised the flag because this site is revered as the burial place of a beloved saint, and it is a last vestige of the location's long devotional history. Scattered around the ruins are numerous modern graves, placed here in the hope that the *baraka*, or sacred

Figure 1.1 *Balis* mashhad, *main* miḥrāb. *Photo: Drew Stauss, Departure Studio*

Figure 1.2 *Modern graves near Balis* mashhad. *Photo: Drew Stauss, Departure Studio*

emanations, from the holy person's tomb will bless the souls of the deceased (Fig. 1.2). Still, in spite of these continued local devotional practices, the ruin seems a rather sad and neglected locale, located far on the periphery of the centres of Syrian religious practice.

Stepping back somewhat, a different picture comes into focus. Just north of the pile of masonry and attached to it is a small, tripartite prayer hall. A closer look reveals traces of elegantly carved stucco decoration still clinging to the remains of one of its tall, pointed-arched *miḥrāb*s (prayer niches) (Fig. 1.3). Stretching out behind the prayer hall are the low walls of a recently excavated series of rooms, arranged around a pillared central space, apparently a courtyard (Fig. 1.4). Each room is graced by its own small *miḥrāb*, a niche indicating the direction of Mecca used to orientate worshippers during prayer. At the centre of the courtyard is a hole that was once the opening to a carefully constructed cistern, designed to hold water for the numerous visitants to this holy place (Fig. 1.5). Although today, reverence for the shrine has taken on a local character, it would seem from the substantial remains of this building that this was not always so. And indeed, this shrine was once a critical node in the vast network of sites making up Syria's holy landscape, a landscape characterised by a vibrant and flourishing system of shrines, pilgrimage places, mosques and *madrasa*s.

In many ways, this nameless shrine is emblematic of the phenomenon of medieval Syrian devotional culture and its architectural manifestations as a whole. The Balis shrine, like many hundreds of others, arose at the end of the eleventh century, during a period of

Figure 1.3 *Traces of stucco decoration at the base of the* miḥrāb.
Photo: Drew Stauss, Departure Studio

Figure 1.4 *View from prayer hall northward, showing east-central room
(on the right) and central room (partially excavated) on left. Photo: Drew
Stauss, Departure Studio*

intensive – and apparently intentional – sanctification of the Islamic
holy landscape. Like many of these shrines, this one manifested
as an ʿAlid site at a time when Sunnism was ascendant across the
Islamic world. Although initially a humble foundation, within a

Figure 1.5 *View south across central room. East-central room is on left, prayer hall at top of frame and hole of cistern at centre-right. Photo: Drew Stauss, Departure Studio*

very short period of time it was visited so extensively that it benefited from numerous and intensive patronage activities, performed with an eye to expanding or modifying the shrine to accommodate increasing numbers of pilgrims. Indeed, it was heavily visited and repeatedly altered right up until 1259, when the city of Balis and the surrounding countryside were abruptly abandoned in anticipation of the Mongol advance. And yet, considering the questions historians and art historians often ask, and the assumptions commonly made about this middle period in Islamic history, such a shrine, and the general flourishing of ʿAlid devotion of which it was a part, appears at first to be something of an anomaly.

The Balis shrine is also important from the perspective of the methodology employed in its study, a methodology explored in detail in the following pages. Shrines, as a type, are perhaps the consummate 'living' buildings, meaning they are sites of continuous and ongoing devotional practice, a tradition that plays a critical and enduring role in the life of contemporary religious practitioners today as it did in the medieval period. For most still functioning Islamic devotional sites, the disturbances an archaeological investigation would bring are outside the boundaries of acceptability. This means it is difficult or impossible to precisely delineate the chronology of construction and patronage of any given building. At the same time, and perhaps somewhat ironically, the shrines' central role in devotion also means that even were such investigations possible, the buildings would hardly remain static long enough to carry them out.

The architectural and archaeological reality of such buildings is, in fact, a continuous state of flux, for few building types are as intensively patronised and re-patronised, as are shrines. Indeed, finding a methodological response to the limitations imposed by the study of 'living' buildings is one preoccupation of this study, and frequently the framework employed in the following pages is a response to the question of how to study buildings that are continuously visited and constantly transformed. The Balis *mashhad*, as an archaeological site, presents a singular opportunity to study such a locale unencumbered by many of the constraints imposed on living buildings, and thus allows us to re-imagine this lost shrine from a perspective rarely employed in the study of this building type. The story that unfolds from the excavation of the Balis shrine will serve as our template for the other medieval sites in Syria. Before we turn to the shrine, however, some information about the history of the city in which it was built is in order, for unlike Damascus and Aleppo, the unimposing medieval settlement of Balis is little-known, even among specialists in the field.

A brief history of Balis

The Islamic ruins of Balis are located approximately 100km east of Aleppo and a few kilometres north-east of the dusty modern market town of Meskene, which straddles the road leading eastwards to al-Raqqa, just at the point where the Euphrates stops flowing south and turns eastwards (Map 1). Today, the area of the medieval city is largely flooded as a result of the closing of the Tabqa dam in 1973–4. The dam created a vast, 100km-long reservoir in its wake, which inundated both archaeological sites and modern villages all along the upper Euphrates valley. Balis, however, was not completely submerged. Presently, an imprecise triangular area of approximately 150m north to south by 100m east to west emerges out of the eastern shore of the reservoir (Fig. 1.6), while the remains of the ruined city wall mark out its western perimeter. A tall, remarkably intact Byzantine *praetorium* and a fortified bastion stand at the north and south corners, respectively, of the ruined eastern wall, lending the site a picturesque air (Figs 1.7 and 1.8).

This location had a long occupational history prior to the Islamic period. Strategically situated on a rise that once overlooked the Euphrates river plain, at the boundary of Syria and Mesopotamia just at the point where the riverine and land routes intersected, the city has always been an important centre for trade connecting the Mediterranean coast to the lands further east. On the western flank of the medieval ruins rises a prominent tell, which has been identified as the early and middle Bronze-age city of Emar, occupied since at least 2500 BC (Fig. 1.9). There, an important cache of some 800 cuneiform tablets was discovered in French excavations carried out

Figure 1.6 *Ruins of the city of Balis, seen from Lake Assad. Photo: Drew Stauss, Departure Studio*

Figure 1.7 *Ruins of the Byzantine praetorium. Photo: Drew Stauss, Departure Studio*

Figure 1.8 *View south along eastern city wall of Balis, from within the praetorium. Corner bastion and surrounding Lake Assad are visible in the distance. Photo: Drew Stauss, Departure Studio*

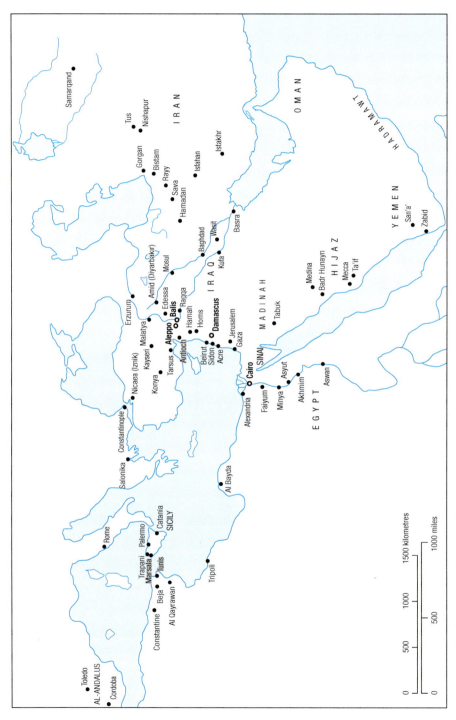

Map 1 *Medieval pilgrimage places. Balis is located slightly north of the turn of the Euphrates, north-west of Raqqa. After J. Sourdel-Thomine,* Guide des lieux de pèlerinage

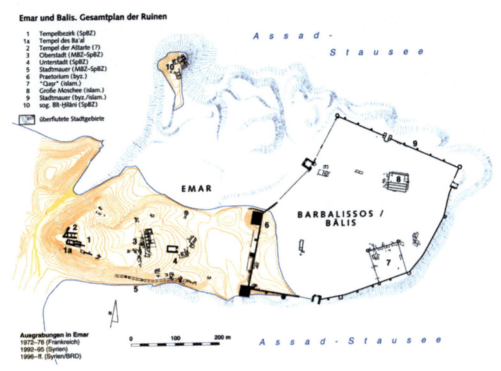

Figure 1.9 *Plan, Emar and Balis. Illustration: Hans Birk. Permission: Thomas Leisten*

in the 1970s.[1] Ancient Emar was destroyed in a catastrophic event, probably a major fire, in 1187 BC and was, apparently, not reoccupied for over a millennium.

The next mention of the site belongs still to ancient times, when it reappears with a new name derived from Aramaic and Greek. Called BYT BLS (Bayt Bales) and Barbalissos, the oldest reference to the city appears to be in the writings of the Greek historian Xenophon (d. 355 BC), who indicates a governor of Syria named Belesis who had a castle at the spot.[2] The city functioned as a frontier town along the *limes* throughout the Roman and Byzantine period. It was mentioned in the *Notitia Dignitatum* as part of the eastern administrative districts belonging to the Roman province of *Augusta Euphratensis*. Later, in the Byzantine era, the town flourished as a significant Christian pilgrimage centre, for it conserved the relics of the martyr Bacchus, who died with his comrade Sergius, interred at nearby Rusafa/Sergiopolis (Fig. 1.10).[3] Balis was pillaged at least twice by Sasanian invasions, the second time in 540 by the armies of Khusrau II Anushirwan. After this incident, which must have devastated the city, the walls were rebuilt by Justinian as part of his effort to fortify towns along the *limes* (Fig. 1.11).[4] It is likely that the massive *praetorium* and tower along the western wall of the city can be attributed to Justinian.

Figure 1.10 *SS Sergius and Bacchus Photo: after Robert S. Nelson and Kristen M. Collins, eds,* Icons from Sinai *(Los Angeles, CA, Getty Publications, 2006), plate 3, p. 126*

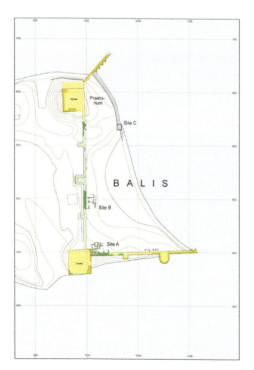

Figure 1.11 *Plan of excavations in 1996 and 1998. Permission: Thomas Leisten*

Our knowledge of the history of Balis becomes considerably richer after the Muslim conquest. The city surrendered peacefully in 636 to the army of the Muslim general Abu 'Ubayda, who installed a garrison there. In the Umayyad period, the city and its hinterland became the *qaṭīʿa* (feudal estate) of Maslama Ibn 'Abd al-Malik, the son of the Caliph 'Abd al-Malik, and after his death in 738 it passed to his heirs. Maslama invested in the agriculture of the region by building a canal, the Nahr Maslama, as well as a *qaṣr* (fort or palace) on a hilltop overlooking the city.[5] In the Islamic era, by the ninth and tenth centuries, the city was no longer a frontier town and had evolved rapidly into an important centre for trade. Its advantageous location at the point where the Euphrates turns east after flowing south from Asia Minor meant that it was the last stop on the river along the great route that brought goods from the Persian Gulf via Baghdad or Mosul, to destinations in Aleppo or the Mediterranean ports of Antioch or Lattakia. The Arab geographers refer to it as 'the port of Syria on the Euphrates'.[6] It is called 'the first city of Sham [Syria]' from the direction of Iraq, located two days from Aleppo, two days from Raqqa and five days from Kufa.[7] Its fortified location overlooking a rich agricultural plain meant that even in difficult times the city was self-sufficient and produced its own wheat and barley, among other products. Undoubtedly this gave the city a measure of stability; its real importance, however, was in trade.

This trade made Balis a cosmopolitan place, in spite of its rather modest size. International commerce brought people and goods from all corners of the known world. Merchants passing through the city sent slaves, brocade, skins and spices from the west, and brought back musk, aloe wood, camphor and cinnamon. Several pieces of Song dynasty porcelain and a single sherd of celadon found during excavations at Balis attest to trade in luxury goods from the Far East: in fact Balis is one of only two sites on the upper Euphrates to have produced sherds of Chinese porcelain.[8] Benjamin of Tudela writes of a small community of Jews in the city.[9]

Adding to Balis's cosmopolitan air was the fact that the tenth century also saw the city become a centre for scholarship. Sam'ani lists ten scholars with the name al-Balisi, seven of which belong to this period. Ibn 'Asakir identifies sixteen shaykhs active at the time, and thirteen *muhaddithūn* (transmitters of *hadīth*, or exemplary traditions of the Prophet). Indeed, families of scholars are known, as for example the family of Ahmad b. Bakr, a *muhaddith* before the year 873.[10] This seems to have remained the case throughout its history, through to the early thirteenth century. The medieval biographer al-Subki devotes a seventeen-page entry to the life of the Shaykh Abu Bakr al-Balisi, born in 1188, who had so many followers that he could rally them for major public works projects, as when they excavated a canal to bring water to the city after their request was refused by the Sultan al-Malik al-'Adil.[11] The city became a centre for the transmission of *hadīth*, and as such – like bigger cities such as Damascus, Aleppo and Jerusalem – it was a destination for scholars travelling in search of traditions.[12]

The middle of the tenth century saw a Shi'i dynasty, the Hamdanids of Mosul, having more or less direct control over Balis. Wars against the Byzantines fought by the Hamdanid Sayf al-Dawla, as well as that ruler's harsh policy of taxation, exacted their toll on the city, which was several times ravaged by battle. Nevertheless, the medieval geographer al-Muqaddasi was in Syria at the time and calls the city prosperous.[13] After the middle of the eleventh century, Balis, along with the rest of the region, descended into a period of political fragmentation and instability, with Kurdish Marwanids in control of Diyar Bakr, Arab 'Uqaylids in the Jazira and another Shi'i dynasty, the Mirdasids, having control over Aleppo and its hinterland, including Balis. In this period, and perhaps for some time previously, the region of northern Syria seems to have had a notably Shiʿi character. The *khutba* (Friday sermon) had been said either in the name of the Fatimid imam or using a Shiʿi formula almost without interruption since 977.[14] When the Shiʿi Mirdasid Mahmud joined forces with the Sunni Seljuk Alp Arslan in 1070 and adopted the Sunni ʿAbbasid *khutba* in Aleppo, he had to put down a rebellion by Shiʿi partisans. Shiʿi propaganda was widespread: an Ismaʿili *dār al-daʿwa* (propagandistic mission) was installed in Aleppo, and Balis also was a centre for the diffusion of the Druze doctrine, an offshoot of Shiʿism.[15]

Balis was subject to several indecisive incursions by the Franks during the Crusader era in the early part of the twelfth century, until it came under the control of the Zangids and Ayyubids, who gained dominance in the area beginning in 1128. The twelfth century ushered in a time of stability and prosperity for Balis, particularly in the period following the reign of Nur al-Din (1147–74). Balis was once again given in *iqtāʿ* (feudal possession) to a succession of Zangid and Ayyubid rulers.[16] Although Friedrich Sarre and Ernst Herzfeld infer a decline of the city during the Ayyubid period, based on Yaqut's use of the term *balda* (town) in his account of Balis and the fact that the Euphrates began to change its course (to eventually flow some 8km from the city), André Raymond has argued that the effects were not as serious as have been supposed. The two major Aleppan historians of the period, Ibn Shaddad and Ibn al-ʿAdim, employ the word *madīna* (city) in their description of Balis. In fact, Balis had always been separated from its port on the Euphrates by a rich agricultural plain and this had never harmed its prosperity.[17]

During the Ayyubid period, Balis was approximately 450m east to west by 400m north to south. André Raymond has estimated that, assuming a density of 400 inhabitants per hectare, the population of the city can be placed somewhere in the vicinity of 5,000 residents. Based on these estimates and information on the fiscal revenue of Balis provided by Ibn Shaddad, he proposes it was a city of medium size and importance in this period, with a steady and reliable source of income from trade and agriculture.[18] This trade continued to lend the city a cosmopolitan character: estimates of the tax paid by non-Muslims suggest they numbered in the range of 750 to 1,200 – a significant percentage of the total – and Ibn al-ʿAdim mentions a remark by the geographer al-Yaʿqubi that suggests as much: 'its population was a mix of Arabs and non-Arabs' (*wa-ahlaha ikhlāt min al-ʿarab wa-l-ʿajam*).[19] Interestingly, even after some 100 years of 'Sunni Revival' under the Zangids and Ayyubids, the Shiʿi inclination of the residents seems to have remained strong. The inscription on the minaret of the Great Mosque, built by the Ayyubid sovereign al-Malik al-ʿAdil in 1210–11, was decorated with an inscription that has clear Shiʿi associations (Fig. 1.12).[20] This rare and beautiful

Figure 1.12 *Minaret at Balis. Photo: Author*

octagonal brick minaret, showing influence from the Iranian architectural tradition, was rescued from the rising waters in the 1970s
and is preserved today on a hilltop overlooking the city.[21]

Balis appears to have been completely abandoned in 1259 in fear
of the advancing Mongols.[22] After that point, it ceases to appear in
historical sources as a living city. Ibn al-ʿAdim, who died in Cairo in
1262, writes that 'in our time, its wall is in ruins, there is not a single
scholar or prince remaining'.[23] Archaeological findings provide proof
of this: excavation has recovered no evidence of Mamluk or Ottoman
occupation, with the exception of a small fort whose construction
in the Ottoman period was never completed. The city did not even
appear in the Mamluk administrative reorganisation of Syria.[24]
Thus, Balis lay in ruins, traversed only by itinerant herders and the
occasional western explorer, for over half a millennium before it was
once again inhabited – this time, by archaeologists.

Balis

Archaeological investigation

The first archaeological excavation of the Islamic city of Balis was carried out in 1929, under the direction of Eustache de Lorey, then director of the Institut Français d'Archéologie et d'Art Musulman, and Georges Salles, director of the Louvre. With the exception of two short notices in the journal *Syria*, these excavations have never been published, and the notes are believed lost.[25] Scattered references to the French excavations, along with several photographs, survive in a few early-twentieth-century books and journals.[26] Later in the twentieth century, as part of the Tabqa Dam salvage project, rescue excavations were conducted at the site by another French team from the Institut Français d'Études Arabes de Damas. Four campaigns were pursued under the direction of Lucien Golvin and André Raymond, from 1971 to 1974. From those excavations, a catalogue of the coin finds and of the excavation of two trenches has been published. Still unpublished are the remainder of the excavation areas and a catalogue of the ceramics.

In 1996, Princeton University began a new exploration of the ruined city, in cooperation with the Syrian Antiquities Authority. The original goal of the Syrian-Princeton excavation was modest: to determine the relationship between the Byzantine wall and later Islamic settlement. The team also hoped to recover some evidence of pre-Ayyubid occupation, for which there is abundant textual evidence, but for which no significant traces or monuments related to these periods had yet been identified or published. With these goals in mind, three areas were opened in the 1996 and 1998 campaigns: two on the city wall, and one near the shoreline of the reservoir (now called Lake Assad) that had submerged the remainder of the site. In this third trench, a deep sounding was made with the object of finding pre-Ayyubid levels of occupation (Fig. 1.11).

Also in 1998, and coincident with research on Balis *intra muros*, a trench was opened on a hilltop approximately 2km south of the city. In the 1970s, as part of the rescue excavations, the minaret from the soon-to-be-submerged mosque had been relocated to the hilltop. In the process of digging a foundation trench for the minaret, the engineers had encountered walls and evidence of settlement, but the area had not been properly explored.[27] The 1998 excavations revealed a *castrum*-type building c. 77m square that was designated the *Qasr* (palace). Thereafter, from the 1999 season until 2008, research in the lower city was largely abandoned in favour of exploring the *Qasr*, and a significant portion of the building has now been exposed. The results of the excavation have proved to be extremely enlightening both architecturally and historically, for they reveal a rare example of a single-occupation Umayyad site largely undisturbed by later

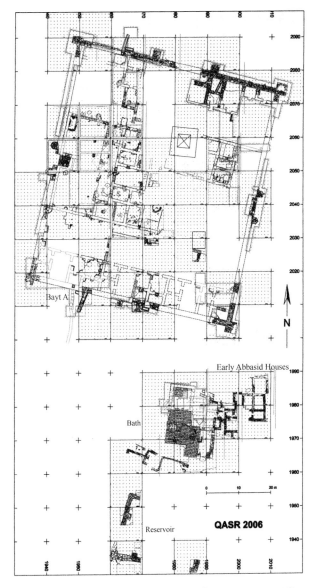

Figure 1.13 *Plan, Qasr. Illustration: Hans Birk. Permission: Thomas Leisten*

settlement (Fig. 1.13). This *Qasr* is as notable for its central reception area graced by intact early Islamic frescos as it is for the surrounding structure containing an elaborate system of canalisation and a sequence of built-in 'wet rooms'– perhaps used for the processing of wool or felt. This dual 'high/low' function of the *Qasr* illustrates the method of Umayyad administration wherein the ruling class sought to promote social and political cohesion in the heartland by sponsoring and redeveloping the Levantine agricultural economy.[28]

The exploration of the *Qasr* was coincident with a survey of the area around Balis. During this survey, the ruins of the small, partially excavated mosque or shrine described at the beginning of this chapter were discovered on a hillside overlooking Lake Assad, just over a kilometre east of the *Qasr*. Between 2005 and 2009, this building was also excavated, and it is to this structure that we will now turn our attention in detail. Despite its small size, the shrine's history is rich and complex, and that history begins not in Balis, but in Damascus.

Which mashhad *at Balis?*

On any given day, a visitor to the National Museum in Damascus may round a corner and encounter a beautiful and important artefact from Balis's past. Taking up much of one wall in the second room of the Islamic galleries is a near-complete group of stucco panels (Fig. 1.14). The catalogue offers the information that the panels were presented to the museum in the 1930s by Georges Salles, the first excavator of Balis:

> Façade en stuc d'une mosquée trouvée au cours des fouilles effectuées en 1932 par MM. Eustache de Lorey et Georges Salles à Meskanah (Balis) sur l'Euphrate. Une inscription en coufique fleuri montre qu'elle date du 11e siècle.[29]

This description provokes more questions than it answers. It does not put forward any information about the structure, nor about the precise location in Balis from which the panels were removed, nor about the content of the inscriptions, epigraphy (aside from the

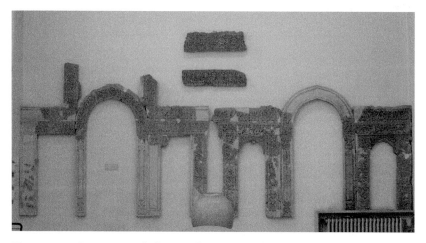

Figure 1.14 *Stucco panels from Balis, National Museum of Damascus.* Photo: Author

mention that it is floriated Kufic) nor any of the decorative elements carved in deep relief into the stucco. Thus, the stucco panels, aside from their aesthetic value, remain essentially – frustratingly – mute. In the absence of an unambiguous provenience for the panels, a question for the Syrian-Princeton excavation team was: could these panels have come from the small shrine discovered at Balis? The answer was important, for it had potential to reveal information about the sectarian composition of the medieval city.

In the late 1990s, the *mashhad* at Balis was a striking sight. Like many holy places in the Islamic world, the shrine had originally been built at the crest of a hill. It was situated outside of the ruins of the city, about 2km to the south, with what must have been in medieval times a magnificent view north towards the city of Balis and east down over the green plain of the Euphrates. In the years following the filling of the reservoir, the location of the shrine had become even more dramatic. The encroachment of Lake Assad had turned the once-sloping hillside into sharply defined, low cliffs on three sides, making the shrine seem to sit atop a peninsula jutting precariously out into the water (Fig. 1.15). Year by year, as the water lapped at the shore, a bit more of the hillside sheared off into the lake below and a decision was made that excavations should be pursued before further damage was done to the structure.

However, the Syrian-Princeton team was not the first to excavate at this site atop the hill. When the team encountered the shrine, not only was it decorated with a green flag and surrounded by modern

Figure 1.15 *View of cliffs near the* mashhad. *Photo: Drew Stauss, Departure Studio*

Figure 1.16 *South-east corner of prayer hall prior to Syrian-Princeton excavations. Central mihrab is visible on right. Photo: Author*

graves, as described previously, but also the entire southern section, which appeared to be a small prayer hall, had been systematically cleared of its dirt and debris. It was not apparent when this excavation had taken place, but it was obvious from the precision of the work that it had been archaeological in nature and that it had happened some time in the past century (Fig. 1.16). Yet, no publication had made reference to excavations at a shrine south of the city. This cleared area exposed a tripartite sanctuary with a tall central *miḥrāb* flanked by two piers that projected northwards by about a metre. To the east and west, flanking each of the projecting piers and also in the south wall, were two more, smaller, niches. Thus the prayer hall was divided into three sections, each containing a niche in its southern wall. To the north of the prayer hall, the uneven contour of the ground and the scattering of bricks and pottery made it clear that the rest of the building lay just under the surface.

Although in the 1930s the De Lorey-Salles team had excavated a *mashhad* they claimed was located north of Balis, and the present shrine was located about 2km to the south, some compelling evidence indicated that this shrine and the one from which the stucco panels in the museum had come might, in fact, be the same. If so, the excavators in the 1930s had simply made an error when reporting the location of the site. The strongest argument for this interpretation was that surviving photographs taken during the De Lorey-

Salles excavations showed stucco panels that closely matched a few remaining fragments from Balis and the panels on display in the Damascus museum. Furthermore, the arrangement of the panels made them seem likely to fit the form of the excavated south wall of the shrine at Balis. Still, the evidence was far from conclusive.

Interestingly, the provenience of the Damascus museum stucco panels was not only important for the research of the Syrian-Princeton team. Their wider historical relevance had already been illustrated elsewhere. The museum's panels had been the focus of a separate study in the 1970s by the French scholars Dominique Sourdel and Janine Sourdel-Thomine, who presented them as part of a constellation of evidence pointing to the Shiʿi character of northern Syria during the eleventh and twelfth centuries.[30] Sourdel and Sourdel-Thomine cited a previous study in which they had examined numerous indicators, including the 'Shiʿi' inscriptions of the Ayyubid minaret from the mosque at Balis, the patronage of Shiʿi shrines in Aleppo at the end of the twelfth century by its mayor Tariq al-Balisi – whose family apparently originated in Balis[31] – as well as accounts by medieval authors.[32] Now, they argued persuasively that the inscriptions from the stucco panels from Balis were further evidence of the Shiʿi confession of the majority of the population.

Indeed, a direct reading of the inscriptions on the museum's stucco panels leaves little room for doubt that they had been commissioned by a figure or figures that, at the least, had strong ʿAlid sympathies:

> *Left panel, lower band, right of miḥrāb*:
> This is the *mashhad* of al-Khidr. May God have mercy upon him and (upon) the Pure Family . . .
> *Centre Panel, around arc of miḥrāb*:
> . . . Muhammad and ʿAli and Fatima and al-Hasan and al-Husayn, and ʿAli and Muhammad and Jaʿfar and Musa and ʿAli and Muhammad.[33]

These inscriptions contain several valuable pieces of information (Fig. 1.17). First, they establish that the *mashhad* was one for al-Khidr. Al-Khidr is a Muslim saint, sometimes linked with the Biblical Elijah and sharing many of his roles and functions, including associations with esoteric knowledge and eternal life. Islamic exegetical literature identifies al-Khidr as the unnamed 'servant of God' who appeared to Moses in the Qurʾan and reveals to him the limits of his wisdom.[34] He was revered by both Sunnis and Shiʿis and was especially important in Sufi thought, where he was regarded as an initiating shaykh.[35] Al-Khidr is associated in extra-Qurʾanic literature with a story in which he searches for the water of life, and upon finding it, is granted immortality. It is perhaps this aspect for which he is revered among the Shiʿa: for his eternal life mirrors and presages the occultation of the twelfth Imam al-Mahdi, who

Figure 1.17 *Damascus Museum stucco panels, central* miḥrāb.
Photo: Author

is believed to be hidden, yet still alive and awaiting a time shortly
before the Day of Judgement to return, much as Elijah's attainment
of eternal life presaged that of Jesus in Christianity.

Yet, the most remarkable feature of the inscriptions cannot be
appreciated by reading the text alone. For although it makes clear
the shrine is a *mashhad* to al-Khiḍr, the placement of his name on
the inscription panel is such that his name is hardly the focal point
of the composition. Located unobtrusively to the right of the central
miḥrāb, 'al-Khiḍr' is just one word in a crowded line of text that is
not differentiated in any way from the sentence in which it is a part.
Indeed, the focal point of the stucco composition is not the first,
but the *second* line of text quoted above. This lists the names of the
Family of the Prophet – including each of the twelve Imams of the
Shiʿa, in the order of their succession, beginning with the Prophet
Muhammad and ending with the twelfth Imam Muhammad al-
Mahdi, the figure whose eschatological role al-Khiḍr may have been
believed to presage. These names have been carefully arranged so
that they fit precisely into the arch of the *miḥrāb*, which would have
been the central feature of the prayer hall. Their beautifully floriated
calligraphy braids its way around the arch, transforming the names
of the Prophet's family into the most prominent visual element of
the composition. The first name, of the Prophet Muhammad, just
above the right springing of the arch, and the final name, of the

twelfth Imam Muhammad al-Mahdi, just above the left springing, thus echo each other across the *miḥrāb* in perfect symmetry.

The theme of the Prophet Muhammad's mission is taken up in the other line of inscriptions in this panel, located in a second band just above the one already discussed. It initially follows the line of text below it, but when it reaches the springing of the arch for the *miḥrāb*, turns sharply upwards and proceeds vertically towards what must once have been a tall rectangular frame surrounding the *miḥrāb* arch. Its top portion is missing, however it contains a Qur'anic quotation that is easily reconstructed:

> *Right half, horizontal band:*
> In the name of God, the Compassionate, the Merciful. Oh Prophet!
> *Right half, vertical band:*
> We have sent you as a wit . . . *ness and a bearer of happy tidings and an admonisher, and to call (men) to God by His leave, and as a lamp resplendent. Give glad tidings to the believers that there is. . .*
> *Left half, vertical band:*
> . . . great bounty for them in God. Do not listen . . .
> *Left half, horizontal band:*
> . . . *to the un . . .* believers . . . nor to the hypocrites . . . *ignore what they do to hurt you, and put your trust in God. God is sufficient as protector.*[36]

This is Qur'an 33:44–8, a powerful invocation of the prophetic mission of Muhammad and an acknowledgment of the supreme power of God in the face of oppression. This panel seems highly appropriate for a Shiʿi context, with its deep reverence for the Prophet and especially its reminder that persecutors are to be ignored and dismissed as unbelievers and hypocrites, and its assurance that God will protect the true believer. In fact, at about the same time, a near-identical inscription appears in Damascus in what was probably also a Shiʿi context: on the cenotaph of a descendant of the Prophet named Sukayna bt. al-Husayn, located in the cemetery of Bab al-Saghir.[37]

According to the notice published by Georges Salles, the overseer of the 1929 excavations, this stucco panel was located in the central room of a tripartite prayer hall. This indicates that the *miḥrāb* of the stucco composition, with its paean to the Family of the Prophet and its assurance of protection for those who suffer, was the central focus not only of the individual panel but of the entire monument as a whole.[38] Thus, although the shrine was in name devoted to al-Khidr, it was clearly also, and arguably primarily, envisaged as a place of devotion to the ʿAlids, or the Family of the Prophet.

In the room to the right of the central panel was a second stucco panel, a decorative composition that has not been preserved in the

museum. This panel is only known from the photographs published
in the preceding notice by Salles.[39] Its primary importance is that it
gave an artist's signature and a date of 1071–2.[40]

The third stucco panel in the Damascus museum, now displayed
to the right side of the central panel but according to the excavators originally located in the room to the left of it, has a corpus of
inscriptions bearing a similar message to the central panel described
above. It also had a date slightly later than the second panel, that of
1076–7. Its inscriptions include, yet again, the invocation of blessings on the Prophet and his family on the right half of the panel.
The central arc over the *miḥrāb* bears a band repeating the names
of the twelve Imams, once again placing the names of the Prophet
and his family at the centre of the composition. The inscriptions on
the left half derive largely from Qurʾan 2:144. This reads '. . . those
who are recipients of the Book surely know that this is the truth
from their Lord . . .', and is a fragment of a verse which speaks of the
establishment of Mecca as the *qibla* and of the duty of believers in
the Book (the Qurʾan) to turn towards it in prayer. On the surface,
this fragment seems largely devoid of polemical content, but it is
interesting to note that two verses later in the same chapter, there is
a strong condemnation of those who claim to believe in the Book yet
knowingly conceal the truth.[41]

Clearly this *mashhad* to al-Khidr represents a strong current of
ʿAlid devotion that characterised the population of northern Syria
in the late twelfth century. The inscriptions of its beautiful stucco-
decorated prayer hall are quite insistent in their emphasis on the
Family of the Prophet, even in a shrine that ostensibly honours a
figure unrelated to that family altogether, like al-Khidr. And yet,
our exploration of these panels so far reveals only tantalising clues.
For despite the intriguing content of their inscriptions, the question
remains: did these stucco panels come from the shrine discovered by
the Syrian-Princeton team? To answer this question, we must return
once again to Balis.

A *mashhad* at Balis: The Syrian-Princeton excavations

According to the medieval pilgrimage guide author ʿAli al-Harawi,
the people of Balis venerated several ʿAlid *mashhad*s. 'The city of
Balis,' he wrote,

> contains the shrine of ʿAli ibn Abi Talib, the Shrine of the
> Miscarried Foetus (*mashhad al-tirḥ*) and the Shrine of the Rock,
> upon which it is said al-Husayn's head was placed when the cap-
> tives (of the Battle of Karbalaʾ) passed through.[42]

It is notable that al-Harawi does not mention a single non-ʿAlid
shrine in the vicinity of Balis. The *mashhad* of ʿAli, it goes without

saying, falls into the ʿAlid category, and the *mashhad* of the Miscarried Foetus is a reference to a shrine for al-Muhassin, the son of al-Husayn (or, alternatively, the son of ʿAli) believed to have been miscarried as a result of the shock to his mother following the tragedy at Karbalaʾ. This tiny martyr had a more famous burial place in Aleppo, which is also the location of a better-known Shrine of the Rock for al-Husayn.[43] Although al-Harawi does not mention the *mashhad* of al-Khidr, we have already pointed to the strongly ʿAlid inflection for that shrine evident in its inscriptions. Thus, while there are a number of possibilities for the identification of the shrine excavated by the Syrian-Princeton team, the available evidence indicates that it was likely to have been an ʿAlid *mashhad*.

Following on that assumption, the Syrian-Princeton excavations are most notable for what they say about the history of such places of pilgrimage. The excavation confirms that like many other shrines, the *mashhad* was an extremely dynamic structure that experienced continuous growth and modification from the time of its founding until Balis was abandoned in the mid-thirteenth century. The excavations took place during the summers of 2005–9. Archaeologist David Lineberry excavated the *mashhad*, with the assistance of local workmen hired from the nearby villages of Samuma and Hottin. Professor Thomas Leisten from Princeton University and Mr Jamil Massouh of the Syrian Antiquities Authority oversaw the excavation.[44] The ceramic material was processed, recorded and analysed by the author.

By the autumn of 2006, approximately two-thirds of the *mashhad* had been excavated (Fig. 1.18). As noted above, the size and general orientation of the building was discernible on the surface, and the area of the south-facing prayer hall had already been excavated at some unknown point. From the piles of rubble and depressions visible on the surface, the building appeared to be square or rectangular in plan, with nine rooms distributed in a three-by-three pattern stretching northwards from the prayer hall. The prayer hall was a long, rectangular room perpendicular to the courtyard and stretching along the *qibla* wall. This room, although open in plan, was nevertheless articulated somewhat by the intrusion of two brick buttresses on either side of the central *miḥrāb* (Fig. 1.16). Aside from the main prayer hall, this three-by-three pattern indeed proved to be the case once the building was excavated, however there was great variability in the size and shape of these rooms and each had certain unique characteristics.

Based on the initial observations noted above, a 10m grid was laid out, and excavation of the rooms proceeded moving roughly from the south-east of the structure towards the north-west, using 9 × 9m squares with a 1m baulk buttressing the trenches. As is common architectural practice, each square was excavated following the manifestation and distribution pattern of individual loci. This means

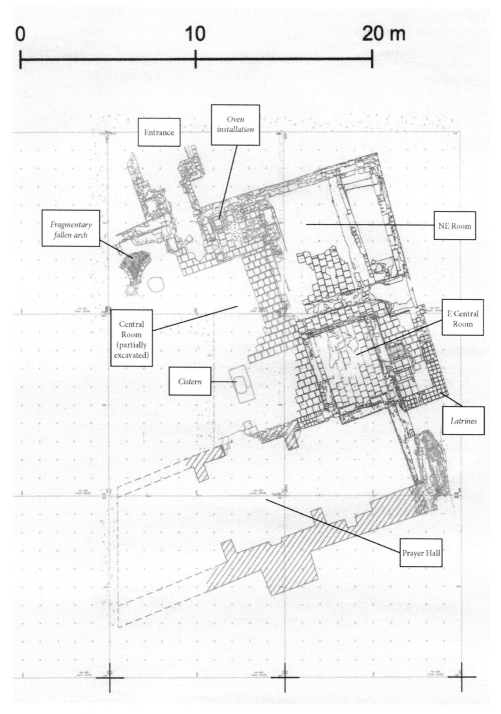

Figure 1.18 *Plan of* mashhad *as partially excavated in 2006. Tripartite prayer hall is visible along south-east wall, with east-central and north-east rooms on right and entrance on north-west wall. Illustration: Hans Birk. Permission: Thomas Leisten*

that within a trench, a locus is defined as a specific and distinct horizontal and vertical area: for example a particular colour or consistency of fill of a room between the north and south wall. A locus is also always defined vertically so the depth of strata is known. Using loci the team was able to excavate the building according to its unique plan and depositional history and to keep careful account of any artefacts associated with the room or feature in which they may have been deposited.

Quite rapidly, a general fill pattern emerged that was largely consistent across the rooms of the *mashhad*. It consisted of three levels. First, the archaeologists encountered a thick layer of dirt and brick rubble. In the southern room, this lay over a dark, brownish-black layer of humus containing animal and rodent bones and sheep excrement. Below this was a 10cm-thick layer of brown, silty dirt that directly covered the tile floor.

This depositional record was largely consistent across the building. It was closely watched, and it plays an important role in the interpretation of the structure's history. The top layer was read as rubble from the collapse of upper layers of the building. The layer of dark organic material, which appeared only in the southern room (the prayer hall), was seen as an indication that the building was used secondarily following its abandonment – but before its collapse – by herders who penned their sheep there. Perhaps, given the fact that the organic material existed only in the southern room, the more northerly rooms had already collapsed by the time this secondary use occurred. The lowest, silty layer was interpreted as fill that was laid down during a period of neglect following the abandonment of the building, but before its collapse. The lack of brick and mortar in the dirt confirms it as a pre-collapse deposition, and its thickness indicates a substantial period of abandonment. This silty layer was the lowest layer of soil deposition, beneath which was a tile floor in most rooms. Below this, with a few exceptions to be detailed below, was the untouched soil of the hillside, made up of hard, red dirt with numerous chert cobble inclusions. It was determined that the exterior walls of the *mashhad* rested on this 'virgin' soil.

Numerous phases of construction were evident in the erection of the walls of the *mashhad*. These indicated that the building had not been built in a single phase, but had been built and rebuilt repeatedly. Not only were additions made, but long-extant walls were also thickened and strengthened in many places. The quality of this work varied widely. In the south-east corner, the eastern wall became gradually thinner and thinner until it met the much thicker southern wall. On the interior face, the bricks of the southern and eastern walls were in bond and the corner was firmly interlaced by patterns of intersecting brick. However at some later point, or perhaps at two different points, both the east and south wall were thickened and added to with a shoddier form of brick and rubble construction,

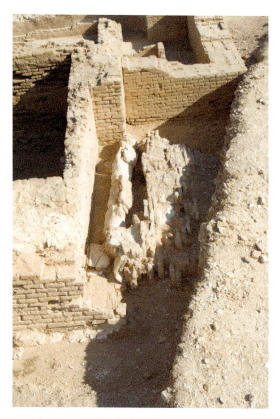

Figure 1.19 *View showing collapsed exterior wall at south-east corner, which was not in bond with the interior wall.*
Photo: Drew Stauss, Departure Studio

meaning that the exterior section of the wall was not in bond (Fig. 1.19). A bird's-eye view down on the southern wall shows a clear line of mortar between these two walls, built flush up against each other in an attempt to strengthen and thicken the southern wall. In the south-east corner of the building is also evidence of another modification: the addition of another, smaller and shallower, niche to supplement the central *miḥrāb* (Fig. 1.20). The south-west room also had such a niche, bringing the total number of niches in the southern wall to three. Both of these lateral niches were cut into the brick of the wall at some later date and plastered over to give the desired form. Perhaps it was because these niches weakened the structure that the south wall was thickened.

Excavation then moved to the east-central room (Fig. 1.18), which was found to have also undergone repeated renovations. This room was square in plan, with a *miḥrāb* niche cut into its southern wall (Fig. 1.21). The floor was tiled in baked terracotta and the niche still had traces of plaster decoration adhering to its base (Fig. 1.3). This floor was raised above the rest of the floors in the building, forming

Figure 1.20 Miḥrāb *niche cut into south wall of prayer hall, south-east corner. Photo: Drew Stauss, Departure Studio*

Figure 1.21 *East-central room, view towards south, with* miḥrāb *niche visible at centre of south wall, while main prayer hall is visible immediately behind. Photo: Drew Stauss, Departure Studio*

Figure 1.22 *Hallway on north side of east-central room. Thin curtain wall is on right. Photo: Drew Stauss, Departure Studio*

a kind of platform. On the north side of the room, a thin curtain wall separated the room from a narrow hallway leading eastwards (Fig. 1.22). This hallway ran between the north curtain wall of the east-central room and a thicker wall marking the south boundary with the north-east room, until it rounded a corner and ran southwards for a few metres along the east wall of the east-central room (Fig. 1.23). At the end of the hallway were two stalls raised up on two small platforms, each of which had originally been enclosed by thin walls (Fig. 1.24). The floors of the platforms were made of two slabs of limestone. Between the two slabs was a slit, which opened into what was once a hole below. These stalls were determined to be latrines. They were only partially excavated because of the danger of collapse.

The north-east room also had a raised floor tiled in terracotta, but the floor tiles were not continuous, and disappeared towards the northern and eastern portions of the room. This

Figure 1.23 *View east over east-central room showing hallway on north and east leading to latrines. Photo: Drew Stauss, Departure Studio*

Figure 1.24 *Latrines, view looking south-west. Note that the corner at the top left is not in bond. Photo: Drew Stauss, Departure Studio*

Figure 1.25 *North-east corner of north-east room showing earlier wall structures below floor. Photo: Drew Stauss, Departure Studio*

room also had a *miḥrāb* niche cut into the brick and plaster of its south wall, bringing the total of niches in this small building so far to five. Beneath the tiled floor the excavators uncovered remnants of earlier wall structures (Fig. 1.25). There was a massive limestone

Figure 1.26 *Central area (courtyard) looking south, showing east-central room on left, doors to prayer hall at top of frame and hole revealing cistern on right. Photo: Drew Stauss, Departure Studio*

wall with a few layers of tile brick on top running north to south, about a metre and a half inside of the east exterior wall. This massive limestone wall is deeper than the exterior walls and at a different angle. Furthermore, when excavating the latrines outside of the east central room, a limestone wall was also found. This limestone wall was in line with the limestone wall in the north-east room. Apparently, when the latrines were added, the original east exterior wall was cut down to the foundations and the entire east wall of the building was extended outwards so that the new exterior wall would be contiguous.

The central room of the *mashhad* was also floored in terracotta (Fig. 1.26). This area was likewise square in plan, with two wide doorways in its south wall revealing a view of the central *miḥrāb*. Beneath the floor tiles was a large, well-constructed cistern, visible via a hole in the floor. This cistern was excavated to reveal a deep, square pit with a carefully built, pointed-arched ceiling (Figs 1.27 and 1.28). Its walls were mortared with waterproof cement and sealed with a waterproof plaster different from the plaster used in the rest of the building. The top of this cistern had been broken open, probably by the building's collapse. This theory was confirmed during excavation, as the fill produced from the cistern consisted of building debris, including many heavy stone architectural elements. Below this fill was a dark brown, silty layer that was full of pottery and metal pieces. This brown layer was quite thin, suggesting the cistern was not in long use before the building was abandoned. Pottery from

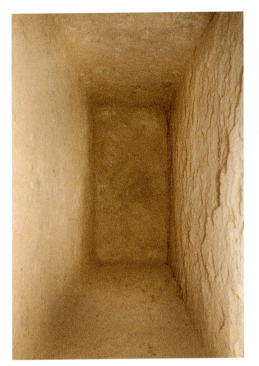

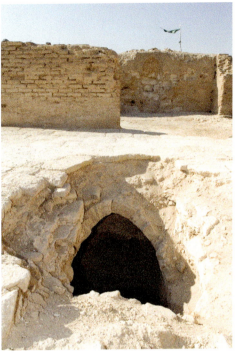

Figure 1.27 *View down into cistern. Photo: Drew Stauss, Departure Studio*

Figure 1.28 *View southward across central area (courtyard), with prayer hall and central mihrab visible in the background. In the foreground is the opening of the underground cistern, showing its vaulted ceiling. Photo: Drew Stauss, Departure Studio*

this locus confirms that the cistern fill can be dated to the mid-thirteenth century.

In the north-central area of the structure, the main entrance to the *mashhad* is visible at the centre of the north wall (Fig. 1.29). The entrance is a complex, multi-period structure including a threshold flanked by two thin walls on the interior and a pivot hole for a door. Just inside and to the east of the doorway, between its thin wall and the exterior wall of the north-east room, was an unusual installation. Raised on a small platform and accessed by a single step, a platform with a small arch a single brick wide was discovered. Behind this arch, on the platform, was found burned plaster, ashes and rounded flint cobbles (Fig. 1.30). The construction details indicate this was an oven that would once have had thin walls and a chimney. This oven was built adjacent to the original door leading to the north-east room, and partially blocked it. It is thus interpreted as a secondary construction, built into the existing *mashhad* plan at some later date.

Figure 1.29 *Main entrance, view towards south. Photo: Drew Stauss, Departure Studio*

Figure 1.30 *Oven installation east of the main entrance. Photo: Drew Stauss, Departure Studio*

The north part of the central room also contained a large pit feature, 5.5m deep, in its floor, of unknown use (Fig. 1.31). When found, the opening of the pit had been sealed by a large basalt column, which had fallen across it during the building's collapse.

Figure 1.31 *Pit feature, showing collapsed arch on upper left, main entrance at top, right of centre and oven installation on upper right. Column bases are visible on right and left. Photo: Drew Stauss, Departure Studio*

When the excavators returned the morning after its discovery, this column had fallen into the pit. It was determined that this pit was too dangerous for excavation and it was sealed off. However, just west of the pit was another intriguing feature: a massive section of brick arch, which had not broken apart entirely when the walls fell. These two features, the column and the arch, provided the excavators with a useful idea of the upper walls and ceiling elements of the *mashhad*. Furthermore, the 'central' and 'north-central' rooms were determined to be a single open space, tiled in terracotta and articulated by the bases of two basalt columns along the east and west walls. One of their columns was assumed to be that which fell into the pit; while another could well have been crushed in the collapse, as many pieces of broken basalt were found in the rubble of the room.

Thus the central area of the *mashhad* was one large room, most likely a courtyard that formed the first area entered by a visitor to the *mashhad*. This room had a large cistern, perhaps indicating it once had a fountain for ablutions. The walls were articulated with columns and, apparently, arches. Perhaps this courtyard had a vaulted ceiling or perhaps it was an open courtyard bordered by a portico. At some point, an oven was installed near the doorway.

The external side of the doorway was also a complex structure that revealed several phases of modifications, apparently designed to monumentalise the entrance of the shrine. Its remaining walls

Figure 1.32 *Reused basalt block in western face of doorway. Photo: Drew Stauss, Departure Studio*

extended outward in jagged, ill-constructed courses of brick (Fig. 1.29). In the course facing the west side of the door was a reused basalt block with carved decorative elements indicating it was robbed from an earlier structure (Fig. 1.32). In the fill of the doorway were two intact plastered brick quarter-domes, suggesting that the doorway had once been ornamented with squinches or *muqarna*s (Fig. 1.33). These squinches imply that a dome or half-dome probably surmounted the door, and they are a strong indication that the doorway was monumentalised in some way at a point after the initial foundation of the shrine.

During the excavations, the team frequently encountered graves. There were graves in the area of the latrines, which had been cut into when the latrines were installed, there were graves under the foundation walls and there were graves in the untouched soil outside of the *mashhad*'s walls. Most graves were left unexcavated out of respect for local sensibilities, and when excavation of a grave was unavoidable, the bones exhumed were later returned to their original location and reburied.

These graves are important, however, for they give a clue to the first phase of use of this area: as a graveyard. Because Islamic tradition requires that the deceased be wrapped only in a simple white shroud and interred without grave goods, it is difficult to date these graves. Similarly, it is impossible to know whether it was first a graveyard, and that at a later date the graveyard was seen as a suitable place for a shrine, or whether the shrine came first and the graves

Figure 1.33 *Fallen squinches in rubble of doorway. Photo: Drew Stauss, Departure Studio*

followed. Logically, the second speculation is perhaps slightly more likely, but the first is certainly a common enough occurrence and is perhaps indicated by the presence of some graves under the walls or cut into by the foundations of the *mashhad*.

A first phase of use of this area can be proposed based on the discovery of deeper foundation walls below the current walls of the *mashhad*. These walls, which did not align with the current walls of the shrine, are set directly into the untouched soil in the eastern third of the building and are the first construction phase for this structure. They too are difficult to date with any certainty. However they stand as evidence that the shrine was modified considerably from its original configuration.

Following the erection of this original structure, the pattern of continuous alteration seems to have become normative for the *mashhad* overlooking the city of Balis. At some point the original structure was either entirely torn down to its foundations, or the eastern wall was extended outward to accommodate an expansion of the shrine that added two latrines and expanded the area of the north-east room. A hallway was carved out of the interior spaces, between the north-east room and the east-central room, leading from the courtyard to the new latrines located on the east wall. Subsequently, the south-east corner of the east wall, along with the southern wall, would, for reasons unknown, be buttressed by thickening both the south and east faces with another layer of brick and mortar. This may have been added simply because the wall was weak, but it may also have reflected a desire to build a more monumental, perhaps vaulted, roof structure.

The central and northern areas also show repeated modifications, especially around the main entrance located at the middle of the large central room. This doorway seems to have been built as a more modest structure that was later monumentalised with the addition of a dome or half-dome on squinches. Its poor, uneven brick and rubble construction and the use of *spolia* point, however, to hasty or local workmanship. Stepping through this doorway into a central room or courtyard, the visitor would have encountered yet another modification in the form of a small, finely built cistern at the centre of the room, undoubtedly with some sort of water-drawing fixture such as a well, pool or fountain. Perhaps this was added at the same time as the doorway was expanded and the east-south wall area was modified, or perhaps each of these modifications took place separately. And it was here, too, that another modification was made: the installation of an oven in the north-east corner. Furthermore, the archaeologist identified the large pit feature in the north-west area of this room as another cistern. If so, it would indicate that at some point the small central cistern was not sufficient and it was necessary to build a larger one. Thus, it speaks of yet another phase of expansion or modification of the shrine.

According to the ceramic evidence, this shrine was probably founded some time before the eleventh century, and used continuously up until the time of the abandonment of Balis in anticipation of the Mongol invasion in 1259. Furthermore, the pattern of occupation described above indicates that the building was intensively utilised, to the degree that it was repeatedly found lacking, and expanded or modified in order to accommodate the needs of its growing number of devotees. Such a pattern points to a shrine that was much beloved and heavily visited, probably by local as well as non-local participants in *ziyāra* (shrine visitation). Many of these modifications seem designed to respond to the needs of visitors far from their homes: for example the latrines, the cisterns and the oven, which was perhaps used for baking bread. But these modifications may just as well have reflected an act of charity for the local poor, as it was not uncommon for a pious person to designate a sum of their income in perpetuity for the provision of charitable activities such as a furnace for making bread or other facilities.

There were also modifications which seem to have been intended to increase the shrine's aesthetic impact: the thickening of the south wall, perhaps to support a more substantial roof structure, and the monumentalisation of the main entrance to include a dome or half-dome. Another indication of the heavy visitation this shrine must have received can be found in the numerous *miḥrāb*s, eventually installed literally in every room of the building. In fact, only the main central *miḥrāb* appears to be original, and the two others in the

Figure 1.34a and 1.34b *Details of main* mihrāb *showing faint traces of painted decoration below a subsequent layer of plaster. Photos: Author*

prayer hall and the two in the east-central and north-east rooms were later additions. Even the main *mihrāb* shows evidence of at least two phases of re-ornamentation: behind the cement to which the stucco forming the latest decorative element of the *mihrāb* was attached, one may see traces of earlier, painted decoration (Figs 1.34 a and b). These many *mihrāb*s are initially a puzzling and unusual phenomenon. Why would so many prayer niches be needed in such a small building? Were they merely decorative, or did they have some more complex explanation? While their interpretation is difficult, one possibility is that the shrine was simply so crowded that it was not possible for many visitants to reach the main prayer hall. Auxiliary rooms would thus form an alternative place in which to pray.

This evidence of continuous and intensive visitation, devotion and patronage demonstrates that devotional activity was as meaningful and important a part of life in the medieval Islamic world as it is today, and that the Balis shrine was a beloved and popular site for such activities. It also forms an important template for the kind of intensive patronage that will be the hallmark of the shrines considered in subsequent chapters, for the Balis shrine is but one example of the continuous patronage that shrines, and particularly ʿAlid shrines, enjoyed throughout the medieval period and until today.

Nevertheless, none of the evidence so far in the excavation of the shrine helps resolve the original question: whether this was the shrine from which the stucco decoration in the Damascus museum was taken. This is a critical question to answer: for on its resolution hangs the possible identification of the shrine. Furthermore, if this shrine can be determined to be that from whence the stuccos came, we will know that it was an 'Alid shrine, and that, according to its archaeology, it remained popular in northern Syria throughout the period of the 'revival' of Sunnism. If the stuccos indeed came from the prayer hall at Balis, many pieces of the puzzle of the shrine will fall into place.

Unfortunately, however, the answer will not come so easily. For as we shall see, the stucco frieze from the Mashhad al-Khidr and that from the prayer hall at Balis seem to be parts of two separate and distinct buildings. The archaeologists' initial assumption that the stuccos were from the Balis shrine was based on several lines of evidence. The first was the simple fact that the prayer hall of the Balis *mashhad* had been excavated, clearly in modern times. While the excavations of the De Lorey-Salles expedition in 1929 had never been fully published, meaning it was impossible to verify that this shrine

was the same as the one the stuccos had been taken from, the fact that the Balis prayer hall had been previously excavated (and that there was no record of another shrine excavation at Balis) seemed to suggest, *prima facie*, that this might be the shrine excavated in 1929. Second, when the Syrian-Princeton team first arrived at Balis, traces of the stucco decoration were still visible on the *miḥrāb* of the prayer hall and in other places throughout the shrine. As excavations proceeded, more stucco fragments were found. The pattern of decoration and style of carving from the stucco of the Balis *mashhad* and the Khidr stucco frieze were so similar as to be nearly identical (Fig. 1.35). And third, before measuring the shrine, the general configuration of the prayer hall seemed to match up quite nicely with that of the Khidr frieze, with a central *miḥrāb* flanked by two smaller niches. Excavation proceeded on the assumption that the frieze had most likely come from the shrine under study.

Figure 1.35 *Stucco fragments from Balis* mashhad. *Photo: Drew Stauss, Departure Studio*

However, when evaluated empirically, the stucco frieze and the *mashhad*'s plan and elevation are not compatible. In the summer of 2007, I conducted a survey of both sites, expecting to find a correspondence between their dimensions that would definitively prove that the shrine of the Syrian-Princeton excavations was the original location of the Khidr frieze excavated by the De-Lorey Salles team. Carefully measuring both the plan and elevation of the Balis prayer hall, I then went to the museum in Damascus and took measurements of the Khidr frieze.[45] The results of these measurements demonstrate that the dimensions of the Khidr frieze are slightly too large for the corresponding spaces in the Balis *mashhad*. This evidence confirms that the Khidr frieze came from some other location in Balis. Indeed, as noted previously, the single brief notice of the excavations published by Georges Salles in 1935 clearly indicated that the shrine that was excavated in 1929 was located 'four miles north of Balis', while our little *mashhad* is located about two miles south.[46] Were the measurements from the museum to correspond exactly, or even were they to be slightly too small but still within the realm of possibility, this topographical notice could have been written off as an error on the part of Georges Salles. But the measurements indicate that the Khidr stucco frieze would not even have fitted into the prayer hall at Balis.[47]

How then, can we identify the shrine excavated by the Syrian-Princeton team? Aside from the certainty that it was built some time in the eleventh century and intensively used until the Mongols arrived in the mid-thirteenth century, it has left no trace of inscriptions, no dates and no direct way to connect it with any known particular building. This means there is no way to identify it with absolute certainty. However, some circumstantial evidence has been left to us by a medieval source, namely the topographer and historian Ibn Shaddad (d. 1284). His topographical and historical work the *A'laq al-Khatira* confirms what the pilgrimage guide author al-Harawi (d. 1215) had reported about the three 'Alid shrines at Balis: that there was a Mashhad al-Tirh (miscarried foetus), a Mashhad al-Hajar (devoted to al-Husayn) and a Mashhad 'Ali ibn Abi Talib.[48]

In addition, Ibn Shaddad elaborates on al-Harawi's account by presenting several enlightening details about one of these shrines. He says that a certain 'al-Safi Abu Sa'd ibn al-Rajjaj constructed a *madrasa* inside the city, and outside (of the city), a *mashhad* for 'Ali (MPBUH) on the mountain of Khuzam'.[49] Ibn Shaddad further notes that prior to the abandonment of the city the shrine had attracted many pilgrims. Could the Balis shrine perhaps have been this Mashhad 'Ali, devoted to the Prophet's nephew and son-in-law 'Ali ibn Abi Talib? We have already demonstrated that the Balis shrine appears to have been heavily visited by pilgrims, tracing the architectural and archaeological response to that visitation in its many acts of patronage and expansion. Furthermore, the Balis shrine is indeed located on one of the highest points of the bluffs overlooking the plain of the Euphrates. Today, this is a prominent projection surrounded by water, but in the medieval period it would certainly have fitted Ibn Shaddad's claim that it was located on a mountain. As noted previously, the shrine sits on a high, mountainous outcropping clearly visible from the city walls of Balis two miles north.

Moreover, of the three shrines recorded by al-Harawi and confirmed by Ibn Shaddad, the shrine of ʿAli is the only one that fits the architectural evidence provided by the Syrian-Princeton team's excavations. This is because the two other shrines probably had features such as tomb chambers that were not found in the excavation of the Balis shrine. The Mashhad al-Tirh, or Shrine of the Miscarried Foetus, would likely have had a cenotaph or other evidence of burial. It was not only a shrine, but also a burial place: built around the belief that a small member of the Prophet's family was actually interred there. An example can be seen in the plan of the Mashhad al-Muhassin in Aleppo, also devoted to a miscarried foetus (further discussed in Chapter 2), which has a tomb chamber containing a cenotaph appended to the main prayer hall of the shrine. The other possibility, the Mashhad al-Hajar, would also probably have been planned around some sort of special area or room designed to accommodate the central object of devotion: a sacred stone upon which the decapitated head of al-Husayn had rested as it was carried from the Battle of Karbalaʾ to the seat of the Umayyad Caliphate in Damascus. But a Mashhad ʿAli, though it might also have been built around a relic, was far more likely to have been exactly the kind of construction found at Balis – the kind of building implied, incidentally, by the word *mashhad* itself: from the Arabic root *shahada* ('to witness'), a place of witnessing, perhaps meant to memorialise the appearance of ʿAli in a dream or vision on the spot, but not necessarily connected to a physical relic *per se*. Thus, a small, multi-room structure with a prayer hall, of the sort uncovered by the Balis excavation, would have served the purposes of the pilgrims well. Although it cannot be demonstrated with certainty, based on the evidence of its plan, location and architectural characteristics it seems likely the Balis *mashhad* is the same as the Mashhad ʿAli described by Ibn Shaddad.

Perhaps most importantly, however, Ibn Shaddad gives us the name of the patron, a person by the name of al-Safi Abu Saʿd ibn al-Rajjaj. And interestingly, this patron, unlike the majority of the inhabitants of northern Syria at this time, may well have been a Sunni. Although he is an unknown figure, and we thus cannot be sure of his sectarian affiliation, his name is not an overtly Shiʿi one. But, most tellingly, Ibn Shaddad informs us that he was the sponsor of a *madrasa*, a school for the teaching of Sunni law and a building associated from at least the Seljuk era with the restoration of Sunnism in Syria. Thus, it seems reasonable to propose that he may have been a Sunni. If so, his patronage would not be unusual.

Indeed, the remainder of this research is devoted to exploring this very phenomenon: the intersectarian nature of the patronage of ʿAlid shrines in Syria. In the end, regardless of its patron, the list of ʿAlid figures revered at Balis – as recorded by authors like al-Harawi and Ibn Shaddad – shows that the Balis *mashhad* was almost certainly devoted to some member of the Prophet's family and that it was visited, endowed and patronised extensively throughout the period of the 'restoration' of Sunnism in Syria.

Conclusion

The Balis shrine is but a single locale, situated within a rich constellation of at least forty still-extant medieval ʿAlid devotional sites distributed throughout Syria and the Levant that collectively form a rich network of interlinked pilgrimage itineraries. Undoubtedly, as the rediscovery of the shrine at Balis testifies, there were countless others. The exploration of a number of these still-extant shrines is the focus of the remainder of this study. These shrines, while each having their own particularities, share with the Balis shrine the characteristic of continuous renovation and renewal. Many of them are still deeply beloved and heavily visited, and, as such, the study of their past is limited to the architectural analysis of their most recent incarnations and the inconsistent notices left by the medieval Arabic sources. The rare opportunity to excavate a medieval ʿAlid shrine archaeologically has provided researchers with the ability to analyse, in detail, aspects of patronage and use that are hinted at by more conventional source material.

The Syrian-Princeton excavation reveals that the Balis shrine fits neatly into this pattern of continual and repeated patronage activity, a phenomenon that was a key aspect of the rapid formation and consolidation of the medieval Levantine sacred landscape. This phenomenon's primary characteristic was the repeated and intensive founding, discovery and renewal of sites of devotion, and ʿAlid shrines appear to have been among the most heavily patronised. This intensive patronage activity swiftly became normative following its apparent inception some time around the eleventh century, but it continued with some intensity into the Mamluk era. In the case of the shrine at Balis, the phenomenon was cut short by the invasion of the Mongols, but there is every indication that it was continuously and vigorously propagated right up to the eve of their conquest. Numerous indicators from the excavation support this observation, the most prominent among them being the thin layer of fill in the cistern, which demonstrates that this significant feature had been only recently installed when the shrine was abandoned. The ceramic material also lends weight to this assertion, for it represented types that were manufactured in the middle of the thirteenth century, just before the abandonment of the site. In this regard, the Balis shrine is a singular example of the kind of extraordinarily detailed information that can be gained through the archaeological exploration of a pious locale. This concrete example of the multi-phased process of the generation of holy sites will serve as a prototype for many of the other shrines to be explored in subsequent chapters.

But many questions remain unanswered, beginning with the firm identification of the shrine itself. The evidence presented here has established that it is most likely not the *mashhad* to al-Khidr whose beautifully ornamented stuccos hang in the Islamic galleries of the National Museum of Damascus. Instead, information about the location of a shrine on a hilltop outside of the city, provided by the medieval historian and topographer Ibn Shaddad, as well as an analysis of the physical characteristics of the shrine itself, indicate it may have been a shrine to 'Ali ibn Abi Talib, the Prophet Muhammad's nephew and son-in-law. There is abundant confirmation that the shrine was heavily patronised, and that at times these acts of patronage were substantial endowments. If this is indeed the shrine for 'Ali mentioned by Ibn Shaddad, we know the name of at least one patron, al-Safi Abu Sa'd ibn al-Rajjaj. It seems intuitive that any patron of an 'Alid shrine would have been Shi'i by confession, and indeed, the area of northern Syria appears to have remained largely Shi'i even long after other areas of Syria had turned towards the Sunnism of the Seljuks and their successors the Zangids and Ayyubids. However, this assumption may not be correct, for this Ibn al-Rajjaj, in addition to sponsoring the *mashhad* 'Ali, was also the patron of a consummately Sunni building, the *madrasa*. For this reason, there is a strong likelihood that the sponsor of the Mashhad 'Ali was a Sunni.

This pattern, it will be shown, was not uncommon. At Balis, we have only sparse information about patrons and their activities. But the shrines to be studied in the following pages are far more generously described in the sources and provide us with abundant references to patrons and their activities in their inscriptions, their architecture and the medieval sources. As will be shown, the vast majority of these 'Alid shrines were endowed, renewed and supported, sometimes in perpetuity, not by Shi'i, but by Sunni patrons. Yet from time to time, Shi'is were also patrons of these holy sites, and the pious contributions of Shi'i figures shows that even in times when Sunnism was ascendant, shrines for the 'Alids were distinct in being uniquely polysemous spaces, capable of encompassing multiple meanings, sectarian associations and forms of piety.

Indeed, the influence of the Shi'is of Balis was also felt in more distant locales. In 1197–8, one of Balis's most illustrious sons would make a remarkable contribution to the sustenance of Shi'i devotional practice in medieval Syria. In that year, the mayor (*ra'is*) of Aleppo, Safi al-Din Tariq b. 'Ali b. Muhammad al-Balisi – an appointee of Saladin who was known by the name Ibn Turayra – demolished the existing door on the Mashhad al-Muhassin in Aleppo and erected a magnificent new one vaulted in stone *muqarnas*. How and why this Shi'i mayor of the capital city of northern Syria found it meaningful to take such an action will be the subject of the next chapter.

Notes

1. Jean Margueron, 'Les fouilles françaises de Meskéné-Emar (Syrie)', *Comptes rendus de l'Académie des Inscriptions et Belles-Lettres*, April–June 1975, 202–3. Widespread looting of the site in the late 1970s and 1980s led to the discovery of many more tablets and their distribution on the international art market. To date, some 1,170 tablets have been identified as originating from Emar. 'Emar, History of the City', home page of the Syrian-German excavations at Emar / Meskene, Syria, accessed 29 September 2007. www.uni-tuebingen.de/emar/en/history. html#
2. Ernst Herzfeld, 'Balis', *Encyclopaedia of Islam*, 1st edition [hereafter *EI1*], ed. M. Th. Houtsma et al. (Leiden: Brill, 1913–38), p. 634.
3. Alois Musil, *The Middle Euphrates, a Topographical Itinerary* (New York: American Geographical Society of New York, 1927), pp. 314–18.
4. Janine Sourdel-Thomine, 'Balis', *Encyclopaedia of Islam*, 2nd edition [hereafter *EI2*], ed. P. Bearman et al. Brill Online, http://reference works.brillonline.com.ezproxy.lib.utexas.edu/entries/encyclopaedia-of-islam-2/balis-SIM_1147 (accessed 1 August 2013).
5. Musil, *Middle Euphrates*, p. 316.
6. René Dussaud, *Topographie Historique de la Syrie Antique et Médiévale* (Paris: P. Geuthner, 1927), p. 453.
7. André Raymond and J. L. Paillet, *Balis II: histoire de Balis et fouilles des îlots I et II.* (Damascus: Institut français de Damas, 1995), p. 26.
8. I am the ceramicist at Balis and have identified these Chinese wares. See Uwe Finkbeiner and Thomas Leisten, 'Emar and Balis 1996 and 1998: a preliminary report of the joint Syrian-German excavations in collaboration with Princeton University', *Berytus* 44 (1999–2000), 53. The other site to produce Chinese wares is Qal'at Ja'bar, just a few kilometres south of Balis, also on the Euphrates. See Christina Tonghini, 'Recent excavation at Qal'at Ja'bar: New data for classifying Syrian fritware', in K. Bartl, *Continuity and Change in Northern Mesopotamia* (Berlin: Dietrich Reimer, 1996), p. 291.
9. He passed through Balis in 1170, and estimated there were around a dozen Jews in the city. Benjamin of Tudela, *The Itinerary of Benjamin of Tudela*, ed. M. N. Adler (New York: P. Feldheim, 1907), p. 32.
10. Raymond, *Balis*, pp. 26–7.
11. Taj al-Din al-Subki, *Tabaqat al-Shafa'iyya al-Kubra*, ed. A. al-Hilu and M. al-Tanahi (Cairo: 'Isa al-Bab al-Halabi, 1964–76), vol. 8, pp. 401–18. The story of the digging of the canal, thereafter called the Nahr al-Shaykh, appears on pp. 403–4.
12. Prophetic *hadith*, an essential building block of both Islamic juris-prudence and the practice of daily life, are transmitted orally from scholar to scholar in chains of transmission stretching back to a direct eyewitness in the time of the Prophet. They therefore had to be learned in person from a scholar who had attained the title of *muhaddith*. A *muhaddith*, according to a famous statement by the founder of one of

the Islamic schools of law, Muhammad ibn Idris al-Shafiʿi, was a person who had memorised a minimum of 400,000 narrations along with their accompanying chains of transmission.

13. Muhammad ibn Ahmad Al-Muqaddasi, *The Best Divisions for Knowledge of the Regions: A Translation of Ahsan al-taqasim fi maʿrifat al-aqalim*, ed. and trans. Basil A. Collins (Reading: Centre for Muslim Contribution to Civilization/Garnet Publishing, 1994), p. 143.

14. Kamal al-Din ʿUmar ibn al-ʿAdim, *Zubdat al-Halab min Taʾrikh Halab*, ed. Sami al-Dahhan (Damascus: al-Maʿhad al-Faransi bi-Dimashq lil-Dirasat al-ʿArabiyya, 1951–68), vol. 1, p. 172.

15. Raymond and Paillet, *Balis*, p. 35.

16. Muhammad ibn ʿAli ibn Shaddad, *al-Aʾlaq al-Khatira fi Dhikr ʾUmaraʾ al-Sham wa-l-Jazira*, ed. Y. ʿAbbara (Damascus: Wizarat al-Thaqafa wa al-Irshad al-Qawmi, 1978), vol. 3, part 1, p. 119.

17. Raymond and Paillet, *Balis*, p. 42.

18. Ibid., p. 44.

19. Kamal al-Din ʿUmar ibn al-ʿAdim, *Bughyat al-Talab fi Taʾrikh Halab*, ed. Suhayl Zakkar (Damascus: S. Zakkar, 1988–9), p. 123. See also Anne-Marie Eddé, 'Notes sur la fiscalité de l'État ayyoubide d'Alep au XXXIe siècle', in Philippe Contamine, Thierry Dutour and Bertrand Schnerb, eds, *Commerce, finances et société (XIe–XVIe s.). Recueil de travaux d'histoire médiévale offert à M. le Profeseur Henri Dubois* (Cultures et Civilisations Médiévales, 9) (Paris: Presses de l'Université de Paris-Sorbonne, 1993), pp. 251–2.

20. It reads, in translation, 'There is no God but God, One, without partner, Muhammad is the Messenger of God, ʿAli is the Friend (*wali*) of God'. Max Van Berchem, 'Arabische Inschriften', in Friedrich Sarre and Ernst Herzfeld, *Archäologische Reise im Euphrat-und Tigrisgebiet* (Berlin: D. Reimer, 1911–20), vol. 1, p. 3.

21. Janine Sourdel and Dominique Sourdel, 'La date de construction du minaret de Bâlis', *Les Annales Archéologiques de Syrie* 3 (1953), 103–5. The minaret was removed from the great mosque in Balis to a location south of the city, and reconstructed on a hill overlooking the site. Also see Van Berchem, 'Arabische Inschriften'. This inscription is no. 3828 in the *Répertoire chronologique d'épigraphie arabe*.

22. Muhammad ibn ʿAli ibn Shaddad, *Al-Aʾlaq al-Khatira, Wasf li-Shamal Suriyya* (Northern Syria), ed. Anne-Marie Eddé, *Bulletin d'Études Orientales* 32–3 (1981–2), 397, 399; trans. Anne-Marie Eddé-Terrasse as *Déscription de la Syrie du Nord* (Damascus: Institut français de Damas, 1984), pp. 5, 13.

23. Ibn al-ʿAdim, *Bughyat al-Talab*, p. 119.

24. Sourdel-Thomine, 'Balis', *EI2*.

25. Georges Salles, 'Les missions archéologiques en Syrie en 1929', *Syria* 10 (1929), 370; 'Nouvelles archéologiques: Les fouilles et recherches archéologiques en 1931, en Liban et Syrie', *Syria* 13 (1932), 112.

26. Cf. René Dussaud et al., *La Syrie antique et médiévale illustrée* (Paris: 1931), plates 107 and108; Georges Salles, 'Les décors en stuc de Balis', in *IIIe congrès international d'art et d'archéologie iraniens: mémoires, Leningrad, septembre 1935* (Moscow & Leningrad: Académie des sciences de l'URSS, 1939), pp. 221–6 and plates 99–102.

27. The relocation of this minaret was reported in Lucien Golvin and André Raymond, 'Meskene/Balis', in *Antiquités de l'Euphrate. Exposition des découvertes de la campagne international de sauvegarde des antiquités*

de l'Euphrate (Aleppo: Direction Générale des antiquités et des musées de la République Arabe Syrienne, 1974), p. 108; Raymond and Paillet, *Balis*, plates 5 and 6; A. Bahnassi, 'La sauvetage des vestiges de la zone de submersion du barrage de Tabqa sur l'Euphrate', *Monumentum. International Council on Monuments and Sites* 17 (1978), 63–6.

28. Thomas Leisten, 'For prince and country(side) – the Marwanid mansion at Balis on the Euphrates', paper delivered at the Colloquium on Late Antique and Early Islamic Archaeology in Bilad al-Sham, Deutsches Archäologisches Institut, under the aegis of the Ministry of Culture – Directorate General of Antiquities and Museums in Syria. Damascus, 5–9 November, 2006. I thank Professor Leisten for providing me with a copy of this paper.

29. Abu'l Faraj al-ʿUsh et al., *Catalogue du Musée National de Damas, publié à l'occasion de son cinquantenaire* (Damascus: Direction générale des antiquités et des musées, 1969), p. 255.

30. Dominique Sourdel and Janine Sourdel-Thomine, 'Un sanctuaire chiite de l'ancienne Balis', in P. Salmon, ed., *Mélanges d'Islamologie* (Leiden: Brill, 1974), pp. 247–53. For more on the subject of medieval Shiʿism in northern Syria, see Chapter 2.

31. Ibid., p. 105, n. 2. This was the mayor (*raʾis*) of Aleppo Safi al-Din Tariq b. ʿAli b. Muhammad al-Balisi, an appointee of Saladin who was known by the name Ibn Turayra and who contributed extensively to the renovation of the Mashhad al-Husayn and Mashhad al-Muhassin at the end of the twelfth century. See Chapter 2 for specific information about his patronage activities.

32. J. and D. Sourdel, 'La date de construction du minaret de Bâlis'. Frustratingly, they do not reproduce the text of the minaret's inscriptions, but only assert that it is 'a eulogy and formula of a Shiʿi tendency'. However the full text is reproduced in Van Berchem's translation; see note 21 above.

33. Sourdel and Sourdel-Thomine, 'Un sanctuaire chiite', pp. 249–50. Translation from the French is my own, however there seems to be an error either in their reproduction of the Arabic (on p. 249) or, more likely as far as I can see, a 'scribal error' in the stucco panel itself. Where it should be 'the Pure Family' (*al-ʿāʾila al-tahira*), the character for the Arabic letter *lām* is missing in the word 'family' (*ʿāʾila*). The Sourdels reproduced this word as *ʿatara*, which as far as I am aware is not a word. Despite their reproduction of the error in the Arabic, their French translation provides the word 'family' and this is clearly what was meant, indeed the expression 'the Pure Family' is a common Shiʿi epitaph. For more on this epitaph and its 'Shiʿi' interpretation, see Chapter 3, section on the cenotaph of Sukayna.

34. Surat al-Kahf (Qurʾan 18:60–82).

35. John Renard, 'Khadir/Khidr', *Encyclopaedia of the Qurʾan*, ed. Jane Dammen McAuliffe, Brill Online, http://referenceworks.brillonline.com.ezproxy.lib.utexas.edu/entries/encyclopaedia-of-the-quran/khadir-khidr-SIM_00248 (accessed 31 October 2007). See also Josef Meri, 'Re-appropriating sacred space: Medieval Jews and Muslims seeking Elijah and al-Khadir', *Medieval Encounters* 5 (1999), 237–64.

36. Text in italics represents the reconstructed parts of the verse.

37. See Chapter 3 below, section on the cenotaph of Sukayna, for a more expansive discussion of this verse.

38. Salles, 'Les décors en stuc', pp. 222–4, plate 99, upper photograph.

39. Ibid., p. 224. The inscription is no. 2678 of the *Répertoire chronologique d'épigraphie arabe*, but without an indication of provenience beyond the place name of Meskene. Sourdel and Sourdel-Thomine, 'Un sanctuaire chiite', p. 251, n. 11.

40. Salles, 'Les décors en stuc', p. 224.

41. Qurʾan 2:146–7, which reads 'Those to whom We have sent down the Book know this even as they know their sons. Yet a section among them conceals the truth knowingly. The truth is from your Lord, so be not among those who are sceptics.' This verse is clearly intended to refer to the *ahl al-kitāb*, the People of the Book, i.e. the Jews and Christians to whom God had also revealed a sacred text but who had gone astray, but it could equally well refer to Muslims who did not follow the Qurʾan's precepts. In a Shiʿi context, perhaps this was meant as a condemnation of misguided Muslims like the Sunnis.

42. ʿAli Ibn Abi Bakr Al-Harawi, *Kitab al-Isharat ila Maʿrifat al-Ziyarat*, ed. Janine Sourdel-Thomine (Damascus: al-Maʿhad al-Faransi bi-Dimashq, 1953), p. 61; ed. and trans. Janine Sourdel-Thomine, *Guide des lieux de pèlerinage* (Damascus: Institut français de Damas, 1957), p. 55; and Josef Meri, *Lonely Wayfarer's Guide* (Oxford: Oxford University Press, 2004), p. 156. Ibn Shaddad also quotes this passage, see Muhammad ibn ʿAli ibn Shaddad, *al-Aʿlaq al-Khatira fi Dhikr ʾUmaraʾ al-Sham wa-l-Jazira* (Aleppo), ed. Dominique Sourdel (Damascus: al-Maʿhad al-Faransi bi-Dimashq, 1953), vol. 1, part 1, p. 59.

43. Both are discussed in detail in Chapter 2.

44. For the following section I am grateful to David Lineberry for providing me with his excavation notes, upon which, in addition to my own observations from the site, I rely for the description of the archaeology here.

45. I thank the National Museum of Damascus for permission to measure the frieze.

46. Salles, 'Les décors en stuc', pp. 221–6 and plates 99–102.

47. The measurements are very close. For example, the distance between the left corner of the Khidr frieze (the one hanging on the right side in the museum, but originally located on the left) and the edge of the central *miḥrāb* is 112cm, while the same distance in the Balis *mashhad* is 105cm. Still, 7cm is quite a bit too long to account for in any reasonable way. Furthermore, the extreme left edge of the Khidr frieze is broken off and its inscription and decoration seems to have continued further to the left, meaning it was actually longer than 112cm. Similarly, the central *miḥrāb* of the same frieze in the museum has a width of 84cm while the central niche in the Balis *mashhad* has a width of 60cm.

48. Ibn Shaddad, *Aʿlaq* (Aleppo), p. 59.

49. Ibn Shaddad, *Aʿlaq* (Northern Syria), ed. Eddé, p. 399; trans. Eddé-Terrasse, *Déscription*, pp. 15–16.

CHAPTER TWO

Aleppo: An Experiment in Islamic Ecumenism

ALEPPO ONCE HAD two medieval gates in its western wall (Map 2). The southernmost of these gates still stands, at the western terminus of the main market street that leads from the citadel. As in the medieval period, it is known today as the Bab Antakya (Antioch Gate). Exiting this gate, a pilgrim today will find a road that crosses over the river Quwayq and follows the river's winding path as it eventually turns southward. About 1.5 km from the city wall, this southbound road passes near a low hill. On the eastern flank of the hill, which was known in the medieval period as the Jabal Jawshan, sit two medieval shrines overlooking the city. The larger, northernmost shrine commemorates al-Husayn. About 300 m to the south is another shrine devoted to al-Muhassin, the stillborn son of al-Husayn. Before 2011, over a million pilgrims a year from many locations throughout the Islamic world participated in organised tours to these sites, and a visitor could observe these pious supplicants as they emerged in a seemingly incessant stream from the tour buses and cars that continuously parked in the large car park in front of the site. Although Aleppo once had many Shi'i shrines, including two shrines to 'Ali, a *mashhad* to Sidi Ghawth[1] and others, the shrines to al-Husayn and al-Muhassin on the Jabal Jawshan were the largest and most significant, and they remain so today.[2] In the Seljuk, Zangid and Ayyubid eras, they were the locus of medieval Syria's most highly invested experiment in pragmatic toleration and cooperation between Sunnis and Shi'is.

The architects of this experiment were a group of Aleppo's rulers in the period from the late tenth to the twelfth century. One of these sovereigns consciously used the shrines to promote such cooperation as part of a larger project of sectarian conciliation. The actions of several other rulers indicate that such cooperation was probably an implicit motivation for their act of patronage. In the end, two buildings of extraordinary beauty emerged from these multiple investments, one of them a true masterwork of Ayyubid architecture. Yet it is a bit strange that such lavish buildings would be erected to commemorate an obscure figure and an ephemeral event that were otherwise unknown in Islamic history. In an ironic inversion of the

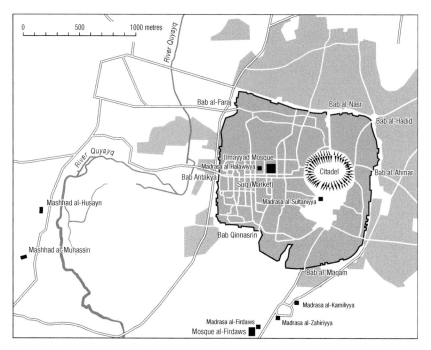

Map 2 *Plan of Aleppo, showing the Bab Antakya west of the citadel and the road leading west and then south along the river Quwayq. The Mashhad al-Muhassin is visible on the hillside on far left, and the Mashhad al-Husayn is directly north of it.*

expected, the ʿAlid shrines of Aleppo, devoted to relatively little-known episodes of Shiʿi martyrology, are far more elaborate than their counterparts in Damascus, where – as we shall see in the following chapter – the remains of much more important ʿAlid figures were housed in strikingly small-scale, modest constructions.

This irony is perhaps explained by a simple fact of demography, for Aleppo, unlike Damascus, was a Shiʿi-controlled city for much of its medieval history. Thus, these shrines are the product of a particular moment in that history in which it was advantageous to propitiate the city's Shiʿi population. In this environment, Aleppo's patrons had far greater freedom to endow projects that benefited Shiʿi practice than did their Damascene equivalents. Indeed, by the Ayyubid period, the population of northern Syria and Mesopotamia had a long-established inclination toward Shiʿism. A large proportion of the Muslims of Aleppo were Shiʿi, as were the inhabitants of numerous surrounding towns.[3] In the mid-eleventh century, Nasir-i Khusrau reports that the cities of the Syrian littoral, such as Tripoli, Baalbek, Sidon, Tyre and Tiberius, had a majority of Shiʿis.[4] Many inland towns, such as Homs, Hama and Damascus, sheltered a significant, and vocal, Shiʿi minority. This so disturbed a staunch

Sunni like Ibn Jubayr (d. 1217) that he paused in his travel narrative to grumble about their excessive numbers and sue for preservation from their heresies:

> In these lands the Shi'is are an astonishing phenomenon. They are more numerous than the Sunnis, and they have disseminated their doctrines everywhere. They are divided into different sects . . . the Rafidis . . . the Imamis, the Zaydis . . . the Isma'ilis, the Nusayris – who are infidels because they attribute divinity to 'Ali (may God be pleased with him) – . . . the Ghurabiyya – who claim that 'Ali resembles the Prophet PBUH . . . as well as other sects one shrinks from enumerating. God has misled them and has misled many of his creations. We beg of God to protect us in (true) religion and seek refuge in Him from the deviations of the heretics (zaygh al-mulḥidīn).[5]

No doubt this apparent flourishing of Shi'ism was encouraged by the fact that Syria was under the political control of Shi'i dynasties for much of its medieval history, although precisely how and to what degree this officially sanctioned Shi'ism succeeded in winning over the general population is somewhat unclear. However it is apparent that in northern, central and coastal Syria, as well as selected cities in other areas, Shi'i rule had a palpable effect on conversion. In some cities, it seems Shi'ism made inroads at an early stage: al-Muqaddasi (d. c. 1000) reports that

> regarding allegiance to theological schools, the people of Syria are rightly guided, and upholders of authority and tradition [i.e., Sunni]. The people of Tiberias, however, and half the population of Nablus and Qadas, and most of the people of 'Amman, are Shi'a.[6]

However, Shi'i political control – if it were indeed an impetus for Shi'i popular allegiance – did not have the same outcome in southern Syria as it did in the area of north-central Syria and the Jazira. Though the Isma'ili Fatimids controlled southern Syria until the mid-twelfth century, Shi'ism remained a marginal presence there, with the exception of the Shi'i movement of the Druze, which became entrenched in the area of the Hawran under the rule of the Fatimid Caliph al-Hakim (r. 996–1021). This heterodox faction, along with some small groupings of Imami (Twelver) Shi'is, seems always to have been a minority in the south, which remained predominantly Sunni.[7] In particular, the large cities such as Damascus maintained a strong commitment to Sunnism and sheltered only a small minority of Shi'i inhabitants.

In north-central Syria and the Jazira, however, the strength of Shi'ism was such that the Shi'a were able to practise openly for many centuries, encouraged by the leadership of several Shiʿi dynasties. In Mesopotamia, the Shiʿi Hamdanids had become the ʿAbbasid amirs of Mosul in 905 and slowly extended their reach, capturing Aleppo, Antakya and Homs in 944. The Hamdanid ʿAli ibn ʿAbdallah, who took the regnal title of Sayf al-Dawla, met little resistance when he captured Aleppo. He made the city his capital and surrounded himself with a glittering court that included the most famous poets, philosophers and litterateurs of the day. He also encouraged the immigration of Shiʿi ʿulamaʾ, thereby directly influencing the numerical expansion of Shiʿism in northern Syria. In 977, the mosques of Aleppo began to use the Shiʿi formulas ʿCome to the best of works' and 'Muhammad and ʿAli are the best of men' as part of the call to prayer.[8]

The decline of the Hamdanids after the death of Sayf al-Dawla in 967 did not bring a reversal of this trend. The Hamdanids were replaced in 1024 by the Shiʿi Mirdasids, who ruled for a further sixty years, and later by the ʿUqaylids, also Shiʿi, who held the city until the Sunni Seljuks captured it in 1090. These Shiʿi dynasties presided over a population that, as Ibn Jubayr grumbled, also tended to be Shiʿi, or at least one that had powerful and vocal Shiʿi factions. In 1069, the Mirdasid prince Mahmud ibn Nasr, sensing the political winds were beginning to shift in favour of Sunnism, ordered that the invocation of the *khuṭba* should no longer honour the Fatimid caliph, and should name instead the ʿAbbasid caliph and the Seljuk amir. The response of the attendees at Friday prayer was telling: they snatched up their prayer mats and said, 'These are the mats of ʿAli ibn Abi Talib. Let Abu Bakr bring mats for the people to pray upon.'[9] In cities like Aleppo, though we do not know whether they ever achieved numerical majority, Shiʿis held many of the prominent political and religious positions and thus wielded power disproportionate to their numbers.[10] Furthermore, despite their external demonstrations of allegiance to the Ismaʿili Fatimid caliph, the Shiʿis of Aleppo tended to be what we might rather anachronistically call 'bourgeois' Imamis – in other words, Aleppo was a city of merchants who favoured a conservative theological moderation.[11]

The capture of Aleppo by the Sunni Seljuks did not diminish the region's Shiʿi tendencies. It seems, for example, that in the tenth and eleventh centuries, most of the tribal groups on the desert fringes were Shiʿi, many of them Ismaʿili or heterodox branches.[12] The last Seljuk prince of Aleppo, Ridwan ibn Tutush (r. 1095–1113) found himself under such strong local Shiʿi pressure that he actually ordered that the *khuṭba* be pronounced in the name of the Fatimid caliph, demonstrating that several decades of Sunni rule had done little to alter local allegiances.[13] Shortly thereafter, even the archetypal Sunni ruler Nur al-Din hesitated to enforce official Sunnism on the city. According to the twelfth century Shiʿi chronicler Ibn Abi Tayyiʾ, Nur al-Din initially conformed to the attitude of his father ('Imad al-Din Zangi), with full regard for the Aleppan Shi'is, and, far from troubling them, let them practise their prayer openly in conformance with their rites in the eastern part of the great mosque, and make the call to prayer from the minarets of Aleppo according to their formula 'Come to the best of works!'[14]

Ibn Abi Tayyi' continues that his father had told him that in his time, even the mosque of the citadel (the residence of the Sunni ruler of Aleppo) still used the Shi'i formula.[15] This was allowed to continue until political expediency intervened in 1146–7, when Nur al-Din wished to consolidate his position by making a treaty with the Sunni prince of Damascus. The liaison was threatened by an alliance of Aleppan and Damascene Sunni notables, who conspired to pressure Nur al-Din to renounce what they felt was his too-favourable attitude toward the Shi'is of Aleppo.[16]

Even so, the edict against the Shi'i call to prayer was not seriously enforced until two years later in 1148. Despite considerable political pressure from the Sunnis, Nur al-Din had been reluctant to follow through, as he feared loss of control over the city, and he was right. When he finally prohibited the Shi'i formula, riots erupted, and Nur al-Din was forced to exile some Shi'i leaders who stubbornly refused to conform. Later, after Nur al-Din died, the population's apprehension about the policies of his successor al-Salih Isma'il, who had a strong attachment to Sunnism, provoked yet another a violent reaction from the Shi'is of Aleppo. According to Ibn al-'Adim, they 'pillaged the houses of [prominent Sunnis] Qutb al-Din Ibn al-'Ajami and Baha' al-Din Abu Ya'li Ibn Amin al-Dawla'.[17] In retaliation, the soldiers of the citadel were ordered to destroy the house of Abu'l-Fadl Ibn al-Khashshab, the Shi'i $q\bar{a}d\bar{\imath}$ who had led the mob.[18] Nevertheless, it was only a temporary setback and the Shi'is eventually regained some of the privileges revoked under Nur al-Din, including the right to pray in the eastern part of the great mosque.[19]

At about this time, in the second half of the twelfth century, Aleppo also became an important centre for Shi'i scholarship. This was due to the residence there of several important scholars, chiefly Abu'l-Makarim Hamza ibn 'Ali al-Halabi, who was known as Ibn Zuhra (d. 1189), and Muhammad ibn 'Ali al-Sarawi al-Mazandarani, or Ibn Shahrashub (d. 1192). Because of their influence, for nearly half a century Aleppo was among the predominant centres of Shi'i learning in the Islamic world.[20]

Nur al-Din's control over Aleppo came to an end with his death and the acquisition of the city as the capital of an Ayyubid principality. It was during the Ayyubid period that Sunni tolerance toward the Shi'is of Aleppo reached its zenith, particularly under the rule of the Ayyubid al-Malik al-Zahir, who received the principality of

Aleppo from his father Saladin in 1176. Nowhere was al-Zahir's pragmatically tolerant attitude more evident than in his patronage of the shrines of al-Muhassin and al-Husayn on the Jabal Jawshan. Nevertheless, long before the actions of al-Zahir, these shrines had already accumulated a complex prior history of both Sunni and Shi'i patronage.

The Mashhad al-Muhassin (Mashhad al-Dikka)

The first sovereign to take an interest in building Shi'i shrines in Aleppo was the Shi'i Hamdanid ruler of Aleppo, Sayf al-Dawla (r. 944–67). He prefigured the twelfth century trend toward the 'discovery' of holy sites when he founded the Mashhad al-Muhassin, which commemorates a previously unknown, stillborn child of al-Husayn (Figs 2.1, 2.2 and 2.3). The shrine is located at the southern end of Jabal Jawshan and its main entrance is accessed by a long flight of stairs, making the front façade difficult to see properly from the base of the hill. The shrine is built around a rectangular courtyard and consists of a domed tomb chamber on the south-east corner accessed through a slightly smaller domed vestibule, a triple-domed prayer hall on the south wall, and latrines and facilities for cooking and study in the north-east, north and west (Fig. 2.2). Its rather austere stone *muqarnas* portal is among the earliest in Islamic architecture (Figs 2.4 and 2.5).[21] The *mashhad*'s physical structure and constitution, as well as the architectural phasing, have been recorded and analysed twice: first by Ernst Herzfeld in the 1950s, and more recently by Terry Allen.[22] There are two published plans of the building, one a less detailed version by Jean Sauvaget, and the other, depicting accurate projections of the vaulting, by Herzfeld (Fig. 2.2).[23]

The shrine was originally called the Mashhad al-Dikka because Sayf al-Dawla had a terrace or *dikka* there from where he watched horse races below. It was 'rediscovered', according to a common *topos*, when Sayf al-Dawla had a dream about the site. In the dream, he stood on the balcony of his house overlooking the town and saw lights repeatedly descend at a location on the Jabal Jawshan.[24] When he awoke, he rode personally to the place he had dreamed about and began digging there. To his amazement a tombstone was found precisely where the lights had descended, engraved in the name of a certain al-Muhassin b. al-Husayn b. 'Ali b. Abi Talib, designating this location as his grave.[25]

Visions, dreams and miraculous occurrences are common features of Shi'i shrine foundation stories. The phenomenon seems not to have been as prominent in Sunni piety. If we include the Mashhad al-Muhassin, Ibn al-Shaddad records seven instances of miraculous, dream-inspired Shi'i architectural foundation stories in Aleppo, five of them involving visions of 'Ali, the sixth the flashes of light seen

Figure 2.1 *Mashhad al-Muhassin, view of entrance portal and east wall. The inscription of Zangi is visible in the frame on the left, above a blocked entrance into the tomb chamber. Photo: Terry Allen*

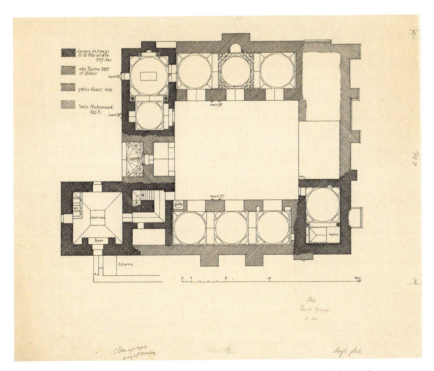

Figure 2.2 *Aleppo, Mashhad al-Muhassin (Mashhad al-Dikka), plan. Illustration: The Ernst Herzfeld Papers. Freer Gallery of Art and Arthur M. Sackler Gallery Archives. Smithsonian Institution, Washington, DC*

Figure 2.3 *Mashhad al-Muhassin, tomb chamber. Photo: Terry Allen*

by Sayf al-Dawla and the seventh a shepherd's dream of an unidenti-
fied man, who appears in the foundation story of the Husayn shrine
(to be discussed below).[26] Although Sunnis also had miraculous
dreams and visions, they appear to have been used less frequently to
spur or justify the foundation of shrines.[27] The tenth to thirteenth
centuries saw a great increase in the experience of such events by
medieval Muslims.[28]

Despite the ubiquity of such accounts, the story of the discovery of
this site and the identity of the holy figure buried there was the cause
of some controversy. Ibn al-ʿAdim (d. 1262) notes that he had read 'in
the writings of one of the Aleppans' that it was 'a worthless place,
until the prisoners of al-Husayn and his wife and children (peace be
upon them) passed there (on their way to Damascus following the
battle of Karbalaʾ)'. According to this account, there was a mine on
the mountainside near where the Karbalaʾ prisoners camped. Thirsty
from the journey, the pregnant wife of al-Husayn approached the
miners and asked them for water. The miners refused her request
and abused her. Presumably because of this incident, which implies
she was raped, she miscarried her child and buried him near the
camp on the mountainside. She cursed the miners, and in a stroke

Figure 2.4 *Aleppo, Mashhad al-Muhassin, portal. Photo: Terry Allen*

of poetic justice their mine was thereafter as barren as her womb, for 'whoever works on it gains nothing but exhaustion'. Ibn al-ʿAdim adds that this story was confirmed directly for him by one of the Shiʿi shaykhs of Aleppo.[29] The story has many of the hallmarks of Shiʿi

Figure 2.5 *Aleppo, Mashhad al-Muhassin, portal, elevation and section. Image: The Ernst Herzfeld Papers. Freer Gallery of Art and Arthur M. Sackler Gallery Archives. Smithsonian Institution, Washington, DC*

martyrology and probably grew from a desire to explain the presence of an abandoned mine near the shrine.

This foundation story reappears in the sources a generation later, in Ibn Shaddad's history of Syria and the Jazira, but this time the source for the hagiographic material is explicit. He writes on the authority of the Shi'i historian Ibn Abi Tayyi' (d. 1228–33) that when Sayf al-Dawla found the grave marker, he queried the Shi'i leaders of Aleppo about the existence of a son of al-Husayn named al-Muhassin. Their response seems to reflect some ambivalence:

> Some of them replied: 'We have not heard this, but we have heard that Fatima (peace be upon her) was pregnant and the Prophet (peace be upon him) said: in your belly is al-Muhassin. And when the Day of (swearing the oath of) Allegiance (*yawm al-bay'a*) arrived, they forced their way into her house to bring 'Ali (peace be upon him) out to swear the oath, and she miscarried.' And others of them said: 'It is possible that when the captive women of al-Husayn arrived in that place one of his women miscarried that boy.'[30]

Others pointed out that the writing on the stone was ancient, indicating the locale was of great antiquity. The phrases 'some of them/ others of them' make clear there was dissent between the city's Shi'i leaders regarding the authenticity of the shrine. There also seems to have been uncertainty as to whether it was a son of 'Ali or a son of al-Husayn that was buried there, as indicated by the account of Fatima's miscarriage.[31] At this point in the narrative, for the first time, there is mention of the body of an actual miscarried foetus, whose miraculous lack of decay the Shi'i scholars used to bolster the argument that it was that of the son of al-Husayn. Despite these scholarly controversies, among the people, the wondrous story quickly spread, and there was growing pressure to build a *mashhad*. Sayf al-Dawla appears not to have taken sides. He simply remarked that 'God has given me permission to build in this place in the name of the *ahl al-bayt*!' and began construction.

Nothing remains from Sayf al-Dawla's original construction, and the building that stands today is a palimpsest of later additions and renovations (Fig. 2.2). Ibn Shaddad reports that the Shi'i historian Ibn Abi Tayyi' claimed to have visited it in the days when the portal of Sayf al-Dawla still stood. He described the portal:

> I entered the door of that *mashhad*. It is a small door made of black stone with a vault over it. There is a broad inscription in Kufic writing on it (which reads): 'This blessed *mashhad* was built for the purpose of turning toward (*ibtighā'an wijhata*) God most high and becoming closer to Him, in the name of our Master al-Muhassin ibn al-Husayn ibn 'Ali ibn Abi Talib (peace be upon him). The most exalted Amir Sayf al-Dawla Abu al-Husayn 'Ali ibn 'Abdallah ibn Hamdan.'[32]

Ibn Abi Tayyi' adds that in the days of the Mirdasids (r. 1023–79) the shrine gained a large structure in its northern section. But like the work of Sayf al-Dawla, this structure is now gone, and the building as it stands today is entirely the work of Sunni patrons.[33] Nor were these patrons' acts mere token gestures, but rather they represented a major investment of private and state resources. These acts were ongoing throughout the period of Sunni Revival.

The first Sunni to contribute was the Seljuk governor of Aleppo, Qasim al-Dawla Aq Sunqur, who ensured the functionality of the shrine by adding a cistern on the south (qiblī) side in 1089. He also entirely rebuilt the southern wall, which was beginning to fall, built a small enclosure around the tomb that was ornamented with silver colonnettes, donated a fine cloth cover for the cenotaph and endowed the shrine with the income from fields and a mill to ensure its upkeep.[34]

In 1124, after the death of the Seljuk emir Ridwan b. Tutush – the emir who had briefly allowed the khutba to be said in the name of the Fatimid caliph (see above) – the crusader Count Joscelin I of Edessa laid siege to Aleppo. During the siege an interesting episode occurred at the Mashhad al-Muhassin. As the blockade wore on, the Crusaders burned and pillaged the shrines on the outskirts of the city. But when they came to the shrine of al-Muhassin, instead of sacking it straightaway, they entered the tomb area and excavated the grave. This looks at first glance like a simple act of desecration, but Ibn al-ʿAdim, who reports the episode in both of his histories of Aleppo, each time ends the account by saying 'they descended into it [the grave], and didn't find anything (or did not see anything) in it, so they burned it'.[35] The description of this event suggests that the Crusaders pillaged the shrine only after ensuring that the grave did not contain the body of a holy figure. It is difficult to find an unambiguous explanation for this, but it suggests that for the Crusaders there was some value or interest in verifying claims made about holy sites. In any case, the pillaging of the Mashhad al-Muhassin provoked a well-known episode of Christian persecution in Aleppo, as reported by Ibn al-ʿAdim:

> When (the Seljuk regent and Shiʿi qāḍī) Abu al-Fadl ibn al-Khashshab was deputised and managing the affairs of the city during the siege, he changed the churches of the Christians in Aleppo into mosques by ordaining for them mihrābs facing the qibla. I heard this from my father, may God have mercy upon him, and he heard it from his father.[36]

This vengeful action, which included the conversion of the great Byzantine cathedral founded by Flavia Helena Augusta, the mother of the Byzantine Emperor Constantine, testifies to the importance of the shrines, and perhaps in particular of the shrine to al-Muhassin, for the people of Aleppo.[37]

Following this incident, the shrine continued to benefit from the interest of Sunni rulers. In the mid-twelfth century, although rather unusually the Arab chroniclers do not report it, the Atabeg Zangi funded work on the shrine, as is evident from an inscription, probably not *in situ*, located on the eastern external wall of the tomb chamber, above a blocked doorway (Fig. 2.1). It is a large inscription, in Kufic contained within a frame, and it records unspecified work on the shrine in Zangi's name in the year 1142–3. Just below this inscription is evidence that Zangi's son Nur al-Din also contributed to the upkeep of this ʿAlid shrine. The inscription is small and rather disfigured, but according to Ibn Shaddad, Nur al-Din ordered the construction of a cistern and a spacious latrine or area for ablutions with multiple stalls (*mīdā fīhā buyūt kathīra*), a gesture for which both pilgrims and residents were grateful.[38] This is probably the present groin-vaulted cubical projection the north-east corner of the building. Herzfeld records the presence of latrines, however none is visible today.[39] Relying on these inscriptions, Herzfeld thought that the tomb chamber, which consists of a domed room on squinches preceded by a smaller domed anteroom, also on squinches, must be attributed to Zangi, but Terry Allen has disputed this, proposing a slightly later date.[40] The architectural details of the tomb area, with its small squinches set on little projecting knobs at their springing, and tiny, single *muqarnas* cells at the point of transition to the dome, are consistent with a twelfth-century date (Fig. 2.3).[41] Another notable feature of this tomb chamber are two marble columns with lyre-shaped capitals, which support the transverse arch dividing the anteroom from the main tomb area. As several scholars have noted, lyre-shaped capitals are rare in Syrian monuments and are more typically associated with Mesopotamia.[42]

After these interventions, the shrine grew in importance, and by the Ayyubid period, the Mashhad al-Muhassin had become one of the most beloved Shiʿi pilgrimage sites in Aleppo. Ibn al-ʿAdim writes that in the thirteenth century 'the Shiʿis of Aleppo have great veneration for it and make many visits there'.[43] Several major expansions occurred during the period of Ayyubid sovereignty. In 1197–8, the mayor (*raʾīs*) of Aleppo, Safi al-Din Tariq b. ʿAli b. Muhammad al-Balisi, an appointee of Saladin who was known by the name Ibn Turayra, demolished the original portal built by Sayf al-Dawla and added an impressive new one vaulted in stone *muqarnas* (Figs. 2.3, 2.4 and 2.6). This is the portal remaining today, notable for being one of the earliest preserved stone *muqarnas* vaults in Syria.[44] The mayor's nephew, Wali al-Din Abu al-Qasim ibn ʿAli, who was himself mayor a decade later, tore down the door of the reservoir that had been built by the Seljuk Aq Sunqur in 1089, and rebuilt it in his name. He was later buried there, though no trace of the tomb or of the reservoir on the south side remains.[45]

A few years later, in 1212–13, al-Malik al-Zahir Ghazi (r. 1186–1216), the son of Saladin and the Ayyubid sultan of the principality of Aleppo, undertook a major restoration of the *mashhad* after the

Figure 2.6 *View upward into stone* muqarnas *dome over entrance. Photo: Author*

south wall collapsed. He entirely rebuilt the sanctuary on the south side of the building, adding a triple-domed prayer hall (Fig. 2.7).[46] Inside, the south courtyard wall still bears an inscription in his name, confirming him as patron and noting the date of the work (Figs 2.8 and 2.9). This inscription is *in situ* and thus the sanctuary area dates to the early thirteenth century.[47] This sanctuary is a small, triple-domed prayer hall, with a central dome over the *miḥrāb*. The ante*miḥrāb* dome is set on *muqarnas* pendentives, while the two side domes rest on split pendentives. The *miḥrāb* is a simple niche devoid of decoration, and the prayer hall, aside from its simple *muqarnas* ornament, has a rather sober aspect (Fig. 2.10).

Another Ayyubid sultan, the son of al-Malik al-Zahir, al-Malik al-ʿAziz (r. 1216–36), rebuilt the north wall of the courtyard, which had fallen down, in 1234–5 (Fig. 2.11).[48] This wall bears what is possibly the Mashhad al-Muhassin's most remarkable feature: an inscription near its north-east corner in the name of the Sunni Sultan al-ʿAziz, which praises the twelve Shiʿi Imams, to which we shall return later (Fig. 2.12). Regarding the patron, the architectural and the textual evidence are at odds. Ibn Shaddad records that the reconstruction of the north wall was done not by al-ʿAziz, but by his son, al-Malik al-Nasir Yusuf, who also built the contemporaneous cupola (*rawshan al-dāʾir*) in the prayer hall of the courtyard (*bi-qāʿat al-ṣahn*). This, incidentally, would also mean that the ante*miḥrāb* dome was built,

Figure 2.7 *Mashhad al-Muhassin, view from the west. The domes of the sanctuary rebuilt in the early seventh/thirteenth century are visible in the foreground, with the two domes of the tomb chamber behind them. Photo: Author*

Figure 2.8 *Mashhad al-Muhassin, south wall of courtyard (exterior of prayer hall), showing inscription panel at top, left of centre. Photo: Author*

Figure 2.9 *Inscription of al-Malik al-Zahir, dating sanctuary to 1212–13. Photo: Author*

or rebuilt, a few decades after al-Zahir's complete rebuilding of the sanctuary. Ibn Shaddad's statement is thus not in conformity with the epigraphic evidence given by the inscription, which clearly credits the refurbishing of the north area to al-Nasir's father al-ʿAziz.[49] In any case, like the prayer hall to the south, this northern area consists of a domed portico with three bays. There is no architectural decoration, and the domes rest on simple squinches.

However, one detail indicates that there may have been two phases in the creation of this north wall, namely that the inscription itself seems to have been carved into the wall at a later

Figure 2.10 *Mashhad al-Muhassin, view east from under main dome of prayer hall. Photo: Creswell Archive, Ashmolean Museum. Image courtesy of Special Collections, Fine Arts Library, Harvard University*

Figure 2.11 *Mashhad al-Muhassin, north wall of courtyard showing inscription of al-ʿAziz (632/1234–5). Photo: Creswell Archive, Ashmolean Museum. Image courtesy of Special Collections, Fine Arts Library, Harvard University*

Figure 2.12 *Mashhad al-Muhassin, north wall of courtyard. Inscription of al-ʿAziz praising the Twelve Shiʿi Imams. Photo: Author*

date. Unlike the inscription of al-Zahir located across the courtyard, which was carved on a single stone tablet that was built into the wall, the inscription of al-ʿAziz is carved directly into the stones of the north wall. Its frame even extends rather awkwardly downwards, cutting into the stones of the arch over the two doors. Perhaps this north wall was begun by al-ʿAziz, and continued by his son al-Nasir Yusuf, who later added an inscription in his father's name.

The Mashhad al-Muhassin continued to be the object of elite Sunni patronage well into the Mamluk period. In 1260, another catastrophe befell the shrine: 'When the Mongols captured Aleppo they came to the *mashhad* and plundered the silver ornaments (*awānī al-fiḍḍa*) and carpets (*busuṭ*), opened the tomb and enclosure (*jidār*) and ruined its door.'[50]

The depredations of the Mongols thus destroyed much of the shrine, including its portal, and specifically desecrated the tomb itself. Probably not long afterwards, the Mamluk Sultan al-Malik al-Zahir Baybars (r. 1260–77) repaired the *mashhad*, rebuilt its door and appointed an imam, a caretaker and a muezzin.[51] If, as is suggested by Ibn Shaddad, the enclosure around the tomb was destroyed by the Mongols, it was perhaps also during Baybars' reconstruction that a beautiful, and little-known, carved wooden cenotaph was added. Although the cenotaph has no date, a direct parallel can be found in the tomb of Khalid ibn al-Walid, today located in the Damascus museum but originally placed in Khalid's tomb in Homs, commissioned by Baybars and dated to the mid-thirteenth century.[52] It bears a similar pattern of lamps set within recessed and lobed arches. On the basis of the close iconographic parallels between the two it seems reasonable to date the Muhassin cenotaph to Baybars' reign. The proposal that the cenotaph dates to the Mamluk period is bolstered by the flowing style of *naskhī* writing and the presence of repeating motifs of *fleurs de lys*, a common Mamluk blazon.[53]

Today this cenotaph is rarely seen; it sits at the centre of the domed tomb chamber behind a metal enclosure, hidden beneath heavy carpets. On a visit in 2005, however, the caretakers were kind enough to open the enclosure and lift the carpets.[54] Sauvaget published partial photographs and translations of a fragment of the text of the cenotaph in the 1920s.[55] Though missing its top and portions of the side panels, it is otherwise relatively well preserved. It is a rectangular carved wooden casket measuring 2.16m by 89cm, with a height of 89cm.[56] The decoration is lost on the short faces of the cenotaph. The ornament of the long faces consists of a series of vertically orientated, rectangular panels, divided by scrolling vegetal ornament. A line of *naskhī* calligraphy, which has not yet been read, borders each panel. Sauvaget was able to decipher a fragment of a Qurʾanic phrase, which he attributed to the 'lower band' of calligraphy, though it is not clear to which part of the cenotaph this refers. According to him it bears a fragment of the *sūrat al-nūr* or Light

Verse (24:36), which is common in funerary contexts and particularly logical in relation to the cenotaph's primary iconographic elements. These elements are located within each of the vertical panels and consist of a niche with a lamp hanging from its apex, flanked by two candlesticks.

The motif of the lamp within the niche is the cenotaph's most notable feature, and connects the Mashhad al-Muhassin to its neighbour the Mashhad al-Husayn, where the same motif appears on the portal (see below). It is common in funerary contexts, and as Nuha Khoury has shown this iconography of light is an important sign 'by which shrines, tombs, and mausolea can be immediately recognized'.[57] Khoury distinguishes between actual *miḥrāb*s and their representational counterpart the '*miḥrāb* image', which was a functional, aesthetic and semiotic distinction made by some medieval Muslims such as Ibn Battuta and Ibn Taymiyya.[58] The *miḥrāb* image differed in function from its counterpart the actual *miḥrāb* because it was not intended to indicate the direction of prayer. Rather, it functioned to mark a space that was connected with death, commemoration and eschatology.

The overwhelming majority of such images occur within shrines as commemorative or devotional objects and as grave markers and on cenotaphs. Although Khoury claims the image of a lamp within a niche was neutral from the perspective of sectarian associations and was not 'attached to any single esoteric Muslim perception',[59] a survey of the examples she provides in her article suggests otherwise. Of the sixteen shrines she presents that contain this image, ten are spaces devoted to the ʿAlids or to members of the *ahl al-bayt*.[60] It is reasonable then to propose that the image held special significance for Shiʿi worshippers, particularly considering that ʿAli and the twelve Imams are often described as being the bearers of 'divine light' and that the Imamate was passed from one Imam to the next via the transmission of such light. Husayn is often described as shining with divine light, or as himself being a light, and imagery of the light of God inhabiting the bodies of holy ʿAlid figures is common in Shiʿi religious literature.[61] The image of a lamp within a niche and its association with the *sūrat al-nūr*, then, could have been meant to function as a polyvalent sign that simultaneously marked the space as a locus of general holiness and commemoration; made general reference to the light of God for Sunnis via the *sūrat al-nūr*; and for Shiʿis, reminded the viewer that al-Muhassin, as an ʿAlid descendant, was designated as both the recipient and the point of emanation of such holy light. Shiʿi esoteric references to the ʿAlids as the 'Lights of the Faith' are common.[62]

The Mashhad al-Muhassin was therefore the locus of a series of ideological acts of patronage, initiated by a succession of Aleppo's rulers. For its founder the Hamdanid Sayf al-Dawla, it was an expression of personal piety and a manifestation of a growing trend towards the foundation of new shrines. His action bore the hallmarks of many contemporary Shiʿi foundation stories: instigated by a vision of divine light descending on the site and confirmed by the discovery of the tablet inscribed in the name of a previously unknown child of al-Husayn.

Explaining this Shiʿi ruler's intervention is not difficult. More intriguing are the acts that gave the shrine its present form: the intervention of various Sunni sovereigns in the years after the return of Aleppo to Sunni political control. Ibn al-ʿAdim's statement that the shrine was beloved and visited by the Shiʿa, and the knowledge that Aleppo had a large and powerful Shiʿi population in the medieval period, provides the first explanation for why the shrine continued to be patronised during the period of the Sunni Revival. Clearly, Sunni rulers saw that it was to their political advantage to invest in ʿAlid shrines in a city that was apparently majority Shiʿa. Furthermore, this investment was probably also an act of sincere piety on the part of these rulers: a reflection of general Sunni reverence for the *ahl al-bayt*. However, a hint that something more complex might have been at work comes in the form of the inscription on the north wall, commemorating the Ayyubid Sultan al-Malik al-ʿAziz, the one that praises the twelve Shiʿi Imams. Generalised Sunni reverence for the *ahl al-bayt* is one thing, but actually praising the competing leaders of a rival Islamic sect is quite another. What can have been a Sunni ruler's motivation for such an action?

The answer may be found in the Mashhad al-Muhassin's neighbour on the Jabal Jawshan: the Mashhad al-Husayn. There, a similar Shiʿi inscription, ordered by yet another Ayyubid sultan, greets visitors as they enter its magnificent thirteenth-century inlaid *muqarnas* portal.

The Mashhad al-Husayn

The Mashhad al-Husayn is located about 300m north of the Mashhad al-Muhassin on the Jabal Jawshan (Fig. 2.13). It is, in Tabbaa's words, 'the most important medieval Shiʿi structure in all of Syria . . . and the largest, most complex, and most enigmatic religious monument in Ayyubid Aleppo'.[63] Though analogous in some details of plan, it is considerably larger and more elegantly proportioned than the Mashhad al-Muhassin. Indeed, the Mashhad al-Husayn is one of the great Ayyubid-era buildings and in sheer aesthetic splendour easily competes with, and even eclipses, many of the more famous contemporary *madrasa*s. Several scholars have studied it, and yet it rarely appears in standard textbooks or architectural surveys.[64] This is probably because there is no ready explanation in the historiography of the Ayyubid era – focused as it is on the revival of Sunnism and the repression of Shiʿi political power – for the appearance of such a noteworthy 'Shiʿi' building.

Figure 2.13 *Aleppo, Mashhad al-Husayn, east façade: view towards the city centre, with citadel on horizon to the right. The raised roof shading the centre of the courtyard is a modern addition. Photo: Author*

In plan, the shrine consists of numerous interconnected spaces (Fig. 2.14), and represents several phases of construction. At its heart, the *saḥn* or courtyard of the main shrine area is surrounded by an expansive *iwān* (barrel-vaulted hall) on the west, with a five-domed sanctuary on the south side and a complex sequence of vaulted areas on the north. This main shrine area is accessed via a tall portal (Figs 2.15 and 2.16). The portal, elaborately carved and inlaid with stone interlace and a *muqarnas* hood, is the most prominent feature of a large walled enclosure that stretches eastwards from the main shrine area, and which acts as both frame and shelter for it.

Like the Mashhad al-Muhassin, the Mashhad al-Husayn's foundation story accords with the literary *topos* regarding the rediscovery of ʿAlid shrines. It, too, is a colourful anecdote: in 1177, a young shepherd named ʿAbdallah, who lived in the neighbourhood of the North African immigrants (*darb al-maghāriba*, probably meant to underscore his status as a simple pauper), was tending his goats on a low hill overlooking the city of Aleppo. He had just returned from the noon prayer, and lay down to have a nap. As his eyes began to get heavy, he slipped into a dream. In the dream, he saw a man emerging from a cleft in the rock nearby. The man suddenly reached out and snatched up one of ʿAbdallah's goats. 'Excuse me sir,' ʿAbdallah said, 'but what are you doing with my goat?' As if he had not heard the question, the man replied in a commanding voice, 'Tell the people of

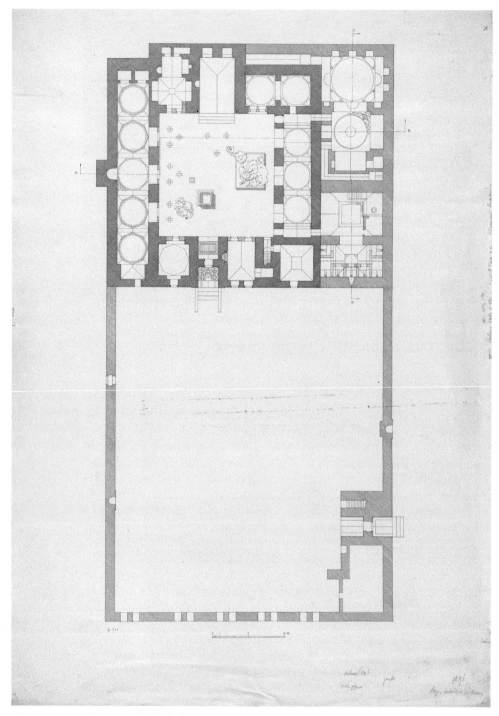

Figure 2.14 *Aleppo, Mashhad al-Husayn, plan. Illustration: The Ernst Herzfeld Papers. Freer Gallery of Art and Arthur M. Sackler Gallery Archives. Smithsonian Institution, Washington, DC*

Figure 2.15 *Mashhad al-Husayn, exterior courtyard, showing entrance to shrine in east wall. Photo: Author*

Aleppo to built a shrine here and call it the Mashhad al-Husayn!' The shepherd replied, 'But why would they listen to me?' The man then seized the hapless goat, and, lifting it into the air, threw it forcefully towards the ground. The goat's hooves sunk deep into the earth. 'Tell them to dig here!' he commanded.

'Abdallah awoke and saw that one of his goats was indeed stuck up to its knees in the dirt of the hillside. He grasped it around the middle and pulled, and from the hole where the goat's hooves had been, a spring of water began to gush forth. 'Abdallah dropped the goat and ran towards town. When he reached the main mosque, he told the miraculous story. Within days, the people of the city began feverish construction on the *mashhad*. They hired an architect, who piously (and perhaps rather extravagantly) declared, 'I would build this shrine even if the people of Aleppo wanted it made from gold!'[65]

The foundation of the shrine was truly a communal project. Each willing Aleppan was assigned one day a week to labour on the shrine. The skilled craftspeople of the city contributed their arts to the embellishment of the building. To defray expenses, the merchants of Aleppo's *sūq* added a surcharge to the goods they sold and donated it. Thus it was that almost overnight, Aleppo gained a *mashhad* for another member of the *ahl al-bayt*.[66] Unlike the Mashhad al-Muhassin, however, no holy figure was buried there. It was probably,

Figure 2.16 *Mashhad al-Husayn, main portal giving entrance to shrine area.*
Photo: Author

like many other shrines for the head of al-Husayn that appeared in this era, meant to mark the place where the head rested on its journey from Karbalaʾ to Damascus. Today, the *mashhad* honours a place where a drop of blood fell from the head of the martyr.[67]

Once construction was underway, it quickly attracted the interest of Sunni patrons. In fact, several of these figures also contributed to the improvement of the Mashhad al-Muhassin. The earliest donors were members of the local elite. First in line was the Shaykh Ibrahim Ibn Shaddad, the grandfather of the famous medieval historian. He bequeathed a large sum of money. Immediately thereafter, one of the urban notables, a silk merchant named Abu Ghanaʾm ibn Shaqwayq, donated funds for the construction of an *iwān* or hall (Fig. 2.17).[68] This donation was once commemorated in a small inscription placed high on the western wall of the *iwān*, visible in early photographs, but now missing.[69]

Not to be outdone, the mayor himself jumped into the fray. This was the same *raʾīs* al-Balisi, or Ibn Turayra, who would go on to rebuild Sayf al-Dawla's portal in the Mashhad al-Muhassin a few years later in 1197–8.[70] He demolished the portal that was already under construction at al-Husayn and built it higher in 1189–90. This door was the focus of much of the patronage activity at the shrine. Just seven years later, in 1195–6, it was torn down and built again, according to the foundation inscription located just above the entrance to the shrine from the outer courtyard (Fig. 2.16). There is some ambiguity surrounding the patron of the final phase of construction of this portal, because it does not specify that al-Zahir himself was the patron of the door, only that it was built 'during his reign' (*fī ayyām dawlat mawlānā al-malik al-Ẓāhir*). Furthermore, there is a discrepancy between the dates provided by Ibn Shaddad, who says specifically that 'in that year 1189–90 construction was completed' but makes no mention of al-Zahir as the builder of the portal, and the date provided from the foundation inscription.[71] Tabbaa writes that the later date, the one on the portal, must refer to completion of the portal begun by al-Balisi, which would therefore have been seven years under construction if it had been begun in 1189–90,[72] but Ibn Shaddad's account, which gives this as the completion date, not the date of its initiation, belies this. Despite the ambiguity of the inscription, then, it makes most sense to assume that the current portal is to be attributed to the Sultan al-Zahir.[73] Perhaps the strongest argument in favour of this conclusion is the architecture of the portal itself: its elaborate decoration and extraordinary height are characteristics usually associated with sultanal foundations. This will be explored further in a moment.

If this reading is accurate, the sovereign may have been inspired by his illustrious father Saladin. Saladin had made *ziyāra* to the shrine when he captured Aleppo in 1183, and contributed 10,000 dirhams

Figure 2.17 *Mashhad al-Husayn, interior courtyard, view towards western iwān (reconstructed). Photo: Author*

to it. Ibn Shaddad does confirm al-Zahir was one of the shrine's most generous benefactors:

> when (Saladin's) son al-Malik al-Zahir became ruler of Aleppo, he took an interest in (the Husayn shrine) and gave a mill, named al-Kamiliyya, to it in *waqf*, the proceeds from which amounted to six thousand dirhams per year. He set this money aside for the purchase of cookies and sweets on Friday nights for those who came there.[74]

Al-Zahir specified that the Shi'i leaders, the Naqib al-Ashraf Shams al-Din Ibn Zuhra and the *qāḍī* Baha' al-Din Ibn al-Khashshab, should administer the matter.[75] Indeed, the shrine's continuing upkeep was due entirely to the beneficence of the Ayyubid ruler.

Thus there were at least three phases in the construction of the portal: that of the townspeople, that of the *ra'īs* al-Balisi and that of the Sultan al-Zahir. At that time, the *mashhad* consisted only of the courtyard and the domed rooms immediately surrounding it on the north and south, along with the portal and the *iwān* on the east and west. A few years later, during the rule of al-Zahir's son al-'Aziz, the *qāḍī* Ibn al-Khashshab asked permission to build an extension to accommodate the pilgrims and others who wished to stay at the shrine. Al-'Aziz granted this request and the vaulted and elevated area to the north was begun. The Mongols, however, interrupted this work before it could be completed. Ibn Shaddad writes that:

> when they occupied (Aleppo) they entered the *mashhad* and took what the people had given to it in *waqf*, the hangings and carpets and mats and copper objects and gold and silver candlesticks and the candles. The things that were there were uncountable and without limits.[76]

The shrine fell into ruin for a brief time before it, like the Mashhad al-Muhassin, was restored by the Mamluk Sultan Baybars. In the modern period, it was restored by the Ottoman Sultan Abdülhamid, who was also a patron of the shrines of the Bab al-Saghir in Damascus.[77]

The portal of al-Zahir

From a purely aesthetic perspective, the entrance to the shrine is graced by a magnificent portal, a tour de force of Ayyubid architecture and ornament (Fig. 2.16). Speaking of it, Allen writes that:

> the vault of the portal is by far the most elaborate in Ayyubid architecture, the relief carving of the portal is particularly rich, and the portal is unusually tall . . . Because of its location, visible from a great distance, its unusual depth, and the *ablaq* surround of its frontal arch, this portal seems more monumental than any other extant twelfth-century portal.[78]

The portal is the main focal point of the spacious enclosure that welcomes pilgrims before approaching the main body of the shrine. The entrance is today located a bit left of centre, because the northerly addition of the *qāḍī* Ibn al-Khashshab disturbed the symmetry of the original building, but it would originally have bisected the façade directly on its central axis. It is approached via a flight of stairs

that further emphasise its already considerable height. The entire
structure is situated on the slope of the hillside, and the three main
sections are terraced upwards from the outer enclosure facing the
portal to the interior courtyard to the western *iwān* via yet another
short flight of steps. The portal is thus visible above the exterior wall
of the enclosure and can be seen from a great distance, even, if one
had good eyes, from the city walls, the citadel and the road at the
foot of the Jabal Jawshan, which winds its way westwards from the
Bab Antakya. Perhaps only the monuments of the citadel have such
a prominent visual profile.[79]

The portal's decoration is also intended to attract attention. Its pro-
portions are unusual in that the vault covers a square bay, rather than
the more typical rectangular one, and the decoration stretches across
nearly two-thirds of the bay (Fig. 2.18).[80] This gives the already atten-
uated vault a further aspect of unusual depth and expansiveness. The
portal is composed of several elements. The first, located just above
the door, is a broad area of grooved interlace ornament that stretches
across the entire back face of the bay and frames the foundation
inscription. This is the inscription, noted above, that refers to the
building as a *mashhad* and confirms that it was built during the era
of al-Zahir (Fig. 2.19).[81] The interlace is crowned by a frieze of small
lamps carved in deep relief (Figs 2.20 and 2.21). Above the frieze of
lamps is a band of delicate, stylised scrolling ornament, consisting of
grape vines and leaves within a pearl-decorated band. Superimposed
over the frieze is a tier of large, inscribed *muqarnas* cells interspersed
with brackets (Figs 2.20 and 2.22–2.24). And crowning these large
cells are four more tiers of smaller, more complex *muqarnas* interspersed with small domelets with projecting brackets. At the apex is
a small polylobed dome (Figs 2.18, 2.20 and 2.25). The entire portal
is bordered by a wide foliate arch that becomes a barrel vault at the
apex, the front corner of which is faceted in triangular segments (Figs
2.18, 2.20 and 2.25). Crowning this barrel vault, on the flat face of the
wall above it – as if mirroring in two dimensions the plastic contours
of the baroque *muqarnas* dome behind it – are five bands of zigzag
and polylobe inlaid stone decoration, bordered by a polylobed double-
dentillated moulding (Figs 2.16 and 2.18).

In addition to this complex decorative scheme and the considerable skill it would have required to execute the portal's hundreds of
interlocking and inlaid stone elements, al-Zahir's portal is notable
for another reason. For it is here that the Shi'i encomium similar to
the one in the Mashhad al-Muhassin appears. This inscription runs
in bold Ayyubid *naskhī* on both lateral faces of the portal bay, just
below the carved moulding decorated with hanging lamps (Figs 2.20
and 2.21). It reads:

> Bismillah . . . Oh God! Give your blessing to Muhammad the
> prophet, 'Ali the mandator; al-Hasan the trustworthy, the poisoned,

Figure 2.18 *Portal of al-Husayn, elevation and section drawing. Illustration: The Ernst Herzfeld Papers. Freer Gallery of Art and Arthur M. Sackler Gallery Archives. Smithsonian Institution, Washington, DC*

Figure 2.19 *Mashhad al-Husayn, foundation inscription. Photo: Author*

al-Husayn the martyr, the oppressed; ʿAli Zayn al-ʿAbidin;
Muhammad al-Baqir, the standard of religion; Jaʿfar al-Sadiq,
the commander; Musa al-Kazim, the loyal; ʿAli the pure, the
contented; Muhammad the reverent, the pious; ʿAli al-Hadi the
pure; al-Hasan al-ʿAskari; and the Master of Time, the Authority,
al-Mahdi; and pardon whoever has worked for this shrine with his
person, his opinion, and his fortune.[82]

This overtly Shiʿi text is paired with three further inscriptions.
These appear on the back face of the portal bay, just above the carved
moulding with the lamp decoration, each line contained within
one of the three large cells of the first tier of *muqarnas* (Fig. 2.20).
They are, by contrast, strongly Sunni in content, for they praise
Muhammad, his family and the first four Sunni caliphs:

Oh God, give your Blessing to our master Muhammad and to the
family of Muhammad and offer them peace (Fig. 2.22),
May God be pleased with Abu Bakr, and ʿUmar, and ʿUthman, and
ʿAli (Fig. 2.23),
May God be pleased with all the companions of God's Prophet
(Fig. 2.24).[83]

At first glance seeming contradictory, these two inscriptions have
been interpreted in various ways. Herzfeld remarked that the Sunni

Figure 2.20 *Mashhad al-Husayn, view into main portal. Inscription praising the Twelve Imams is just visible on lateral faces of the bay, below the frieze of lamps. Copyright: Creswell Archive, Ashmolean Museum. Image courtesy of Special Collections, Fine Arts Library, Harvard University*

Figure 2.21 *Mashhad al-Husayn, detail, right lateral face of portal bay. Frieze of lamps, scrolling decoration and detail of inscription praising the Twelve Imams. Photo: Author*

Figures 2.22 and 2.23 *(from right to left): Mashhad al-Husayn, details, forward face of portal bay. (From right) right and central inscribed muqarnas cells under dome, praising the Four Rightly Guided Caliphs. Photo: Author*

Figure 2.24 *Mashhad al-Husayn, detail, forward face of portal bay. Left and final inscribed muqarnas cell, reading, 'May God be pleased with all the companions of God's Prophet'. Photo: Author*

taṣliya (epitaph) – located above the lamp-decorated frieze and thus directly facing entrants to the shrine on the back face of the portal – is placed above the Shi'i one, and that the Sunni inscription therefore was intended to 'neutralise' the Shi'i words of praise. But such an explanation seems weak and tendentious, and seems to stretch the evidence to fit a preconceived notion of contentious relations between Sunnis and Shi'is in this period. In truth, the Shi'i

Figure 2.25 *Mashhad al-Husayn, view upward into* muqarnas *dome. Photo: Author*

encomium is far more visually bold, harmonious and certainly more legible, its two halves facing each other in broad bands of *naskhī* across the lateral faces of the portal. The Sunni *taṣliya*, on the other hand, is brief and disjointed, and spreads its abbreviated phrases over three separate cells of *muqarnas*. Without knowing better one might even mistake it for a later inscription. Furthermore, it is difficult to argue that an inscription that begins by praising the Family of the Prophet (as the Sunni litany does) can 'neutralise' an inscription that is itself primarily concerned with praising the Family of the Prophet.

Tabbaa agreed with Herzfeld that the Sunni formula should be seen as cancelling out the Shiʿi one, and cited similar examples of the use of this Sunni formula on late- eleventh-century tomb-stones and in Nur al-Din's reconstruction of the Umayyad mosque, carried out in 1159.[84] However both these examples are somewhat removed from the Husayn shrine temporally, spatially and especially contextually, and are arguably weak comparisons.

On the other hand, Tabbaa continues by making an important observation, although he does not expand on it:

> By the early Ayyubid period, this form of Sunni *taṣliya* seems to have become a necessary feature of the Friday sermon, as indicated by Ibn Jubayr's descriptions of the sermons at al-Azhar mosque in Cairo and at the Haram of Makka. In all these instances, the main purpose of the formula, which often also included al-

Hasan, al-Husayn and Fatima, was not to gloat over the victory of Sunnism but rather to present a compromise that moderate Shi'is might accept.[85]

Indeed, for this combination of inscriptions on the Husayn portal, the notion of compromise has greater explanatory power than the notion of a triumphant Sunnism. In fact, the inscriptions on this portal probably refer to the main point of popular ideological conflict between Sunnis and Shi'is in the medieval period: namely, the Shi'i practice of the cursing of the *saḥāba* or Companions of the Prophet Muhammad who, according to Shi'is, had behaved in ways injurious to the *ahl al-bayt*. Devin J. Stewart has written about this aspect of medieval polemic:

> This process of religio-historical interpretation created a body of material designed to impugn the characters of the first three caliphs and those of the Companions who opposed 'Ali, showing them in the most unfavourable light possible. The Shi'is' chief targets for criticism were the first three caliphs Abu Bakr ... 'Umar ... and 'Uthman ... While the Imamate became a major issue in Islamic theological polemics, the cursing, deprecation, and vilification of preeminent Companions of the Prophet was one of the most prominent popular manifestations of Shi'i identity throughout medieval Islamic history.[86]

In seeking to interpret these inscriptions, it is important to remember that Aleppo was strongly Shi'i in this period. In light of the Shi'i practice of the cursing of the first three caliphs and certain companions of the Prophet and the prominence of this ritual practice in popular sectarian disputation, the Husayn portal's inscriptions perhaps may have served a clear purpose. For al-Zahir's portal inscriptions not only praise the twelve Imams of the Shi'a, but its encomium for the first three caliphs begins, pointedly, by calling down blessings on the Prophet Muhammad and his family, and ends with an unambiguous statement that not just some, but *all* the companions of God's prophet (*aṣḥāb rasūl Allah ajmaʿīn*) are to be respected. Thus, the message al-Zahir meant to impart would seem to be not one of division but one of conciliation and coexistence. All of the companions and 'Alid descendants, the portal seems to say, are worthy of praise and deserving of reverence.

A deeper understanding of how this portal functioned is revealed when its inscription is read with attention to the spatial orientation of its various epigraphic elements. Indeed, the physical arrangement of, and aesthetic relationship between, the two inscriptions reveals a more complex understanding of how they spoke to viewers. Despite their apparently contradictory character, the arrangement of the two inscriptions indicates they were intended to be read as unified, and that they communicated a single message. And the vehicle of that unification was, in fact, the frieze of *miḥrāb* images that decorates the portal, which consists of a series of lamps hanging within intricately carved, multilobed niches (Figs 2.20 and 2.21). This frieze runs just above the Shiʿi inscription and just below the Sunni one – as if connecting, physically linking and visually mediating the two apparently opposing sectarian positions. In fact, viewers cannot read the Shiʿi inscription in full without first pausing at its midpoint and lifting their eyes upwards to read the 'Sunni' encomium for the *ṣaḥāba*, before continuing with the second half of the 'Shiʿi' inscription along on the left lateral face of the portal. Thus, the *miḥrāb* image itself becomes the very thing that unites the two sectarian positions. For viewers, the process of actively reading the inscriptions, guided by the *miḥrāb* image, literally integrated two opposing viewpoints on figures revered by the different sects. It spoke to viewers, worshippers and pilgrims as a unifying rhetorical device intended to emphasise the possibility for coexistence and respect between the two seemingly opposite positions.

But perhaps the strongest evidence for the Mashhad al-Husayn's role as a tool of sectarian conciliation is not the inscriptions on its walls, but the general attitude and policies of its most illustrious patron, the Ayyubid Sultan al-Zahir. Particularly revealing is the close relationship he cultivated with his contemporary, the Sunni ʿAbbasid caliph in Baghdad, al-Nasir li-Din Allah (r. 1180–1225). Al-Nasir has long been credited with the introduction of policies aimed at the rapprochement between Sunnis and Shiʿis. The caliph created a policy of sectarian inclusiveness which had at its heart a tolerant Sunni ecumenism that embraced the more moderate forms of Shiʿism, and even, to some degree, more radical groups such as the Ismaʿilis.

For the Caliph al-Nasir, who came to power in 1180 nearly ten years after the fall of the long-weakened Fatimids, any viable, organised Shiʿi threat to the Caliphate must have seemed a thing of the past.[87] In fact, his behaviour toward Shiʿism was so sympathetic that he may be the only ʿAbbasid caliph who was accused of being crypto-Shiʿi himself.[88] Whatever his personal inclinations, his policy of tolerance was politically advantageous. It was probably a reaction to concrete realities, for 'if al-Nasir wanted to raise the Caliphate in Baghdad to a real and effective power, he could only succeed by taking into account *and* by exploiting the interests of the Shiʿis who formed about half of Baghdad's population'.[89]

The means by which he did so were the reorganisation of the *futuwwa* (guild-like medieval orders of brotherhood), the direct sponsorship, support and sometimes even the conversion of prominent Shiʿis, and his patronage of important pilgrimage places. As we shall see, each of these policies was supported and, in some cases, directly imitated by the ruler of Aleppo, al-Zahir. The political and social actions of these two sovereigns make clear that their use of architectural patronage to propagate a message designed to unite the believers was only one aspect of a broader policy. A survey of these policies illustrates the broadly inclusive commitments of these two sovereigns and allows us to place their initially puzzling intersectarian acts of patronage back into their broader social and political context.

The reorganisation of the *futuwwa*

Perhaps the most effective, and the best known, of the Caliph al-Nasir's policies was his reform and restructuring of the *futuwwa*. Under al-Nasir, the *futuwwa* was transformed from a phenomenon of heterogeneous and rowdy urban gangs – occasionally loyal to various Sufi orders or Shi'i charismatic leaders – into a viable means of hierarchical organisation and state control under the caliph's exclusive purview.[90] This seems to have been a specific and thoughtfully planned reform which al-Nasir carefully implemented over a period of twenty years, beginning when he joined a Sufi-influenced branch of the *futuwwa* in 1182, two years after his accession as caliph, and culminating in his installation as the head of a newly consolidated universal *futuwwa* around 1203. With the weakening of central authority that characterised the pre-Ayyubid centuries, this organisation of young men *(fityān)* had come to have almost the role of a local police force or militia, alternately providing protection to the merchants of the souks or pillaging them, as local allegiances shifted. Such groups existed in most cities of the medieval Middle East and were an important element of social organisation, and they included both Sunnis and Shi'is.

The reorganisation of the *futuwwa* gave al-Nasir the framework for

> a new awareness of solidarity among Muslims of all confessions and social ranks up to the princes . . . the renewed rules of this new community, related directly to the person of al-Nasir, entailed dependence on the 'Abbasid caliph as the highest authority *(qibla)* in the Islamic world.[91]

As suggested above, this concept of a universal *futuwwa* depended for its success on the welcoming of groups representing multiple sectarian persuasions, and encouraged the attitude of inclusion that came to characterise al-Nasir's caliphate:

> By indicating himself as the highest authority for all *fityān*, al-Nasir established a relation between *sharī'a* and *futuwwa*. For this, it was necessary to find a compromise between Sunnis and Shi'is. Inside the *futuwwa* the caliph could not favour one group

over the other, nor could he accept both groups as being independent from each other if he wanted to attain his aim, namely, keeping the community of the believers within the structure of the state ... Al-Nasir thus created a powerful organisation which, more than his army, made his Caliphate acceptable as a binding form of sovereignty for all religious and political factions in Baghdad and in the Islamic lands.[92]

Al-Nasir's self-identification as the *qibla* was elaborated and given legal justification by the Sufi Shaykh Abu Hafs ʿUmar al-Suhrawardi (d. 1234), another supporter of the union between the Sunnis and moderate Shiʿis. Suhrawardi's *Rashf al-Nasaʾih al-Imaniyya wa Kashf al-Fadaʾih al-Yunaniyya,* a polemic against philosophy, is also an elaboration of al-Nasir's conception of the Caliphate. In that work, the caliph's relation to his people is much like that between shaykh and *murid,* with the caliph occupying the role of mediator. It is a surprising departure from standard Sunni law, in that it gives little regard to consensus (*ijmāʿ*), and in fact closely resembles some Shiʿi premises about the imam, who is considered by Shiʿis to be beyond consensus.[93]

According to Diyaʾ al-Din Ibn al-Athir (d. 1239), who worked for a period in the Aleppan chancery, al-Zahir rallied to al-Nasir's cause.[94] Between 1205 and 1210, the two sovereigns exchanged numerous letters and embassies. In one of the earliest of these, al-Zahir asked to be ceremonially inducted into the *futuwwa,* by entreating him to send the pantaloons (*sarawil*) of the order.[95] Later, in 1207–8, the embassy sent by al-Nasir to confirm al-Malik al-ʿAdil in Cairo stopped in Aleppo. At its head was the same ʿUmar al-Suhrawardi who had already proven himself a great propagandist for the Caliph al-Nasir. He met with the sultan and delivered a moving sermon. Then, in 1210–11, a new embassy arrived in Aleppo to grant al-Zahir's desire to be inducted into the *futuwwa.* The sultan drank from the cup of the *futuwwa* and received the ceremonial *sarawil.* He instructed the population to follow suit.[96] Clearly, al-Zahir, like al-Nasir, saw political advantage in allying himself with this symbolic reorientation of the Islamic community toward the caliph. Both al-Zahir and al-Nasir probably saw the *futuwwa* as an effective means of bringing together disparate elements of the Islamic community under a religiously neutral umbrella. In strongly Shiʿi Aleppo, as in Baghdad, the *futuwwa* was a method of social organisation that depended for its survival on the inclusion of multiple groups. Embracing this group was one way to make official a policy of rapprochement toward moderate Shiʿism in Aleppo.

Sponsorship and support of 'good' Shiʿis

Perhaps the most visible element of this policy of accommodation is al-Nasir and al-Zahir's sponsorship and support of prominent Shiʿis. There are numerous examples of Shiʿis who served as important members of their intimate circle, enough to imply that moderate Shiʿism was certainly no hindrance to caliphal or sultanal service. Not only did al-Nasir and al-Zahir welcome Shiʿi scholars at their courts, they also maintained cordial, at times even warm, relationships with Shiʿi urban notables in Baghdad and Aleppo. One of these Shiʿi scholars was yet another Suhrawardi, Shihab al-Din Yahya al-Suhrawardi, the illuminationist philosopher who had tried to implement many of the political aspects of his philosophy by directly teaching it to a number of late-twelfth-century rulers, including the young al-Zahir. He was enthusiastically welcomed at al-Zahir's court until the prince's father Saladin grew concerned and insisted on the philosopher's execution, which took place in Aleppo in 1191.[97]

Al-Suhrawardi's fate, however, was likely the result of his rather extreme philosophical stance rather than his Shiʿism, for a number of other Shiʿis were found among al-Zahir's close companions. These Shiʿis adhered to moderate, Twelver Shiʿism, avoiding (at least openly) many of the more contentious aspects of Shiʿi practice, in particular the cursing of the Companions of the Prophet. Indeed, time and again Aleppan Shiʿi notables are said to be 'well respected by both Sunnis and Shiʿis alike' because they were known for never having insulted the Companions of the Prophet. This was the case with the Shiʿi qāḍī Bahaʾ al-Din Ibn al-Khashshab, the same qāḍī who administered the Mashhad al-Husayn and who built the north wing. He was popular with both Sunnis and Shiʿis because of his respect for the Companions. The leader of the Shiʿis under al-Zahir, the naqīb al-ashraf ʿIzz al-Din al-Murtada, went so far as to severely punish a Shiʿi faqīh for insulting the companions.[98] Such examples argue strongly for the general acceptability of moderate Shiʿism on the popular as well as the official level, and give an insight into the nature of the inclusive sectarian climate of northern Syria in the twelfth and thirteenth centuries.

The conception of the Caliphate promulgated by the philosopher ʿUmar al-Suhrawardi, with its equivocal stance regarding the issue of ijmāʿ (consensus of the Islamic community, a main point of doctrinal dispute between Sunnis and Shiʿis) may have made the Sunnism of al-Nasir more palatable even to some of the more radical Shiʿi figures he courted, perhaps most prominently Hasan III of Alamut, the leader of the Nizari Ismaʿili sect (known also as the Assassins). This policy succeeded when Hasan famously converted to Sunnism (or perhaps to Twelver Shiʿism, the evidence is unclear) in 1211–12.[99] This was a remarkable achievement for al-Nasir, who thereby gained as a loyal ally the leader of a group that had tormented his

predecessors. Al-Nasir enthusiastically supported Hasan's conversion, seeing that the Ismaʿilis were given full rights as Muslims.[100]
This was yet another realm in which al-Zahir followed the lead of
the caliph, indeed

> the striking trait of the Ayyubid epoch is the relative good feeling
> between the Aleppan leaders and the sect of the Assassins ... the
> reign of al-Zahir was marked by a complete absence of aggression
> on the part of the Assassins in the territory of Aleppo.[101]

Later, al-Zahir saved the Nizaris from a Frankish attack in 1214,
even helping them reconstruct their fortress and restock provisions.
Al-Nasir considered it his greatest religious victory.[102]

Some of these 'good Shiʿis' were patronised and supported by both
al-Nasir and al-Zahir, for example ʿAli al-Harawi (d. 1215), the com-
poser of the only known medieval pilgrimage guide that treats the
entire Islamic world and the Mediterranean.[103] Although nominally a
Sunni, the obvious Shiʿi tendencies in al-Harawi's writing have been
remarked upon.[104] Born in Mosul, al-Harawi first gained renown as
a preacher in Baghdad, where his Friday sermons brought him to the
attention of al-Nasir. He then undertook a wandering, ascetic existence, which allowed him on several occasions to serve prominent
leaders on missions to obtain secret information or as arbiter in
delicate political negotiations. He served in that function for Saladin,
and later made his way to the court of the Ayyubid prince of Hama,
al-Mansur al-Muzaffar.[105] His pilgrimage guide is a record of his wide
travels. The fact that he dedicated it to the caliph in Baghdad may
indicate that it was commissioned by al-Nasir himself.[106]

He eventually made his way to Aleppo, where he spent his
last days at the court of al-Zahir. During his years there, al-Nasir
appointed him *khaṭīb* of Aleppo and *muḥtasib* for all Syria, though
these appear to have been largely honorary positions, perhaps related
to his unstated role as propagandist for the caliph's social and religious policies.[107] Certainly his pilgrimage guide fulfilled that role,
for in contrast with other Sunni visitors to the same localities (such
as the pious Maliki Ibn Jubayr), al-Harawi paid particular respect to
the ʿAlid sanctuaries, the tombs of the *ahl al-bayt* and the twelve
Imams.[108] Further evidence for the guide's role as part of al-Nasir's
programme is to be found in the structure of the work itself. Unlike
some later guides, whose clear delineation of distances and road-
markers make obvious their authors' intent that they be used as
actual guidebooks, al-Harawi's guide gives few such indicators. It
rather emphasises descriptions of the sanctity and beauty of holy
places, including miraculous accounts of appearances of saints and
cures attributed to certain localities as well as accounts of proper
conduct while visiting. Rather than a practical handbook to guide
pilgrims, al-Harawi's *Kitab* seems something more like a beautiful

honorary volume for the caliph's private consumption, or, perhaps, for him to disseminate to others. Like the shrines themselves, the guide created an ideological map to the sacred landscape of al-Nasir's domain.

Patronage of pilgrimage places

We have seen how the rulers of Aleppo were conscientious patrons of shrines and holy places, including Shi'i sites, beginning with Sayf al-Dawla, probably in response to the Shi'i allegiance of Aleppo's population. But it does not necessarily follow that the Ayyubids, too, should have been devoted patrons of these same shrines, and even less so that the 'Abbasid Caliph al-Nasir himself should become one of the most generous patrons of Shi'i holy places. And yet, al-Nasir was the direct patron of numerous Shi'i places of pilgrimage, for he is known to have directly contributed to the founding, restoration and upkeep of at least seven 'Shi'i' architectural projects. Such projects, though generally well received, were not met with universal approval, and some Sunni scholars accused him of having 'Shi'i' tendencies.[109] Whatever his personal propensities, the shrines he chose to renovate were not minor foundations, and in fact were among the most prominent holy places for Shi'i *ziyāra* (visitation) in the entire Islamic world. The grandest of these architectural projects was the tomb of the twelfth Imam at Samarra, the Ghaybat al-Mahdi, which al-Nasir ordered to be expensively renovated and enlarged to include a *mashhad* in 1209.[110] This *mashhad*, next to the tombs of the tenth and eleventh imams 'Ali al-Hadi and Hasan al-'Askari, is a mosque built over the *serdab* (cave) into which the twelfth Imam disappeared. The inscription, which the caliph had carved onto a gate built inside the cave, designates al-Nasir as builder and protector of the Shi'i sanctuary (Fig. 2.26).[111]

Al-Nasir's other projects were no less ambitious, and included the restoration of the *mashhad* of Musa b. Ja'far, the Mashhad 'Ali and the Mashhad Husayn in northern Baghdad in the Kazimayn quarter, all lavish projects on which he expended around 10,000 dinars.[112] Other projects included tombs for 'Alid descendants such as 'Aun and Mu'in. Even al-Nasir's own gravesite was to be near the tomb of Musa b. Ja'far, a preference that the caliph made clearly known during his lifetime.[113]

Conclusion

Al-Nasir's policies had an overtly political goal: to unify the fractured Islamic community under the single banner of the caliph in Baghdad, and thereby to strengthen the weakened Caliphate. The means by which he did this included the creation of military-religious orders loyal to the caliph known as the *futuwwa*, the formulation of a

384. Sardāb des Mahdi . . (In blau: bb der Ghaibat al-Mahdi, Inschrift des
      Nāṣir ≈ 481)

Figure 2.26 *View of the Caliph al-Nasir li-Din Allah's inscription on the
gate of the* serdab *(cave) of the shrine of Imam al-Mahdi, Samarra, Iraq.
Illustration: The Ernst Herzfeld Papers. Freer Gallery of Art and Arthur M.
Sackler Gallery Archives. Smithsonian Institution, Washington, DC*

policy of religious tolerance, which he propagated through loyal religious scholars and thinkers, and the active courtship of groups who
might be inclined to rise up in discontent, chief among them the
Shiʿa. He also reformed religious education in the capital, collected
and disseminated his own collection of *ḥadīth*, and surrounded
himself with both Sunni and Shiʿi scholars. Furthermore, as we have
seen, the Caliph al-Nasir was an active patron of architecture, and
his policy of ecumenism was evident here as well in his generous
investment in at least seven Shiʿi shrines. Each of these policies
was supported and imitated by his Aleppan ally, the Ayyubid Sultan
al-Zahir.

But why were shrines seen as the means of communicating this
policy? As noted previously, the twelfth and thirteenth centuries
saw a remarkable proliferation of pilgrimage sites and shrine complexes. There was enormous popular support for such projects, and
shrines favoured by Shiʿis seem to have been patronised as readily
as Sunni ones.[114] Furthermore, though ʿAlid shrines may have had
special significance for the Shiʿa and may have directly benefited
Shiʿi communities, such shrines were also visited by Muslims of
all sectarian persuasions, making *ziyāra* to such places a distinctly
supra-sectarian activity. It is for this reason that the patronage of

Shiʻi shrines was such a politically shrewd move on the part of al-Nasir and, in turn, al-Zahir. For while sponsorship of Shiʻi shrines certainly would have given these Sunni rulers political capital with the Shiʻi community, it also acted as a form of symbolic appropriation, bringing Shiʻi popular practice within the realm of official Sunni religious policy. Indeed, the building and renovation of such shrines functioned as the material and spatial manifestation of the caliph's broader policy of Sunni ecumenism.

Thus, al-Zahir's support of these ʻAlid shrines was both part of an emerging tradition of Sunni patronage of Shiʻi holy sites throughout the Islamic lands and at the same time an attempt to ally himself with the religious policy of the ʻAbbasid caliph in Baghdad. By choosing to support the most important Shiʻi holy sites, the two sovereigns could simultaneously provide for the upkeep of popular shrines visited by Muslims of all sectarian stripes, propitiate the local Shiʻi population, and situate Baghdad and Aleppo within the wider sacred landscape of Shiʻi pilgrimage that stretched from Iraq to Egypt. Following the lead of the caliph in Baghdad, al-Zahir's patronage of these shrines powerfully reorientated the sacred geography of his realm in such a way that he and his Ayyubid allies were the primary benefactors of both Sunni and Shiʻi popular practice. As we shall see in the next chapter, even in a strongly Sunni city like Damascus, such ecumenism was also embraced: although there, its impetus was far more spontaneous and organic.

Notes

1. Some remaining fragments of this shrine were documented by Ernst Herzfeld, *Matériaux pour un Corpus Inscriptionum Arabicarum*, pt 2, *Syrie du Nord. Inscriptions et monuments d'Alep* [hereafter *MCIA-Alep*] (Cairo: Institut français d'archéologie orientale, 1954–6), pp. 271–3.
2. Today, the shrine of al-Husayn has acquired a large Shiʻi school, attached directly to its southern wall.
3. Yaqut ibn ʻAbdallah al-Hamawi (d. 1229) reports that in the eleventh century the Aleppan *fuqahā'* (legal scholars) gave rulings according to the Imami ('Twelver' Shiʻi) school. *Muʻjam al-Buldan*, ed. Muhammad Aman Khanaji (Cairo: Matbaʻa al-Saʻada, 1906), vol. 3, p. 313; Carole Hillenbrand, 'The Shiʻis of Aleppo in the Zengid Period: Some unexploited textual and epigraphic evidence', in Hinrich Biesterfeldt and Verena Klemm, eds, *Difference and Dynamism in Islam. Festschrift for Heinz Halm on his 70th Birthday* (Würzburg: Ergon-Verlag, 2012), pp. 163–79.
4. Moojan Momen, *An Introduction to Shiʻi Islam* (New Haven, CT: Yale University Press, 1985), p. 88; Nasir-i Khusrau, *Safarnama*, ed. Mahmud Ghanizada (Berlin: Chapkhana Kaviyani, 1922), pp. 18, 20–1, 25.
5. Ibn Jubayr, *Rihla* or *The Travels of Ibn Jubayr*, ed. William Wright (Leiden: 1907 [reprinted 1973]), p. 280.
6. Muhammad ibn Ahmad al- Muqaddasi, *Ahsan al-Taqasim fi Maʻrifat al-Aqalim*, ed. M. J. de Goeje (Leiden: Brill, 1967) pp. 179–80 and *The*

Best Divisions for Knowledge of the Regions: A Translation of Ahsan al-taqasim fi maʿrifat al-aqalim, ed. and trans. by Basil A. Collins (Reading: Centre for Muslim Contribution to Civilization/Garnet Publishing, 1994), pp. 162–3.

7. Tables listing geographical origins of Twelver Shiʿi ulama in various cities are given in Momen, *Introduction*, pp. 84, 91 and 97.

8. Kamal al-Din ʿUmar Ibn al-ʿAdim, *Zubdat al-Halab min Taʾrikh Halab*, ed. Sami al-Dahhan (Damascus: al-Maʿhad al-Faransi bi-Dimashq lil-Dirasat al-ʿArabiyya, 1951–68), vol. 1, p. 172.

9. Ibid., vol. 2, pp. 16–18; ʿIzz al-Din Ibn al-Athir, *Al-Kamil fi-l-Taʾrikh*, ed. C. J. Tornberg (Beirut: Dar Sader and Dar Beirut, 1965–7), vol. 10, p. 63.

10. Anne-Marie Eddé, *La Principauté ayyoubide d'Alep* (Stuttgart: Steiner, 1999), p. 436.

11. H. M. Khayat, 'The Siʾite rebellions in Aleppo in the 6th A. H./12th A. D. century', *Revista degli Studi Orientali* 46 (1971), 170.

12. Clifford Edmund Bosworth, *The New Islamic Dynasties* (New York: Columbia University Press, 1996), p. 85.

13. Although it seems that a generous bribe from the Fatimid vizir was also an enticement. Ibn al-ʿAdim, *Zubdat al-Halab*, vol. 2, pp. 127–8.

14. Eddé, *Principauté*, p. 436. See also Claude Cahen, 'Un chronique chiʿite au temps des Croisades', *Comptes rendus des Séances de l'Académie des inscriptions et des Belles-Lettres* (1935), 265; Yasser Tabbaa, *The Transformation of Islamic Art During the Sunni Revival* (Seattle, WA: University of Washington Press, 2001), p. 60, and 'Monuments with a message: propagation of Jihad under Nur al-Din', in V. Goss and C. Vézar-Bornstein (eds), *The Meeting of Two Worlds: Cultural Exchange between East and West during the Period of the Crusades* (Kalamazoo, MI: Medieval Institute Publications, Western Michigan University, 1986), p. 224.

15. Khayat, 'Siʾite rebellions', 176.

16. Cahen, 'Chronique chiʿite', 264.

17. Kamal al-Din ʿUmar ibn al-ʿAdim, *Bughyat al-Talab fi Taʾrikh Halab*, ed. Suhayl Zakkar (Damascus: S. Zakkar, 1988–9), vol. 4, p. 1823.

18. Ibid., vol. 4, p. 1823; Eddé, *Principauté*, p. 437, n. 674. Khayat, 'Siʾite rebellions', 191.

19. Eddé, *Principauté*, p. 437, n. 674.

20. Momen, *Introduction*, p. 88.

21. The earliest source to mention the shrine is ʿAli Ibn Abi Bakr al-Harawi (d. 1215), *Kitab al-Isharat*, ed. Janine Sourdel-Thomine (Damascus: al-Maʿhad al-Faransi bi-Dimashq), 1953, p. 4, and *Guide des lieux de pèlerinage*, ed. and trans. by Janine Sourdel-Thomine (Damascus: Institut français de Damas), p. 4; and Josef Meri, *A Lonely Wayfarer's Guide to Pilgrimage* (Oxford: Oxford University Press, 2004), pp. 12–13. Other sources that mention the shrine are Ibn al-ʿAdim, *Zubdat al-Halab*, vol. 2, pp. 144–5 and *Bughyat al-Talab*, vol. 1, pp. 411–12; Muhammad ibn ʿAli Ibn Shaddad, *Al-Aʿlaq al-Khatira fi Dhikr ʾUmaraʾ al-Sham wa-l-Jazira* (Aleppo), ed. Dominique Sourdel (Damascus: al-Maʿhad al-Faransi bi-Dimashq, 1953), vol. 1, pp. 48–50; Ibn al-Shihna, *al-Durr al-Muntakhab fi Taʾrikh Mamlakat Halab*, ed. Yusuf Sarkis (Beirut: Al-Matbaʿa al-Kathulikiyya, 1909), and trans. by Jean Sauvaget as 'Les perles choisies' d'Ibn ash-Shichna (*Mémoires de l'Institut français de Damas: Matériaux pour*

servir à l'histoire de la ville d'Alep, I.) (Beirut: Institut français de Damas, 1933), pp. 85–8 (this source largely copies Ibn Shaddad). Secondary sources include Moritz Sobernheim, 'Das Heiligtum Shaikh Muhassin in Aleppo', *Mélanges Hartwig Derenbourg (1844–1908)* (Paris: Ernest Leroux, 1909), 379–90; Jean Sauvaget, 'Deux sanctuaires chiites d'Alep', *Syria* 9 (1928), 319–27; *Répertoire chronologique d'épigraphie arabe* [hereafter, *RCEA*] 10 (3791), 134; Nikita Elisséeff, 'Les monuments de Nur ad-Din', *Bulletin d'études orientales* 13 (1951), 7, no. 1; Heinz Gaube and Eugen Wirth, *Aleppo: Historische und geographische Beiträge zur baulichen Gestaltung, zur sozialen Organisation und zur wirtschaftlischen Dynamik einer vorderasiatischen Fernhandelsmetropole* (Wiesbaden: Ludwig Reichert, 1984), no. 652; and Lorenz Korn, *Ayyubidische Architektur in Ägypten und Syrien: Bautätigkeit im Kontext von Politik und Gesellschaft 564–658/1169–1258* (Heidelberg: Heidelberger Orientverlag, 2004), vol. 1, p. 63, vol. 2, p. 220.

22. Herzfeld, *MCIA-Alep*, pp. 193–201; Terry Allen, *Ayyubid Architecture* (Occidental, CA: Solipsist Press, 2003), 7th edition, chapter 4, 'The Ornamented Style and the Plain Style in Aleppo and Damascus', s.v. 'Mashhad al-Muhassin'. Online at www.sonic.net/~tallen/palmtree/ayyarch/ch4.htm#alep.mashm (accessed 10 February, 2006).

23. Herzfeld, *MCIA-Alep*, plate LXXX; Sauvaget, 'Deux sanctuaires'. Herzfeld's plan has been reproduced by Yasser Tabbaa, *Constructions of Power and Piety in Medieval Aleppo* (University Park, PA: Pennsylvania State University Press, 1997), fig. 82.

24. According to al-Muqaddasi, Sayf al-Dawla's palace was near where the river Quwayq enters the town, which would place it on the western side of the city, i.e. directly facing the Jabal Jawshan. See al-Muqaddasi, *Ahsan al-Taqasim fi Ma'rifat al-Aqalim*, p. 155 and Collins, *Best Divisions*, p. 143.

25. Ibn Shaddad here quotes the Shi'i historian Ibn Abi Tayyi' (d. 1228–33), whose work is no longer extant except as preserved by later medieval historians. Cf. Muhammad ibn 'Ali ibn Shaddad, *Al-A'laq al-Khatira fi Dhikr 'Umara' al-Sham wa-l-Jazira* (Aleppo), ed. Dominique Sourdel (Damascus: al-Ma'had al-Faransi bi-Dimashq, 1953), pp. 48–9.

26. Ibn Shaddad, *A'laq* (Aleppo), pp. 42–50; Tabbaa, *Constructions*, p. 111 n. 21.

27. Some examples of various Sunni dreams and miraculous visions are discussed in Josef Meri, *The Cult of Saints Among Muslims and Jews in Medieval Syria* (Oxford: Oxford University Press, 2002). See pp. 76, 105 and 136. For Sunni shrines founded in obedience to instructions received from holy figures in dreams see pp. 178–9, 181–3 and 188–9. Tabbaa writes that the phenomenon of dream visions and their role in the foundation of shrines 'has no parallel in Sunni piety': however, the previous examples show that it was a common enough occurrence. Tabbaa, *Constructions*, p. 111, n. 21.

28. Daniella Talmon-Heller, 'Graves, relics and sanctuaries, the evolution of Syrian sacred topography', *ARAM Periodical* 19 (2007), 107–10.

29. Ibn al-'Adim, *Bughyat al-Talab*, 411.

30. Ibn Abi Tayyi' in Ibn Shaddad, *A'laq* (Aleppo), p. 49.

31. Another Mashhad al-Muhassin exists in Mosul, this one commemorating the legendary son of 'Ali and Fatima. Meri writes that Wilferd Madelung had informed him that the belief that 'Ali and Fatima

had a son named al-Muhassin precedes the belief that al-Husayn had a son by that name. Meri, *Cult of Saints*, p. 184, n. 255; Louis Massignon, 'al-Muhassin b. ʿAlī', *Encyclopaedia of Islam*, 2nd edition [hereafter *EI2*], ed. P. Bearman et al. Brill Online, http:// referenceworks . brillonline . com . ezproxy . lib . utexas . edu / entries / encyclopaedia-of-islam-2/al-muhassin-b-ali-SIM_5429 (accessed 22 July 2013).

32. Ibn Abi Tayyiʾ quoted in Ibn Shaddad, *Aʿlaq* (Aleppo), p. 49.
33. This is according to Terry Allen, who made a painstaking physical survey of the architectural phasing of the building. In my direct observation of the shrine I have found no reason to disagree with his meticulous evaluation and rely on his conclusions here.
34. Ibn al-ʿAdim, *Bughyat al-Talab*, vol. 1, p. 12. Ibn Abi Tayyiʾ in Ibn Shaddad, *Aʿlaq* (Aleppo), p. 49. Aq Sunqur's patronage is also noted in another work by Ibn Shaddad: his *Taʾrikh al-Malik al-Zahir*, ed. Ahmad Hutayt (Wiesbaden: Franz Steiner, 1983), p. 68; and in Ibn al-ʿAdim, *Bughyat al-Talab*, vol. 1, p. 412.
35. Ibn al-ʿAdim, *Bughyat al-Talab*, vol. 1, pp. 411–12; and *Zubdat al-Halab*, p. 214.
36. Ibn al-ʿAdim, *Bughyat al-Talab*, vol. 1, p. 412.
37. The mosque on the site of the cathedral of St Helena was subsequently converted by Nur al-Din into the *Madrasa* al-Halawiyah.
38. Ibn Abi Tayyiʾ in Ibn Shaddad, *Aʿlaq* (Aleppo), p. 49.
39. Terry Allen believes this entire wing has been replaced since Nur al-Din's time and notes that neither the latrines nor the north door visible on Herzfeld's plan are to be found in the building today. A distinctive characteristic of this room are the trilobed arches with inverse keys located high on the walls. Allen believes they can be associated with a specific architect or workshop, that of Qahir ibn ʿAli. Allen, *Ayyubid Architecture*, 'Mashhad al-Muhassin', s.v. 'Northeast Wing'.
40. Herzfeld thought the inscription on the exterior of the tomb chamber was in its original location and accordingly attributed its construction to Zangi, but Terry Allen argues that the inscription is not *in situ* and suggests the tomb chamber could just as easily have been built later, during the intervention of Nur al-Din. Allen, ibid.
41. Allen, ibid.
42. Sauvaget, 'Deux sanctuaires', 323; Allen, *Ayyubid Architecture.*, s.v. 'Northeast Wing'.
43. Ibn al-ʿAdim, *Bughyat al-Talab*, vol. 1, p. 412.
44. Tabbaa, *Transformation*, p. 152, where he claims it is *the* earliest, giving a date of 585/1189. Tabbaa cites Herzfeld for this date, both here and in *Constructions*, p. 109 n. 18. However, according to Allen, Herzfeld relied on a faulty manuscript of Ibn Shaddad for this early dating of the portal. Lorenz Korn has re-read the inscription and favours the later date (1197–8), as does Allen. This door was rebuilt or repaired in 1896–7. That work was commemorated in the inscription just above the door's segmental arch. At that time the original twelfth-century foundation inscription was moved upwards and is now located just under the springing of the dome, while a new inscription was inserted in its place commemorating the late-nineteenth-century restoration. See Allen, *Ayyubid Architecture.*, s.v. 'Northeast Wing'; Korn, *Ayyubidische Architektur*, vol. 2, pp. 218–19.

45. Ibn Shaddad, *A'laq* (Aleppo), p. 50. There is a discrepancy in the dates here: Ibn Shaddad writes that Wali al-Din carried this work out in 1216, however the next section records that al-Zahir's work occurred in 1212–13; this earlier date is reinforced by the inscription.
46. Ibn Shaddad, *A'laq* (Aleppo), p. 50.
47. Although the ante*mihrāb* dome may be later, as discussed below.
48. Following the reading of the inscription on the north wall of the courtyard.
49. Allen suggests that Ibn Shaddad could have confused the work of the father for that of the son, or alternatively that perhaps the work was started under al-ʿAziz and completed under al-Nasir. Allen, *Ayyubid Architecture.*, s.v. 'Prayer Hall'.
50. Ibn Shaddad, *A'laq* (Aleppo), p. 50.
51. Ibid., p. 50.
52. Herzfeld, 'Damascus: Studies in Architecture II', *Ars Islamica*, 66–9; Sauvaget, 'Deux sanctuaires', 325; Abu'l Faraj al-ʿUsh, 'Les bois de l'ancien cénotaphe de Khalid ibn al-Walid à Hims', *Ars Orientalis* 5 (1963), 11–39; Tabbaa, *Constructions*, p. 109, n. 17. Tabbaa says the date is twelfth century, but this must be an error.
53. For more on the cenotaph, see Mulder, 'Seeing the light: enacting the divine at three medieval Syrian shrines', forthcoming in David J. Roxburgh, ed., *Envisioning Islamic Art and Architecture: Essays in Honor of Renata Holod* (Leiden: Brill, 2013).
54. However I was unable to photograph the cenotaph.
55. Sauvaget, 'Deux sanctuaires', 324. In this article Sauvaget continuously expresses dissatisfaction with the caretakers, who, he reported, because of a problem with their 'attitude', hesitated to reveal the cenotaph to the light of full art historical scrutiny.
56. Sauvaget, 'Deux sanctuaires', 324.
57. Nuha N. N. Khoury, 'The *mihrāb* image: commemorative themes in medieval Islamic architecture', *Muqarnas* 9 (1992), 11–28.
58. Ibid., 12 and 23, n. 8.
59. Ibid., 22.
60. These are: Panja ʿAli at Mosul, Sitt Zaynab at Sinjar, Imam Reza at Mashhad , *mihrāb*s from Qum and Najaf, Masjid ʿAli at Kuh-i Rud, al-Aqmar Mosque in Cairo, Mashhads al-Husayn and Muhassin in Aleppo, Imam ʿAli al-Hadi in Mosul.
61. Early Shiʿi sources such as Ibn Rustam Tabari (d. 923) use such imagery, for example in his description of the *ahl al-bayt*: '7,000 years before the creation of the world, Muhammad, ʿAli, Fatima, Hasan and Husayn (as) figures (*ashbāh*) of light, praised and glorified the Lord before His throne. When God wished to create their forms (*suwar*) He forged them like a column (*ʿamūd*) of light.' Ibn Rustam Tabari, *Dalaʾil al-Imama* (Najaf: al-Matbaʿa al-Haydariyya, 1949), pp. 71–80. Certain Shiʿi traditions also describe the Prophet's family as 'beings of light', for example Furat ibn Ibrahim ibn Furat al-Kufi, in his *Tafsir Furat al-Kufi*, on which see Shafique Virani, s.v. 'Ahl al-Bayt', in *Encyclopedia of Religion*, 2nd edition, ed. Lindsay Jones (Detroit, MI: Macmillan Reference USA, 2005), vol. 1, p. 199. See also section 'The Legend of al-Husayn' in L. Veccia Vaglieri, '(al-)Husayn b. ʿAlī b. Abī Ṭālib', *EI2*, http://referenceworks.brillonline.com.ezproxy.lib.utexas.edu/entries/encyclopaedia-of-islam-2/al-husayn-b-ali-b-abi-talib-COM_0304 (accessed 22 July 2013).

62. Rashid al-Din ibn Shahrashub, a (probable) Twelver Shiʿi writer who died in 1192, includes stories describing the transfer of light in just such a way. Such imagery seems to have been elaborated in large part by the *ghulaṭ* ('extremist' Shiʿis), but was apparently embraced by many Twelver Shiʿis as well. See Ibn Shahrashub, *Manaqib Al Abi Talib* (Najaf: al-Matbaʿa al-Haydariyya, 1956), vol. 3, pp. 230–4; Caroline Williams, 'The cult of ʿAlid saints in the Fatimid monuments of Cairo, Part I: the mosque of al-Aqmar', *Muqarnas* 1 (1983), 46. See also F. B. Flood, 'The iconography of light in the monuments of Mamluk Cairo', *Cosmos* 8 (1992), 175.

63. Tabbaa, *Constructions*, p. 110.

64. Sauvaget, 'Deux sanctuaires', 224–37; Herzfeld, *MCIA-Alep*, pp. 236–48, plate 237; Sauvaget, 'Inventaire des monuments musulmans de la ville d'Alep', *Revue des Études Islamiques* 5 (1931), 59–114, no. 20; Gaube and Wirth, *Aleppo*, p. 410, no. 651; Gaube, *Arabische Inschriften aus Syrien (Beiruter Texte und Studien*, vol. 17) (Beirut: Orient-Institut der Deutschen Morgenländischen Gesellschaft, 1978), later inscriptions, nos 33 and 34; Korn, *Ayyubidische Architektur*, vol. 2, pp. 218–19.

65. Ibn Shaddad, *Aʿlaq*, vol. 1, p. 51; Ibn al-Shihna, *al-Durr al-Muntakhab*, vol. 1, p. 87 ff.

66. Ibn al-ʿAdim, *Bughyat al-Talab*, vol. 1, pp. 412–13; Ibn Shaddad, *Aʿlaq*, vol. 1, p. 50; Ibn al-Shihna, *al-Durr al-Muntakhab*, vol. 1, p. 87.

67. The *mashhad* was used as a storage facility for munitions in the Ottoman period and in July 1920 it exploded, killing as many as 500–600 Aleppans who had taken refuge there during the uprising against the French. Al-Kamil ibn Husayn al-Ghazzi, *Nahr al-Dhahab fi Taʾrikh Halab*, ed. Mahmud Fakhuri and Shawqi Shaʿath (Aleppo: Dar al-Qalam al-ʿArabi, 1991), vol. 3, pp. 212–13; James L. Gelvin, 'The other Arab nationalism: Syrian/Arab populism in its historical and international contexts', in Israel Gershoni and James Jankowski, eds, *Rethinking Nationalism in the Arab Middle East* (New York: Columbia University Press, 1997), pp. 231–48. Their bones were still visible among the ruins according to Sauvaget who visited and photographed the shrine not long after; see 'Deux sanctuaires', 226. Sauvaget also published a sketch plan showing which parts were damaged in the explosion; see ibid., plate LXIV. It was carefully, though not perfectly, reconstructed in the 1970s by ʿAli Summaqiya of the Directorate General of Antiquities and Museums. Particularly the eastern wall of the *iwān* was altered; today there are windows where once there were niches. In the early 1990s, a stone covered with the blood of al-Husayn was placed on the southern wall of the large *iwān* on the west side of the building. It is enshrined within a small metal enclosure next to the *miḥrāb* and is today the focus of Shiʿi devotional practice. Yasser Tabbaa tried to prevent the insertion of this devotional object along with the steel-framed canopy that now covers the courtyard, claiming they rendered the *mashhad* 'an aesthetic ruin', Tabbaa, *Constructions*, p. 111, n. 20. However the large numbers of pilgrims who visit the shrine do not seem perturbed by the enclosure and rest, eat and pray peacefully in the shade of the canopy.

68. Ibn Shaddad, *Aʿlaq*, vol. 1, p. 51; Ibn al-Shihna, *al-Durr al-Muntakhab*, vol. 1, p. 87 ff.

69. For the text of the inscription, see Herzfeld, *MCIA-Alep*, 1, 228, *RCEA*,

3027 and Tabbaa, *Constructions*, p. 112. A photograph is also published by Tabbaa, fig. 97.

70. See note 44 above regarding the re-dating of the al-Muhassin portal by Korn and Allen.

71. Ibn Shaddad, *A ʿlaq*, vol. 1, p. 51; Ibn al-Shihna, *al-Durr al-Muntakhab*, vol. 1, p. 87 ff.

72. Tabbaa, *Constructions*, p. 113.

73. Allen, *Ayyubid Architecture*, chapter 5, 'al-Malik al-Zahir and the Ornamented Style', s.v. 'Mashhad al-Husayn: History and Construction Campaigns'.

74. Ibn Shaddad, *A ʿlaq*, vol. 1, p. 51; Ibn al-Shihna, *al-Durr al-Muntakhab*, vol. 1, p. 87 ff.

75. Note that this is *not* the same Abu'l Fadl Ibn al-Khashshab who changed the churches of Aleppo to mosques in the Seljuk period (see prior section on the Mashhad al-Muhassin).

76. Ibn Shaddad, *A ʿlaq*, vol. 1, p. 52; Ibn al-Shihna, *al-Durr al-Muntakhab*, vol. 1, p. 87 ff.

77. Sauvaget, 'Deux sanctuaires', 226. Abdülhamid's patronage is explored in depth in Chapter 2.

78. Allen, *Ayyubid Architecture*, chapter 5, s.v. 'Portal'. The portal was 'pulverised' by the explosion of 1920, according to Sauvaget, who could only describe it on the basis of small fragments littering the courtyard. 'Deux sanctuaires', 227.

79. This visual profile has been much altered today by the building of residential neighbourhoods on the Jabal Jawshan.

80. Allen, *Ayyubid Architecture*, s.v. 'Portal'.

81. Full Arabic text and translation are in Tabbaa, *Constructions*, p. 113.

82. Tabbaa's translation, *Constructions*, p. 116. See note 33 on that page for his commentary on Herzfeld's erroneous reading. It seems to me there is a minor error in Tabbaa's translation: after the name 'al-Hasan', I do not see the word 'al-Amin' or 'the trustworthy' but only 'al-Masmum' or 'the poisoned'.

83. Translated by Tabbaa, *Constructions*, pp. 115–16.

84. Ibid., p. 116.

85. Ibid., p. 116.

86. Devin J. Stewart, 'Popular Shiʿism in medieval Egypt, vestiges of Islamic sectarian polemics in Egyptian Arabic', *Studia Islamica* 84 (1996), 37. For a more general analysis of Shiʿi attitudes toward the ṣaḥāba, see Etan Kohlberg, 'Some Imami Shiʿi views on the Sahaba', *Jerusalem Studies in Arabic and Islam* 5 (1984), 143–75.

87. Angelika Hartmann, 'Al-Nasir li Din Allah', *EI2*, http://reference-works.brillonline.com.ezproxy.lib.utexas.edu/entries/encyclopaedia-of-islam-2/al-nasir-li-din-allah-COM_0854 (accessed 22 July 2013). Hartmann writes that 'from al-Nasir's religious policy it is clear that he did not consider the Shiʿis as a threat and an undermining influence in the Muslim community'.

88. Marshall G. S. Hodgson, *The Order of Assassins. A Struggle of the Early Nizari Ismaʿilis Against the Islamic World* (The Hague: Mouton & Co., 1955), p. 223; Angelika Hartmann, *An-Nasir li-Din Allah* (Berlin and New York: Walter de Gruyter, 1975), pp. 136–72.

89. Hartmann, 'Al-Nasir'.

90. Hartmann, *An-Nasir*, pp. 96–9.

91. Hartmann, 'Al-Nasir'.

92. Hartmann, 'Al-Nasir'. See also Hartmann, *An-Nasir*, p. 103.

93. Hartmann, *An-Nasir*, pp. 111–13. This is not Shihab al-Din Yahya al-Suhrawardi, the famous philosopher, who will make an appearance below.

94. Diyaʾ al-Din Ibn al-Athir, *Rasaʾil Ibn al-Athir*, ed. Anis al-Maqdisi (Beirut: Dar al-ʿIlm lil-Malayin, 1959), pp. 235–7.

95. To be inducted into the order required a rite of initiation that included a number of symbolic components, of which the bestowal of the *sarawīl* seems to have been the most prominent. Hartmann, *An-Nasir*, pp. 246–7.

96. Eddé, *Principauté*, p. 348.

97. Anne-Marie Eddé, 'Hérésie et pouvoir politique en Syrie au XIIe siècle: l'exécution d'al-Suhrawardi en 1191', in André Vauchez, ed., *La religion civique à l'époque médiévale et moderne (chrétienté et islam)* (Rome: École française de Rome, 1995), pp. 237–8. The young al-Zahir spent so many hours in discussion and argument with al-Suhrawardi that the local ʿulamaʾ became alarmed, accused the scholar of heresy, and wrote to Saladin, imploring him to intervene.

98. Musa ibn Muhammad Al-Yunini, *Dhayl mirʾat al-zaman.* (Hyderabad: Matbaʿat Majlis Dayrat al-Maʿarif al-ʿUrthmaniyya, 1960), vol. 3, pp. 439–40. Eddé, *Principauté*, p. 439.

99. Hodgson speculates that this may have been the case, *Order of Assassins*, p. 223.

100. Ibid., p. 223.

101. Eddé, *Principauté*, p. 447.

102. Nasseh Ahmed Mirza, *Syrian Ismailism* (Richmond: Curzon, 1997), pp. 44–7; Hartmann, 'Al-Nasir'.

103. Josef Meri, 'A late medieval Syrian pilgrimage guide: Ibn al-Hawrani's *al-Isharat ila Amakin al-Ziyarat* (Guide to Pilgrimage Places)', *Medieval Encounters* 7 (2001), 5.

104. Al-Harawi, *Kitab al-isharat*, XV. This seems all the more plausible since Shiʿis often chose to join the Shafiʿi *madhhab*: upon his arrival in Aleppo al-Harawi installed himself in a Shafiʿi *madrasa* there. For references to Shiʿis practicing *taqiyya* by 'passing' as Shafiʿis, see Devin J. Stewart, *Islamic Legal Orthodoxy: Twelver Shiʿi Responses to the Sunni Legal System*. (Salt Lake City, UT: University of Utah Press, 1991), pp. 61–109.

105. Eddé, *Principauté*, pp. 443–4.

106. Youssef Raghib, 'Essai d'inventaire chronologique des guides à l'usage des pèlerins du Caire', *Revue des Études Islamiques* 41 (1973), 272–3. The guide says 'a dear and wise friend asked me to write for him an accounting of the places of pilgrimage which I had piously visited' and continues with long paragraphs of praise for al-Nasir, whom he calls the 'Imam of the Muslims'. Al-Harawi, *Kitab al-Isharat*, p. 4; Meri, *Cult of Saints*, p. 144.

107. Al-Harawi, *Kitab al-Isharat*, pp. XIX–XX.

108. Ibid., p. XXI; Eddé, *Principauté*, p. 444.

109. Hartmann, 'Al-Nasir'. He was accused of being 'mutashayyiʿ', or it was said of him 'kāna yatashayyaʿu'. It is interesting to consider that it was these acts of architectural patronage, apparently more so than other aspects of his policy, that seem to have been most disturbing to Sunni partisans.

110. Hartmann, *An-Nasir*, p. 166; Momen, *Introduction*, p. 162.
111. Hartmann, *An-Nasir*, p. 166; Ernst Herzfeld, *Die Ausgrabungen von Samarra* (Berlin: D. Reimer, 1921–1948), p. 288.
112. Hartmann, *An-Nasir*, p. 167.
113. Apparently, however, the implications of a Sunni caliph's burial at the grave of a Shi'i saint were a bit too uncomfortable for his descendants, who had the body properly buried in the tomb of the Abbasid caliphs. Hartmann, *An-Nasir*, p. 168.
114. Talmon-Heller, 'Graves, relics and sanctuaries'. Meri, *Cult of Saints*, pp. 258–9.

CHAPTER THREE

Eclectic Ecumenism: The Cemetery of Bab al-Saghir in Damascus

AMONG THE ANCIENT gates of Damascus, there is one known as the Small Gate, or Bab al-Saghir, located in the south-western portion of the city wall. It was the old Roman Gate of Mars, and it served as the main entrance to the city along the road from the south in pre-Islamic times. Reconstructed by Nur al-Din in 1156 as part of his refortification of the defences of the city, it still rests on the foundations of the Roman gate and the demarcation between the Roman and Islamic stonework is clearly visible. It was further heavily restored under the Ayyubids, and the inscriptions commemorating these reconstructions are legible on the interior of the gate, in the tympanum of the arch.

A bit to the south-west of the gate is one of Damascus's largest cemeteries, known since medieval times as the cemetery of Bab al-Saghir (Maps 3 and 4). According to the medieval topographer Ibn Shakir al-Kutubi, during the Arab siege of Damascus in 635–6, the army of Yazid ibn Abi Sufyan camped outside the walls, and it was through the gate of Bab al-Saghir that they entered the city, victorious.[1] It is said that during the battle, the soldiers of Yazid's army were buried where they fell in the field outside the gate.[2] If so, they were the first to be interred in what would later become perhaps the most important cemetery in the city, and a potent sacred site for native Damascenes and pilgrims alike. It has been in use at least since the time of the first Umayyad caliphs, as the graves of Mu'awiya and the purported grave of 'Umar ibn 'Abd al-'Aziz attest.[3] Also believed to be buried there are numerous other figures important for the early history of Islam, including a number of the *ṣaḥāba* or Companions of the Prophet, three of his wives (Hafsa, Umm Salama and Umm Habiba), the Prophet's first muezzin Bilal al-Habashi and numerous 'Alid figures. Later, the sanctity of these holy persons' graves attracted the burial of countless scholars, Sufis, preachers and other religious figures, along with wealthy and important members of the Damascene elite.

For the Shi'a, the importance of the cemetery is perhaps even more profound. In fact, the cemetery of Bab al-Saghir, along with several other holy sites in Damascus, is arguably the most important

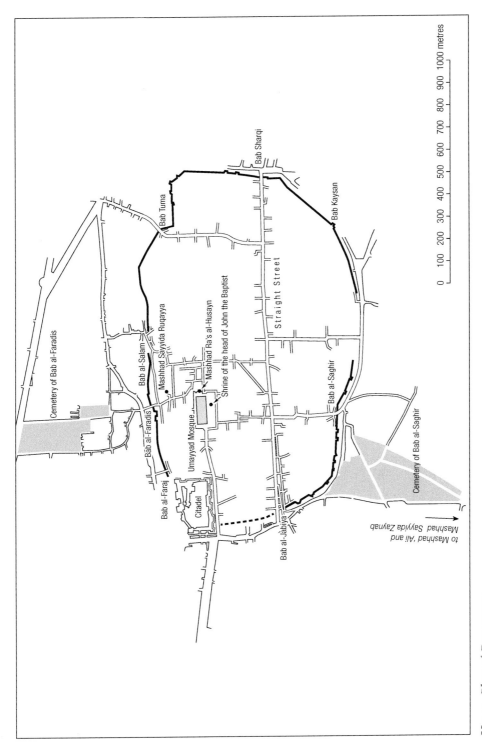

Map 3 *Plan of Damascus.*

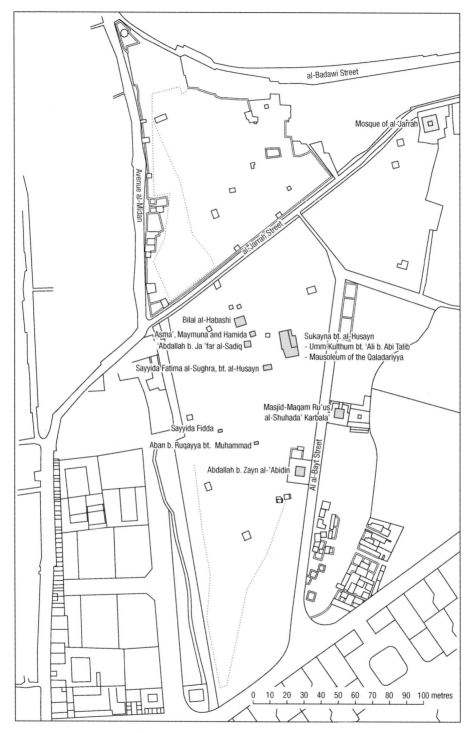

Map 4 *Damascus, plan of cemetery of Bab al-Saghir. After Moaz and Ory,* Inscriptions, *plate II*

Shiʿi pilgrimage place outside of Najaf, Karbalaʾ and Mashhad. This is because Damascus was the capital of the Umayyads during the crucial years of the formation of Shiʿi religious identity, and after the battle of Karbalaʾ the heads of many martyrs, including that of al-Husayn, as well as captive ʿAlid women and children, were brought back to Damascus by the Umayyad Caliph Yazid. A number of these holy figures eventually died and were buried there. Thus, Damascus is a critical *locus sanctus* for the formation of Shiʿi identity and an important site of communal mourning.[4]

Despite this long history, the cemetery, like many holy sites in the Islamic world, seems to have undergone a process of particularly intensive sanctification and renewal beginning in the eleventh century, and continuing through to the fifteenth century. This process involved the discovery of new shrines, a revived interest in shrine construction and a newly ecumenical approach to the commemoration of holy figures, both Sunni and Shiʿi alike. During this period, sacred space was literally created, reinforced and reconfirmed through the building and renovation of shrines for holy figures of many sectarian stripes.[5] However, unlike in Aleppo, this ecumenism took place within the context of a city that had been predominantly Sunni throughout its Islamic history. Even under Fatimid rule, the city's Muslim inhabitants remained Sunni and the city's Shiʿi population seems always to have been an intermittently embattled minority.[6]

Thus, in Damascus, the motivation for such an attitude of ecumenism must have been something other than the need to appease a possibly restive Shiʿi population or to unite the Muslims under the aegis of a single Islamic polity, as seems to have been the situation in Aleppo. In fact, the reasons for the patronage of the shrines of Bab al-Saghir are as varied and eclectic as the patrons themselves. Furthermore, given the ostensibly beleaguered position of Shiʿism in predominantly Sunni Damascus, it is remarkable to note that Shiʿis were apparently capable of significant acts of patronage. This is an important observation, for it directly contradicts much of the textual evidence regarding the situation of Shiʿism in this Sunni city and opens up the possibility that at least some Shiʿis had greater access than is usually supposed to the social capital and financial means necessary for such endowments.

The apparent contradiction between the textual and architectural evidence highlights a significant methodological problem for the history of architecture in medieval Damascus, namely the lack of a sectarian history for the city. The *prima facie* assumption that Damascus was always a Sunni city has meant that evidence for the survival and continuity of Damascene Shiʿism after the Seljuk conquest has been largely neglected.[7] This lack of corresponding historical context has meant that the architectural evidence is sometimes difficult to interpret, but at the same time has opened up

2

a remarkable opportunity for the architecture to tell a story about sectarian exchange and interaction that the textual sources alone cannot.

Thus, the remaining physical and textual evidence for the shrines in the cemetery of Bab al-Saghir is more difficult to interpret than that for Aleppo. In addition to the lack of sectarian history noted above, there are several additional reasons for this difficulty. The first is that the buildings were built on a much more modest scale than their Aleppan counterparts. Many of them are simple, one-room, dome-on-square structures. Rather than reflecting the status of the holy figures buried there, however, this small scale probably points to the fact that within the cemetery, a strong cultural sanction against moving the bodies of the dead meant there was little room for expansion into the area around the shrines. Such speculation may be validated by the many instances of lesser holy figures elsewhere that nevertheless received large shrines, for example the large shrine to al-Muhassin, the stillborn son of ʿAli located in Aleppo and discussed in the previous chapter. Another problem is that unlike the Aleppo shrines, those in the cemetery of Bab al-Saghir have experienced continuous renovation and rebuilding over the course of many centuries. In several cases, such renovation is taking place even today. This means that few of these shrines preserve their medieval fabric intact. While this continuous reconstruction is undoubtedly evidence of how beloved these shrines were, and of perpetual care and investment by their patrons, it makes an understanding of their historical and architectural sequencing a complex process of inference and association.[8]

Nevertheless, enlightening conclusions can be drawn from paying close attention to the varied and subtle clues those patrons left behind. As noted above, given the few studies on the sectarian history of Damascus, these shrines present a unique opportunity to make a contribution to our understanding of the relationship between Sunnis and Shiʿis in the medieval period. In order to do so, one must cast as wide a methodological net as possible. Thus this study draws on evidence from the medieval Arabic sources, measured architectural drawings, archaeological analysis, epigraphy and the interpretation of inscriptions, and analysis of the spatial relationships within and between buildings. How and why these patrons chose to invest in such projects will be explored here, in a study of ten ʿAlid shrines in the cemetery of Bab al-Saghir. Each of the following entries will present what is known about these shrines and reconstruct their histories from the Arabic sources, read and analyse their inscriptions (many have not previously been published), assess the remaining architectural evidence and present information regarding the buildings' patrons.

Shrines of known provenance

Bilal al-Habashi

Bilal al-Habashi was an early convert from Ethiopia and the first muezzin of Islam. While not belonging to the Prophet's family, and thus not an ʿAlid, he is of interest here because he is among the handful of Sahaba (Companions) who are deeply revered by the Shiʿa, in this case for his loyalty to the Prophet and the Prophet's family. According to Shiʿi tradition, he refused to recite the *adhān* (call to prayer) after Muhammad's death, as a protest against the usurpation of ʿAli's right to succession. The Imam Jaʿfar al-Sadiq is said to have praised Bilal for his love of and loyalty to the *ahl al-bayt*. In addition, popular tradition associates Bilal's tomb with an ʿAlid grave, that of Abdallah b. Jaʿfar al-Tayyar, the nephew of ʿAli and the husband and cousin of Sayyida Zaynab. Abdallah's father, Jaʿfar al-Tayyar, incidentally, had at Muhammad's injunction led one of the early Islamic emigrations to Habasha or Ethiopia, where Bilal was from. Today, as in the medieval period, Bilal's tomb is part of the usual itinerary of Shiʿi visitors to Damascus.[9]

The mausoleum is located in the cemetery of Bab al-Saghir south of the al-Jarrah road and north-east of the mausoleums of Sukayna and Asma (Map 4, Fig. 3.1).[10] It consists of a square domed building,

Figure 3.1 *Mausoleum of Bilal al-Habashi, north elevation. Western extension is visible to the right. Photo: Author*

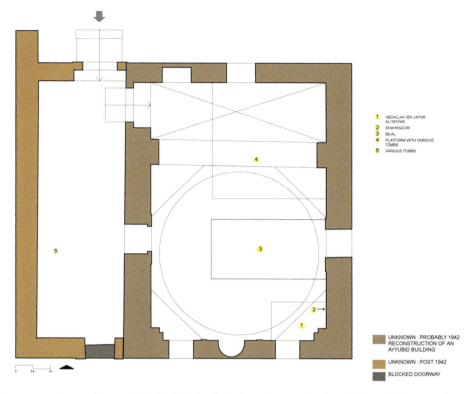

1 ABDALLAH IBN JAʿFAR AL-TAYYAR
2 SHAHRAZURI
3 BILAL
4 PLATFORM WITH VARIOUS TOMBS
5 VARIOUS TOMBS

UNKNOWN : PROBABLY 1942 RECONSTRUCTION OF AN AYYUBID BUILDING

UNKNOWN : POST 1942

BLOCKED DOORWAY

Figure 3.2 *Mausoleum of Bilal al-Habashi, plan. Image: Author, Milena Hijazi and Irina Rivero*

built of *ablaq* masonry, with a northerly extension in the form of an open, groin-vaulted rectangular space. At some later date, a flat-roofed extension was added to the west side of the building, presumably to shelter some graves there (Fig. 3.2). The building has a *miḥrāb* of Ottoman appearance, bordered on both sides by vertical panels of simple, geometric decoration in relief. Directly under the dome is the massive cenotaph belonging to Bilal. In the south-east corner of the room is the cenotaph which popular tradition attributes to ʿAbdallah b. Jaʿfar al-Tayyar.

The building and the tomb of Bilal were at least partially destroyed in a fire that took place in 1942. The Department of Islamic Waqfs, 'preserving what could be preserved of the old style', immediately restored it.[11] This does not seem to have been much; other than its inscriptions it would appear the building has little medieval fabric remaining. The small-scale, uniform *ablaq* masonry of the exterior is of indeterminate date, and is almost entirely absent of decoration. It seems unlikely to be anything more recent than late Ottoman, and probably dates to the 1942 restoration.[12]

A single line drawing from Herzfeld's 'Damascus: Studies in Architecture – III' depicts an Ayyubid arch with joggled voussoirs

that once graced the western doorway
of the tomb (Fig. 3.3). This has entirely
disappeared today, though the inscription he associates with this door survives and will be discussed below.
Fortunately, Herzfeld also published
a sketch-plan of the mausoleum that
confirms that the post-fire restoration
closely followed the plan of the original
building.[13] Thus, we have two lines of
evidence for reconstructing the history
of this building: the historical inscriptions, of which several are preserved,
and the Arabic sources.

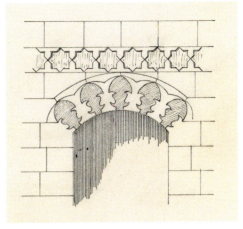

Figure 3.3 *Herzfeld's drawing of the
Ayyubid arch that once framed the
entrance to the tomb of Bilal al-Habashi.
Illustration: The Ernst Herzfeld Papers.
Freer Gallery of Art and Arthur M. Sackler
Gallery Archives. Smithsonian Institution,
Washington, DC*

The earliest dated inscription in
the mausoleum is located just above
the cenotaph popularly attributed to
ʿAbdallah b. Jaʿfar al-Tayyar, on the
east wall in the far south-east corner of
the mausoleum (Fig. 3.4). This inscription is in fact not for Jaʿfar al-Tayyar,
but instead bears an epitaph for the
qāḍī Muhammad b. ʿAqil b. Zayd al-Shahrazuri (d. 1061), a well-
known eleventh-century religious figure in Damascus (Fig. 3.5).[14]
This epitaph is clearly not *in situ*, however Shahrazuri was probably
buried somewhere very near Bilal. This is confirmed by an anecdote
from Ibn ʿAsakir, whose father once met a Persian pilgrim crying by
Shahrazuri's grave. When Ibn ʿAsakir's father asked why she was
crying, she reported that after making *ziyāra* to the tomb of Bilal,
the Prophet had appeared to her in a dream, saying, 'You visited
the tomb of Bilal, yet you have not visited that of his neighbour!'
Thus, she had returned to visit the grave of Shahrazuri.[15] Moaz and
Ory speculate that since Shahrazuri's grave had become the object
of pilgrimage, the epitaph was preserved by being inserted into the
wall when the mausoleum for Bilal was erected. It is a short funerary
inscription on a limestone plaque, written in Kufic, and is the second
oldest inscription in the cemetery.

Bilal's cenotaph bears a small (39cm × 34.5cm) rectangular
marble inscription at its foot, facing west (Fig. 3.6). It consists of
four lines of large floriated Kufic separated by raised horizontal
borders. The inscription is carved in relief on an excised field. It reads
simply:

Bismillah al-raḥman al-raḥīm
This is the tomb (*qabr*) of Bilal ibn
Hamama the *muʾadhdhin* of the Messenger of God.
May God bless him and be pleased with him.

Figure 3.4 *Inscriptions for Ibn ʿAqil and al-Shahrazuri in south-east corner of the mausoleum of Bilal al-Habashi. The cenotaph for Ibn ʿAqil (revered as that of ʿAbdallah ibn Jaʿfar al-Ṭayyar) is in the foreground with the upper left corner of its inscription (located on the front face of the cenotaph) barely visible, and al-Shahrazuri's inscription is inserted in the wall above. After Moaz and Ory,* Inscriptions, *plate XX B*

Figure 3.5 *Inscription for al-Shahrazuri. After Moaz and Ory,* Inscriptions, *plate VI A*

Although lacking a date, two thirteenth-century authors specifically mentioned this inscription, Ibn ʿAsakir and Ibn Jubayr, so we may presume it was at least prior to that date.[16] On epigraphic grounds alone, the date of this Kufic inscription can be pushed back by a further hundred years: to the first half of the twelfth century.[17] However, other evidence suggests an even earlier date could be proposed, if not for the inscription, at least for the presence of a mausoleum for Bilal in the cemetery. Indeed, several clues point to the existence of a mausoleum or tomb on the spot by at least the mid-eleventh century.

The first clue is the burial of the Shaykh Shahrazuri there. While the proximity of the tomb of Shahrazuri to that of Bilal could be coincidental, it is perhaps more likely that he was buried there because of a desire to be near the holy figure. Furthermore, that some sort of tomb for Bilal existed prior to the burial of al-Shahrazuri nearby is confirmed by the medieval author al-Rabaʿi, who gives us the earliest textual reference to Bilal's tomb in his treatise on the virtues of Damascus. Since al-Rabaʿi's *fadāʾil* work was written some time before his death in the mid-eleventh century,[18] we may conclude that a well-known tomb existed by that time, if not a

A – Ins. n° 29 – 6e/12e s.   (Cl. S. Ory)

B – Fac-similé de l'ins. n° 29.

Figure 3.6 *Mausoleum of Bilal al-Habashi, inscription at foot of his grave. After Moaz and Ory,* Inscriptions, *plates XXIII A and B*

full-scale mausoleum. The style of the Kufic inscription on Bilal's grave is certainly not out of line with such a date.[19] The convergence in the early to mid-eleventh century of the burial of Shahrazuri, the textual reference from al-Raba'i and the style of the Kufic inscription at the foot of Bilal's cenotaph all point to the establishment of some sort of memorial at the site at around or prior to the mid-eleventh century. However as yet there is no evidence regarding the patron of the enterprise.

Our next bit of information relates to the stone cenotaph located just below the epitaph of Shahrazuri, in the south-east corner of the mausoleum (Fig. 3.4). Though, as noted above, this cenotaph is popularly associated with 'Abdallah b. Ja'far al-Tayyar, the nephew of 'Ali and the husband of Sayyida Zaynab, there is no archaeological evidence to support this claim.[20] Rather, the cenotaph's inscription commemorates yet another shaykh, Diya' al-Din Abi al-Hasan 'Ali b. 'Aqil b. 'Ali b. Hibat Allah al-Shafi'i (d. 1205), known as Ibn 'Aqil, who according to his epitaph was the imam of the *mashhad* of Zayn al-'Abidin in the Umayyad mosque (see Chapter 4).[21] The stone epitaph, located at the foot of the cenotaph and carved in Ayyubid *naskhī*, contains the Basmallah, a Qur'anic quotation and a few short lines of blessing. A secondary wooden coffer dedicated to the 'Alid 'Abdallah b. Ja'far al-Tayyar once covered the shaykh's cenotaph. The Antiquities Service removed this coffer some time prior to the late 1970s.[22] Despite the present visibility of the inscription, it is still venerated by pilgrims as though it were the cenotaph of 'Abdallah.[23]

We get a bit more information about the history of this shrine with our next dated inscription. Today, it is located over the entrance portal to the mausoleum proper, on the northerly portion of the west wall, inside the Ottoman extension (Fig. 3.7). The inscription is written on a single block of masonry, which serves as the lintel for the door. It bears five lines in Ayyubid *naskhī*:

> *Bismillah* ... 'For this the toilers should strive' (Qur'an 37:61).
> This is the tomb (*qabr*) of Bilal b. Rabah
> the muezzin of the Messenger of God (PBUH) the seal of the prophets and lord of the messengers.
> He was the freedman (*mawla*) of Abu Bakr ibn al-Sadiq the caliph of the Messenger of God. Bilal died in the year 20
> of the *hijra* of the Prophet (640–1) and his birth was at al-Sharat. At the time of his death he was sixty and some years and he was buried in this mausoleum (*turba*).
> The name of Bilal's mother was Hamama, may God grant them both his compassion. This place (*makān*) was restored (*juddida*) in the year 625 (1228).[24]

The phrase *juddida hadha al-makān*, which appears in the final line, is both enlightening and frustrating. On one hand, its use of the word *juddida*, or 'restored', clearly indicates that there was some sort of structure extant by 1228 which was in need of restoration: the inscription does not use the term *buniya*, meaning something built from scratch. On the other hand, it uses the neutral word *makān*, or 'place', to refer to this structure, rather than something more specific like 'mausoleum' or 'shrine'. However, in line four of

Figure 3.7 *Inscription on lintel of west-facing entrance to mausoleum of Bilal al-Habashi. After Moaz and Ory,* Inscriptions, *plate XXIV A*

the inscription, the structure is specifically referred to as a *turba*, a word that by the thirteenth century is associated with mausolea. From this we may deduce two things: that by the thirteenth century, a mausoleum of some sort had been built on the site – possibly as early as the mid-eleventh century, as suggested by the information from al-Rabaʿi above – and second, that the mausoleum had been in existence for a long enough time that it was in need of restoration by the early thirteenth century, a task that was completed in 1228. Ernst Herzfeld briefly noted this inscription and associated it with a feature (noted above) that is no longer present in the mausoleum: a classically Ayyubid arch, consisting of joggled voussoirs and a row of eight-pointed stars. It was apparently destroyed in the fire that took place in 1942 or obscured by the subsequent restoration,[25] but it gives some sense of the richness of the original decoration and further confirmation of a major renovation to the shrine in the year 1228.

There are repeated references to this shrine in the Arabic sources following those of al-Rabaʿi, Ibn ʿAsakir and Ibn Jubayr mentioned above. However, few offer clues to patronage or to the nature of the structure itself. The medieval pilgrimage guide author al-Harawi (d. 1215) notes its existence in a list of shrines located in Bab al-Saghir,[26] as do several later medieval authors, some of whom relied on al-Harawi as their source.[27] One writer, Ibn al-Mibrad (d. 1503), calls the structure a mosque (*masjid*), suggesting the presence of a *miḥrāb* by the early sixteenth century. Ibn al-Hawrani notes

Figure 3.8 *Inscription in the name of ʿUthman Agha (located just above that in Figure 3.7), over the west-facing entrance to the mausoleum of Bilal al-Habashi. Photo: Zaher al-Saghir*

that it was a popular and well-visited site that had a reputation for effective intercession, and further added that the people provided endowments for it, indicating the mausoleum was the beneficiary of dependable financial support.[28] However, given the few clues in the Arabic sources relevant to its architecture, to understand its patronage history we must rely on the evidence of the building itself and its inscriptions.

For the pre-modern period, we have one inscription, and it is here that we gain some clarity regarding the building's Sunni patrons. This inscription is located above the entrance to the tomb chamber, on the western wall of the mausoleum and inside the western extension, immediately above the thirteenth-century inscription quoted above (Fig. 3.8). It reads: 'This noble dome (*al-qubbat al-sharīfa*) was renovated by ʿUthman, *agha dār al-saʿāda bi-l-bāb al-ʿālī* in the year 1007 of the *hijra* of the Prophet (1598)'.[29]

Here we find a very interesting patron indeed. ʿUthman (Osman) Agha was the *Agha dār al-saʿāda*, or Chief Black Eunuch in charge of the harem at the Topkapı Palace in Istanbul, and the first eunuch entrusted with supervision of the royal *waqf*s (pious endowments).[30] He was the slave of Safıye, a noblewoman from Venice who had been captured by corsairs and brought to the imperial harem. Famous for her beauty, she became the chief consort of the Sultan Murad III (1574–95) and Valide Sultan after the birth of her son Mehmed

III.[31] Osman was thus one of the most highly placed officials in the Ottoman Empire, a powerful and successful man whose origins as a black slave perhaps made his patronage of the shrine for the Ethiopian freedman Bilal particularly meaningful. Osman Agha's inscription confirms that by the late sixteenth century, a domed building existed over the tomb of Bilal: for a *qubba* is specifically mentioned as the object of 'renovation'. Most likely his renovations were made to the same building Ibn al-Mibrad referred to as a *masjid* a century earlier (see above).

There are two modern patrons, each of whom left an inscription on the exterior of the building. One of these, located over the entrance to the western extension to the mausoleum, which today is the main entrance, mentions work done rapidly in the early nineteenth century, though without naming a patron:

> This is the *maqam* of our Master (*sayyidna*) Bilal al-Habashi, may God be pleased with him, the muezzin of our Master the Messenger of God, PBUH. It was renovated in seven days in Dhu al-Qaʿda of the year 1248 (1833).

Another patron left evidence of a renovation in the form of an inscription placed over the entrance to the mausoleum proper, just over that of ʿUthman Agha cited above:

> This noble dome was renovated by the heirs (*waratha*) of the late (*al-marḥūm*) Sulayman Pasha, Commander of the Army (*raʾis al-orduwī*) on Thursday the fifteenth of Shaʿban in the year 1289 (17 October 1872).[32]

The preceding information allows us to draw the following general conclusions: a mausoleum, or at least a memorial of some sort, for Bilal existed by the first half of the eleventh century, when it was noted by the *fadāʾil* author al-Rabaʿi. It had attracted the devotion of important religious figures by the time of the death and burial of al-Shahrazuri nearby in the mid-eleventh century. It was a beloved pilgrimage site by the early thirteenth century, as the story about the Persian pilgrim told by Ibn ʿAsakir's father illustrates. It remained an important destination for pilgrims and visitors throughout the medieval period, for it is renovated in the thirteenth century and continuously mentioned in the medieval sources as a locus of *ziyāra*. Finally, it was the object of patronage at least three times in the pre-modern and Ottoman periods.

We also have evidence that it was the focus of patronage by prominent Sunni figures. The first bit of evidence comes in the form of the thirteenth-century inscription cited above. Although we are in the dark as to the name of the patron, this inscription refers to a significant renovation to the shrine. This supposition is further verified by

Herzfeld's drawing of the now-lost Ayyubid arch over the door that once ushered pilgrims into the tomb (Fig. 3.3). The reason Herzfeld mentions this arch in the mausoleum of Bilal is that it was an important parallel for more prominent contemporary foundations, such as the *Madrasa* al-Atabakiyya in the Salihiyya area of Damascus, built by the grandniece of Nur al-Din Turkan Khatun (d. 1242) and the *Maristan* (hospital) al-Qaymari (1248–58), also in Salihiyya, built by an amir of al-Malik al-Salih and al-Malik al-Nasir Yusuf, the last Ayyubid to rule Damascus.[33] The tomb of Bilal shared with these buildings a feature that presages later Mamluk architectural decoration: an arch with elaborately joggled voussoirs forming an ornamental pattern. The parallel between the arch over the door of Bilal and that of the Maristan al-Qaymari is particularly marked, to the degree that the voussoirs are cut into a nearly identical pattern. Since such costly and elaborate architectural decoration is typically found only on Ayyubid buildings endowed by high-ranking members of the Sunni Ayyubid elite, it seems we have a strong circumstantial case at the tomb of Bilal for patronage by a person of such stature. Furthermore, we also have evidence of Sunni patronage in the form of the Ottoman official 'Uthman Agha's intervention in the sixteenth century.

For the tomb of Bilal, such Sunni interest seems entirely natural. Bilal, though dearly beloved by the Shi'a, is an equally important figure for Sunnis. Nevertheless, such sustained interest in this tomb would have benefited the Shi'i community of Damascus and the many Shi'i pilgrims who came to visit it, as well as the culture of *ziyāra* in Damascus more generally. Our next example of the patronage of an 'Alid shrine in the Cemetery of Bab al-Saghir is a bit more ambiguous.

Sukayna bt. al-Husayn/Umm Kulthum bt. 'Ali b. Abi Talib/ Mausoleum of the Qalandariyya

The most prominent of the shrines in the cemetery of Bab al-Saghir is a large double-domed mausoleum dedicated to Sayyida Sukayna, the daughter of al-Husayn, and Umm Kulthum, the daughter of 'Ali (Fig. 3.9). Sukayna was one of the *grandes dames* of Islam. Numerous biographies have been devoted to her; they praise her beauty, her cultivated spirit and her courage, not to mention her sauciness.[34] She was apparently a strong-minded woman who was a great patroness of the arts, and she refused to wear the veil. The sources are not unanimous in fixing the place of her death and her sepulchre, but most of them opt for the city of Medina, where she died in 735. Nevertheless, by the twelfth century the tradition relating her death in Damascus and the placement of her tomb in the cemetery of Bab al-Saghir was already known, and was reported by the Damascene historian Ibn 'Asakir.[35] The authors of the Damascene works of *fadā'il* and

Figure 3.9 *Western elevation of mausoleum of Sukayna and Umm Kulthum and mausoleum of the Qalandariyya. Photo: Author*

ziyārāt also opt for the tradition of locating the tomb of Sukayna in Damascus, although mention of it is absent in the earliest *faḍāʾil* works, such as that of al-Rabaʿi.[36] Based on Janine Sourdel's dating of the epigraphy of the splendid walnut cenotaph in the crypt, it is clear there was a shrine at this location at least by the first half of the twelfth century, when Damascus was under the rule of Seljuk governors and their Atabeg successors.[37]

After Ibn ʿAsakir, the tomb of Sukayna appears reliably in the sources, though usually without mention of her companion. It is listed in the late twelfth and early thirteenth centuries by Ibn ʿAsakir, al-Harawi and Ibn Jubayr.[38] Later, in the early sixteenth century, it is briefly noted by al-Badri, Ibn al-Mibrad and al-Nuʿaymi, all of whom locate it near the grave of Bilal. Al-Nuʿaymi refers to the building as a mosque (*masjid*).[39] Later authors mention Sukayna's 'tomb' or her 'grave' in the cemetery but give no further information.[40]

Today, this mausoleum is part of a double-domed complex that pairs it with a shrine dedicated to Umm Kulthum, the daughter of Imam ʿAli and sister of al-Hasan and al-Husayn (Fig. 3.10). However, it seems that the belief that Umm Kulthum was buried in this place is a recent one, for the medieval Arabic sources do not name Umm Kulthum as the inhabitant of a tomb in the cemetery of Bab al-Saghir. Ibn ʿAsakir (d. 1176) mentions a domed building near Sukayna's tomb, but reports that it belonged to another, otherwise

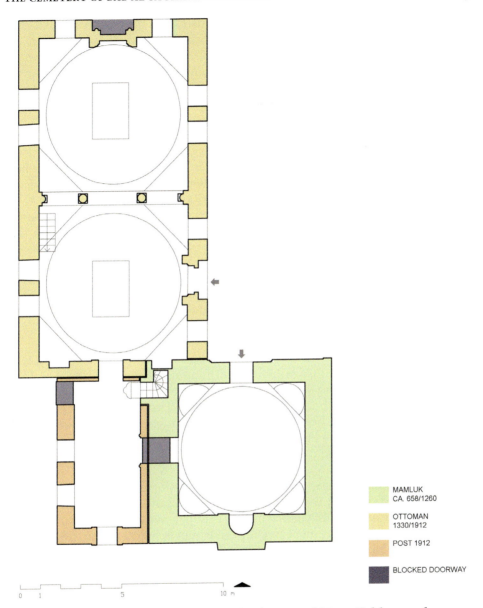

Figure 3.10 *Plan, upper level, mausoleum of Sukayna and Umm Kulthum and mausoleum of the Qalandariyya. Image: Author, Milena Hijazi and Irina Rivero*

unknown female member of the *ahl al-bayt* known as Buriha bt. al-Husayn.[41] He later notes that this attribution is likely false, since 'the scholars of genealogy do not mention (a Buriha) among the children of al-Husayn ibn 'Ali ibn Abi Talib'.[42] Buriha is not mentioned in later sources describing the cemetery, but there was evidently a domed building near Sukayna's tomb dedicated to some female member of the *ahl al-bayt* by the late twelfth century.

So it seems there was a confusion in the sources themselves about who was buried in the mausoleum next to Sukayna's in Bab al-Saghir, as is illustrated by Ibn ʿAsakir's entry above. The uncertainty may have resulted from a mixing up of female members of the *ahl al-bayt*, several of whom were named Zaynab and/or Umm Kulthum. For example, the third child of ʿAli and Fatima was named Zaynab, but she also had the nickname 'Umm Kulthum' even though Umm Kulthum was also the *given* name of their fourth child.[43] In the late fifteenth century, one author, al-Badri, mentions the grave of 'Zaynab, the daughter of Imam ʿAli' in a list of holy figures buried in the cemetery of Bab al-Saghir, though a few pages later he also says she is buried in Rawiya south of Damascus,[44] but in general when the sources mention a shrine to Umm Kulthum, it is nearly always the mausoleum to Sayyida Zaynab in Rawiya they are describing, not the one that exists today in the cemetery of Bab al-Saghir. Because of this medieval habit of referring to the Rawiya shrine as 'Umm Kulthum', it is usually only the accompanying information about the location of the mausoleum that allows us to confirm they mean the shrine known today as Sayyida Zaynab. Ibn Jubayr, however, gives a fuller account:

> Among the other monuments to members of the family of the Prophet is that of Umm Kulthum, daughter of ʿAli b. Abi Talib, who is also known as Zaynab al-Sughra (the little Zaynab);[45] Umm Kulthum is a *kunya* (nickname) that the Prophet gave to her because of her resemblance to his daughter Umm Kulthum. And God knows best. Her venerated monument is in a village in the south of the city, called Rawiya, at a distance of a parsang.

Similar notices are given by Ibn al-Mibrad (d. 1503), al-Nuʿaymi (d. 1520) and Ibn al-Hawrani (d. 1592), all of whom refer to Umm Kulthum or Zaynab Umm Kulthum's tomb in Rawiya, and who make no mention of an Umm Kulthum in Bab al-Saghir.[46] So it seems we have one notice for a Zaynab (but not an Umm Kulthum) next to Sukayna's tomb in the cemetery in the early fifteenth century, but she then disappears from view.

However, al-Nuʿaymi does mention a Zaynab when describing the *zāwiya* of the Qalandariyya, built next to the mausoleum of Sukayna in the second half of the thirteenth century (discussed below).[47] He notes that a Sufi shaykh used to live part of the time in the cemetery of Bab al-Saghir near the *zāwiya* of the Qalandariyya, and the rest of the time 'in the *qubba* of Zaynab bt. Zayn al-ʿAbidin', yet another Zaynab, this one the daughter of the fourth Shiʿi Imam and thus the great-granddaughter of ʿAli.[48] Unfortunately it is not explicitly clear from this entry if the *qubba* he mentions is the one next to Sukayna's mausoleum, but it does seem to indicate the possibility. And finally, according to Moaz and Ory, who mapped the cemetery in the 1970s, a 'cenotaph in the name of Zaynab' existed in the crypt facing that of Sukayna. It did not possess an inscription, and if one exists, the wooden screen that has been built around it obscures it today.[49]

From this confusing sequence of references, we may establish the following: the mausoleum of Sukayna was paired with a mausoleum devoted to some other female 'Alid, either side by side or as part of a single complex, in the twelfth century. The shrine of Sukayna is consistently mentioned in the Arabic sources, but that of her neighbour is not. At some point, this neighbouring mausoleum was dedicated to Zaynab/Umm Kulthum, the daughter of 'Ali, perhaps through confusion over different female 'Alids bearing these names or nicknames. We may never know the medieval identification of the second shrine with certainty, but it serves as an excellent example of how shrines could survive and even thrive despite the absence of a clear identity. For our purposes, the important information is that from the medieval period, there existed two domed mausolea, either side by side or part of a single complex. As noted above, Ibn 'Asakir confirms this was the case from at least the twelfth century.

This text-based information accords well with the architectural evidence. Today, above ground, one sees a spacious Ottoman double-domed structure attached to a small, one-room Mamluk mosque, which will be discussed below (Fig. 3.9). Inside the Ottoman building, against the western wall, a narrow flight of stairs leads down to a tripartite underground chamber or crypt containing the cenotaphs of Umm Kulthum and Sukayna (Figs 3.10 and 3.11). This crypt consists of a long hallway orientated east–west with two doorways opening from the north and south walls of the hallway into two small rooms, each containing a cenotaph (Fig. 3.12).

The crypt of Sayyida Sukayna, accessed through the north doorway (Fig. 3.13), is a small, flat-roofed space that shelters the cenotaph with just enough room for circumambulation. The magnificent walnut cenotaph, which appears to be *in situ*, dates to the twelfth century. The room is orientated so that its only entrance – a curious multi-arched structure that is clearly the result of several phases of buttressing or rebuilding (Fig. 3.14) – almost directly faces the entrance to the crypt of Umm Kulthum, which has a more regular arrangement consisting of a single interior arch framing the doorway. Umm Kulthum's crypt also contains a *mihrab* in the southern wall and a wide arch in the eastern wall (Fig. 3.15).

In plan, the crypt of Umm Kulthum is far more regular than that of Sukayna (Fig. 3.12). In the crypt of Umm Kulthum, two arches, one over the *mihrab* and one over the doorway, face each other across the room. The only point of irregularity in the plan of Umm Kulthum's crypt is the wide arch in the eastern wall, which is not replicated to the west.

Figure 3.11 *Hallway in crypt of Sukayna and Umm Kulthum, view from stairway, facing east. Doorway to crypt of Umm Kulthum is visible on right. Renovation was underway when these photos were taken. Photo: Author*

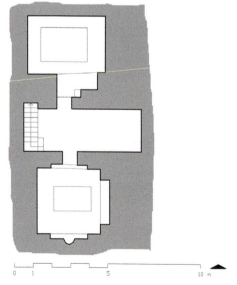

Figure 3.12 *Plan, crypt of Sukayna and Umm Kulthum. Image: Author, Milena Hijazi and Irina Rivero*

Figure 3.13 *Doorway to crypt of Sukayna, as seen from the hallway, facing north. Cenotaph is visible at centre. Photo: Author*

Figure 3.14 *View of multiple phases of buttressing, looking out door towards hallway from inside crypt of Sukayna. Renovations often appear to be ongoing. Photo: Author*

Figure 3.15 Miḥrāb *in crypt of Umm Kulthum. Photo: Author*

Sukayna's crypt, at least as it stands today, is less rationally organised. While the crypt of Umm Kulthum approaches a square plan, that of Sukayna is more rectangular, its close walls on the north and south providing only the narrowest of passageways around the cenotaph. Its doorway opens to the south, meaning that today at least the room has no *miḥrāb*. Unlike the crypt of Umm Kulthum, with its regular arrangement of arches, in Sukayna's crypt there are only two interior arches, both framing the doorway (Fig. 3.14). Beginning on the eastern side, the first and wider arch disappears into the western wall, and the second, narrower one into the ceiling of the doorway. Clearly this is not the original configuration of the crypt. These two arches must once have completed their arc and come to rest at a point now buried within the western wall. The most likely explanation is that this western wall is not original, and that it was inserted at some later date, thereby blocking part of the arches. The reason for this seems obvious from the plan: in order to provide more solid support for the stairway. But why, if the crypt and mausoleum above were constructed at the same time, would such an unusual doorway configuration have been chosen?

One possibility is that these crypts were not originally crypts at all: but buildings that were once above ground. In addition to the architecture of the crypts themselves, there are some compelling observations to be made in support of this proposition: first, the simple fact that from an archaeological standpoint a cemetery, with its constant acts of burial and reburial, is one of the most rapidly 'built up' areas of a city. Throughout the area, there are numerous indications that the level of the cemetery of Bab al-Saghir has risen at a steady rate: for example the tomb dedicated to the Umayyad Caliph ʿUmar b. ʿAbd al-ʿAziz contains two stone cenotaphs contemporary with the twelfth century wooden cenotaph of Sukayna. These are now at least 2–3m below the current level of the cemetery.[50] Even structures dating to the mid-nineteenth century, for example the ornate, wrought-iron tomb canopies that grace some graves, have been partially buried. Walkways throughout the cemetery often seem on their way to becoming tunnels, as the level of the graves on either side have risen up around them, sometimes by a metre or more.

A second line of reasoning derives from the architecture of the crypts themselves, which display doors, windows and arches that appear to have once given passage or opened to the outside. Unfortunately, the masonry of the crypts has been obscured by plaster or marble panelling, making this theory impossible to verify. However, simple formal analysis of the architecture of the crypts supports the proposal that the crypts are the remains of above-ground structures.

If so, the nature of both doorways suggests that these crypts may once have been a type of canopy tomb. These would have been open on one side; and the form of the crypt of Umm Kulthum makes the strongest case for this interpretation. If this were the case, its broad eastern arch may once have been the entrance arch, with the two narrower ones over the *miḥrāb* and current door providing support for a small dome. Such simple canopy tombs were probably still common in the early twelfth century, though they seem a bit old-fashioned at this point: the Fatimid mausolea at Aswan, for example, are already 100 years old and such dazzling Seljuk/Zangid-era innovations as the *muqarnas* domed mausolea of Iraq are more in step with the times. But this comparison is intriguing: it suggests two possibilities. The first is that the building surrounding the cenotaph is older than the cenotaph itself, and that it was built some time before the twelfth-century cenotaph in the crypt of Sukayna was installed. The second is that the building is contemporary with the cenotaph, but was deliberately constructed in an archaising style that was reminiscent of the Fatimid mausolea of Cairo. Because the interiors of both crypts are today lined with marble, the masonry cannot be evaluated, and neither of these hypotheses can be proven without archaeological investigation.[51] For now, however, the relevant point

Figure 3.16 *Cenotaph of Sukayna. Photo: Author*

is that for these buildings, we can securely date a significant act of patronage to the Seljuk period or earlier in Damascus, based on the association of the cenotaph with the crypt of Sukayna and the plan and structure of the crypts themselves.

The inscription on this cenotaph unfortunately gives no indication of the patron, but it does bear three verses from the Qur'an that were common in pro-Shi'i polemic. The cenotaph, a complex and beautiful example of medieval woodcarving, is today preserved under glass and is openly visible in the crypt of Sukayna (Fig. 3.16). The cenotaph is in a fragile state; in many places the wood has already decayed and the lower area of the north face along with certain areas of the south face have been lost entirely due to time and wear. Its four sides are ornamented with Kufic inscriptions, of a post-Fatimid type sometimes called *atābakī*; this is carved in relief on a dense ground of scrolling vines. The text is distributed in three registers. The first register is narrow and runs along the top of the cenotaph, and its small and elegant characters are separated from the monumental register below it by a raised band. Running among the uprights of the bold characters in the monumental lower register is a third and much smaller inscription. The characters of the monumental register extend over the entire lower surface of the cenotaph.[52]

The content of the inscriptions is almost entirely Qur'anic and devotional. However, the verses chosen were not neutral, for in fact they represent important proof-texts in medieval Sunni–Shi'i polemic. The top register contains the *āyat al-kursī* or Throne Verse

(Qur'an 33:46–7), a majestic paean to the infinite power and inimitability of God. At the end of the *āyat al-kursī*, in smaller script,
we find the artist's signature, which reads simply 'This is the work
of Muhammad b. Ahmad b. 'Abd Allah, may God be pleased with
him.'

In addition to the *āyat al-kursī* the cenotaph bears three other
Qur'anic inscriptions, all with Shi'i significance. The first of these
is also located in the upper register, on the east panel – immediately
following the *āyat al-kursī* and the artist's signature. It is Qur'an
33:46–7:

> Oh Prophet, We have sent you as a witness and a bearer of happy
> tidings and an admonisher, and to call (*dā'iyan*) (men) to God by
> His leave, and as a lamp resplendent.

The monumental inscription in the bottom register of the cenotaph
is devotional in content. Beginning with the south side, it reads:

> *Bismillah.* This
> is the tomb of Sukayna bt. al-Husayn
> b. 'Ali b. Abi Talib. May God's blessings be upon them
> all, and upon their pure family (*ālihim al-ṭāhirīn*).

Interspersed among the uprights of this inscription we find the last
part of Qur'an 33:33, sometimes known as the *āyat al-rijs*, reading
from the south and west sides:

> God desires to remove impurities from you, *ahl*
> *al-bayt*, and to purify you completely.

Then, continuing on the north and east sides, also interspersed
among the uprights, we have the following, from Qur'an 33:40:

> Muhammad is not the father of any man among you, but a
> messenger of God, and the seal of the prophets.
> God has knowledge of every thing.

These inscriptions have two themes. The first is the power, infal-
libility and greatness of God, as expressed in the *āyat al-kursī*. The
Throne Verse occurs as an inscription in religious contexts with
relative frequency – in fact, technically, it is the second most popular
Qur'anic inscription for mosques – but this status by no means
indicates it is universally invoked in such contexts. Indeed, this
second-place ranking seems to be a reflection of the infrequency of
epigraphic repetition in mosque architecture generally, rather than
a true index of its popularity: one study shows that of over 4,000
mosque inscriptions from across the Islamic lands, there were a mere

thirty occurrences of the *āyat al-kursī*.[53] The most popular verse for mosque inscriptions is *al-Tawba* (9:18) with 110 occurrences: thus the *āyat al-kursī* is a very distant second indeed and a small proportion of the overall total.[54]

This evidence makes it possible that this verse was chosen intentionally, with a specific message in mind, rather than merely by default – as a common choice for inscriptions. Indeed, the *ayat al-kursī* played a key role in medieval polemic because its vivid imagery of God's throne sparked debate over the nature of divinity.[55] The central question revolved around whether the imagery of God's throne implied His possession of physical form. For the most literal of interpreters, for example traditionalists like members of the Hanbali legal school, the answer was that indeed, such Qurʾanic references meant that God had physical form. This led to the levelling of charges of anthropomorphism against these literalists, considered a grave heresy by groups such as the Shafiʿi Ashʿaris. The Ashʿari position, integrated with the Shafiʿi school by the mystic and theologian al-Ghazali in the eleventh century, was a middle ground between literalist interpretations and the more extreme rationalising ones advocated by groups such as the Muʿtazila. Followers of Ashʿarism felt that God, in His greatness and inimitability, could not possibly resemble humans, and that such verses could be accepted as factual only *bi-lā kayf* – without asking how – thus acknowledging human limitations of understanding. Thus, God might be described as having a hand, but this could not be a hand in the sense that we humans understand a hand. The Shiʿa, who generally supported the Muʿtazili theological school, also favoured the argument that all such Qurʾanic references must be interpreted metaphorically. Thus, the inclusion of this particular verse on the cenotaph of a prominent member of the *ahl al-bayt* may not have been a neutral act. But which position is being advocated here, and how can this help us understand the intent of the cenotaph's patron?

To answer this question, we must turn to the second theme within these inscriptions: repeated references to the role of the Prophet and his family, the *ahl al-bayt*. The first inscription of this nature, Qurʾan 33:46–7, follows immediately after the *āyat al-kursī* and is an explication of the role God envisions for His Prophet: he is to be a witness, a bearer of happy tidings and an admonisher, a *dāʿī* (one who calls people to God), a resplendent lamp, shining in the darkness of ignorance. This reference to the Prophet as a *dāʿī* literally means 'one who summons' to the true faith, but by this period such a term was undoubtedly also associated with the propagandistic mission of the Fatimids. Furthermore, Muhammad is likened to a lamp, and light is a common Shiʿi symbol for the continuity of the Imamate. The twelve Imams are often described as being the bearers of 'divine light' and the Imamate was passed from one Imam to the next via the transmission of light. Indeed, as noted previously, imagery of the light of God inhabiting the bodies of holy 'Alid figures is common in Shi'i religious literature.[56]

The next inscription containing references to the *ahl al-bayt* is the monumental devotional inscription that occupies the majority of the cenotaph's surface. As though expanding on the theme of the previous inscription, it praises Sukayna the daughter of Husayn and calls down blessings upon her and her family, i.e. the Prophet and his descendants – who are presumably worthy of such blessings by virtue of their close association with God's Prophet whose role had been carefully delineated in the previous inscription. This inscription ends with what has been called the classic Shi'i *taslīya* or eulogy, reading 'May God's blessings be upon them all, and upon their pure family (*ālihim al-ṭāhirīn*)'.[57]

This monumental inscription is complemented by the two interspersed among its uprights. The first, verse 33:33, once again refers to the *ahl al-bayt* and their purity. Qur'an 33:33, sometimes called the *āyat al-rijs* (verse of [cleansing from] impurity), is probably the most common inscription to appear in shrines for the *ahl al-bayt*. It is a verse that Shi'i exegetes often evoke as evidence for Shi'i claims to the Imamate of 'Ali and his descendants, specifically 'Ali, Fatima, al-Hasan and al-Husayn. Shi'i exegesis interprets the verse through the *ḥadīth al-kisā'* or the Hadith of the Mantle, which describes a time when the Prophet enveloped himself along with these four family members in his cloak and recited verse 33:33. According to Shi'i exegesis the Prophet then said, 'This is my house', indicating the verse referred specifically to them.[58] Thus the claim is made that God has lifted moral impurity from His descendants through Fatima, and, thus purified by Him, they should be seen as infallible and perfect.

The final verse once again takes up the theme of the role of the Prophet as a seal and messenger, but in a way that also emphasises the role of the *ahl al-bayt*. Verse 33:30 contains the phrase 'Muhammad is not the father of any man among you'. Al-Tabari's exegesis of this verse, along with that of many other scholars, emphasises it as proof that Muhammad is the seal of the prophets, a role confirmed by his lack of male offspring. Like the previous verse, verse 33:40 is part of the *Surat al-Ahzab*, and the context of the verse refers specifically to Muhammad's adoption and later repudiation of a slave named Zayd ibn Haritha. The repudiation of Zayd as a lawful son of Muhammad established Islamic legal guidelines for adoption in which the adopted child is not considered a true child because he retains his original family affiliation, even while being raised by a new family. Later Sunni exegesis explains the incident as necessary to the establishment of Muhammad as the final 'seal' of the prophets, for only if Muhammad had no son could prophethood come to an end.[59] From a Shi'i perspective, however, this verse had deeper meaning, for it emphasises that Muhammad's only surviving children were female, most prominent among them Fatima, and it is through her marriage to ʿAli that the *ahl al-bayt* were perpetuated.

The accumulation of evidence based on the interpretation of the verses on Sukayna's cenotaph points to a Shiʿi patron. Without a patron's name, it is of course impossible to confirm such a reading, and the interpretation of inscriptions is always an indeterminate business. But here, while the patron could possibly have been an ʿAlid Sunni, the strongly Shiʿi flavour of the inscriptions makes it seem likely that the patron of the cenotaph, and perhaps also the patron of the building that surrounded it (today's crypt), was very likely to have been Shiʿi. This is remarkable for the evidence it provides about the position of the Shiʿi community in Damascus during the medieval period. According to Pouzet, the community of Shiʿis in Damascus was virtually non-existent, and, if present, subject to persecution.[60] But here, in essence, we have evidence of at least some members of the Shiʿi community in Seljuk Damascus with the means to fund such a project and the freedom to be able to do so. Certainly a community suffering discrimination or persecution could not have been in a position to commission such an exquisite piece of woodwork, nor a building to shelter it. The cenotaph's pronouncement of a Shiʿi creed was thus a bold claim to these sites as Shiʿi space within a majority Sunni city, in the heart of a period long thought to be inimical to Shiʿism in Syria.

But as was usual in these cases, shrines marked the landscape not as fixed but as fluid sites of identity. For in the Mamluk period, the mausoleum was the beneficiary of a clear act of Sunni patronage. Any visitor to the site cannot help but notice that attached to a corner of today's Ottoman building is a small, single-room Mamluk mosque (Fig. 3.17). Above its door, carved in magnificent Mamluk *naskhī* on the stone lintel, are the words 'the Sultan al-Malik al-Zahir Baybars al-Salihi' (Figs 3.18, 3.19 and 3.20). How is it that the great Mamluk Sultan Baybars came to patronise our little mausoleum of Sukayna?

Al-Nuʿaymi, a historian of Damascus, reports that around 1219, the founder of the Sufi brotherhood of the Qalandariyya, a fraternity infamous in the medieval period for their proto-hippie asceticism – which included such disturbing antisocial behaviour as shaving the head and eyebrows, and wearing rings on their wrists, ears and genitals – decided to take up residence in the tomb of one Zaynab bt. Zayn al-ʿAbidin.[61] One of the successors of this founder was a shaykh by the name of Muhammad al-Balkhi, who was well known in Damascus and highly esteemed by Baybars. Upon his accession to the Sultanate, Baybars demanded that the shaykh come live with him, but the shaykh refused this offer on the grounds that he wanted to devote himself entirely to the ascetic life. Baybars then constructed the *qubba* for the shaykh and his companions. He consecrated for the building a sum of money deriving from the funds of the Great Mosque and gave a pension to the shaykh of ten dirhams

Figure 3.17 *South-eastern corner of mausoleum of the Qalandariyya.*
Photo: Author

per day as well as a provision of thirty measures of wheat per year. In addition, each time Baybars visited Damascus from Cairo he made a donation of one thousand dirhams and two tapestries for the upkeep and maintenance of the building.[62] It is interesting to note that Baybars was also the major Mamluk-era patron of the Mashhad s al-Muhassin and al-Husayn in Aleppo (see Chapter 2). In this case, his interest in the shrine of Sukayna is personal, pious and clearly linked to his desire to support a beloved shaykh, not to some wider political

Figure 3.18 *Entrance to mausoleum of the Qalandariyya, with entrance to Sukayna and Umm Kulthum on right. Photo: Author*

goal, as was the case with the Ayyubid-era patrons of the Aleppan shrines. Nevertheless, his action contributed to the monumentalisation of the site. Baybars left his mark here in the form of his name and his personal herald: two lions rampant, blazoned on each side of the door.

The decision of the Sufi shaykh, who could certainly have chosen numerous locales to practice his asceticism, to situate himself at the grave of 'Zaynab bt. Zayn al-ʿAbidin', a somewhat remote ʿAlid

Figure 3.19 *Entrance to mausoleum of the Qalandariyya, with Baybars' inscription on the lintel. Photo: Author*

descendant, is a telling one and raises the interesting issue of the connections between presumably Sunni Sufis and Shiʿis in this period. Although it has long been noted for the modern period, recently, several scholars working on medieval Egypt and Iran have argued that Sufi and Shiʿi thought and practice were often remarkably interconnected in the medieval period as well.[63] Asma Afsaruddin has shown, for example, that the shared respect of Sunnis and Shiʿis for the *ahl al-bayt* could be a fruitful meeting ground for groups often ideologically opposed.[64] Some Sufi thinkers took this general respect a step further, evincing a liberal interest in Shiʿism and, in the case of one medieval Egyptian Sufi, even adopting Shiʿi philosophical positions.[65] This is particularly true during the fourteenth and fifteenth centuries, a time when Baghdad under the Mongols became a centre for an open climate of debate and exchange between Sunni and Shiʿi

Figure 3.20 *Detail, inscription of Baybars. Photo: Author*

scholars.[66] In many cases, as we have seen in the previous chapter on Aleppo, this openness manifested itself in the form of architectural patronage. That was certainly the case at the shrine of Imam ʿAli b. Musa al-Rida in Mashhad, which was the site of continuous Sunni and Shiʿi intervention and interaction throughout the medieval period.[67] Within this context, the Sufi Shaykh al-Balkhi's decision to take up residence at the grave of an ʿAlid seems explicable and even logical. His decision was the impetus for Baybars' generous act of patronage, an act that grew out of the sultan's personal attachment to this shaykh and his fraternal order, rather than a commitment to a broader theological or sectarian position.

In the early twentieth century, this shrine – among several others in the cemetery of Bab al-Saghir – was supported by yet another Sunni patron: the Ottoman Sultan Abdülhamid II (r. 1876–1909). Four shrines in the cemetery, as well as that of Sayyida Zaynab in Rawiya, have been the family trust of the Murtadas, an established Damascene Shiʿi family who have controlled the shrines for at least four generations. Today, the overseer of the shrine of Sukayna and Umm Kulthum is Sayyid Waʾel Salim Murtada. During interviews, he recounted the family history of the shrines. According to Murtada, in the early years of Abdülhamid's reign his great-grandfather Sayyid Salim became distressed by the state of decay afflicting the shrines of the *ahl al-bayt* in the cemetery. Having little personal means with which to intervene, the sayyid decided to do something about it, and journeyed to Istanbul. There, he tried unsuccessfully to gain an audience with the sultan. One day, in frustration, as the sultan passed through the streets of Istanbul in a ceremonial procession, Sayyid Salim elbowed his way through the crowd surrounding the sultan and, when close enough, threw a letter of petition in his direction. The sultan's guards reacted quickly, seizing the old sayyid and carting him off to prison. The sultan apparently received the letter, however, and upon reading it released the sayyid from prison and brought him for an audience. The sayyid pleaded for the sultan to intervene, arguing that the shrines' state of decay was a blot on Islam. Convinced, the sultan allocated funds for the construction of four new buildings in the cemetery, among them the shrine of Sukayna and Umm Kulthum. Construction was completed in 1912, and it is Abdülhamid's building that one sees today in the cemetery. Clearly, well into the Ottoman period, Sunni interest in these ʿAlid shrines was a critical factor in their continued preservation and continuity.[68]

The shrine to Sukayna and Umm Kulthum was thus the locus of multivalent architectural and devotional practice. The initial act of patronage in the Seljuk period was probably due to a Shiʿi benefactor, who built either an archaising Fatimid-style canopy tomb complex or commissioned a cenotaph for a pre-existing Fatimid-era structure. This cenotaph, with its Shiʿising inscriptional programme, bore a sectarian message for visitors to the tomb, who, in a city such as Damascus, undoubtedly included many Sunnis. The ability of a Shiʿi patron to make such a statement suggests a wider latitude for Shiʿi devotional practice than is often assumed for this period of the Sunni Revival. Evidence of further Sunni interest in the shrine came in the form of the Sufi shaykh who took up residence there in the early thirteenth century. His residency was the impetus for further Sunni intervention, and the Mamluk Sultan Baybars was the shrine's most illustrious medieval patron. His devotion is the outcome of particular and personal circumstances that were probably related more to his interest in supporting his beloved shaykh than to affection for Sukayna or Umm Kulthum/Zaynab themselves. And finally, in the modern period, the buildings benefited from the patronage of the Ottoman Sultan Abdülhamid, who, as the perpetuator of the Caliphate on earth, was the most prominent Sunni of his day. Such was the complex mix of motivations and interests that conspired to generate Sunni support for the shines of these two ʿAlid descendants.

We will now turn to the three other ʿAlid mausolea the Murtada family was responsible for. Like the mausoleum of Sukayna and Umm Kulthum, each of these was built or renovated by the Ottoman Sultan Abdülhamid. Yet, as we shall see, they share a common problem: a lack of unambiguous evidence for their existence before Abdülhamid's intervention.

Sayyida Fatima al-Sughra, bt. al-Husayn

The previous sentence is not entirely accurate, for one shrine, at least, existed from the Fatimid era. In fact, the extraordinary stone cenotaph in its crypt bears the oldest inscription in the cemetery, and, with the exception of the foundation texts for the Umayyad mosque, is the oldest inscription in Damascus.[69] However, its current identity as the grave of an ʿAlid lady does not seem to have solidified until the early twentieth century, some time just before the Sultan Abdülhamid's intervention.

Fatima al-Sughra was the daughter of al-Husayn and the sister of Sukayna. Her mausoleum is located in the centre of the cemetery, just south-west of the shrine of Sukayna and Umm Kulthum. Above ground, it consists of a small dome on squinches preceded by a small, flat-roofed anteroom (Figs 3.21 and 3.22). A grille separates these two rooms and the area of the cenotaph is elevated by a single step up from the anteroom. The anteroom today consists of a small, office-like area for the mausoleum's guardian to the south, and stairs descending to the crypt on the north. Descending the stairs, we encounter an almost identical layout: an anteroom preceding the area of the sarcophagus, raised up by a single stair (Fig. 3.23). The cenotaph itself is, somewhat unusually, not in the centre of this

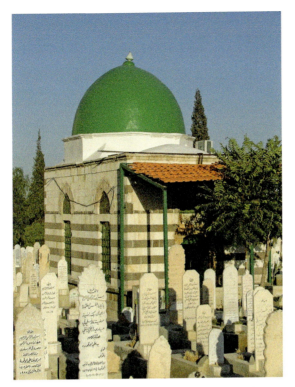

Figure 3.21 *Mausoleum of Fatima al-Sughra. Photo: Author*

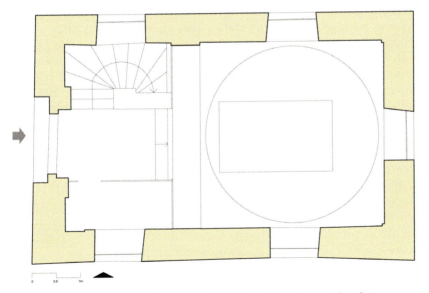

Figure 3.22 *Mausoleum of Fatima al-Sughra, plan of upper level. Image: Author, Milena Hijazi and Irina Rivero*

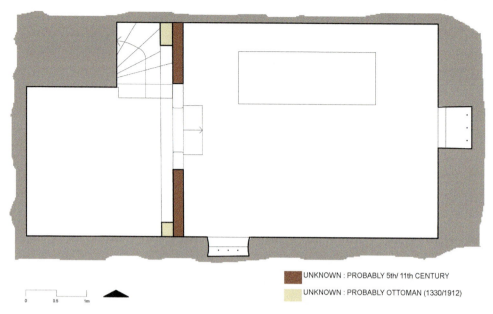

UNKNOWN : PROBABLY 5th/ 11th CENTURY

UNKNOWN : PROBABLY OTTOMAN (1330/1912)

Figure 3.23 *Mausoleum of Fatima al-Sughra, plan of crypt level. Image: Author, Milena Hijazi and Irina Rivero*

room but located in its northern portion, almost against the northern wall.

Yet again, the walls of the crypt are covered by thick painted plaster. There is no exposed masonry, making architectural analysis a challenge. Unlike in the crypt of Sukayna and Umm Kulthum, there is no unambiguous evidence that this crypt was once above ground. By analogy it is likely that it was, since it is in the immediate neighbourhood of the crypt of Sukayna and also of Asmaʾ, yet another mausoleum with a crypt (to be discussed below). Nevertheless the passage from the anteroom of the crypt to the area housing the sarcophagus makes clear that this crypt was constructed in two phases, for at this point of juncture we find two unevenly proportioned arches which have been built flush up against each other. The innermost arch is the one that provides passage into the area of the cenotaph, and is the narrower of the two. The second arch is much wider, spanning almost the entire eastern wall of the anteroom. It is unclear when this anteroom was added to the crypt, however the logical assumption is that it is an Ottoman addition meant to provide a foundation for the anteroom above as well as providing access from the stairway to the crypt below.

The eastern room of the crypt is probably associated archaeologically with the exquisitely carved stone sarcophagus, firmly dated to the late eleventh century by the inscription on its face (Fig. 3.24). It seems logical that this sarcophagus is *in situ*, for there are no signs it

A_ Ins. n° 1: Cénotaphe de Fāṭima (face est).   (Cl. J. Dufour)

B_ Ins. n° 1: Cénotaphe de Fāṭima (face sud).   (Cl. J. Dufour)

Figure 3.24 *East and south faces of stone sarcophagus in mausoleum of Fatima al-Sughra. After Moaz and Ory,* Inscriptions, *plate V*

has been moved or reassembled in the past. Furthermore, the alternative, that a special crypt was excavated and the stone sarcophagus installed within it, is unlikely. The most sensible conclusion is that the crypt represents either a building that was once above ground, as at Sukayna and Umm Kulthum, or the original crypt of a Fatimid-era building; however, as noted previously, there are no contemporary Fatimid mausolea with crypts. Thus it seems likely we have another example of an original building becoming a crypt over time.

The sarcophagus's inscription is executed in large-format Kufic distributed along two registers separated by a raised stone band.[70] Above the letters and sometimes intertwined with their uprights – though not growing out of them directly in the manner of true floriated Kufic – are scrolling vines ornamented with polylobed leaflets and palmettes. The inscription itself reads:

Western Face:
This is the tomb of Fatima *ibnat* Ahmad
Ibn al-Husayn al-Subki.[71] She passed away,
May God be pleased with her, in Rajab of the year
439 (January 1048).

This is followed, on the north, east and south faces, by the *āyat al-kursī*. Here, lacking further evidence of the sort found in the inscriptions on the cenotaph of Sukayna, it is not possible to infer any sectarian meaning for this inscription. However, the cenotaph was clearly not dedicated to Fatima bt. al-Husayn as is claimed today, and this is a puzzle. Who is the Fatima being commemorated here? Fortunately, we have some information about who this particular Fatima might have been, thanks to her family name al-Subki.

The Subki family originated in the town of Subk al-Dahhak in Lower Egypt, and produced a celebrated group of scholars and jurists belonging to the Shafi'i school. They rose to prominence in the Mamluk period, their most illustrious member being the *qāḍī* Taj al-Din al-Subki (d. 1369), who wrote the great biographical dictionary of Shafi'i scholars, the *Tabaqāt al-Shafi'iyya*. From the beginning of their ascent in the early fourteenth century, nearly every one of the illustrious members of this family had appointments as *mudarrisūn*, *qāḍī*s, *muftī*s or *khaṭīb*s in Damascus.[72] The problem is that our Fatima appears to have passed away 250 years before the era of the Subki family's glory. The medieval sources provide no information about the Subki family in Damascus prior to the early fourteenth century. Thus, while we may infer that she represents a prior ancestor of the Subki scholars, we cannot identify her with certainty.

Furthermore, despite the plainly worded epitaph dedicating the sarcophagus to Fatima al-Subki, at some point popular tradition came to associate this tomb with Fatima bt. al-Husayn. Fatima bt. al-Husayn, who is called 'al-Sughra' to distinguish her from Fatima al-Kubra, the daughter of the Prophet Muhammad, died in 735. As noted above, the inscription indicates that the Fatima of this shrine died in 1048. Thus, even ignoring the evidence of her name on the sarcophagus, it is obvious that the Fatima buried here is a different person. When the transference occurred is also not clear. Not a single medieval Arabic source mentions the grave of Fatima bt. al-Husayn in Bab al-Saghir. The first mention of it comes in 1943, in As'ad Talas's *Dhayl* (Postscript) to Ibn al-Mibrad's topographical dictionary *Thimar al-Maqasid fi Dhikr al-Masajid*.[73]

Nevertheless, one clue survives in the form of another inscription, located above ground over the entrance to the mausoleum. It reads:

> This is the tomb of Sayyida Fatima al-Sughra, daughter of the Prince of the Martyrs Imam al-Husayn,
> Martyr of Karbala'. May peace be upon them both. This noble *maqam* was built (*tashayyada*) in the year 1330 (1912).

According to the year of its dedication, this shrine should probably also be associated with Abdülhamid's renovation project, the same project undertaken for Sukayna and Umm Kulthum in response to Sayyid Murtada's entreaty.[74] The foundation inscriptions for the four buildings under the Murtadas' care are notable for not mentioning the true patron – Abdülhamid – by name. Furthermore, it is a highly 'Shi'ising' inscription, naming Husayn as 'Imam' and 'Prince of the Martyrs': hardly distinctions a Sunni patron would bestow upon a member of the *ahl al-bayt*, however beloved. This points to minimal involvement on behalf of Abdülhamid, who may well have simply provided the funds for the renovations, leaving the details to the Shi'i Sayyid Salim Murtada. The shrine itself must have lost its original identity and become associated with Fatima bt. al-Husayn at some point between the seventeenth century – when the most recent pilgrimage guide was produced in which it is not mentioned – and the intervention of Abdülhamid.[75] No record of it prior to the early twentieth century exists. In fact, as we shall see, the remaining two commissions by Abdülhamid are similarly unknown before the twentieth century.

Masjid Maqam Ru'us al-Shuhada' Karbala'

On the east side of the road which cuts south through the cemetery, known today as the Street of the Ahl al-Bayt, south-east of the mausoleum of Sukayna, is a shrine complex that includes a mosque and *maqām* (Fig. 3.25). This site is today renowned for being the place of burial of the heads of the martyrs of Karbala', not including the head of al-Husayn and his youngest son, 'Ali al-Asghar, the infant

Figure 3.25 *Distant view from the north-west, Masjid Maqam Ru'us al-Shuhada' Karbala'. Photo: Author*

brother of Sukayna and Fatima al-Sughra.[76] The heads of the Karbalaʾ martyrs were brought to Damsascus, along with the captive ʿAlid women and children, by the soldiers of the Umayyad Caliph al-Yazid after the battle.

Medieval sources speak of a burial place for 'the *shuhadā*'' in the cemetery of Bab al-Saghir. Al-Harawi (d. 1215) reports a rumour that seventy 'men from among the companions' are said to be buried in the cemetery.[77] The earliest source to specifically mention 'martyrs', however, is al-Nuʿaymi (d. 1521). He reports that the Damascene historian Ibn ʿAsakir was buried in the cemetery 'near the *shuhadā*''.[78] This would seem to be the strongest confirmation for the existence of the tomb in the medieval period, for indeed one may see the grave of Ibn ʿAsakir – today rather forlornly confined to a small roundabout in the southernmost part of the cemetery – a few hundred metres south of the mausoleum of the Karbalaʾ martyrs.

Today this complex is by far the largest in the cemetery (Fig. 3.26). It is arranged around two spacious colonnaded courtyards. The first courtyard, that closest to the street, is entered via a large, arched, modern portal containing a fountain. This courtyard surrounds a domed Ottoman-era mausoleum facing north (Fig. 3.27).[79] From this courtyard, one ascends a short flight of stairs to another, narrower

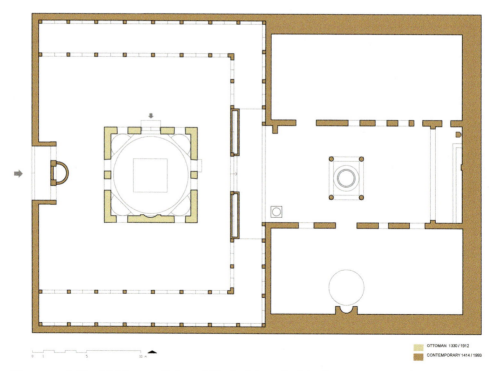

OTTOMAN 1330 / 1912
CONTEMPORARY 1414 / 1993

Figure 3.26 *Masjid Maqam Ruʾus al-Shuhadaʾ Karbalaʾ, plan. Image: Author, Milena Hijazi and Irina Rivero*

Figure 3.27 *Ottoman mausoleum in first courtyard of Masjid Maqam Ru'us al-Shuhada' Karbala'. Photo: Author*

courtyard (Fig. 3.28). Within this courtyard is a covered well in the south-west corner (Fig. 3.29), a stone upright bearing an inscription in the north-east corner (Fig. 3.30) and, at the centre, a cupola sheltering an enormous monolithic basalt basin (Figs 3.28, 3.31). Much of the eastern wall is taken up by an ablutions area. On the south side of this courtyard a door opens to a long prayer hall with a *miḥrāb* and

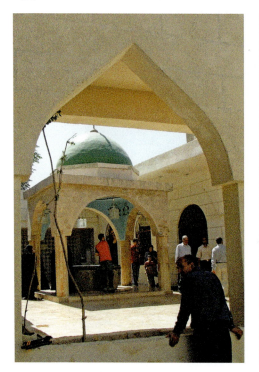

Figure 3.28 *Maqam Ru'us al-Shuhada' Karbala', view from first courtyard into second courtyard, with cupola at centre and entrance to prayer hall on right. Photo: Author*

Figure 3.29 *Well in south-east corner of second courtyard. Photo: Author*

a modern concrete dome. The north side opens into a series of small rooms, offices and latrines.[80] These courtyard areas, including the colonnades, the dome over the basalt basin, the prayer hall and ablutions area, and the offices and latrines, are newly built in concrete, which in places has been faced with marble or kiln-fired contemporary tiles. In fact, final touches on a new renovation were still being applied in the spring of 2005, though construction probably began in 1993.[81]

Considering the large area carved out of the cemetery to accommodate these courtyards and the presence within the second courtyard of three pre-modern features (the basin, the upright inscribed stone and the well), it seems likely that these courtyard areas and their attendant structures existed in some form before this most recent renovation. They existed in the 1970s, for the complex appears, with much the same double-courtyard plan as today, on a plan of the cemetery published by Moaz and Ory in 1977.[82] However with the exception of the features noted above, nothing remains in the architecture itself to confirm or deny the existence of any previous structures.

Figure 3.30 *Stone upright in north-east corner of second courtyard. Photo: Author*

Figure 3.31 *Basalt basin under cupola at the centre of second courtyard. Photo: Author*

Today, the second courtyard is held by many Shiʿa to be the place where those *ahl al-bayt* who had been brought back from Karbalaʾ were imprisoned. The three features of this courtyard noted above are interpreted in such a way as to reinforce this narrative: the basin is the one in which the heads of the martyrs were washed before burial (Fig. 3.31); the well is the place from which the water was gathered (Fig. 3.29); and the stone the one to which the Imam Zayn al-ʿAbidin was chained (Fig. 3.30). Other attributions exist as well: Asʿad Talas, writing in the 1940s, wrote that the basin was believed to be the drinking vessel (*tāsa*) of the *ahl al-kahf*, or People of the Cave, a reference to a popular tradition inherited from Byzantium about the Seven Sleepers, seven young Christian men whom God spared from persecution.[83] The basalt stone basin is likely to be the oldest of these features, and is also probably *in situ* or near its original position. Because of its association with the Karbabaʾ martyrs, it is venerated by pilgrims, along with the other features in the courtyard (Fig. 3.32). Its massive size and weight would have prevented it from being moved with any frequency. The well is not possible to date, although the marble structure which covers it today

Figure 3.32 *Pilgrim tying fabric to a metal pipe inside the basalt basin. Such gestures are intended to mark a vow or secure a request for intervention. Photo: Author*

appears to be contemporary with the Ottoman shrine in the first courtyard. The stone upright bears a one-line inscription which has not yet been deciphered but which appears to be either late Mamluk or early Ottoman in date.[84] Its general shape and size and its location near the modern ablutions fountain indicate it is some remnant of a previous fountain, possibly a seat for resting while washing the feet and hands.

The Ottoman building in the first courtyard is a medium-sized structure with a dome raised on a low octagonal drum on squinches. On the exterior corners are four miniature domed tower-like structures bearing blind arches on their upper levels (Fig. 3.27). Inside, the shrine contains a *miḥrāb* and a large, silver, jewelled *ḍariḥ* or *maqṣūra* (latticed burial enclosure) of recent manufacture. Like the mausolea for Fatima and Sukayna/Umm Kulthum, this shrine bears a foundation inscription above the door, dating it to the year of Abdülhamid's renovation, but crediting only Sayyid Salim Murtada (Fig. 3.33):

(Two lines of poetry)
This is the Shrine of the Heads of the Sixteen Martyrs (*maqām ruʾūs al-shuhadāʾ al-sittata ʿashar*) of the People of (*ʿubayy?*) who became martyrs on the day of the Plain (*taff*) of Karbalāʾ alongside Imam al-Husayn ibn al-Imam ʿAli ibn Abi Talib, upon

Figure 3.33 *Inscription over entrance to Ottoman shrine in first courtyard, Masjid Maqam Ruʾus al-Shuhadaʾ Karbalaʾ. Photo: Author*

them be peace. This holy *maqām* was built (*tashayyada*) by the efforts of (*bi-masʿan*) al-Sayyid Selim Effendi ibn al-Sayyid Husayn Murtada, the overseer of the *maqām*s/mausolea (*qāʾim maqām marāqid*) of the *ahl al-bayt*, upon them be peace, in Shawwal of 1330 (August–September 1912).

Above this inscription is another one, dating to 1993. It commemorates the renovation of the mausoleum and the donation of the new *maqṣūra*, which replaced an Ottoman one, by the sultan of the Bohras, Jawhar Muhammad Burhan al-Din, with the assistance of Muhammad Salim Ibn Rida Murtada, another descendant of Sayyid Salim.

ʿAbdallah b. Zayn al-ʿAbidin

The fourth mausoleum built by the Ottoman Sultan Abdülhamid in the cemetery is that of ʿAbdallah b. Zayn al-ʿAbidin, the son of the fourth Shiʿi Imam Zayn al-ʿAbidin.[85] Zayn al-ʿAbidin, a nickname meaning 'jewel of the worshippers', was the son of al-Husayn. Thus,

Figure 3.34 *Mausoleum of 'Abdallah b. Zayn al-'Abidin. Photo: Author*

'Abdallah is the grandson of al-Husayn. Beyond this, little is known of him.

His mausoleum is located on the western side of the Street of the Ahl al-Bayt, south-west of the shrine to the heads of the Karbala' martyrs (Fig. 3.34). Despite his seemingly minor importance, his mausoleum is substantial and almost matches that of the Karbala' martyrs in scale. It sits at the centre of a small, tree-shaded courtyard

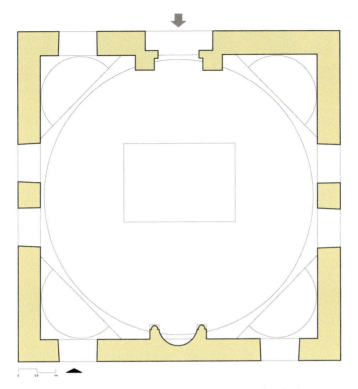

Figure 3.35 *Plan, mausoleum of ʿAbdallah b. Zayn al-ʿAbidin.*
Image: Author, Milena Hijazi and Irina Rivero

with a modest fountain in front of the door. Like that of the Karbalaʾ
martyrs, the shrine is square in plan, covered by a low dome raised
on a short drum on squinches (Fig. 3.35). Inside, the building has a
miḥrāb and a recently added golden *ḍarīḥ* or *maqṣūra* that appears to
be Iranian. The dome has been recently repainted in bright colours,
but this repainting has preserved what appear to be elements of the
original Ottoman design. It includes the names of the twelve Imams
in small cartouches around the drum of the dome (Fig. 3.36), once
again an indication that Abdülhamid probably gave the shrine's
builders considerable freedom in the execution of the project. A
curious motif of the interior painted stucco decoration is a series
of small palm trees in the spandrels between the squinches and
windows of the interior (Fig. 3.37).

No medieval source mentions a grave to ʿAbdallah in the cemetery. Although undoubtedly there was some sort of structure
previous to Abdülhamid's intervention, it would seem that the
tradition of associating this site with the grave of ʿAbdallah appeared
quite recently. It is unclear why he was considered deserving of
such a comparatively opulent mausoleum. The building bears two

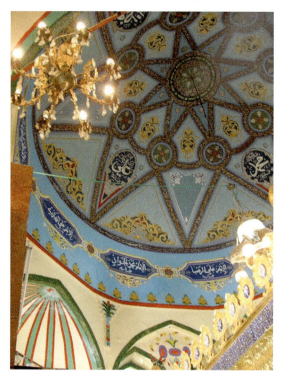

Figure 3.36 *Dome of mausoleum of 'Abdallah b. Zayn al-'Abidin.*
Photo: Author

inscriptions. The first, above the entrance portal, is a virtual copy of
the one over the portal to the Karbala' martyrs (Fig. 3.38):

> This is the shrine (*maqām*) of Sayyidna 'Abdallah ibn al-Imam
> Zayn al-'Abidin 'Ali ibn al-Imam al-Husayn ibn al-Imam 'Ali
> ibn Abi Talib, may peace be upon them. This noble *maqām* was
> built (*tashayyida*) by the efforts of (*bi-mas'an*) al-Sayyid Selim
> Effendi Ibn al-Sayyid Husayn Murtada, the overseer of the maqam/
> mausolea (*qā'im maqām marāqid*) of the *ahl al-bayt*, upon them
> be peace, in the year 1330 (1912).

A further inscription to the left of the door records the most recent
intervention:

> This noble *maqām* was renovated by the efforts of Muhammad
> Salim Ibn Rida Murtada, overseer of the maqam-mausolea (*qā'im
> maqām marāqid*) of the *ahl al-bayt*, upon them be peace, 1419
> *hijrī* – 1998 *mīladī*.

There is no indication of a previous structure or of the prior existence
of this mausoleum.

Thus, so far we find that in the cemetery there were four shrines patronised by the Ottoman Sultan Abdülhamid: Sukayna and Umm Kulthum, Fatima al-Sughra, Ruʾus al-Shuhadaʾ Karbalaʾ and ʿAbdallah ibn Zayn al-ʿAbidin. Of these four, the last two have an almost identical pattern of intervention: first, the initial expansion and building of the mausoleum under Abdülhamid, which was apparently carried out in practice by the Sayyid Salim Murtada. The sayyid received his Sunni patron's largesse and created from it distinctly Shiʿi spaces, such as the mausolea of ʿAbdallah ibn Zayn al-ʿAbidin and the Karbalaʾ martyrs: sites of devotion specific to critical figures and events in the history of Shiʿi martyrology. Such spaces are marked by invocations to the twelve Shiʿi Imams. Later, toward the end of the twentieth century, we find these shrines maintained and renovated through the effort of a descendant of that same Sayyid

Figure 3.37 *Palm tree motif in the spandrels of the interior arches. Photo: Author*

Figure 3.38 *Foundation inscription, mausoleum of ʿAbdallah b. Zayn al-ʿAbidin. Photo: Author*

Salim, Muhammad Salim Ibn Rida Murtada. But though the presence of some features indicates a longer history, the structures are essentially Ottoman ones.

On the other hand, Sukayna and Umm Kulthum and Fatima al-Sughra are examples of a different pattern altogether, although their recent history is much the same. In the case of Sukayna we have a mausoleum of demonstrated medieval provenance, probably built originally by a Shiʿi patron, expanded by the Mamluk Sultan Baybars and, much later, the beneficiary of Abdülhamid's attention before reverting once again to the care of the Shiʿi Murtada family. Fatima al-Sughra, on the other hand, seems to be a somewhat unique example. There, by appropriating and investing with new meaning a mausoleum that had previously commemorated an unknown member of the Subki family, the combined efforts of the Ottoman sultan and the Damascene sayyid created an entirely new Shiʿi devotional space.

Shrines of unclear provenance

In addition to those cited above, the cemetery of Bab al-Saghir also contains a group of shrines about which we have very little information other than that given by their inscriptions (which rarely specify their patrons) or their architectural features. Although some of these shrines are mentioned in medieval sources, such mention tends not to include information about their foundation or restoration. However, two of these shrines contain at least some information in the form of their architecture or other features within the mausolea.

Aban ibn Ruqayya bint Muhammad

South-west of the mausoleum of Fatima is a small cupola devoted to Aban, who according to popular tradition was the son of Ruqayya and the third Caliph ʿUthman b. ʿAffan (Fig. 3.39).[86] Ruqayya was the Prophet Muhammad's second daughter, and is not to be confused with Ruqayya bt. al-Husayn, commemorated in a well-known shrine in the old city of Damascus (see Chapter 4). Aban was a famous traditionist and one of the *tābiʿūn* or Followers of the Companions of the Prophet. He died in Medina in 723–4. Thus this mausoleum is probably attributed to him erroneously, and indeed no medieval Arabic source refers to a mausoleum for him in the cemetery. However, today the Shiʿa visit Aban's tomb since he is believed to be a descendant of the Prophet's daughter Ruqayya.

The building itself is of small size and extremely simple construction (Fig. 3.40). It consists of a tall, narrow stone structure with a dome raised on an octagonal drum on squinches. Today, its exterior masonry has been painted in black and white *ablaq* imitation. It is unclear whether this paint replicates the colour of the

Figure 3.39 *Exterior, mausoleum of Aban ibn Ruqayya. Photo: Author*

stone underneath. The building's entrance faces east. Inside, the
interior above the springing of the arches and the dome is beautifully
painted, and it appears this paint is original to the late Ottoman
period in the early twentieth century (Figs 3.41 and 3.42). If so, it is
the only mausoleum in the cemetery with its original interior decoration intact. Unlike the mausoleum of ʿAbdallah b. Zayn al-ʿAbidin,
described above, the decoration of which praised the twelve Imams,
the painted cartouches of the dome of Aban praise the four Rightly-
Guided caliphs and Hasan and Husayn.[87]

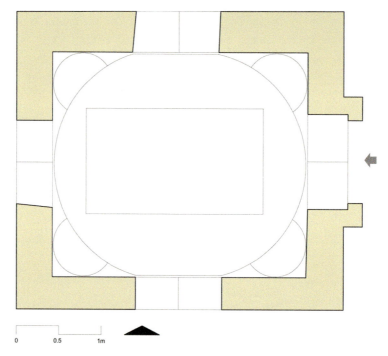

Figure 3.40 *Plan, mausoleum of Aban ibn Ruqayya. Image: Author, Milena Hijazi and Irina Rivero*

Figure 3.41 *Aban ibn Ruqayya, Ottoman-era painted dome with inscriptions praising four Sunni caliphs. Photo: Author*

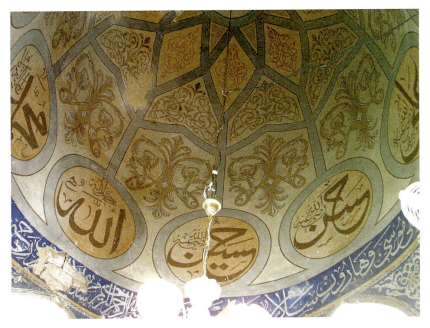

Figure 3.42 *Inscriptions praising al-Hasan and al-Husayn. Photo: Author*

The mausoleum's primary historical and art historical importance rests on a medieval stone cenotaph (Fig. 3.43) that closely resembles the sarcophagus of Fatima al-Sughra and the wooden cenotaph of Sukayna, both discussed above. It does not have a date, but has been assigned on the basis of the epigraphy to the twelfth century.[88] At some point in its past the cenotaph of Aban was badly damaged. Its blocks were reassembled incorrectly and certain parts of the inscription were effaced or covered by the cement used to re-join them, in places rendering the text indecipherable. Like the cenotaph of Sukayna, it is written in *atabākī* Kufic on a field of scrolling vines. It contains several verses from the Qur'an. The first is 3:18, a somewhat unusual choice for inscriptions. It refers to the oneness of God, His might and wisdom, but also to the knowledge or learning (*'ilm*) of the angels and of men. This is followed by verses 22:77–8, which contain exhortations to worship God and praise of Him as a friend and helper of the observant believer. This first inscription seems especially appropriate for the tomb of a man famed for his knowledge of *hadīth*. However, as noted previously, on the cenotaph itself there is neither a date nor an epitaph naming the person buried there.

Attached to the surface of the cenotaph on the west side is a quadrangular stela bearing an inscription in six lines of Ottoman *naskhī* (Fig. 3.44). It is here that we find an epitaph identifying the inhabitant of the tomb as Aban, along with his date of death.[89] Though also without a date, based on the style of the cursive characters and their

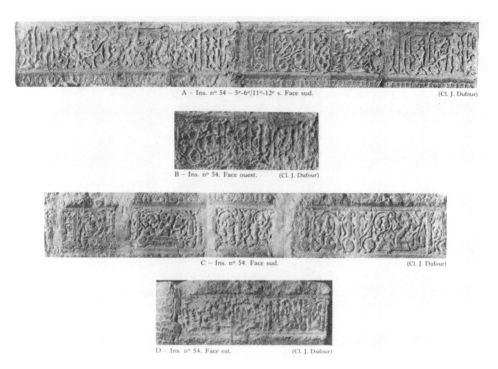

A – Ins. nᵒ 54 – 5ᵉ-6ᵉ/11ᵉ-12ᵉ s. Face sud.   (Cl. J. Dufour)

B – Ins. nᵒ 54. Face ouest.   (Cl. J. Dufour)

C – Ins. nᵒ 54. Face sud.   (Cl. J. Dufour)

D – Ins. nᵒ 54. Face est.   (Cl. J. Dufour)

Figure 3.43 *Cenotaph, mausoleum of Aban ibn Ruqayya. After Moaz and Ory,* Inscriptions, *plate XXXV*

Figure 3.44 *Stela, mausoleum of Aban ibn Ruqayya. After Moaz and Ory,* Inscriptions, *plate XXXVI B*

enclosure within oblong hexagonal cartouches it seems reasonable to assign it to the early Ottoman period.

The poor condition of this cenotaph and its obvious evidence of restoration suggest it has been moved from its original location. Given its twelfth century date, it was probably once located in a mausoleum that slowly became a crypt after the manner of Sukayna and Umm Kulthum and Fatima al-Sughra. For some reason, however, this cenotaph was removed from that crypt and reassembled at the current cemetery level. It is possible that this reconstitution occurred in the early Ottoman period and perhaps this was what is commemorated by the Ottoman stela attached to the twelfth-century cenotaph. In the late Ottoman period the current mausoleum was built around it. Thus, despite a lack of corroborating evidence from the Arabic sources, we can postulate at least three phases of building and renovation for the shrine of Aban: one in the twelfth century, one perhaps around the sixteenth century and a final phase in the early twentieth century.

Regarding a foundation date and patron for the present building, no evidence is available. However, one clue is the marked stylistic similarity between the mausoleum of Aban and a shrine devoted to the Prophet's wife Hafsa, located in the northern area of the cemetery on the other side of the al-Jarrah road. If these two mausolea were indeed built by the same patron, it would be firm evidence that the patron was a Sunni, for Hafsa is particularly reviled by the Shiʿa, because along with the Prophet's wife ʿAisha she is believed to have caused him various sorts of tribulations. She is sometimes even accused of conspiring to poison him. Thus, there is a strong likelihood that her mausoleum, and possibly also that of Aban, was built by a Sunni patron.

Asmaʾ, Maymuna and Hamida

Directly west of the mausoleum of Sukayna are two nearly identical mausolea, one devoted to three ʿAlid women and one devoted to ʿAbdallah ibn Jaʿfar al-Sadiq. The first mausoleum commemorates Asmaʾ bint Umays, the wife of Jaʿfar al-Tayyar (the brother of ʿAli ibn Abi Talib); Maymuna bint al-Husayn, about whom little seems to be known; and Hamida bint Muslim ibn ʿAqil (Fig. 3.45). ʿAqil was the brother of ʿAli, making Muslim ibn ʿAqil the cousin of al-Hasan and al-Husayn. Thus this mausoleum commemorates three lesser-known ʿAlid women who were wives or daughters of the *ahl al-bayt* or their close relatives.

The mausoleum is of medium size and is a simple, elegant dome-on-pendentive construction, built in limestone and a rose-coloured marbled stone. From the exterior, the dome appears raised on a low octagonal drum. Its only decorative feature is alternating *ablaq* masonry around the door and some faceting of the blocks supporting

Figure 3.45 *Mausoleum of Asma', Maymuna and Hamida. Photo: Author*

the lintel. Above the lintel is an inscription upon which is written the names of the women and the year 1912. Inside is a simple modern cenotaph in the centre of the room (Fig. 3.46). To the south, a staircase leads downward to a crypt (Fig. 3.47), which contains yet another cenotaph of modern manufacture. Its western face has three, seemingly recent, inscribed stones with the names of the tomb's inhabitants.

A mausoleum to these 'Alid ladies is not mentioned in the medieval sources. Furthermore, although its foundation inscription gives a date of 1912 – meaning that it corresponds with the year of the works of Abdülhamid – the Murtada family claims this mausoleum was not part of the project which led to the construction of the four other mausolea in the cemetery, including Sukayna and Umm Kulthum nearby, despite their architectural similarities.[90] Thus its Ottoman patron is unconfirmed, though it does seem likely on chronological and formal grounds to be part of the same project.

Despite the lack of medieval sources mentioning a shrine to these three ladies of the *ahl al-bayt*, the crypt of this mausoleum, like that of Sukayna/Umm Kulthum and Fatima, clearly indicates this building has a long prior history. In fact, the architecture of this crypt could well be the strongest evidence in the cemetery in support of the theory that the crypts were once above ground. This evidence comes primarily in the form of a narrow blocked arch in the north wall of the crypt (Fig. 3.48). This arch, precisely the size of

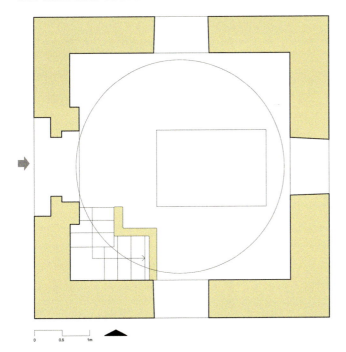

Figure 3.46 *Plan, upper level, mausoleum of Asma', Maymuna and Hamida. Image: Author, Milena Hijazi and Irina Rivero*

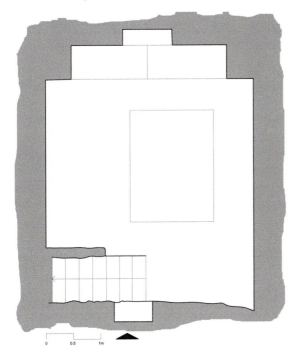

Figure 3.47 *Plan, crypt level, mausoleum of Asma', Maymuna and Hamida. Image: Author, Milena Hijazi and Irina Rivero*

Figure 3.48 *Blind arches in north wall of crypt of mausoleum of Asmaʾ, Maymuna and Hamida. Photo: Author*

a doorway, is set back within a much wider, pointed arch, much as in the crypt of Umm Kulthum. Furthermore (Fig. 3.49), the southern wall and the wall of the stairway are not straight and curve wildly inwards and outwards, perhaps indicating that the stairway was dug as an extension of the crypt or that the structure of the wall was compromised during the building of the stairway. This wall also bears a blind, window-like structure with a curious hollow, slot-like space at the top. Above this blind window is a tiny, arch-shaped open window that lets in a small amount of light.

It seems that here, too, the Ottoman building was built atop a previous, perhaps – by analogy with Sukayna and Umm Kulthum – Seljuk-era crypt. Such speculation is supported by the architecture of the wide pointed archway and blocked door in the northern wall, as well as the highly irregular southern wall. Were this crypt built at the same time as the Ottoman structure above it, the southern wall would have been more regular in plan and there would be no need for the sequence of arches in the north wall. Thus, for the

Figure 3.49 *Crypt, staircase with uneven wall masonry and blind window-like structure on top left. Photo: Author*

mausoleum of Asma', Maymuna and Hamida we may postulate a previous lifetime in which the crypt of today was an original Seljuk-era building. However, given its absence in the sources, just who was commemorated there during that previous life is unclear.

'Abdallah ibn Ja'far al-Sadiq

Just a few metres south-west of the mausoleum of Asma' is a nearly identical mausoleum, dedicated to 'Abdallah ibn Ja'far al-Sadiq, the son of the sixth Shi'i Imam. We have little information about this building, either from the Arabic sources or from the architecture. Like the mausoleum of Asma', Maymuna and Hamida, it is a simple dome-on-pendentive construction, built of limestone and rose-coloured marbled stone, with some decorative *ablaq* masonry around the door and the same faceted stone under the lintel (Fig. 3.50). Unlike that mausoleum, however, it does not have a crypt (Fig. 3.51). Given the striking similarity of its architecture to that of Asma', Maymuna and Hamida, it was probably built in the same year (1912). However, its foundation inscription, if it had one, has been painted over recently and thus the building has no firm date. Today, above

Figure 3.50 *Mausoleum of ʿAbdallah ibn Jaʿfar al-Sadiq. Photo: Author*

the door, one may read the name of ʿAbdallah ibn Jaʿfar al-Sadiq and verse 33:33 of the Qurʾan, 'God desires to remove impurities from you, *ahl al-bayt*, and to cleanse you and bring out the best in you' (Fig. 3.52). As noted previously, this verse has Shiʿi significance, and appears today throughout the cemetery in various contexts.[91]

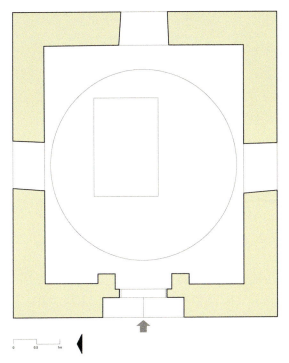

Figure 3.51 *Plan, mausoleum of 'Abdallah ibn Ja'far al-Sadiq.*
Photo: Author

Figure 3.52 *Modern inscription over entrance to mausoleum of 'Abdallah ibn Ja'far al-Sadiq. Photo: Author*

Figure 3.53 *Mausoleum of Sayyida Fidda. Photo: Author*

Sayyida Fidda

South-west of the mausoleum of Fatima al-Sughra and north-west of the mausoleum of Aban is the mausoleum of Sayyida Fidda (Fig. 3.53). Fidda was the maid of Fatima, beloved by the Shiʿa for her devoted service to her mistress, and revered by all for her piety. Her small mausoleum is simply built, of black basalt, with a curving, pointed dome on pendentives (Fig. 3.54).

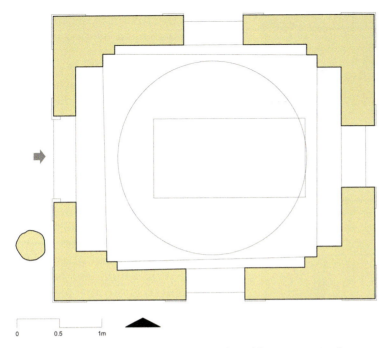

Figure 3.54 *Plan, mausoleum of Sayyida Fidda. Image: Author, Milena Hijazi and Irina Rivero*

A tomb for Sayyida Fidda was recorded in the cemetery since at least the thirteenth century, when it was mentioned by al-Harawi.[92] Subsequently, her shrine appears with relative frequency in the sources: it is cited next in the fifteenth century by Ibn Shahin al-Zahiri in his Mamluk administrative manual for Syria as one of the *mazārāt* of Damascus,[93] and thereafter, it appears regularly in the *ziyāra* literature at least up to the seventeenth century.[94] However, no trace of medieval construction remains today, with the possible exception of a stone upright, cemented into the porch immediately to the right of the front door (Fig. 3.55). This unusual feature is shaped like a roughly hewn, rounded semi-column and is about 80cm high. It has no inscription or other indication of its use. Perhaps it is the remains of some sort of previous grave marker.

Given the well-recorded presence of this grave to Fidda the maid of Fatima in the sources, it is thus somewhat surprising to find that the mausoleum's inscription today names another Fidda. This inscription, in two lines placed over the entrance portal (Fig. 3.56), reads:

This is the mausoleum (*ḍarīḥ*) of Sayyida Fidda, the maid of Sayyidna Muhammad, MPBUH. This blessed *maqam* was founded by the Sultan al-Ghazi Abdülhamid Khan, may God perpetuate his reign, in the year 1327 (1909).[95]

Figure 3.55 *Stone upright to the right of the door of mausoleum of Sayyida Fidda. Photo: Author*

Above the inscription is the *tughra* of Abdülhamid flanked by two crescent moons.

Thus, we have a fifth ʿAlid mausoleum for which the patron was the Ottoman Sultan Abdülhamid. However, it differs from the four previous foundations in several ways. First, it was built three years prior to the four mausolea commissioned by the Sayyid Salim Murtada. Second, it is the only ʿAlid mausoleum built by the sultan that specifically names him as the patron, which suggests Abdülhamid's direct involvement in the project without the intervention of a middleman like Sayyid Salim. It is not clear why the sultan chose to break with the medieval precedent and declare a new affiliation for the tomb's inhabitant.[96] However, it is clear from this and the four previous examples that the Ottoman sultan had an ongoing interest in the maintenance of the ʿAlid shrines in the cemetery of Bab al-Saghir.[97] In this, it seems, he was only following the lead of the Sunni patrons that had preceded him.

Figure 3.56 *Inscription over door of mausoleum of Sayyida Fidda. Photo: Author*

Conclusion

From this evidence it is apparent that an extremely varied set of intentions and motivations informed the patronage of these shrines. While sectarian affiliation certainly played a role, the remarkable constant throughout is the eclecticism of both the identities of the patrons and their motivations, and the type of endowment they made. Sunni patrons appear here more frequently than Shi'i ones, but they often seem to have been motivated by simple personal piety rather than by a desire to achieve some greater political or social end. Furthermore, the appearance of a newly ecumenical approach to holy figures, beginning in the twelfth and thirteenth centuries and continuing through to the Mamluk and Ottoman periods, is readily apparent here. In particular, Sunni patronage of the 'Alid shrines of the cemetery makes this point explicit, for while it seems reasonable that Sunni patrons might invest in a shrine to a prominent figure such as the Prophet's grandson al-Husayn, it is clearly a bit less so for shrines to the many 'second-tier' 'Alid figures buried in the cemetery which are generally revered only by the Shi'a, such as the grandchildren of al-Husayn, the wives of lesser-known 'Alid figures or the sons of the twelve Shi'i Imams. And yet, as far as it is possible to determine, Sunni patronage of such shrines was common in the cemetery of Bab al-Saghir.

Such investment took place within a context of intense competition between Sunnis and Shi'is and between Muslims and Christians in Syria. The arrival of the Crusaders in 1099 had reinforced and brought to the fore an already extant Islamic concept of a 'holy land': an idea that sparked competition between Muslims and Christians for the appropriation and demarcation of holiness within the land of Syria. Over the following two centuries, new shrines and holy sites were discovered, old ones restored and varied projects patronised by an ever-widening group of actors. This undoubtedly made such an ecumenical approach toward holy figures highly desirable, for it opened up a wider number of sites for potential sanctification by Muslims.

Between Sunnis and Shi'is too such rivalries unfolded, particularly in Syria under Fatimid rule, when acts of destruction resulting from Fatimid infighting sparked a revival and reinvestment in holy sites on the part of Damascene Sunnis, a process Josef Meri has called 'reassembling the sacred'.[98] Indeed, the period immediately following the end of Fatimid rule is precisely the time that, according to the sources, several of the shrines in the cemetery of Bab al-Saghir first appear, a fact that is corroborated by the architectural evidence. Furthermore, it seems that in at least one case – namely, the mausoleum of Sukayna bt. al-Husayn – a Shi'i patron found the means and social freedom within predominantly Sunni Damascus to invest quite lavishly in the sanctification of a holy site. Such conclusions suggest a far more fluid interaction between sectarian groups than is often supposed for the city of Damascus in the medieval period. Furthermore, such interaction was not limited to the cemetery, and was a feature of holy sites throughout Damascus and Syria generally. As we shall see in the next chapter, at least three other 'Alid holy sites in the city – the shrine to al-Husayn in the Umayyad mosque, Sayyida Ruqayya near Bab Faradis and Sayyida Zaynab in the Damascus suburb of Rawiya – received similar attention.

Notes

1. Muhammad Ibn Shakir al-Kutubi, *'Uyun al-Tawarikh*, ed. and trans. by H. Sauvaire as 'Description de Damas', *Journal Asiatique* (May–June 1896), 372–3.
2. Ross Burns, *Monuments of Syria* (London & New York: I. B. Tauris, 1999), p. 100.
3. Khalid Moaz and Solange Ory, *Inscriptions arabes de Damas: les Stèles funéraires, I. Cimetière d'al-Bab al-Saghir* (Damascus: Institut français de Damas, 1977), p. 118.
4. Even today, tens of thousands of Shi'is from across the Islamic world congregate in Damascus each year during the month of Muharram to commemorate 'Ashura, the date memorialising the martyrdom of al-Husayn. They make processions through the main market of the city, beating their chests or performing rituals of self-flagellation in sympathy with the suffering of al-Husayn.
5. Josef Meri, *The Cult of Saints Among Muslims and Jews in Medieval Syria* (Oxford: Oxford University Press, 2002), pp. 29–35; 43–7; Daniella Talmon-Heller, *Islamic Piety in Medieval Syria: Mosques, Cemeteries and Sermons under the Zangids and Ayyubids (1146–1260)* (Leiden: Brill, 2007), Chapter 6.
6. Thierry Bianquis, *Damas et la Syrie sous la domination Fatimide (359–468/969–1076)* (Damascus: Institut français de Damas, 1986), pp. 292–5, 349–63.
7. An important exception is Louis Pouzet, *Damas au VIIe–XIIIe siècle: vie et structures religieuses d'une métropole Islamique* (Beirut: Dar al-Machreq, 1988), pp. 245–62. As critical as Pouzet's initial foray is as a starting point, though, it is now over twenty years old and there is much room for further exploration.
8. According to the pilgrimage guide author Ibn al-Hawrani, by the late sixteenth century many shrines had entirely disappeared. He writes that he will only mention 'the famous and patent [*sic*] sites, not of those whose tombs were obliterated and whose cenotaphs (*darā'ih*) are no longer visible'. Ibn al-Hawrani, *Kitab al-Isharat ila Amakin al-Ziyarat*, ed. and trans. Josef W. Meri. *Medieval Encounters* 7, 1 (2001), 33.
9. Ibn 'Asakir recounts an anecdote which confirms the shrine was a destination for Persian pilgrims in his day and that they passed through Damascus on their way to Mecca, although it should be noted that the area of present-day Iran was not predominantly Shi'i until the Safavid period. Moaz and Ory, *Inscriptions*, p. 22.
10. Bilal is also said to be buried in the village of Daraya outside of Damascus. See 'Ali ibn al-Hasan Ibn 'Asakir, *Ta'rikh Madinat Dimashq*, ed. Salah al-Din al-Munajjid (Damascus: Matbu'at al-Majma' al-'Ilmi al-'Arabi, 1951), vol. 2, p. 199. This site is visited by Shi'i pilgrims as well.

11. Muhammad As'ad Talas, '*Dhayl* (Postscript)', in Yusuf ibn Hasan Ibn al-Mibrad, *Thimar al-Maqasid fi Dhikr al-Masajid*, ed. M. A. Talas (Beirut: n.p., 1943), p. 198. Talas reports that the fire took place in 1361 *hijrī* (1942) and notes the restoration of the building. Since Talas's book was published in 1943, the work of restoration must have commenced immediately following the fire.

12. I was unable to determine whether it is the original masonry or a facing.

13. Ernst Herzfeld, 'Damascus: Studies in Architecture III', *Ars Islamica* 9 (1942), 14, 15.

14. Moaz and Ory, *Inscriptions*, pp. 21–2.

15. Ibid., p. 22.

16. Ibn 'Asakir, *Ta'rikh Madinat Dimashq*, p. 196; Muhammad ibn Ahmad Ibn Jubayr, *Rihla*, or *The Travels of Ibn Jubayr*, ed. William Wright (Leiden: Brill, 1907, reprinted 1973), p. 279.

17. Moaz and Ory, *Inscriptions*, p. 77.

18. 'Ali ibn Muhammad Al-Raba'i, *Fada'il al-Sham wa-Fadl Dimashq*, ed. Abi 'Abd al-Rahman 'Adil ibn Sa'd (Beirut: Dar al-Kutub al-'Ilmiyya, 2001), p. 86.

19. Moaz and Ory were uncertain as to the dating of this inscription, noting that it was impossible to situate with certainty. However they opted for the first half of the twelfth century. See Moaz and Ory, *Inscriptions*, p. 77.

20. Medieval authors – for example Ibn Jubayr – place his grave in Mecca. Ibn Jubayr, *Rihla*, p. 196.

21. Moaz and Ory, *Inscriptions*, pp. 60–2 and plates XX, A and B.

22. It is perhaps this coffer that produced the dark stain visible on the lower portion of the epitaph of Shahrazuri. See Moaz and Ory, *Inscriptions*, plates VI, A and XX, B. This supposition is confirmed by Talas in his 'Postscript (*Dhayl*)' to Ibn al-Mibrad's *Thimar al-Maqasid*, p. 198. In the early 1940s, when noting the existence of the eleventh-century epitaph, Talas writes that it was impossible to read because it was obscured by the wooden coffer in front of it.

23. If asked, the caretakers of Bilal's shrine will confirm the cenotaph is Ibn 'Aqil's, but most Shi'i pilgrims seem unaware the cenotaph is not for 'Abdallah and treat it as though it is. It is frequently attributed to 'Abdallah on Iranian *ziyāra* websites.

24. My translation. See also Lorenz Korn, *Ayyubidische Architektur in Ägypten und Syrien: Bautätigkeit im Kontext von Politik und Gesellschaft 564–658/1169–1258* (Heidelberg: Heidelberger Orient-verlag, 2004), vol. II, p. 139, no. 147.

25. Talas, 'Postscript (*Dhayl*)', in Ibn al-Mibrad, *Thimar al-Maqasid*, p. 198.

26. 'Ali Ibn Abi Bakr Al-Harawi, *Kitab al-Isharat ila Ma'rifat al-Ziyarat*, ed. J. Sourdel-Thomine (Damascus: al-Ma'had al-Faransi bi-Dimashq, 1953), p. 13; *Guide des lieux de pèlerinage*, ed. and trans. Janine Sourdel-Thomine (Damascus: Institut français de Damas, 1957), p. 32; ed. and trans. by Josef Meri, *Wayfarer's Guide*, p. 30. On p. 4 of the Sourdel-Thomine edition, Al-Harawi notes that Bilal also had a shrine in Aleppo, but expresses some doubt as to its authenticity.

27. Ibn Battuta, *Rihlat Ibn Battuta al-Musamma Tuhhfat al-Nuzzar fi Ghara'ib al-Amsar wa-'Aja'ib al-Asfar*, ed. Abd al-Hadi al-Tazi (Rabat: Al-Mamlaka al-Maghribiyya, 1997), vol. 1, p. 320; Ghars al-Din Khalil Ibn Shahin al-Zahiri, *Zubdat kashf al-mamalik*, ed. Paul Ravaisse (Paris: E. Leroux, 1894), p. 46; 'Abdallah ibn Muhammad Al-Badri,

Nuzhat al-Anam fi Mahasin al-Sham, ed. and trans. by Henri Sauvaire as 'Description de Damas', *Journal Asiatique* 9 (May–June 1896), 450; Ibn al-Mibrad, *Thimar al-maqasid*, p. 160; ʿAbd al-Qadir ibn Muhammad Al-Nuʿaymi, *Al-Daris fi Taʾrikh al-Madaris*, ed. Jaʿfar al-Hasani (Cairo: Maktabat al-Thaqafa al-Diniyya, 1988), vol. 1, p. 252; Mahmud ibn Muhammad Al-ʿAdawi, *Kitab al-Ziyarat bi Dimashq*, ed. Salah al-Din al-Munajjid (Damascus: Al-Majmaʿ al-ʿIlmi al-ʿArabi bi-Dimashq, 1956), pp. 13 and 23.

28. Ibn al-Hawrani, *al-Isharat*, the tomb of Bilal is noted again on p. 38.

29. Talas, *Dhayl* (Postscript), in Ibn al-Mibrad, *Thimar al-Maqasid*, p. 198.

30. Baki Tezcan, 'Dispelling the darkness: The politics of 'race' in the early seventeenth-century Ottoman Empire in the light of the life and work of Mullah Ali', in Baki Tezcan and Karl K. Barbir, eds, *Identity and Identity Formation in the Ottoman World: A Volume of Essays in Honor of Norman Itzkowitz* (Madison, WI: University of Wisconsin Press, 2007), p. 79.

31. On the household of Valide Sultan Safiye, see Maria Pia Pedani, 'Safiye's household and Venetian diplomacy', *Turcica* 32 (2000), 9–32. Osman was also patron of the Mosque of al-Malika Safiyya in Cairo, completed after his death by Safiye around 1610. See also Caroline Williams, *Islamic Monuments in Cairo* (Cairo & New York: American University in Cairo Press, 2002), p. 132.

32. Talas, *Dhayl* (Postscript), in Ibn al-Mibrad, *Thimar al-Maqasid*, p. 198. Talas quotes the inscription incompletely and with an error (he writes *al-marsūm* instead of *al-marhūm*). I am grateful to Dr Abraham Marcus of the University of Texas at Austin for help with the interpretation of this inscription, particularly the Ottoman Turkish word 'orduwī'. At some point around the same time work may have also been done by the Damascus governor or city council, see Stefan Weber, *Damascus: Ottoman Modernity and Urban Transformation (1808–1918)* (Aarhus: Aarhus University Press, 2009), vol. 1, p. 142 and vol. 2, p. 247.

33. Terry Allen, *Ayyubid Architecture* (Occidental, CA: Solipsist Press, 2003), 7th edition, Chapter 10, 'Bimâristân al-Qaimarî'. Online at www.sonic.net/~tallen/palmtree/ayyarch (accessed 10 February 2006).

34. See in particular Rida Kahhala, *Aʿlam al-Nisaʾ fi ʿAlamay al-Arab wa-l-Islam* (Damascus: al-Matbaʿah al-Hashimiyah, 1959), vol. 2, pp. 202–24; A. Arazi, 'Sukayna bt. al-Husayn', *Encyclopaedia of Islam*, 2nd edition [hereafter *EI2*], ed. P. Bearman et al. Brill Online, http://referenceworks.brillonline.com.ezproxy.lib.utexas.edu/entries/encyclopaedia-of-islam-2/sukayna-bt-al-husayn-SIM_7140 (accessed 22 July 2013); Leone Caetani, *Chronographia Islamica* (Paris: P. Geuthner, 1912), vol. 5, p. 1478.

35. Ibn ʿAsakir, *Taʾrikh Madinat Dimashq*, vol. 2, pp. 80 and 199.

36. See al-ʿAdawi, *Ziyarat bi-Dimashq*, p. 25; Ibn Shakir al-Kutubi, *ʿUyun al-Tawarikh*, pp. 387, 391.

37. Moaz and Ory, *Inscriptions*, 124.

38. Ibn ʿAsakir, *Taʾrikh Madinat Dimashq*, vol. 2, pp. 198–9; al-Harawi, *Kitab al-Isharat*, ed. J. Sourdel-Thomine, p. 13; ed. and trans. by J. Sourdel-Thomine, *Guide*, p. 34; ed. and trans. by Meri, *Wayfarer's Guide*, p. 30. Ibn Jubayr, *Rihla*, ed. W. Wright, p. 281; *Voyages*, ed. and trans. by Maurice Gaudefroy-Demombynes (Paris: P. Geuthner, 1949), vol. 3, p. 326. Ibn Jubayr seems to have made a topographical error here; cf. *Rihla*, p. 281, where he locates the tombs of Bab al-Saghir 'in the

cemetery which is to the west of the city'. As noted previously, the cemetery of Bab al-Saghir is south of the city, albeit more towards the south-west corner.

39. Al-Badri, *Nuzhat al-Anam*, p. 450, though he says Sukayna is the daughter of the Caliph Abu Bakr; Ibn al-Mibrad, *Thimar al-Maqasid*, p. 106. Al-Nuʿaymi, *Daris*, vol. 2, p. 341. Ibn al-Mibrad also notes another mosque dedicated to both al-Khidr and Sukayna, *Thimar al-Maqasid*, p. 106. On shrines to al-Khidr see Meri, *Cult of Saints*, pp. 179–83; the one mentioned by Ibn al-Mibrad is possibly located outside Bab Kaysan.

40. Ibn al-Hawrani, *al-Isharat*, p. 46; al-ʿAdawi, *Ziyarat bi-Dimashq*, p. 25. Ibn al-Hawrani is quoting al-Harawi.

41. Ibn ʿAsakir, *Taʾrikh Madinat Dimashq*, vol. 2, p. 197.

42. Ibid., p. 199.

43. See Ibn Jubayr's note below for a fuller explanation.

44. Al-Badri, *Nuzhat al-Anam*, pp. 450, 452.

45. On this point Ibn Jubayr seems to have been mistaken, for Zaynab/Umm Kulthum bt. ʿAli is usually known as Zaynab al-Kubra. Zaynab al-Sughra is the daughter of Imam al-Husayn.

46. Ibn al-Mibrad, *Thimar al-maqasid*, p. 105; Al-Nuʿaymi, *Daris*, vol. 2, p. 340; Ibn al-Hawrani, *al-Isharat*, pp. 67–8.

47. On this *zāwiya*, see Pouzet, *Damas*, p. 446.

48. Al-Nuʿaymi, *Daris*, vol. 2, pp. 209–11.

49. Moaz and Ory, *Inscriptions*, p. 81, n. 3.

50. For analysis of the epigraphy of these cenotaphs including photographs, see Moaz and Ory, *Inscriptions*, pp. 118–20.

51. The caretaker of the shrine claimed that the long hallway separating the two crypts was actually the beginning of an old tunnel that had at one time led to the shrine of the Shuhadaʾ (Karbalaʾ martyrs). While initially seeming like an urban legend, as noted previously it is true that many pathways through the cemetery have remained stable as the cemetery rose around them, indeed making some passageways seem almost tunnel-like. Investigating this intriguing claim would also require archaeological intervention.

52. H.A.R. Gibb, s.v. 'Kitabat', *EI2*, Brill Online, http://referenceworks. brillonline.com.ezproxy.lib.utexas.edu/entries/encyclopaedia-of-islam-2/kitabat-COM_0525 (accessed 1 August 2013).

53. Hillenbrand's study was based on the indices of *The Image of the Word*, Erica Dodd and Shereen Khairallah's record of religious inscriptions from the Islamic world (Beirut: American University of Beirut, 1981). Robert Hillenbrand, 'Qurʾanic epigraphy in medieval Islamic architecture', *Revue des Études Islamiques* 54 (1986), 171–87.

54. Ibid., 175.

55. Majid Fakhry, *A History of Islamic Philosophy* (New York: Columbia University Press, 2004), pp. 4, 12, 54–7; A. J. Wensinck, *The Muslim Creed: its Origins and Development* (London: Frank Cass, 1965), pp. 67, 90, 93, 115. On the emergence of a clearer definition of Shiʿi thought during and after the period of Sunni revival, see Meir Mikhael Bar-Asher, *Scripture and Exegesis in early Imami-Shiism* (Boston, MA: Brill, 1999); Michel M. Mazzaoui, *The Origins of the Safawids: Shiʿism, Sufism, and the Ghulat* (Wiesbaden: F. Steiner, 1972), pp. 22–40; and Alessandro Bausani, 'Religion under the Mongols', in *The Cambridge History of Iran*, ed. J.A. Boyle (Cambridge: Cambridge University Press, 1968), vol. 5, pp. 538–49.

56. According to early Shiʿi sources such as Ibn Rustam Tabari (d. 923), *Dalaʾil al-Imama* (Najaf: al-MaTbaʿa al-Haydariyah, 1949), pp. 71–80; and Ibn Shahrashub (d. 1192), *Manaqib Al Abi Talib* (Najaf: al-Matbaʿah al-Haydariyya, 1956), vol. 3, pp. 230–4. See Chapter 2, notes 60 and 61.

57. Jonathan Bloom is among those who have claimed this is a Shiʿi *tasliyya*, see 'The Mosque of the Qarafa in Cairo', *Muqarnas* 4 (1987), p. 9. However, this claim is not without ambiguities, as both Jean Sauvaget and Christopher Taylor have argued. See Sauvaget, 'Glanes épigraphiques', *Revue des Études Islamiques* 6 (1941–6), p. 27 and Taylor, 'Reevaluating the Shiʿi role in the development of monumental Islamic funerary architecture: The case of Egypt', *Muqarnas* 9 (1992), p. 7. Acknowledging Sauvaget's differing claim, namely that the *tasliyya* was not a 'significant archaeological index', and cannot be said to be unambiguously Shiʿi, Bloom nevertheless counters that Sauvaget's evaluation was based on stelae covering a period of only twenty years. See Bloom, 'Mosque of the Qarafa', p. 19, n. 19. Although the medieval meaning is not entirely certain, this eulogy is prominent today in Shiʿi contexts. In fact, in 2005, while I was working in the cemetery of Bab al-Saghir, the 'pure family' epitaph was newly appended to many inscriptions, a process that seemed to go hand in hand with the addition of inscriptions praising the Twelve Imams and other actions seemingly designed to mark Shiʿi space.

58. Sunni exegetes also accept this interpretation, but add the wives of the Prophet and sometimes members of the Banu Hashim to those he included under his mantle. Farhad Daftary, 'Ahl al-Kisa', Encyclopaedia of Islam, 3rd edition [hereafter *EI3*], ed. Gudrun Krämer et al. Brill Online, http://referenceworks.brillonline.com.ezproxy.lib.utexas.edu/entries/encyclopaedia-of-islam-3/ahl-al-kisa-SIM_0311 (accessed 22 July 2013); see also C. Williams, 'The cult of ʿAlid saints in the Fatimid mosques of Cairo, Part I: The mosque of al-Aqmar', *Muqarnas* 1 (1983), 44.

59. David S. Powers, *Muhammad is not the Father of Any of Your Men: the Making of the Last Prophet* (Philadelphia: University of Pennsylvania Press, 2009); see especially Chapter 5.

60. Abu Shama reports an incident in which an anti-Shiʿi mob disinterred the corpse of a Shiʿi man buried in the cemetery of Bab al-Saghir and exposed his head hung between two dead dogs. See Pouzet, *Damas*, p. 245.

61. This appears to be yet another example of the confusion over the identity of the occupant of the tomb next to Sukayna's; see discussion above.

62. Al-Nuʿaymi, *Daris*, vol. II, p. 209.

63. Valerie Hoffman-Ladd, 'Devotion to the Prophet and his family in Egyptian Sufism', *International Journal of Middle Eastern Studies* 24 (1992), 615–37; Kamil Mustafa Al-Shaybi, *Al-Sila bayn al-Tasawwuf wa-l-Tashayyuʾ* (Cairo: Dar al-Maʿarif, 1969); Seyyed Hossein Nasr, 'Shiʿism and Sufism', in *Shiʿism: Doctrines, Thought, and Spirituality*, ed. Seyyed Hossein Nasr et al. (Albany, NY: State University of New York Press, 1988), pp. 104–20.

64. Asma Afsaruddin, *Excellence and Precedence: Medieval Islamic Discourse on Legitimate Leadership* (Leiden & Boston, MA: Brill, 2002), pp. 285–6.

65. Richard J. A. McGregor, *Sanctity and Mysticism in Medieval Egypt: the Wafa Sufi order and the legacy of Ibn 'Arabi* (Albany, NY: State University of New York Press, 2004), pp. 19 and 119–55.

66. Tariq al-Jamil's dissertation, 'Cooperation and contestation in medieval Baghdad' (Princeton University, 2004), explores this theme in depth.

67. May Farhat, *Islamic Piety and Dynastic Legitimacy: The Case of the Shrine of 'Ali ibn Musa al-Rida in Mashhad (10th–17th century)*. Unpublished PhD dissertation, Harvard University, 2002.

68. More on Abdülhamid's patronage of the 'Alid shrines of the cemetery of Bab al-Saghir can be found in Mulder, 'Abdülhamid and the 'Alids: Ottoman patronage of "Shi'i" shrines in the Cemetery of Bab al-Saghir in Damascus', *Studia Islamica* 108, 1 (2013), pp. 16–47. An image of the building before the Ottoman reconstruction can be found in Weber, *Damascus*, vol. 2, p. 230.

69. Moaz and Ory, *Inscriptions*, pp. 18–20.

70. This inscription has been published many times. See Eustache de Lorey and Gaston Wiet, 'Cénotaphes de deux dames musulmanes à Damas', *Syria* 2 (1921), 224–5; *Répertoire chronologique d'épigraphie arabe*, vol. 7, no. 2529; Janine Sourdel-Thomine, 'Épitaphes coufiques de Bâb Saghîr', in Jean Sauvaget, *Les Monuments Ayyoubides de Damas* (Paris: E. de Boccard, 1938–48), vol. 4, pp. 147–67, no. 16; G. Conteneau, 'Deuxième mission archéologique à Sidon', *Syria* 5 (1924), 207 and plate LI, 2; Gaston Migeon, *Manuel d'art musulman, arts plastiques et industriels* (Paris: Picard, 1927), vol. 1, pp. 242, 244.

71. There is ambiguity about the reading of Fatima's *nisba*, as it is not clear on the inscription itself whether it should be read al-Subki or al-Sibti. Moaz and Ory leave the question open, recording it as al-Sibti while also presenting information about the al-Subki family. Moaz and Ory, *Inscriptions*, p. 19.

72. J. Schacht and C. E. Bosworth, 'al-Subkī', *EI2*. Brill Online, http://referenceworks.brillonline.com.ezproxy.lib.utexas.edu/entries/encyclopaedia-of-islam-2/al-subki-SIM_7116 (accessed 22 July 2013).

73. Talas, '*Dhayl* (Postscript)', in Ibn al-Mibrad, *Thimar al-Maqasid*, p. 252.

74. This was confirmed in an interview with Wa'el Murtada. However, unlike the three other shrines Abdülhamid renovated, the shrine of Fatima al-Sughra is no longer in the hands of the Murtada family and is today under the care of the Ministry of Waqfs.

75. The most recent pre-modern pilgrimage guide I have checked is the *Ziyarat bi-Dimashq* by al-'Adawi (d. 1623). It does not mention a shrine to Fatima al-Sughra in the cemetery.

76. Al-Husayn's head was brought to Damascus after the battle of Karbala' and is said to have been repeatedly buried and reburied in various locales, including Damascus, Ascalon and Cairo, while the body of his infant son 'Ali al-Asghar was buried in Karbala' immediately following his martyrdom.

77. Al-Harawi, *Kitab al-Isharat*, ed. Sourdel-Thomine, p. 14; Meri, *Wayfarer's Guide*, p. 30.

78. Al-Nu'aymi, *Daris*, vol. 2, p. 302.

79. Weber, *Damascus*, p. 373.

80. I was unable to enter the mosque and the office/latrine areas of this second courtyard. Their representation in Fig. 3.26 is not to scale and is my best estimate of their dimensions. As noted in the text above, the

office/latrine area is partitioned, but as I was unsure of the dimensions of these rooms I have left the interior area empty.

81. This is part of a project undertaken in the late 1990s by Waʾel Murtada, the caretaker of the shrines of Sukayna and Umm Kulthum, Ruʾus al-Shuhadaʾ and ʿAbdallah b. Zayn al-ʿAbidin. He hopes eventually to build a museum, a medical clinic and a library for researchers. Interview with Waʾel Salim Murtada, 21 March 2005.

82. Moaz and Ory, *Inscriptions*, plate II.

83. Talas, 'Dhayl (Postscript)', in Ibn al-Mibrad, *Thimar al-Maqasid*, p. 232. On the Seven Sleepers, see Janine Sourdel-Thomine, 'Les anciens lieux de pèlerinage damascaines d'après les sources arabes', *Bulletin des Études Orientales* 14 (1952–4), 71, and Louis Massignon, 'Les sept dormants d'Éphèse en Islam et chrétienté', *Revue des Études Islamiques* 22–5 (1955–7), 61–112. The story is an enduring one. In addition to the famous shrine for the Sleepers in Ephesus, one also exists in eastern Turkey at Afşin, near Elbistan in Kahramanmaraş province. I visited this second site in the spring of 2005. It consists of a magnificent Seljuk complex built around the cave and includes a mosque, *khan* and *madrasa*, built in part using the *spolia* from the prior Byzantine shrine.

84. Neither I, nor a colleague in Islamic art whose native language is Arabic, have been able to decipher this inscription.

85. Weber, *Damascus*, p. 234.

86. There seems to be some confusion regarding his parentage; see K.V. Zetterstéen, 'Abān b. ʿUthmān', *EI2*, Brill Online, http://reference works.brillonline.com.ezproxy.lib.utexas.edu/entries/encyclopaedia-of-islam-2/aban-b-uthman-SIM_0005 (accessed 22 July 2013), where his mother is given as Umm ʿAmr bint Jundab b. ʿAmr al-Dawsiyah. I am not sure how he came to be claimed as a son of Ruqayya.

87. The practice of praising the Rashidun and adding al-Hasan and al-Husayn seems to be an Ottoman one. According to Yasser Tabbaa, the formulation appears in a number of mid-sixteenth-century Ottoman mosques and mausolea. Tabbaa, posting to H-Islamart listserve, 15 March 2005. Bernard O'Kane points out that it is a feature of the painted decoration on the dome of the mosque of Sulayman Pasha (1528) in the citadel in Cairo. Ibid., 16 March 2005. Another contributor speculated that since the addition of al-Hasan and al-Husayn was largely an eastern Anatolian characteristic, which never appeared in mosques in the Balkans, it was a gesture meant to appease the Shiʿi population of that area. Filiz Yenisehirlioglu, H-Islamart listserve, 20 March 2005. However Gottfried Hagen, who had posted the original query regarding inscriptions on roundels in Ottoman mosques, largely rejected these conclusions. H-Islamart listserve, 20 March 2005.

88. Moaz and Ory, *Inscriptions*, p. 114.

89. Ibid., pp. 114–15.

90. Interview with Waʾel Salim Murtada, 21 March 2005.

91. For example, on the exterior entrance gate leading to the mausoleum of Sukayna and Umm Kulthum. It was also one of the quotations on the twelfth-century cenotaph of Sukayna, discussed above.

92. Al-Harawi, *Kitab al-Isharat*, ed. J. Sourdel-Thomine, p. 13; Sourdel-Thomine, *Guide*, p. 32; Meri, *Wayfarer's Guide*, p. 30.

93. Ibn Shahin al-Zahiri, *Zubdat Kashf al-Mamalik*, p. 46.

94. Ibn al-Hawrani, *Al-Isharat*, trans. J. Meri, pp. 38 and 46; al-ʿAdawi, *Ziyarat*, p. 24.

95. This inscription is badly damaged and broken into multiple pieces, which have been reassembled and cemented back into place. The marble plaque seems to be in its original location, however, since it fits neatly into the space allotted for it over the door. It would seem as though it either fell from its location and shattered, or was deliberately broken and removed at some point in the past. Since there remain nail holes along the edges that probably once attached the slab of marble to the building, the first scenario is the more probable. Such nails could easily have weakened or eroded over time, causing the plaque to fall.

96. According to Moaz and Ory, al-Harawi *does* write of a shrine to Fidda the maid of Muhammad, but they claim he locates it in Homs: see Moaz and Ory, *Inscriptions*, p. 64, n. 1. However this appears to be an error, as the page in al-Harawi cited by Moaz and Ory (*al-Isharat*, ed. J. Sourdel-Thomine, p. 8) does not mention a shrine to Fidda in Homs, nor does J. Meri's translation of al-Harawi, *Wayfarer's Guide*. Ibn Shahin al-Zahiri, *Zubdat Kashf al-Mamalik*, p. 42.

97. He also sponsored the renovation of three other non-ʿAlid shrines in the cemetery, those of the Prophet's wives Umm Salama and Umm Habiba, and that of ʿAbdallah ibn Umm Maktum, a Companion of the Prophet and another of his muezzins. These three were built a year before that of Fidda, in 1909, using the same basalt stone and almost identical inscriptions.

98. For example, the Great Mosque of Damascus was burned to the ground in 1069. Meri, *Cult of Saints*, p. 32.

CHAPTER FOUR

Perpetual Patronage: Four Damascene ʿAlid Shrines

IF THE MONUMENTS of the Cemetery of Bab al-Saghir were, for the most part, rather modest in size and in architectural presence, the same cannot be said for another group of Shiʿi shrines in Damascus. Indeed, the four shrines to be discussed in this chapter were each, at some point in their history, among the most prominent sites of pilgrimage in the region of al-Sham. Two of these, the Mashhad al-Husayn/Mashhad Ruqayya and the Mashhad ʿAli Zayn al-ʿAbidin/Mashhad al-Husayn, are located inside the medieval city perimeter. Two others, the Mashhad ʿAli/Mashhad al-Naranj and the Mashhad Sayyida Zaynab, are located outside the walls. Though spatially separated from each other, they share a similar architectural fate, for they have today been transformed to such a degree that their original plan and constitution is unclear. In one case the shrine has entirely disappeared. But these very acts of transformation are significant, for although they deprive art historians of the ability to analyse these buildings' medieval form or decoration, such a history of constant and ongoing alteration is the strongest evidence for the shrines' prominent social and sectarian role in the life of the city, and no account of the Shiʿi shrines of Damascus would be complete without them.

This perpetual and total kind of renovation is a unique feature of shrine architecture, and one that differentiates it from many other architectural types, such as mosques, *madrasa*s or tombs of historical figures. While such buildings were also frequently renovated or restored, these renovations tended to preserve most aspects of the original plan and appearance of the building in question. Only rarely were non-pilgrimage sites subjected to the kind of total rebuilding that shrines to many holy figures underwent almost as a matter of course. Although a similar form of ongoing patronage was evident in the monuments of Bab al-Saghir, many of those shrines had left traces of their previous incarnations in their plans, crypts or inscriptions, and in this way provided multiple strands of physical evidence. As will be shown, with one exception, this is not the case with the shrines considered in this chapter. But this continuous intervention and the resulting paucity of physical evidence for the medieval form of these shrines should not be cause for their dismissal from art historical purview. On the contrary, the shrines' complex architectural past should be seen as a reflection of their prominence in the Damascene landscape of Shiʿi piety, and the surest testimony for the devotion and affection of pilgrims and local patrons for the *ahl al-bayt*.

Clearly, given the relative lack of material data, the primary line of evidence for the history, patronage and physical form of these buildings must be the Arabic sources. Perhaps ironically, considering the dearth of original architecture, these four buildings are mentioned with greater consistency and detail in the writings of medieval authors than almost all the other shrines we have considered so far. Thus this chapter is primarily an effort towards reconstructive architectural history, based on literary, rather than physical, remains. It is an exercise in the archaeology of texts: an attempt to reconstitute, or re-imagine, important nodes of ritual practice within the lost urban and suburban landscape of medieval Damascus. In a few cases, when physical evidence is present, it will also be considered and interpreted. However, in large part, these re-imagined urban and suburban landscapes are a response to a difficult question: how to study buildings that are continuously in flux? Such buildings have a standard template: they are located within, or linked closely to, an inhabited city fabric, and they share the characteristic of repeated and continuous total intervention. In this chapter, we will track the ongoing health, decline and revival of these shrines over many centuries and in doing so, formulate a method for their study.

Here, several questions will be explored: first, why is it that some loci attract this kind of ongoing and total rebuilding, others have a moment of prominence only to rapidly decline and others still remain largely untouched, preserving the majority of their medieval fabric intact? While of course each building has its own particularities, as noted above it will be shown that this characteristic of perpetual rebuilding is a very common feature of Shiʿi shrines. Their unique building histories reflect the complex set of political, pious and popular motivations behind their founding and renewal. A second theme of this chapter is the fluidity and flexibility of meaning that adheres to Shiʿi devotional structures. While sometimes highly charged with ideological significance, at other times they appear rather as neutral receptacles for generalised notions of piety, devoid of all particularity or sectarian meaning. This makes them uniquely suited as vehicles for a wide range of political or social messages. And finally, another theme explored here is these shrines' contribution to the generation and perpetuation of the urban and suburban landscape. Thus, we will examine the question of intramural vs extramural devotional and architectural practice. 'Shiʿi' shrines are almost always associated with cities, and are rarely found in remote locales (as is frequently the case with Sunni shrines) yet, of the seventeen shrines presented in this study only two are actually located inside the walls of a city. At first glance, it appears possible that shrines to figures beloved by the Shiʿa were 'exiled' in a sense: that is, banished to locations outside the city walls because they were loci of activities defined as 'unorthodox' by some Sunni scholars. But the presence of two important shrines within the city walls, one within the Umayyad mosque itself, argues for a more complex interpretation, and points yet again to the fluidity of meaning and practice that is a hallmark of shrines devoted to the Family of the Prophet.

In order to re-imagine this long-lost urban landscape, it is most fruitful to first orientate ourselves within that landscape as it exists today. Thus, as we explore each of these nodes, our enquiry will begin with a description of the location, surroundings and physical presence of each shrine in its contemporary state. The account will then turn to reconstruct what is known of its medieval history and physical structure, beginning from the date of its earliest appearance in the sources and continuing through to the moment of its most recent mention.

The Mashhad Sayyida Ruqayya bt. al-Husayn/Mashhad Raʾs al-Husayn, Bab al-Faradis

Today, a group of pilgrims, perhaps women from Iran or Pakistan with their families, approaching the city of Damascus from the north are likely to arrive in a bus or taxi after winding their way along the narrow, hectic, traffic-filled road that skirts the northern medieval city wall. They will probably descend from their transport just outside Bab al-Faradis, and, gathering their bags, will cross this congested intersection at considerable peril to themselves and their belongings. They will then make their way towards an unmarked entrance to a dark and narrow market lane, shaded by rusted corrugated tin sheeting. Pushing through teeming crowds of local shoppers, black-clad pilgrims and vendors selling everything from candy floss to freshly slaughtered sheep carcasses and plastic toys from China, they will eventually make their way towards a more substantial monument which looms over the market stalls at the end of the alley: the Bab al-Faradis or Paradise Gate (Map 3). Renovated in the thirteenth century, this simple gate bears a medieval inscription on its heavy lintel.[1] It probably gets its name either from gardens or orchards that used to be outside the gate in Roman and early Islamic times, or from the cemetery north of the gate. This cemetery was once known as the cemetery of al-Faradis and is today called the Cemetery of Dahdah.[2]

Passing under the gate, they enter the quarter of al-ʿAmara, and continue along the market street. Slowly, its character begins to transform. Instead of Arab sweets and vegetables, the stalls now

Figure 4.1 *Damascus, neo-Safavid dome of Mashhad Sayyida Ruqayya.* *Photo: Author*

display shimmering fabrics, plastic shoes and religious memorabilia and souvenirs. Another change is also soon evident: the signs above the stalls are no longer written in Arabic but in Farsi, or in some combination of both languages. Shopkeepers, too, speak Farsi, most of them native Damascene merchants who have learned the language over the past ten to fifteen years, when the transformation of this quarter began in earnest. Indeed, on the left, perhaps 50m down the market lane from the gate, the reason for its transformation becomes visible in the form of an imposing, ivory-coloured, marble-faced wall crowned with a blue-tiled inscription band. It is the north-west corner of the shrine of Sayyida Ruqayya bt. al-Husayn, recently renovated and expanded on a massive scale at the heart of the historic old city of Damascus (Fig. 4.1).

Here, just steps from the Umayyad mosque, the gleaming blue, gold and white surfaces of an Iranian-style neo-Safavid structure rise incongruously from the predominantly beige and brown mosaic of the traditional city fabric, the vision simultaneously jarring and coolly refreshing. Its smooth tile wall stretches ahead, embracing an entire city block (Fig. 4.2). Crowds of pilgrims congregate in clusters in front of the monumental portal, which, like the entire wall of the complex, is angled outwards towards the east out of deference to the original line of the street (Fig. 4.3). Entering the shrine through this tall, mosaic-tiled portal, the angle is brought back to cardinal orientation by a triangular vestibule. Upon passing through the vestibule, our pilgrims find themselves in a clean, peaceful courtyard,

Figure 4.2 *Outside the western wall of the shrine of Sayyida Ruqayya in the evening, where local residents, merchants and pilgrims crowd the passageway of the Old City leading to the main entrance. Photo: Author*

bordered on all sides by a pointed-arched portico. This courtyard serves to continue a process of translation of the pilgrims from the noisy, dusty market street on the exterior to the holy space of the shrine's interior. Facing them across the courtyard is the entrance to the shrine itself, accessed via an opening hung with two magnificent, heavily gilded wooden doors, covered with glass to protect them from the fingers of the thousands more pilgrims that visit the shrine each week. Passing through this portal, the translation is complete, and the pilgrims find themselves in a sparkling, spacious room (Fig. 4.4). The focal point of the room is the golden tomb enclosure of the saint, who reposes serenely there under a low dome, while the lush, glittering, Iranian-inspired mirror mosaic of the ceiling and arches draws visitors' eyes heavenwards.

At prayer time, the shrine fills to capacity with both pilgrims and local people, predominantly Sunni, who pray side by side with Shiʿi pilgrims from remote lands. At other times during the day, women and men enter the shrine incessantly, coming to make entreaty of the Lady Ruqayya, clinging to her tomb enclosure, quietly whispering, reciting devotional prayers and tying small bits of green fabric to

Figure 4.3 *Portal and neo-Safavid dome of Mashhad Sayyida Ruqayya, as seen from surrounding streets. Photo: Author*

its grille. A pregnant woman enters and runs her hands over the grille then passes them over her full belly, seeking to transfer the saintly lady's *baraka* (blessed emanations) to her unborn child. Many, however, come for more mundane purposes: simply to rest, read and talk, their children playing and running freely through the softly carpeted space. It is a relaxed and comfortable setting, and despite the external incongruity of its Iranian-influenced architecture, this building seems at first glance to have incorporated itself effortlessly

Figure 4.4 *Interior of Mashhad Sayyida Ruqayya, showing tomb enclosure and mirror-mosaic dome. Photo: Author*

into the religious and devotional life of the city. In truth, the contemporary transformation of this shrine is a much more complicated tale, achieved by the active, and quite destructive, intervention of former Syrian President Hafez al-Assad as part of a larger political effort to strengthen ties with Iran.[3]

It is not only its contemporary architecture, however, that seems incongruous. Its prior history, as well, is a confusing and complex story of invention, investment, decline and reinvention. Here, we will trace this history in the Arabic sources in an attempt to learn how the total transformation of this site was put into effect, for Sayyida Ruqayya's grave has known many incarnations, from obscure and occasionally visited neighbourhood shrine, to the present glittering and internationally revered site. How did this process unfold, and why did it occur? And how is it that such a rupture with the past and with the local architectural fabric was, apparently, so smoothly integrated into the social and religious life of the old city of Damascus?

According to modern scholarship, a shrine to Sayyida Ruqayya at Bab al-Faradis did not exist at all before the nineteenth century.[4] The contemporary Syrian historian Akram al-ʿUlabi writes in the *Khitat Dimashq*, his topographical work on Damascus, that

> although there is not much historical value to this site, in view of the enormous expansion undertaken today and the fact that it has become holy to the Shiʿa, we include it . . . (however) not a single historian mentions that a grave to Sayyida Ruqayya is (located) in Damascus, nor a mosque, nor a *maqām*, except the Shaykh Muhsin al-Amin (author of the *Aʿyan al-Shiʿa*), and he added to his description the words 'and God knows best' (as an indication of scepticism).[5]

As we shall see, this is not accurate, for the grave of Ruqayya was indeed mentioned by medieval authors. Furthermore, the holy site also seems to have had a prior identity and life before it became sacred to Ruqayya. Indeed, the historian al-ʿUlabi continues his account with a sentence that gives us our first peek into the deeper history of Sayyida Ruqayya: 'This mosque (*masjid*) was called Masjid al-Raʾs and it was said that the head of al-Husayn was in it, and also buried within it was the head of al-Malik al-Kamil al-Ayyubi, who was killed by Hülegü.'[6] Could it be that Sayyida Ruqayya is only the most recent manifestation of an older shrine to the resting place of the head of her father, al-Husayn? In fact, this seems to be the case. But to demonstrate this, we must begin with the earliest mention of the shrine and wend our way systematically forward through the sources.

The earliest reference to a holy site at Bab al-Faradis appears in the great history of Damascus by Ibn ʿAsakir (d. 1176). In fact, Ibn ʿAsakir mentions two mosques in this area. These are his accounts:

The Mosque of Bab al-Faradis, inside the gate and adjacent (*mulāṣiq*) to the rampart. It has a minaret and a canal (*qanāt*).[7]

A large *masjid* outside (*khārij*) Bab al-Faradis, immediately after (*fī 'aqb*) the bridge, to the right of the exit (*'ala yamīn al-khārij*). It is a place of *baraka* and (has) a fountain (*siqāya*). It has an Imam and a *waqf* and administrators (*wazā'if*), and arches (*ṭāqāt*) over the river. It was founded by the Amir Barzan ibn Yamin al-Kurdi.[8]

Thus, from the earliest medieval source, we learn that there were two 'mosques' at the Bab al-Faradis. He also gives very specific information about the locations of these two holy sites: one, known as the Mosque of Bab al-Faradis, is inside the door and attached to the city wall, and one, for which he does not specify a name, is outside the door on the right or eastern side of it, just past the bridge over the river Barada. Notably, Ibn 'Asakir does not mention that either of these sites are places of pilgrimage or holy sites for visitation, but the author commonly conflates categories of buildings that later authors will separate, placing all of them under the heading of 'mosque'. Ibn 'Asakir also records that both places have waterworks, and he uses different words to describe the installations (canal and fountain), perhaps to indicate a more significant feature in the latter mosque. Indeed, several elements of his description suggest that the mosque *extra-muros* was a far more substantial structure than its counterpart inside the gate: namely, the necessity for administrators (*wazā'if*) and the presence of an imam, and the reference to arches (*ṭāqāt*) overlooking the river. And most importantly, in the second notice, Ibn 'Asakir tells us the name of the building's patron: the Amir Barzan ibn Yamin al-Kurdi [*sic*].

This final clue clearly indicates that the second building cannot have been related to our *mashhad* for Ruqayya. The Kurdi mentioned by Ibn 'Asakir was actually Mujahid al-Din al-Kurdu, the Burid governor of Damascus. He oversaw the city in the mid-twelfth century and built a *madrasa*, known today as the *Madrasa* al-Mujahidiyya, at this location in 1144–5, a fact that is today easily confirmed by the presence of an inscription immediately inside Bab al-Faradis to the east. However its location is a bit puzzling, because today this *madrasa* is clearly *not* located on the exterior of the gate. On the other hand, it seems likely that the school was enclosed within the city walls when Bab al-Faradis was rebuilt in 1241. If so, since Ibn 'Asakir died in 1176, the school would still have been outside the walls in his day. This also makes some sense with respect to the first holy site mentioned by Ibn 'Asakir, the Mosque of Bab al-Faradis, because if that mosque were 'adjacent to the rampart' in his day, it would later be located somewhat to the south of it when the gate was rebuilt to the north. In other words, it would assume something like the current location of our shrine to Ruqayya (Map 3). As we shall see, further exploration of this question will move us from the realm of speculation to hard evidence. For now, we can eliminate the 'mosque' patronised by Mujahid al-Din al-Kurdu and focus on the shrine for al-Husayn.

The first notice of a shrine devoted by name to al-Husayn near Bab al-Faradis comes just a few years later, in the pilgrimage guide of al-Harawi (d. 1215). As discussed previously, al-Harawi's guide is notable for its ecumenical approach to mapping the Islamic sacred landscape: he reports Shi'i shrines as frequently as Sunni ones, so consistently that he is commonly assumed to have been Shi'i himself.[9] Al-Harawi's listing simply states that 'at Bab al-Faradis is the Mashhad al-Husayn'. However, when al-Harawi's notice is compared to the commentary by al-'Ulabi cited above – wherein the modern scholar maintains the shine to Ruqayya was previously devoted to al-Husayn – this brief mention by al-Harawi confirms an early topographical correspondence between the shrines' locations.[10] It also establishes that the shrine at Bab al-Faradis, regardless of whom it commemorated, was an important holy site by at least the twelfth century, worthy of mention by this early author of universal pilgrimage literature. As yet, however, a shrine to Ruqayya herself has not been mentioned by medieval writers.

This would change, however, later in the thirteenth century. Another notice of the shrine appears in the historical topography of Syria written by Ibn Shaddad (d. 1284). In the volume on the Jazira, the site is mentioned in Ibn Shaddad's account of the murder of al-Malik al-Kamil, the Ayyubid ruler of the minor principality of Mayyafariqin (r. 1244–60), by the Mongol leader Hülegü. Woven into the tale is a titbit of information about the shrine:

> so (Hülegü) stabbed (al-Kamil) with his sword, and . . . cut off his head, and journeyed with it toward Syria. He travelled around with it throughout the land (ṭafa bihi fī-l-bilād), and it was hung upon Bab al-Faradis in Damascus, where it stayed for a time. Then Majid al-Din – Imam of the Masjid Ruqayya – stole it (saraqahu), and he buried it in the arch (ṭāq) which is next to the miḥrāb of the Mosque. May God grant him mercy.[11]

From this entry, recording an episode only incidentally connected to the shrine, a little is revealed concerning the building's architecture: namely, that it possessed a kind of arch or vault, that it was a building with a miḥrāb and that these two elements were located in close proximity to each other. But most importantly, this is the earliest medieval notice of a shrine associated specifically with Ruqayya. While Ibn Shaddad's entry does not indicate the exact location of the shrine, he does tell the story in such a way that it is clear the shrine was located near Bab al-Faradis, where the head of al-Malik al-Kamil was displayed. Thus, we know that some time before or around 1250, Ruqayya was revered in a shrine with a vault or arch and a *miḥrāb*, and that it was located near Bab al-Faradis. But still, it does not confirm that this is the same shrine as the one for al-Husayn, mentioned previously by al-Harawi and which Ibn Shaddad himself notes briefly in his volume on Damascus.[12]

However, the two shrines are definitively linked by an inform- ant in the fourteenth century. The *mashhad* for Ruqayya was also known as the Mosque of Bab al-Faradis, and thus it appears in the fourth source to mention the shrine. That source is the little-known medieval historian Ibn Shakir al-Kutubi (d. 1363). His universal history the *ʿUyun al-tawarikh* records a 'mosque (*masjid*) of Bab al-Faradis, inside the gate and contiguous with the rampart. It has a minaret, an underground canal and contains a tomb surrounded by a *maqṣūra* . . .'[13] This first part of his entry is a direct copy of Ibn ʿAsakir's notice cited above. Like his predecessor, Ibn Shakir records quite specific topographical information about the location of the site, but unlike Ibn ʿAsakir, who cited two buildings (one outside the walls of the city and one inside, adjacent to the ramparts) this information does not coincide with the present location of the shrine for Ruqayya, today located south of the gate and not at all contiguous with the rampart. Furthermore, Ibn Shakir was a native of Damascus, a book merchant who wrote his scholarly works on the side.[14] He is an informant who lived much of his life in the city, and thus would seem a trustworthy source, but in this respect he appears to have gotten things a bit wrong, because the location he describes corresponds to the coordinates of the *Madrasa* Mujahidiyya.[15] It appears, then, that Ibn Shakir is either conflating two buildings or confusing their locations. After all, it would be easy to do because they were located within 50m of each other.[16]

Despite the topographical error, this source is extremely impor- tant, for two reasons. First – and again belying the claim there is no pre-modern mention of a shrine to Ruqayya – Ibn Shakir expands on Ibn ʿAsakir's notice and specifically associates this shrine with Ruqayya. Here is the continuation of his report:

> It is said that this is the tomb of Ruqayya, the daughter of ʿAli [*sic*]. One may see there a niche (or arch, *ṭāq*) in the southern wall of the mosque, to the right of the *miḥrāb*. It is there, they say, that the head of al-Husayn was buried, PBUH.

This citation also reaffirms the dual identity of the shrine as both a *mashhad* where the head of al-Husayn was interred and (despite Ibn Shakir's error regarding her paternity) the location of the tomb of his daughter Ruqayya. Al-Husayn was decapitated following his martyrdom at Karbalaʾ and his head brought back to Damascus at the request of the Umayyad Caliph Yazid b. Muʿawiya. Its legendary journey from Karbalaʾ to Damascus generated countless Mashhads Husayn (such as that in Aleppo discussed in Chapter 2), for each place the head rested along its journey – or where a drop of blood fell – became holy (Chapter 5). While Damascus also had a number of Husayn shrines, the two most famous seem to have been this one at Bab al-Faradis and the one located inside the Umayyad mosque (discussed below).[17]

The second notable feature of Ibn Shakir's report is his remarkably precise account of the mosque. The problem with his description, of course, is the topographical error discussed previously, for we cannot be entirely certain if he is describing the shrine of Ruqayya or the Mujahidiyya *madrasa*, a building that also contained tombs, a minaret and a canal. However, despite his error in locating the building spatially, the rest of the information in his report and its correspondence with other reports makes it seem more likely he was describing the Ruqayya shrine. One medieval author, Ibn Shaddad, has already confirmed a very specific architectural feature of the shrine to Ruqayya: an arch next to the *miḥrāb* where the head of the Ayyubid ruler al-Kamil was buried. Ibn Shakir also mentions the arch and adds that the head of al-Husayn was also buried under it. Furthermore, from Ibn Shakir's entry we may confirm it was a building with a minaret and a canal, features noted by Ibn 'Asakir in his listing for the 'mosque' at Bab al-Faradis. Inside, the building sheltered a tomb, which was surrounded by a *maqṣūra*, or tomb enclosure.

This particularly rich description enables us to verify that by the Mamluk period, the shrine of Sayyida Ruqayya was a substantial building with a minaret, a tomb with its own enclosure and a canal. It was probably able to accommodate pilgrims as well as local people who might use the shrine as a neighbourhood mosque, a dual role it serves even today. It also suggests that by the Mamluk era, it had been the object of patronage by a significant figure, one with the means to endow the building with the waterworks, minaret and a tomb enclosure. But, like his co-informants, Ibn Shakir does not provide any information about the shrine's patrons.

In the fifteenth century, the Mamluk administrator Ibn Shahin al-Zahiri mentions a shrine to al-Husayn, but he does not indicate its location. In fact, it is more likely the shrine in the Umayyad mosque he refers to.[18] The next figure to describe the *mashhad* at Bab al-Faradis is the Hanbali scholar and topographer Ibn al-Mibrad (d. 1503). His treatise on the mosques of Damascus mentions the site briefly, and adds another relic to the list of objects in the *mashhad*. He writes that '(Bab al-Faradis) has a *mashhad* al-Husayn which . . . has a black rock brought from Hawran, bearing the imprint of the foot of the Prophet PBUH (and God knows best)'.[19] A few decades later, a Mashhad al-Ra's is mentioned by al-Nu'aymi (d. 1521) who notes it twice in his great compendium of the mosques of Damascus, but in one case it is clearly the shrine in the Umayyad mosque that is meant.[20] The other reference is more cryptic; it records the death of a scholar 'in front of the Mashhad al-Ra's'. Although the editor's footnote directs the reader to Ibn Kathir's description of the death of the Ayyubid al-Kamil and the hanging of the sovereign's head on the gate of Bab al-Faradis, there is nothing in the text itself to favour the assertion that al-Nuʿaymi meant the shrine near the gate rather than the one in the Umayyad mosque.[21] However, under the listing 'Masjid Bab al-Faradis' al-Nuʿaymi records that it was located 'inside the gate and adjacent (mulāṣiq) to the rampart. It has a minaret and a canal (qanāt).'[22] This is another word-for-word copy of the earliest source to mention the shrine, Ibn ʿAsakir, and thus adds little to our knowledge about it except to suggest that it was still present in the early sixteenth century.

A few decades later, however, a more substantial reference appears in the pilgrimage guide of Ibn al-Hawrani (d. 1562). While this author does not specifically link the Husayn shrine in Bab al-Faradis with that of Ruqayya, he does something that strongly implies a connection: he follows his description of the Mashhad al-Husayn with an explanatory biography of Ruqayya:

> The Shrine (mashhad) of al-Husayn
> On the interior of Paradise Gate (Bab al-Faradis) is the shrine (mashhad) of al-Husayn which is called 'Mosque of the Head' (Masjid al-Raʾs). It is known at present. It is a shrine (mashhad) replete with loftiness and reverence and possesses an endowment in perpetuity for its upkeep. The people seek it for pilgrimage (yaqṣiduhu al-nās lil-ziyāra), supplication (duʿāʾ), blessing (tabarruk), seeking fulfillment of needs (iltimās al-ḥawāʾij).
> Al-Sayyida Ruqayya
> In Mahd al-Maʿarib fi Fadl al-Imam ʿAli b. Abi Talib of Ibn al-Mabrad [sic], Ibn Abi al-Dunya mentioned from al-Zubayr b. Abi Bakr that two children were born to ʿAli – ʿUmar, and Ruqayya the Elder who were twins. Their mother is al-Sahbaʾ. It is also said that her name is Umm Habib, daughter of Rabiʿa of Banu Thaʿlab of the captives of Khalid b. al-Walid, may God the Exalted be pleased with him.
> Ibn al-Mabrad says in this composition, 'Among them is Ruqayya the Younger'. Al-Dhahabi mentions it and this is reliable. Do not turn to any other view since it is utter nonsense. God knows best.[23]

This is a valuable source, for it is one of only a few which bring the many disparate elements of the Ruqayya shrine's past together into a single narrative. Ibn al-Hawrani does this topographically – by confirming that the Mosque of Bab al-Faradis was located inside the wall and that it was the same as the Mashhad al-Husayn, and also by implying this locale had a connection to Ruqayya. As is appropriate in a pilgrimage guide, he also emphasises the shrine's status as a place of baraka and a beloved destination for pilgrimage and supplication. Thus, it seems that by the mid-sixteenth century the shrine to al-Husayn/Ruqayya, located inside the northern city wall at the Paradise Gate, was an established and venerated Damascene holy site.

The shrine appears as a regular feature of city topographies and pilgrim's guides in subsequent centuries, but little new information is added.[24] In the modern era, the historian Asʿad Talas wrote an addendum to his edition of Ibn al-Mibrad's *Thimar al-Maqasid fi Dhikr al-Masajid*, published in 1943. This addendum provides insight into the later history of the shrine, for it gives a detailed description of the mosque of Sayyida Ruqayya before its recent total renovation. From his description it would seem that much of the medieval fabric remained well into the twentieth century. Talas describes an 'attractive mosque' with a door made of black stone. Entering the door, one passed through a small courtyard (or hall, *nahwa*) which had two doors, one of which led to the caretaker's quarters and one which led to the mosque and shrine of Ruqayya. The most notable features of the mosque, according to Talas, were three inscribed stone markers next to the *mihrab*. The first of these markers commemorated the act of placing a store into *waqf* (a religious endowment) for the benefit of the shrine. This action was taken in the year 1713 by a figure titled His Excellency al-Tawfiq al-Mirza Baba al-Mustawfi al-Kilani. The second marker is a tombstone for al-Malik al-Kamil, the Ayyubid ruler whose head, as previously noted, was buried in the shrine in the thirteenth century. The text of this inscription recorded the burial of al-Kamil's remains in 'this *mashhad* al-Husayni in Bab al-Faradis in ... 888 (1483)'. And on the third tablet, according to Talas, there were four verses of poetry he was unable to read. Perhaps most importantly, Talas gives some further information about the shrine's physical structure:

> In the mosque is an ordinary *mihrab* and *minbar*. As for the dome of the tomb, it is old, (its form is) after the pattern of Mamluk domes (*min tiraz qubab al-mamalik*), but it has been renovated and painted. The tomb is encircled by (a structure made of) decorated brass, and next to it is a stone (*sakhra*), which is said to be from ʿAsir (in Arabia near the border with Yemen), which bears the imprint of the foot of the Prophet PBUH.[25]

From Talas's entry we may surmise the following about this building, as it existed in the 1940s, prior to the contemporary Iranian renovation. It seems it consisted of three separate structures: a mosque, a tomb and caretaker's quarters, enclosed within a single complex accessed through a small courtyard. The main entrance gate had a stone door of some monumentality, the tomb had a dome that may have dated to the Mamluk period and below the dome was a decorated brass enclosure marking the grave, as well as a stone with the footprint of the Prophet. The mosque had an unremarkable *miḥrāb* and *minbar*, and contained three inscribed stone tablets which Talas specifies were located near the *miḥrāb*.

Many of these details accord with the information provided from the primary sources, and bring into focus a number of the elements that have surfaced intermittently in the work of medieval scholars. While the shrine had commemorated al-Husayn from at least the beginning of the thirteenth century (according to al-Harawi), the first author to specify that Husayn's head was buried in the mosque was Ibn Shakir al-Kutubi in the late fourteenth century. Several medieval writers, beginning with Ibn Shaddad already in the late thirteenth century, reported the burial of the Ayyubid al-Kamil's head in the arch next to the *miḥrāb* of the mosque. Ibn Shaddad also specified that the shrine was devoted to Ruqayya, so we may be sure she was revered there, along with al-Husayn, by the early Mamluk era. Furthermore, a number of these authors indicated the head of al-Husayn, and/or of the Ayyubid sovereign, were buried in an 'arch' to the right of the *miḥrāb*: in other words, in the same location as the stone markers noted by Talas in the modern era.

Ibn Shakir also verifies the shrine had an underground canal, implying the presence of the courtyard Talas described, and that the tomb was surrounded by a *maqsūra* or tomb enclosure, as it seems to have been in the modern era. Some time before the sixteenth century, according to the notice of Ibn al-Mibrad, the black rock with the imprint of the Prophet's foot was added to the shrine. And, around the same time, Ibn al-Hawrani specified that the shrine had an endowment in perpetuity for its upkeep, confirming the interest of local patrons and foreign pilgrims that was once again to be reinforced, according to Talas, with the contribution of the patron al-Kilani, recorded on one of the stone tablets in the mosque and dated 1713. Thus the period of greatest efflorescence of the mosque of Sayyida Ruqayya/al-Husayn was the Mamluk era, and the modest mosque and tomb structure built at that time was probably the one that remained – no doubt having undergone numerous restorations – until late in the twentieth century. Then, it would be transformed physically beyond recognition and lose its traditional affiliation with al-Husayn and the footprint of the Prophet. As Yasser Tabbaa has shown, that process, initiated in the mid-1970s by former Syrian President Hafez al-Assad, demolished several city blocks inside the UNESCO-protected quarter of al-ʿAmara in the old city, including two medieval madrasas and dozens of shops and homes. This profound alteration of the quarter continued into the 1990s and even the early 2000s, when the site was expanded to include several new Shiʿi religious schools. As Tabbaa has shown, despite the seeming ease of integration of the shrine into the religious life of the city today, in fact, its transformation was heavily contested and challenged by a range of Syrian actors.[26] Nevertheless, despite the complexity of its past, today it has begun a new life devoted to al-Husayn's daughter alone, the Lady Ruqayya.

Let us turn now to see how another Mashhad al-Husayn – this one located just a few short steps from Ruqayya's shrine – fared over the centuries.

Mashhad al-Husayn/Mashhad 'Ali b. al-Husayn (Imam Zayn al-'Abidin), Umayyad mosque

The vast Umayyad mosque is one of the masterworks of Islamic architecture. Built within the *temenos* of the former Roman temple and utilising its inner curtain wall, the mosque was the largest in the Islamic lands in its day. Today, as in the medieval period, to reach the mosque from the shrine of Sayyida Ruqayya, our pilgrim need only make a brief five-minute walk through the twisting alleyways of the old city (Map 3). Exiting the gate of Ruqayya's shrine, she turns southwards down a busy market street, passing more shops selling cloth, souvenirs and trinkets designed to appeal to pilgrims. At the first corner, perhaps 50m from the southernmost extension of the Shi'i shrine and adjoining the historic Hamam al-Silsila, she encounters a bakery, endowed by the founder of a local Sunni *madrasa*, its employees the students at the school. Turning west, the market street continues. A little further along on her left, she passes near the walls of the crumbling Mamluk *Madrasa* al-Ikhna'iyya. At its western end, a passageway opens up to the south.[27] This passageway is wedged between the wall of the Ikhna'iyya school and the striking *ablaq* masonry of another Mamluk-era *madrasa*, the Jaqmaqiyya, restored and converted to serve today as the Museum of Arabic Calligraphy. Entering the passage, the tomb of Saladin may be seen to the right, across a small courtyard decorated with *spolia*. In front of her is the northern entrance of the Umayyad mosque, guarded by tall brass-plated doors and crowned by the low, square Minaret of the Bride. Removing her shoes, she enters the gate of the mosque, and immediately the noise, dust and crowds of the market are behind her. Now, the view is of a serenely pillared portico, its columns endlessly replicating themselves as they stretch out on either side (Fig. 4.5). She looks ahead into a vast courtyard paved in white marble and usually crowded with visitors. Across this courtyard, on its southern façade, her gaze is drawn upwards by the luminous gold and green mosaic that ornaments the face of the transept of the prayer hall (Fig. 4.6). Entering the courtyard and turning left, she walks along the columns of the portico. Ahead and slightly to the right, she can see the monumental eastern exit of the Umayyad mosque, the Bab Jayrun. Directly ahead of her, at the northern end of the east wall of the mosque, is a door, its surround decorated in an exuberant neo-classical style often (anachronistically) called 'Ottoman Baroque' (Fig. 4.7). The area in front of it is nearly always teeming with

Figure 4.5 *Portico in the courtyard of the Umayyad mosque, gathering of pilgrims in foreground. Photo: Author*

Figure 4.6 *Transept of the prayer hall, Umayyad mosque. Photo: Author*

Figure 4.7 *Shiʿi flagellants during Muharram procession, entering the shrine of al-Husayn and Zayn al-ʿAbidin, Umayyad mosque. Photo: Author*

Figure 4.8 *Inscription over entrance to the shrine of al-Husayn and Zayn al-'Abidin, Umayyad mosque. Photo: Author*

pilgrims and local worshippers. Above the door is a large marble inscription band, which proclaims (Fig. 4.8):

> Within this shrine (*mashhad*) is the mausoleum (*marqad*) of the head of our Lord the Imam Abi 'Abdallah al-Husayn (may God be pleased with him).

Below this inscription, attached to the elegant Ottoman stained glass window that ornaments the tympanum of the arch above the door, is a smaller, black metal sign that reinforces this announcement. It reads simply: 'this is the shrine (*maqām*) of the head of our lord al-Husayn (PBUH)'. Pushing her way through the crowd of worshippers, she enters a large, unremarkable, rectangular prayer hall, panelled with marble and with a modest *mihrāb* (Fig. 4.9). Also ahead of her, in the east wall of this room, is another door, and when she passes through she is in a tall-ceilinged, narrow hallway with small *mihrāb* at its southern end (Fig. 4.10). On its eastern side, against the wall, is a modestly ornamented wooden and glass Ottoman enclosure devoted to Zayn al-'Abidin, which also shelters a *mihrāb* (Fig. 4.11). To the south of this enclosure, in the same wall and located at about chest height, is a cubical, heavily ornamented, silver-lined niche (Fig. 4.12). A few steps past the niche, she again finds a doorway in the eastern wall. Entering this doorway, her journey is complete. She is in a small, domed room. Above her, arched windows in the drum of the dome let in daylight (Fig. 4.13). Another small *mihrāb* graces the southern wall. In the north-west corner of the room is a heavily decorated silver tomb enclosure, enshrining the place where al-Husayn's head either rested or was buried, according to different accounts (Fig. 4.14).

By the twelfth century, the Mashhad al-Husayn in the Umayyad mosque was already an established shrine. Ibn 'Asakir (d. 1176) wrote the following:

Figure 4.9 *Prayer hall, shrine of al-Husayn and Zayn al-ʿAbidin, Umayyad mosque. Photo: Author*

Figure 4.10 *Second prayer hall, shrine of al-Husayn and Zayn al-ʿAbidin, Umayyad mosque. Shrine of Zayn al-ʿAbidin is the glass-walled enclosure on left, while the niche where al-Husayn's head rested is just beyond it, where a pilgrim is inserting her hand. The entrance to the main shrine is just past the head-niche on left. Photo: Author*

Figure 4.11 *Ottoman-era enclosure for Zayn al-ʿAbidin.* Miḥrāb *is visible inside, on right. Photo: Author*

Figure 4.12 *Child placing head into niche where head of al-Husayn rested. Photo: Author*

Figure 4.13 *Dome of Mashhad al-Husayn, Umayyad mosque.*
Photo: Author

Figure 4.14 *Main shrine area and enclosure marking the place*
where al-Husayn's head rested. Photo: Author

> A mosque at the door of the Congregational Mosque, known as the Mashhad al-Ra's. It has a canal, and they say the head of al-Husayn ibn 'Ali (upon him be peace) was placed in it when it was brought to Damascus. It has an imam and a *waqf*.[28]

While Ibn 'Asakir is the earliest source to record the shrine, his mention of the provision of the building with an imam and a *waqf* reveals that the Mashhad al-Husayn was an important holy locale, for it had already benefited from the generous patronage of some unknown individual. Some time before the end of the twelfth century, then, we can say with certainty that this site was already revered and visited by pilgrims and, if the presence of the imam is any indicator, that prayers were held there. At around the same time, the shrine also had a more complex identity. Ibn 'Asakir's contemporary, the pilgrimage guide author al-Harawi (d. 1215), noted that 'inside the Congregational mosque, in its eastern portion, is . . . the shrine of 'Ali ibn Abi Talib, the shrine of al-Husayn and the shrine of ('Ali) Zayn al-'Abidin'.[29] This trio of grandfather, father and son were also the first, third and fourth Imams, respectively, of the Shi'a.

While al-Harawi frequently emphasises Shi'i places of pilgrimage, he was not the only author to invoke multiple figures in relation to this site. Consistently, the sources are somewhat equivocal as to the identities of the holy figures revered in the eastern portion of the Umayyad mosque. For example, the next person to mention one of these figures was another early-twelfth-century traveller, the Spanish pilgrim Ibn Jubayr. He visited Damascus in 1184.[30] As usual, his account is a colourful one, full of pious annoyance at what he perceives to be the deviations of the believers:

> On the eastern side of the courtyard (of the Umayyad mosque) a door gives access to an oratory, the most beautiful in the world, the most magnificently situated and the most perfectly constructed, which the Shi'a pretend is a monument to the presence of 'Ali b. Abi Talib – but this is one of their most ridiculous inventions. Even more extraordinary: facing this monument on the west side, in the corner of the north gallery of the courtyard, just where the end of the north gallery meets the beginning of the west gallery, is a place which is covered with a veil . . . many people imagine that 'A'isha sits there, in order to teach *ḥadīth*. Now, the presence of 'A'isha in Damascus is (about as likely as) that of 'Ali, except that for him, there was an apparent explanation in legend: he was seen in a dream, praying in that place, and thus the Shi'a built an oratory there. As for the place to which the name of 'A'isha is attached, it has no validity, we spoke of it only for the renown that it enjoys in the mosque.[31]

A few pages later, Ibn Jubayr also mentions the Mashhad al-Husayn, and in addition notes a shrine for the Umayyad Caliph 'Umar:

One exits (Bab Jayrun, the eastern gate of the mosque) onto a long paved porch . . . (enclosed by) six tall columns, and on the left side a vast monument (*mashhad*) has been raised, in which was once the head of al-Husayn ibn ʿAli, before it was transported to Cairo. Next to this (*bi-ʾizāʾihi*) is a small oratory (*masjid*) in the name of ʿUmar b. ʿAbd al-ʿAziz. This monument has running water.[32]

Ibn Jubayr's two descriptions are puzzling. They clearly record the presence of three monuments, one for the Caliph ʿUmar, one for ʿAli b. Abi Talib and one for al-Husayn, all located at the eastern end of the Umayyad mosque. Yet today there is evidence of only one of these: the shrine to al-Husayn, which also contains a small memorial for (ʿAli) Zayn al-ʿAbidin. Furthermore Ibn Jubayr's description of the *mashhad* for ʿAli, though dismissive of its historicity, is quite specific (not to mention effusive) in describing it as a remarkably beautiful and impressive site. Nevertheless, aside from the assertion that the shrine was located on the eastern side of the courtyard of the mosque, its precise location is not clear. This suggests two possibilities: that the shrine for ʿAli and the shrine for al-Husayn were the same shrine with two different names, or that they were two separate but adjoining shrines in the same location. Since it seems unlikely Ibn Jubayr would mention the two shrines as separate entities with no notice of a link between them, the shrines for ʿAli and the shrine for al-Husayn were probably two separate shrines. However their spatial relationship to each other has not yet been established. The shrine for al-Husayn, Ibn Jubayr expressly noted, is located just outside the eastern door of the Umayyad mosque (the Bab Jayrun), on the northern end of the Roman-era colonnaded propylaeum that once framed the door, and next to a shrine for the Caliph ʿUmar (no longer extant). The specificity of his account confirms that today's Husayn shrine is the same as the medieval one Ibn Jubayr described. The medieval locations of the glorious shrine to ʿAli and the shrine to ʿUmar, however, remain as yet unclear.

The next source to mention a shrine in the eastern part of the mosque is Ibn Shaddad (d. 1284). He describes the renovation of the 'Mashhad Zayn al-ʿAbidin ʿAli Ibn al-Husayn' at this location in the year 1269. The restoration was carried out, along with a general renovation of the mosque, by none other than the Mamluk sultan Baybars, whose regnal title was al-Malik al-Zahir (r. 1260–77). Ibn Shaddad's account – found in both his history of Damascus and his chronicle of the reign of al-Zahir Baybars – describes the circumstances that motivated the sultan's renovation of the mosque:

(Baybars) was praying (in the Umayyad mosque) after the (Friday) prayer, and he took a walk around it. He saw that the marble of the southern wall had become filthy and that the mosaic that was between it and the gallery was disintegrating. He ordered it all to be repaired: that the columns be washed and their capitals gilded, that the marble that needed replacing should be replaced, and the panelling of the northern wall (which had not previously been panelled) be panelled with marble after the manner of the southern wall, and he caused there to be marble on all sides. He expended on this more than 20,000 dinars.[33]

In addition, as Ibn Shaddad continues in his history of Damascus, Baybars

(re-) built (banā) the mashhad of the Sayyid Zayn al-ʿAbidin, for it was in ruins. He entered it one night dressed in disguise, and he saw some people sleeping in it, and others living in it (wa-l-ākhirīn quyyāman). He ordered that those who had been living there be given an annual charitable stipend (wa ʾamara li-l-quyyām bi-ṣadaqa sanawiyya), and commanded that no one be allowed to live there. The people who had been living there for years were evicted, and no one remained except one man, whom (Baybars) saw was devoted to worship and diligent to such a degree that he could not be turned away. Each person who had lived in (the shrine) had marked out his space and cordoned it off, and built within it a hut and surrounded it with a fence, such that (the shrine) appeared as though it were a khān (caravanserai).[34]

This entertaining story conforms to a popular topos, that of the conscientious ruler visiting his subjects in disguise in order to find out the truth of their situation.[35] But it also gives us a considerable amount of concrete information about a major restoration of the Umayyad mosque and of the shrine of Zayn al-ʿAbidin within it. Finding the mosque in a state of disrepair, the Sultan Baybars decided to use it as an opportunity to both renovate and improve the revered building. Baybars is well known for his extensive building programme, and it is logical that he would also wish to leave his mark on this most famous of Islamic mosques; however it is not obvious that the Sunni ruler should so enthusiastically renovate a shrine for one of the twelve Shiʿi Imams.

Furthermore, the story of Baybars' undercover night visit to the shrine, if true, reveals a desire to make a well-informed decision about the situation of the shrine's inhabitants before embarking on the renovation. Even if not true, it reveals his wish to *appear* to be such a conscientious ruler. From Ibn Shaddad's account it seems Baybars probably became aware of the shrine's disgraceful state when he made his tour around the Umayyad mosque. Probably during the royal tour the shrine had been cleared of its denizens, but following the description of Ibn Shaddad it seems the sultan could see that shrine had been cordoned off to create separately enclosed living quarters for multiple individuals and families, giving it the aspect of a *khan*: a hotel or caravanserai, piled high with goods. Baybars saw the shrine's state of disrepair and apparently decided to return at night to see its real circumstances. Finding it full of poor people, he provided them with a stipend and ordered that they be evicted. Then, as the source says, he 'built' (*banā*) the shrine.

The use of the word *banā* to describe Baybars' action is intriguing, for Ibn Shaddad is usually quite specific when describing the actions of patrons and donors. For example, the entry following that for the Mashhad Zayn al-ʿAbidin specifies that Baybars 'ordered the renovation' (*amara bi-tajdīd*) of another structure, and in his description of Baybars' work in the Umayyad mosque Ibn Shaddad consistently uses the verb *ṣalaḥa* (to repair).[36] Thus the use of the word *banā* was likely meant to indicate Baybars rebuilt this structure anew.

This speculation is strengthened by details of the shrine's architecture (Fig. 4.13), which indicate that the shrine of the head of al-Husayn is a Mamluk structure and that it may well be the original Mashhad Zayn al-ʿAbidin built by Baybars. The shrine is a small, single-room domed structure. As noted above, it is attached on its western side to a small prayer hall, which is, in turn, built directly onto the exterior of the original Roman temple wall (Fig. 4.15). The Roman wall was the eastern wall of the mosque courtyard. On its southern side, the shrine's eastern and western corners are, in fact, the west wall and the corner bastion of the Roman propylaeum. This is the same propylaeum that was still standing in Ibn Jubayr's day, that he described as having six columns and five doors (see above) and which was the location, for a brief period in the twelfth century, of a famous mechanical water clock.[37] The shrine has a slightly rectangular plan, its dome supported by the north and south walls and by two arches erected on the east and west. The low, pointed dome is set back quite far inside a high drum with very thick walls (Figs 4.13, 4.16 and 4.17). The walls of the drum are pierced by eight narrow, deep-set, arched windows. The top edge of this drum has a rather unusual feature on the exterior: a kind of gently curving, v-shaped indentation between each of the windows. This gives the roof of the drum a subtly scalloped appearance against the green of the dome behind it.

A parallel for this building is the mausoleum of the Qalandariyya, located next to the shrine of Sayyida Ruqayya in the cemetery of Bab al-Saghir and discussed in Chapter 3 (Figs 3.17 and 3.18). It was also commissioned by the Sultan al-Zahir Baybars, and it too consists of a single domed room set on squinches. Though a slightly larger building, the Qalandariyya's walls are also extremely thick and the dome sits on a high drum pierced by windows on all sides. Baybars' interest in the mausoleum of the Qalandariyya seems to have been personal and pious, an effort to support a beloved shaykh. However the Qalandariyya mausoleum and other projects commissioned by the sultan also demonstrate that Baybars had a broader

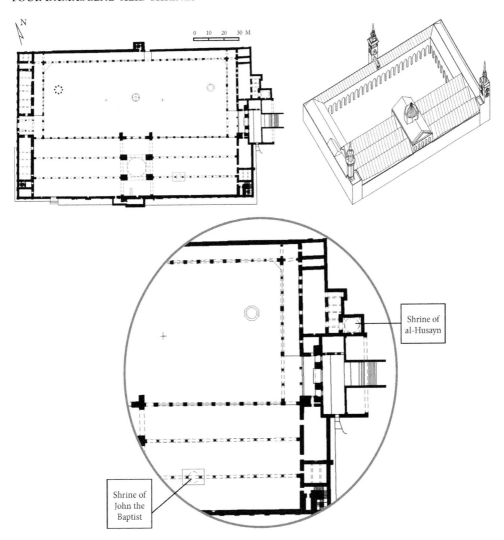

Figure 4.15 *Plan, Umayyad mosque, with detail of north-east corner showing Bab Jayrun and the shrine of al-Husayn just to the north of the gate. Original illustrations: Nasser Rabbat/Aga Khan Program for Islamic Architecture, MIT, found on ArchNet at http://archnet.org/library/images/one-image.jsp?location_id=8854&image_id=150431 and http://archnet.org/library/images/one-image.jsp?location_id=8854&image_ id=150432*

interest in promoting pilgrimage generally and the shrines of the Prophet's family and companions in particular.[38] These parallels lend further weight to the proposition that the building we see today in the Umayyad mosque is to be dated to Baybars' restoration. If the present Mashhad al-Husayn is attributed to this Sunni sovereign, then it, too, joins the ranks of buildings built by prominent Sunnis to commemorate members of the Prophet's family. Furthermore, it

Figure 4.16 *View of eastern side of Umayyad mosque. Dome of Mashhad al-Husayn is visible below wall, just right of centre. Photo: Author*

is important to remember that when he commissioned the building it was not dedicated to al-Husayn, who is broadly revered by Sunnis, but to al-Husayn's son ʿAli Zayn al-ʿAbidin, the fourth Imam of the Shiʿa. Thus Baybars' act of patronage for a Shiʿi figure had a markedly supra-sectarian quality.

The next source to speak of the shrine presents concrete information about the locations of the shrines at the eastern end of the Umayyad mosque. This informant is Ibn Shakir al-Kutubi, a Syrian historian, who died in 1363. A lifelong resident of Damascus, Ibn Shakir is a reliable source with respect to the placement of the various shrines. Here is his notice regarding the buildings at the eastern end of the mosque, outside the Bab Jayrun:

> A mosque at (Bab) Jayrun, between the two doors, small. John b. Zacharias, peace be upon them both, was decapitated there, or so they say. Prayers which are said there are answered.
> A mosque on the fountain (*fawwāra*) stairs, they call it the Mosque of ʿUmar, may God be pleased with him. It was built by a Persian because of a vision he had.

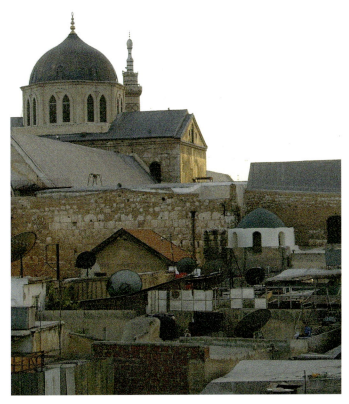

Figure 4.17 *Dome of Mashhad al-Husayn, centre right below wall.*
Photo: Author

> Behind the aforementioned (mosque) is one known by the name
> Mashhad al-Ra's, it has a canal. It is said that the head of al-
> Husayn, the son of 'Ali, may blessings be upon them both, rested
> there when it was brought to Damascus. Its door opens facing the
> Gate of the Clock (Bab al-Sa'at); it is presently blocked. It was
> annexed to the Mashhad 'Ali, PBUH.[39]

Here, Ibn Shakir introduces a new shrine, one devoted to John the
Baptist.[40] This shrine – an analogue for the Mashhad al-Husayn
in that both memorialise the decapitation of their respective holy
figures – serves as the starting point for Ibn Shakir's description.
He would not be the last medieval writer to make the connection
between the two, however. The Mamluk al-Qalqashandi (d. 1418)
recorded that the head of al-Husayn was intentionally placed outside
the door, the same location that John the Baptist's head had rested
after his death.[41] In fact, the 'Bab' Jayrun indeed is composed of two
doors, and the wide space between them could once have accommodated a small shrine. Today, this area is a large, open platform,

Figure 4.18 *Platform outside the Bab Jayrun, Umayyad mosque, view towards the north. Entrance to the mosque is on the left and stairs descending the Roman temenos are on the right (both out of view). Remains of one Roman column in foreground, other Roman architectural elements visible at top right. Just beyond the Corinthian capitals the edge of the dome of the shrine of al-Husayn may be seen. In the wall face directly ahead is a blocked doorway that may once have given access to the shrine. Photo: Author*

bordered on its eastern end by the squat remains of the six pillars of the colonnade that once formed the Roman temple gate and, as the colonnade was still extant in the twelfth century, where the famous mechanical water clock noted previously was installed (Fig. 4.18).[42] It was perhaps this colonnade that Ibn Shakir meant when he referred to the Gate of the Clock.

From this colonnade, the stairs of the Roman *temenos* descend. Today, shops and a venerable old *maqha* (coffee house) known as the Nawfara (fountain) Café are located on the stairs, and at the bottom of the stairs, in fact, a fountain still burbles. No trace of the mosque of ʿUmar remains on the stairs. But this is not the case with the rest of Ibn Shakir's description. Back up on the platform, the wall of the Husayn shrine forms the northern terminus the platform. There, in the wall, a blocked door is visible. This door seems to correspond directly with the intermediary hall of the Mashhad al-Husayn, located between the large hall nearest to the mosque courtyard and the domed room furthest from it. This blocked door would have opened not 'facing' the Gate of the Clock, but rather perpendicular to it, between the outer curtain wall of the mosque and the colonnade. The domed portion of the shrine, then, must have been the Mashhad ʿAli, built by Baybars, to which the Mashhad al-Husayn was annexed. At some later date, the entire shrine was given over to al-Husayn and its original affiliation with ʿAli b. al-Husayn Zayn al-ʿAbidin was forgotten.

This account is strengthened a short time later by the traveller Ibn Battuta (d. 1377), who confirms the presence of the spacious platform, the colonnade, the *mashhad* al-Husayn on the left and, next to it, the mosque of ʿUmar.[43] Later, in the fifteenth century, it was noted by both Ibn Shahin al-Zahiri and Ibn al-Mibrad,[44] who called it the Mashhad al-Raʾs and the Mashhad al-Husayn, respectively. Ibn al-Mibrad adds that it had a canal and an imam and, in a separate entry on the shrine, that there was also a shrine to ʿAli Ibn Abi Talib in the same part of the mosque. This shrine has not been mentioned since the report of Ibn Shaddad in the thirteenth century, and it is not clear how reliable this notation is.[45] Its sporadic mention makes it seem possible that the *mashhad* attributed to ʿAli b. Abi Talib was a confusion with the shrine for ʿAli Zayn al-ʿAbidin, however the fact that Ibn al-Mibrad mentions all three *mashhad*s, one after the other, is an indication that there were likely three separate *mashhad*s (one for ʿAli b. Abi Talib, one for al-Husayn and one for ʿAli Zayn al-ʿAbidin) in the eastern part of the mosque.[46]

The next writer to take notice of the *mashhad*s in the eastern corner of the Umayyad mosque is the historian and topographer al-Nuʿaymi (d. 1521). Much of Nuʿaymi's account is a compilation of previous scholars' work,[47] which means he reports sometimes-conflicting information. However, he does offer some new information about the shrine of ʿAli, as he calls it, in his time.

But first, he presents a bit of older evidence. He begins his account with a brief but entertaining anecdote that sheds light on the popular appeal of this site of pilgrimage. Apparently, in the early thirteenth century, the Shaykh Shams al-Din Sibt Ibn al-Jawzi (d. 1256) used to hold a preaching session every Saturday morning at a column in front of the Mashhad ʿAli Zayn al-ʿAbidin, and – like fans anxious for tickets to hear a favourite band – 'the people used to sleep in the mosque on Friday nights (in order to be able to hear him)'.[48] This quotation reflects the enormous celebrity of some preachers, who must have attracted the kinds of crowds, and apparently the kind of crowd behaviour, reserved today for rock musicians. Indeed, Ibn al-Jawzi's fame in his day rested not on his historical works, but on his eloquence as a preacher, 'moving crowds and princes to tears, urging them to take part in the Holy War, protesting against the giving up of Jerusalem to the Franks, etc'.[49] That the famed preacher, scholar and historian (author of the voluminous universal history the *Mirʾat al-zaman*) would preach at this site may merely be a reflection of the *mashhad*'s location within the Umayyad mosque. However, that it was this holy site, and not one of the several others situated within the mosque (for example, the *maqam* of ʿAʾisha), which Sibt Ibn al-Jawzi chose as his preaching place, is surely also evidence of the Mashhad Zayn al-ʿAbidin's prominence.

Among the earlier writers al-Nuʿaymi cites is the historian Ibn Kathir (d. 1373), who had reported on a restoration to 'the shrine of ʿAli', by which he seems to mean the shrine of ʿAli b. Abi Talib. Here, with Ibn Kathir as his source, al-Nuʿaymi describes the early thirteenth-century transformation of the Mashhad ʿAli into what came to be known as the Dar al-Hadith al-ʿUrwiya or the Mashhad ʿUrwa:

> [Located] . . . on the eastern side of the courtyard of the Umayyad mosque . . . and known in the past as Mashhad ʿAli, may God have mercy upon him. The *ḥāfiẓ* ʿImad al-Din Ibn Kathir recorded . . . for the year 620 (1223) (the obituary of) . . . Sharaf al-Din Muhammad ibn ʿUrwa al-Mawsali. The Mashhad Ibn ʿUrwa in the Umayyad mosque is named after him because he was the first to (re-)open it: for it had been loaded up with the equipment of the mosque. He built the pool (*birka*) in it and provided in the *waqf* of the (Dar al-)Hadith for lessons (*durūs*) and also for its library of books. He had been living in Jerusalem, and was among the most important of the companions of (the Ayyubid Sultan) al-Malik al-Muʿazzam, and he moved to Damascus when the wall of Jerusalem was destroyed . . .[50]

Al-Nuʿaymi continues to say that one of the most important shaykhs of the day was appointed to teach there.[51] The work at the Dar al-Hadith al-ʿUrwiya must have been completed some time between 1200 and the year of Ibn ʿUrwa's death in 1223, for al-Nuʿaymi says it was not yet completed by the first date, when the shaykh passed away before work had finished.[52]

This quotation is notable because we learn that the Mashhad ʿAli underwent a significant restoration less than fifty years before the work of Baybars (discussed above, restored in 1269) on the nearby

Mashhad Zayn al-ʿAbidin. Therefore it seems these shrines attracted repeated, and intensive, patronage during the Mamluk and Ayyubid eras. It is also noteworthy that the person who restored it, Sharaf al-Din Ibn ʿUrwa, was a member of the close coterie of the Ayyubid sultan. Thus, we have evidence of yet another Sunni patron investing in this holy site. The passage also hints at what we might assume to be the usual lifespan for even such a well-known holy site: for if Baybars were appalled at the general condition of the mosque and its shrines in the late thirteenth century, it means that the work of the Ayyubid Ibn ʿUrwa lasted little less than fifty years.

However, the Mamluk Sultan Baybars' restoration apparently endured a bit longer than that of Ibn ʿUrwa, for al-Nuʿaymi also reports that about 130 years later, the Umayyad mosque and its shrines were pillaged during Tamerlane's siege on Damascus in 1401. The shrines were closed and not reopened until nearly thirty years later, in 1429. Then, another patron, who is not named but who, from the dates, is certainly the Mamluk Sultan al-Malik al-Ashraf Barsabay (r. 1422–38), issued a sultanal decree for the restoration of the mosque which included 'some construction' in 'the two eastern *mashhad*s'.[53] This specific mention of 'two' eastern *mashhad*s, presumably the two remaining today (al-Husayn and Zayn al-ʿAbidin), suggests that the siege of Tamerlane perhaps destroyed the Mashhad Ibn ʿUrwa for good. Indeed, it is not mentioned again in the sources.

Only a few later medieval sources mention the *mashhad*s, for example the pilgrimage guide author Ibn al-Hawrani,[54] and they provide little further information. But the sources up to the mid-sixteenth century have provided a vivid picture of the medieval history of the most important shrines in the eastern portion of the Umayyad mosque: the Mashhad al-Husayn/Mashhad ʿAli Zayn al-ʿAbidin, and the Mashhad ʿAli ibn Abi Talib/Ibn ʿUrwa (Table 4.1). Only the location and designation of the Mashhad ʿAli/Ibn ʿUrwa remains somewhat unclear. While it is possible that this shrine's attribution to the Umayyad mosque represents some confusion with the Mashhad ʿAli Zayn al-ʿAbidin, at least three descriptions of the shrines (those of Ibn Jubayr, Ibn Shaddad and Ibn al-Mibrad) list them in sequence and suggest they were present simultaneously and located in the same part of the mosque. Thus they are likely to have been separate and distinct sites. Indeed, the Mashhad ʿAli b. Abi Talib was a prominent shrine in the medieval period. Ibn Jubayr's description of it as a truly magnificent building in the late twelfth century indicates it had already been generously endowed by his day, and it was only shortly thereafter, between 1200 and 1223, that it was once again enlarged and expanded by Ibn ʿUrwa. And yet, it seems that the Mashhad ʿUrwa disappeared at some later date: perhaps by the time of Baybars' work on the nearby Mashhad Zayn al-ʿAbidin around fifty years later, when it is not mentioned, or perhaps during the depredations of Tamerlane at the beginning of the fifteenth century.

Table 4.1 Lifespan of mashāhid located in the eastern part of the Umayyad mosque

Mashhad Name	500s/1100s	600s/1200s	700s/1300s	800s/1400s	900s/1500s
Husayn/Zayn al-ʿAbidin	al-Husayn first mentioned before 572/1172 [Ibn ʿAsakir]; al-Husayn visited in 580/1184 [Ibn Jubayr]	Zayn al-ʿAbidin first mentioned & both shrines visited before 611/1215 [al-Harawi]; Baybars restored 668/1269 [Ibn Shaddad]	Noted some time before 764/1363 [Ibn Shakir al-Kutubi]; again before 779/1377 [Ibn Battuta]	Restored 883/1429 (al-Nuʿaymi); noted again before 872/1468 [Ibn Shahin al-Zahiri]	Noted before 908/1503 [Ibn al-Mibrad]; again before 927/1521 (al-Nuʿaymi); visited before 970/1562 [Ibn al-Hawrani]
ʿAli/ʿUrwa	ʿAli first mentioned in 580/1184 [Ibn Jubayr]	ʿAli visited before 611/1215 [al-Harawi]; Renovated & renamed Mashhad ʿUrwa some time between 597/1200 and 620/1223 [al-Nuʿaymi]			Questionable notation before 908/1503 [Ibn al-Mibrad: but direct copy of al-Harawi [d. 611/1215]]; Possibly present before 927/1503 (al-Nuʿaymi)
ʿUmar	First mentioned before 572/1172 [Ibn ʿAsakir]; visited 580/1184 [Ibn Jubayr]	Visited before 611/1215 [al-Harawi]; noted by Ibn Shaddad (before 685/1284)	Still present before 764/1363 [Ibn Shakir al-Kutubi]; noted again before 779/1377 [Ibn Battuta]		Questionable notation before 908/1503 [Ibn al-Mibrad: but direct copy of al-Harawi [d. 611/1215]]
John the Baptist			Only mention: before 764/1363 [Ibn Shakir al-Kutubi]		

In this respect, it shared the fate of two other shrines which had an ephemeral presence in the eastern portion of the Umayyad mosque: the *mashhad* for the Umayyad Caliph ʿUmar ibn al-Khattab, and the *mashhad* for John the Baptist, neither of which can be given solid provenience in the mosque as independent structures after their last descriptions in the fourteenth centuries.

The Mashhad al-Husayn/Zayn al-ʿAbidin, however, remains until the present day. The Mashhad al-Husayn appears to be the oldest of the Shiʿi holy places in the Umayyad mosque, first described in the twelfth century by the historian Ibn ʿAsakir. Since at that date it already had a canal, an imam and a *waqf*, we may presume it had previously benefited from the generosity of an unknown patron. At nearly the same time – following the effusive description of Ibn Jubayr, who visited Damascus in 1184 – the shrine was described as 'a vast monument'. It seems likely that the building Ibn Jubayr saw reflected that same prior act of patronage. Shortly thereafter, according to al-Harawi, near the beginning of the thirteenth centuries, this shrine was for the first time closely linked, if not sharing the same space, with a shrine to the fourth Shiʿi Imam Zayn al-ʿAbidin. Nevertheless, just over fifty years later, in 1269, the impressive shrine had fallen into ruin, as witnessed by the Mamluk Sultan Baybars. It was that same year that he rebuilt the holy place and contributed generously to its *waqf*s. Baybars' shrine endured until the siege of Damascus by Tamerlane in 1401. Damage to the shrine was apparently so severe that it was closed for nearly thirty years. Its restoration in the year 1429, which is probably to be attributed to the Mamluk Sultan al-Ashraf Barsabay, forms the final act of medieval patronage recorded in the sources.

In all, we may count seven acts of patronage in the medieval period for the shrines in the eastern part of the Umayyad mosque. These include the three endowments of unknown patronage in the late twelfth century for al-Husayn/Zayn al-ʿAbidin, ʿAli and ʿUmar; one for the conversion of ʿAli to the Mashhad ʿUrwa at the beginning of the thirteenth century; one for the rebuilding of Zayn al-ʿAbidin by Baybars in 1269; one more for its restoration by Barsabay in 1429; and one more unknown endowment for the founding of the short-lived shrine to John the Baptist outside the Bab Jayrun mentioned by Ibn Shakir in the early fourteenth century. From this information, we may draw several conclusions.

First, certainly two, and perhaps as many as five, of the seven endowments are clustered in a 100-year period between the late twelfth century and the late thirteenth century (Table 4.1). Even taking the most conservative estimate, acknowledging that the three inferred endowments are of unknown date, the apparently rather short lifespan of many of these shrine endowments probably stretches the time of patronage not much beyond the beginning of the twelfth century. This means that the most intensive episode of patronage activity occurred during the Zangid, Ayyubid and Mamluk periods. Second, we may be nearly certain the three known patrons (Ibn ʿUrwa, Baybars and Barsabay) were Sunni, for one was a close affiliate of the Ayyubid sultan, while the other two were Mamluk sultans. This pattern, of Sunni support for shrines that were particularly revered by the Shiʿa, accords well with evidence from other sites in medieval Syria.

Furthermore, considering the Sunnism of these patrons and the ostensibly highly charged sectarian environment of their contemporary religious milieu, it is illuminating to compare the very different fate of the Mashhad al-Husayn/Zayn al-ʿAbidin (a presumably 'Shiʿi' site) and the Mashhad ʿUmar (a clearly Sunni one). For the Sunni Zangid, Ayyubids, and Mamluks, it would seem logical to have supported the *mashhad* for the early Islamic Caliph ʿUmar – given his role as a beloved figure of early Sunni religious history (and much reviled by the Shiʿa for his usurpation of the rightful place of ʿAli as caliph). And yet, the opposite was the case. The shrine for ʿUmar is consistently described as small and unassuming, and it seems to have endured only a little over two centuries, founded probably some time near the beginning of the twelfth century and disappearing some time near the end of the fourteenth. As far as we know, with the exception of its presumed founding endowment it was never the beneficiary of any patron's purse.

By contrast, the Mashhad al-Husayn/Zayn al-ʿAbidin was repeatedly endowed, and by the most illustrious of patrons. Furthermore, the sources are unequivocal in describing it as a 'lofty' and 'magnificent' shrine, one that dazzled the eye of those who beheld it, and upon which lavish sums of money were expended in its continuous upkeep and beautification. Clearly, shrines such as those for al-Husayn and Zayn al-ʿAbidin were not seen as exclusive to one sect over another, or if they were, their patrons probably tried to coopt those associations and substitute for them a new, and perhaps more inclusive, set of meanings. The shrine of al-Husayn/Zayn al-ʿAbidin – the only holy place to survive today in this once-crowded corner of the Umayyad mosque – probably attracted its patrons because of its very semantic flexibility: its ability to be both a deeply individual expression of sectarian allegiance and, at the same time, a universal and neutral rallying point for the many diverse sects of the Islamic *umma*.[55]

In addition to these shrines located in the heart of the urban fabric, Imam ʿAli and his descendants were also venerated at sites on the outskirts of the city of Damascus. Two of these shrines were of particular prominence: the Mashhad ʿAli and the Mashhad Sayyida Zaynab. But like the many shrines of the Umayyad mosque, they each had very different fates. Today, one has disappeared so completely that we can only speculate as to its location, while the other has become the most important Shiʿi shrine in Syria.

Mashhad 'Ali/Mashhad al-Naranj/Mashhad al-Hajar

Our pilgrim, were she to continue on foot from the shrine of al-Husayn in the Umayyad mosque, could probably walk to the location of the medieval Mashhad 'Ali south of the city within half an hour. Leaving the mosque via its eastern gate (the Bab Jayrun), she turns right, walking briefly south along the vast monument's east wall, then turning left at the Minaret of Jesus on its south-east corner (Map 3). From there, she follows the *qibla* wall of the mosque westwards, passing the Roman temple enclosure's door (now blocked) and continuing until she arrives at the present south door of the mosque located west of the *miḥrāb*, which is open at prayer time. Facing this door is a wide and airy market lane, hung with grapevines, its walls lined with the luminous merchandise of the gold *sūq*: necklaces, earrings, chains and bracelets shimmering under bright lights behind the many stalls' glass windows. Continuing onwards, gold melts into spices, soap, sweets and multi-coloured dried fruit as she passes through the aromatic, covered Suq al-Buzuriyya, or spice market. As she walks, on her left, she goes by the Hammam Nur al-Din, the public bath built by the famous Zangid ruler of Syria in 1172. A few steps further, and she sees the elaborately decorated *muqarnas* portal of the Khan As'ad Pasha (1752–3), one of Damascus's most striking caravanserais, again on her left.

Continuing ahead after crossing the Suq Medhat Pasha (called in the Bible Straight Street), she eventually comes to Bab al-Saghir, the modest southern city gate located near the cemetery discussed in Chapter 3. Exiting via this gate, she walks south through the cemetery, past thousands of tombstones, a number of mosques, a *madrasa* and the domes of the many shrines – not only those sacred to the *ahl al-bayt* or Family of the Prophet, but to shaykhs, caliphs, scholars and other famous and holy figures. As she walks down the street, itinerant vendors call out to her, displaying their wares on all manner of makeshift wooden stands, hoping she will purchase their bolts of cloth, their soft drinks and sweets, or their postcards and other religious memorabilia. After going by the shrine of the Martyrs of Karbala' on the eastern side of the road, she comes to a small roundabout, at the centre of which is a patch of grass surrounding the unprepossessing grave of the famous Syrian historian Ibn 'Asakir (Map 4).

Continuing a bit past his grave, the cemetery becomes narrower and narrower until it finally ends in a kind of triangular area, connecting it to the road on the western side of the cemetery. Somewhere here, a few kilometres beyond the graveyard's southern end, was once the great *muṣalla* of Damascus, a large open space for prayer that provided additional area for the large crowds that would gather during festivals such as Ramadan. Nearby, although in the earliest sources it is not clear exactly where, was once located an important shrine for 'Ali b. Abi Talib, popularly known as the

Mashhad al-Naranj (Shrine of the Orange [Grove])[56] or, sometimes, the Mashhad al-Hajar (Shrine of the Stone). It no longer exists, but frequent notices in the work of medieval historians, chroniclers and topographers make clear that it was once a significant shrine.

Because the shrine no longer exists, it is necessary to reconstruct its location by inference and association based on the clues given in the sources. To begin, the earliest source, Ibn 'Asakir (d. 1176), records that in the twelfth century, the 'Mosque of the Stone (Hajar), known as Masjid al-Naranj' was located 'south of the *musalla* and a bit to the east of it'.[57] Thus, at the outset the topographer provides quite specific information about its location, provided the position of the *musalla* is known, and fortunately, it is. The *musalla* was located south-west of the cemetery, on the eastern side of the main road that took travellers south out of the city from the Bab al-Jabiya.[58] The location of the *musalla* is preserved today because in the early thirteenth century, the Ayyubid Sultan al-Malik al-'Adil Sayf al-Din built a mosque there, which still remains.[59] The mosque, aptly called the Jami' al-Musalla, can be found in the quarter of Midan, just north of the square called Sahat Bab al-Musalla. By way of a physical description of the shrine, Ibn 'Asakir gives a few brief but key details: 'It is large, it has a well and a fountain, and a minaret.'[60] From this sketchy notice we may glean that the shrine was probably a somewhat substantial mosque, probably with a courtyard to accommodate the well and fountain and the architectural presence to justify a *mihrab*.

At about the same time, Ibn 'Asakir's contemporary al-Harawi (d. 1215) adds a bit of colour and complexity to Ibn 'Asakir's stark description. Al-Harawi says that '(Damascus) contains the Shrine of the Orange (Mashhad al-Naranj) in which is a cleft rock (associated with) a story (involving) 'Ali ibn Abi Talib, may God be pleased with him.'[61] This is the first entry that associates the shrine with 'Ali, and also the first to record that it contained a 'cleft rock', but still, al-Harawi provides very little other information, about either the shrine, its architecture or the story about 'Ali.

In contrast, the traveller Ibn Jubayr (d. 1217) left a far more intriguing account when he visited the shrine at the end of the twelfth century. Here is his report, full of his usual scepticism towards all things Shi'i, but remarkably detailed:

> Among the most frequently visited (*ahfal*) of these monuments (to the *ahl al-bayt*) is one consecrated to 'Ali b. Abi Talib – may God be pleased with him – where there has been constructed an impressive oratory, of very beautiful architecture. Next to it is an orchard planted with oranges, watered by a canal of running water, which is especially for the mosque. All around on each of its faces veils are hung, large and small. In the *mihrab* there is an enormous stone that has been cracked in two: the stone was divided

so exactly in two halves that one cannot distinguish one from
the other. The Shiʿa pretend that it was split by ʿAli, by a stroke
of his sword or by some divine intervention realised by his hand.
Now, there is not a single report that ʿAli ever came to this city (of
Damascus). (They get around this) by saying that (he came there)
during his sleep. This dream-state perhaps gave them a certitude,
which the state of wakefulness could not give! It is this stone that
provoked the construction of the oratory.[62]

As is often the case, Ibn Jubayr's description will prove to be the most
comprehensive, and it therefore justifies a careful reading. According
to the traveller, at the end of the twelfth century the shrine was a
substantial and much-beloved monument. Ibn Jubayr makes special
mention of two features of the building: its 'impressive' and 'beautiful' architecture, and the fact that the shrine used fabric as part of
the architectural decoration, to cool the structure and shield the
worshippers from the sun.[63] The other notable aspect of the shrine
was its location within, or next to, a grove of oranges with its own
water supply. The focal point of the shrine was a stone that had been
split into two perfectly matching halves. The perfection of the two
halves, the Shiʿa believed, was evidence that it had been split by
ʿAli's legendary two-bladed sword Dhu al-Fikr, used at the Battle of
Karbalaʾ in 680 and a powerful symbol of honour and martyrdom.

These features together paint a picture of a shrine that was a very
important Damascene site of pilgrimage. It had clearly been the beneficiary of repeated acts of patronage, as is evident from the impres-
sion its beautiful architecture made on the medieval traveller Ibn
Jubayr. The presence of a minaret and particularly the assertion that
the shrine had its own water supply substantiate this picture of the
generosity of an unknown patron or patrons, for the funds for such
monumental features were generally reserved for significant endowments. This is particularly true of the canal that seems to have been
dug specifically to supply the shrine and its grove of oranges with
water. A private water supply is also a feature often associated with
buildings endowed by very wealthy patrons. In this case, the water
supply would have been even more substantial than usual, for not
only was it used for ablutions and a fountain in the courtyard of the
mosque, but it had also to be sufficient for the cultivation of the
grove of oranges.

The shrine was clearly popular and frequently visited. In addition
to Ibn Jubayr's straightforward assertion that this was so, evidence
comes also in the form of the textiles that adorned its walls and
doorways. The presence of such textiles could, perhaps, be said
to be one index of the prominence or popularity of a building, for
an Islamic building without them is probably an abandoned one.
Textiles, among the costliest of the luxury objects in the medieval
world, were donated to shrines, mosques and other holy places as

a sign of piety and a desire to further ornament revered buildings. The Mamluk Sultan Baybars, for example, made a charitable contribution each year to the shrine of Sayyida Sukayna (north of the Mashhad al-Naranj in the cemetery of Bab al-Saghir; see Chapter 3), which included a thousand dirhams, a stipend for its shaykh and his followers, and two carpets.[64] Wall hangings, while still costly, were perhaps often less so than carpets, and could have been within the reach of ordinary pilgrims or local residents of some means. In any case, as a perishable artefact such hangings would have had to be frequently replaced. Their presence suggests an ongoing form of both elite and popular patronage. If so, it is the only patronage we know of for this building, for despite the fact that it was clearly a beloved and much-visited shrine, not a single contributor is mentioned in any source. Nevertheless, a great deal of important information about the shrine and its location can be found among medieval scholars, chroniclers and historians.

This shrine is also interesting for being one of the 'Alid shrines in Syria containing a relic, in the form of the split stone. Sacred stones, particularly stones bearing traces of the past presence of a holy figure, have a prominent place among Islamic sites of visitation – indeed, the Ka'ba in Mecca itself is a shrine built around a black meteorite, the *hajar al-aswad* – and the kissing and caressing of this stone during the *hajj* (pilgrimage) is perhaps the definitive moment of the pilgrim's experience. Sacred stones as relics are not unknown in other civilisational contexts, but in the Islamic world this type of relic seems to appear especially frequently. Syria had a number of holy sites that had such stones as their central devotional object. In Damascus, in addition to the Mashhad al-Naranj, there was the stone bearing a footprint of the Prophet Muhammad at the shrine of Sayyida Ruqayya (discussed above) and a shrine south of the city called the Mashhad al-Qadam or Masjid al-Aqdam that was associated with a stone containing footprints of various prophets where Moses was purportedly buried (an assertion denied, however, by many medieval authors).[65]

In Aleppo, the Mashhad al-Husayn is today situated around a stone bearing the blood from the temporary emplacement there of the severed head of al-Husayn (although there is no evidence of its presence before the late twentieth century), and the Mashhad al-Muhassin was founded because a stone inscribed with the name of al-Muhassin b. al-Husayn b. 'Ali b. Abi Talib was found on the spot.[66] Outside the Bab al-Jinan in Aleppo, a man began digging one day on the instruction of 'Ali ibn Abi Talib, who had appeared to him in a dream. After a time, just as 'Ali had predicted, he unearthed a stone surrounded with soil exuding a powerful scent of musk. Thereafter a Mashhad 'Ali was located there. It was renowned for its curative properties.[67] Another shrine in Aleppo had a stone that was said to be inscribed in 'Ali's hand.[68] The theologically ambiguous position of such apparently pagan holy objects was neatly clarified by the early Islamic Caliph ʿUmar ibn al-Khattab when he said, in reference to the Black Stone in the Kaʿba: 'I know that thou art a stone, that neither helps (mankind) nor hurts, and if the messenger of Allah had not kissed thee, I would not kiss thee.' He then kissed the stone.[69] For ʿUmar, as for many Muslims who made visitation to such sites, holiness was clearly embodied in these objects because they had been touched or been in physical contact with a holy person. Pious believers like the Caliph ʿUmar were discomfited by the similarity between reverence for such stones and the practice of idolatry: the caliph was at pains to clarify that he did not associate any magical properties with the stone and only kissed it out of veneration for the example of the Prophet who had done so before him. But for many ordinary people, these stones, with their ability to create a direct, physical channel between the touch of the holy figure (their *baraka*) and that of the worshipper, were powerful talismans. A visit to them could provide redemption, repentance or cure. The presence of such a stone in the Mashhad al-Naranj further underscores its importance in the medieval period.

The next notice for the Mashhad al-Naranj comes at the end of the twelfth century, and is found in the topographical dictionary of Ibn Shaddad (d. 1284). However, this author and those who come later add little new information. Instead, they tend to repeat the short description by the pilgrimage guide author al-Harawi: that the *mashhad* had a split stone and that it was associated with a story involving ʿAli ibn Abi Talib.[70] One writer, however, al-Nuʿaymi (d. 1521), slightly nuances Ibn ʿAsakir's description of the location of the shrine and thereby helps to clarify it.[71] Al-Nuʿaymi notes that the main road to the side of the cemetery of Bab al-Saghir was the one 'taken to (*al-ākidh ilā*) the Mashhad al-Naranj'.[72] This suggests the building was famous enough to be used as a landmark and that the road was known primarily for its association with the shrine. However, the cemetery is bordered by two roads, and it is not immediately obvious to which the writer refers. From Ibn ʿAsakir (the first author to mention the shrine) came the information that the *mashhad* was near the *muṣalla*. Thus, it was likely the road to the west of the cemetery that was 'taken to the Mashhad '.

A bit later in his narrative, al-Nuʿaymi also notes two other nearby landmarks: the Masjid Khan al-Sabil and the Maydan al-Hasa.[73] This final piece of information helps considerably to narrow the topographical possibilities. The location of the first of these monuments, the Masjid Khan al-Sabil, is not clear. However, the Maydan al-Hasa is known. It was the Zangid-era hippodrome located south-west of the city, in the area known today as the quarter of Midan.[74] Leaving from the Bab al-Jabiya (at the south-west corner of the medieval city wall), the main road leading south is the one bordered on its east side by the cemetery of Bab al-Saghir (Map 3). The *maydan* was located on the western side of this road, a kilometre or two south of the cemetery, its long, narrow outline stretching north–south.

Thus, al-Nuʿaymi's notice defines a southern limit for the location of the shrine. Furthermore, this accords with the information provided by previous sources, which claimed the shrine was near the Mosque of the Musalla. The Mosque of the Musalla, as noted previously, is situated between the southern end of the cemetery and the northern end of the Maydan al-Hasa. Nearby, apparently in the area between the mosque and the *maydan*, the much beloved Mashhad al-Naranj sat, receiving pilgrims in its shady grove of orange trees – just as the earliest source Ibn ʿAsakir said: 'south of the Musalla and a bit east of it'.[75]

The final source to mention the shrine is the pilgrimage guide author al-ʿAdawi (d. 1623), who notes its presence some time in the early seventeenth century in his *Ziyarat bi-Dimashq*. He adds little new information, other than to claim that it was an ancient site and the object of visitation still in his day.[76] Thus, some time in the years between al-ʿAdawi's notation and the present, and for reasons that are entirely unclear, this beautiful and much revered shrine faded from prominence, never to be rebuilt.

The total disappearance of such a prominent shrine is remarkable, though not uncommon in the medieval period. However, perhaps the most striking feature of this shrine's profile in the sources is the stark contrast between the indications of its great popularity and generous endowments, and the lack of acknowledgment of the benefactors. Evidence of the shrine's position include accounts of frequent visitation and of the great esteem in which the shrine was held, as well as secondary evidence: for example, the apparently high aesthetic quality of the building, its minaret and *miḥrāb*, the garden that surrounded it, its private system of waterworks and the fabric hangings that adorned its walls, all of which suggest the hand of one or more patrons. Yet, not a single contributor is mentioned. Generally speaking, information about patronage of sites such as shrines is somewhat rare in the sources, and it is not surprising there is a lack of more specific information, given the absence of any remaining traces of the physical structure itself and the corresponding lack of foundation inscriptions and notices of renovation and restoration usually found on such structures. Nevertheless, what is enlightening is that this shrine, like so many others devoted to the family of the Prophet, could, and did, thrive in such a strongly Sunni city, during a period of heightened Sunni sentiment. It could not have done so without the generous patronage of people from multiple Islamic sects, and once again speaks of the universal appeal of such sites for their members.

Sayyida Zaynab bt. ʿAli (or al-Husayn), Rawiya

In the medieval period, our pilgrim might have left from the doorway of the Mashhad al-Naranj and, turning southwards, would have travelled in some kind of transport out of the city, out of its suburbs and into the lush, green Ghuta, the fertile agricultural oasis that surrounds Damascus on the south. Her journey, if made in the springtime, would have been a notably pleasant one, following a road leading south and slightly east of the walls of the old city, through a flat, verdant plain ornamented by flowering fruit orchards and lush fields, passing one by one through small farming villages. About 7km south of the city walls she would have entered one of these small towns. Immediately, she would probably have sensed something was different about this one. For in the medieval period, as today, the town of Rawiya stood among the most important pilgrimage sites in all of Syria. It owed that fame to a single shrine: one devoted to the veneration of the granddaughter of the Prophet, Sayyida Zaynab bint ʿAli ibn Abi Talib.[77]

Here is where the similarity with the past ends, however. For our pilgrim today would have a very different experience of that shrine than she might have in the medieval period. Beginning in the 1950s and continuing through the final years of the twentieth century, the shrine of Sayyida Zaynab underwent at least two major phases of renovation and expansion that slowly transformed it from a popular, yet quite modest, one-room domed structure into a large, multi-structural pilgrimage complex of international scale and reputation. Like that of Sayyida Ruqayya with which this chapter began, the shrine of Zaynab has in recent years been the beneficiary of an international joint project between Syria and Iran to rebuild and reinvigorate the shrines of the *ahl al-bayt* in Syria.[78] The result of this effort has been one of the most remarkable stories of shrine rejuvenation in the Middle East. The shrine to Sayyida Zaynab in particular was the primary objective of over a million pilgrims who visited Syria annually from all over the Islamic world before the war.[79] This has been especially the case since the beginning of the Iraq war in 2003, when the holiest Shiʿi shrine cities of Iraq such as Najaf and Karbalaʾ became ever more dangerous for visitors seeking to pay respects to Shiʿi holy figures.

Thus, in place of a humble building built in local style, pilgrims from across the Islamic world today encounter a magnificently adorned pilgrimage complex decorated in neo-Safavid style, with a sparkling golden dome, two minarets and a shimmering cloak of blue, yellow and green tiles (Fig. 4.19). A library, research centre, prayer halls and administrative quarters surround the central shrine building. Outside, the streets along the exterior walls of the shrine bustle with a lively trade in pilgrimage souvenirs and trinkets mixed with more earthly merchandise: everything from plastic sandals to Qurʾans to sentimental and evocative images of the *ahl al-bayt* and

Figure 4.19 *Mashhad of Sayyida Zaynab, Rawiya (Qabr al-Sitt), Damascus. Photo: Author*

their sufferings and persecutions.[80] Aside from its centralised plan, this shrine bears almost no relationship whatsoever to the original building.

The first steps toward this renovation, furthermore, were nowhere near as international in scope. Indeed, with few exceptions, throughout its history primarily local or regional patrons have maintained the shrine. The funds for the first modern renovation of the building were gathered locally in the mid-twentieth century, at the behest of the shrine's overseers, Muhsin 'Abbas Murtada and Muhammad

Rida Murtada. The project they undertook will be described below, but it is important to emphasise that unlike some other recently restored sites in Syria, the shrine of Sayyida Zaynab has consistently been among Damascus's most famous sites of visitation. Despite its impressive expansion, it is not a recent reinvention.

The town of Rawiya is more commonly known by the nickname 'Qabr al-Sitt', or 'Grave of the Lady (Zaynab)'. Furthermore, as described in Chapter 3, the lady Zaynab was also commonly referred to by her nickname, one she shared with several other female members of the Prophet's family: Umm Kulthum. Thus the shrine was called by multiple names in the medieval sources and may appear as the Qabr al-Sitt, the shrine of Sayyida Zaynab, the mosque, grave or shrine of Umm Kulthum, and others. The earliest sources, however, call it simply the Masjid (mosque of) Rawiya. The foundation of the shrine stretches back into legend: one report claims Sayyida Nafisa, another descendant of the family of the Prophet, visited the grave of Zaynab as early as 808.[81] It is clear the shrine is very ancient, although the sources make pinning down its precise origins problematic.

Ibn 'Asakir (d. 1176) is the earliest solid source to mention the grave of Sayyida Zaynab/Umm Kulthum. Ibn 'Asakir's entry is unconcerned with the architecture or the aesthetic effect of the shrine. Rather, this first description of the site is confined entirely to establishing the identity of the woman buried there, and he does so via a long paragraph containing all the possible descendants of the Prophet who shared the name Umm Kulthum. This suggests that despite the purported antiquity of the shrine, in the twelfth century its authenticity was still seriously in question. According to Ibn 'Asakir,

(this) Umm Kulthum is not the daughter of the Prophet PBUH, who (married) 'Uthman, for she died within the lifetime of the Prophet PBUH and was buried in Medina. Nor is it Umm Kulthum the daughter of 'Ali and Fatima, whom 'Umar (may God be pleased with him) married, for she died along with her son Zayd ibn 'Umar in Medina on the same day and they were buried in the (Jannat al-)Baqi' (cemetery in Medina). Therefore, she (must be) a woman from the *ahl al-bayt* who had the same name, and her *nisba* (proper name) is not remembered. Her mosque was built by a Qurqubi man from Aleppo (*rajul qurqūbī min ahl Ḥalab*).[82]

Ibn 'Asakir, then, clearly comes down on the side of the shrine's *in*authenticity. While willing to concede it may have been the burial place of an unknown member of the Prophet's family, he unambiguously states that it is neither the grave of the daughter of the Prophet, nor that of the daughter of 'Ali, and he does not mention a third possibility that some later authors will propose, namely a daughter of al-Husayn. Ibn 'Asakir even provides proof of his claim in the form of alternative burial places in Medina, where both Zaynabs, he claims, are said to have died and been interred. This early expression of scepticism about the authenticity of the shrine likely reflects the unstable nature of many shrines in Syria in the twelfth and thirteenth centuries, which were then experiencing a period of intensive investment and expansion. It indicates a desire to weed out the authentic from the spurious among the many competing claims made from shrines from all over the region of al-Sham, and is thus an indication of the value medieval authors placed on establishing the shrines' origins and validity. The tone and insistence of Ibn 'Asakir's entry also suggests that such claims were so common that there was a pressing need to restrain, order and organise them according to a hierarchy of veracity.

He ends his account with an interesting addendum, however, when he proposes a patron for the shrine. It was built, he records, by a 'Qurqubi man from Aleppo'. According to another source, this occurred in the year 1106.[83] Thus, despite his scepticism about its authenticity, Ibn 'Asakir cites the shrine's first known patron. However, he is not a known figure; indeed, according to Ibn 'Asakir his name was already lost in the medieval period, a surprising fact considering that Ibn 'Asakir probably wrote his account not long after the building of the shrine.

The location of the town of Qurqub is also unknown: it is postulated to have been in Iraq and also in Khuzistan, the south-western province of Iran that stretches along the Persian Gulf.[84] Either way, the gentleman in question clearly had family origins outside Syria, and he was not from Damascus, but from Aleppo. As noted in Chapter 2, Aleppo in the twelfth century was a strongly Shi'i city, to the degree that even the staunchly Sunni ruler Nur al-Din had trouble bringing it under a Sunni yoke, and had to make numerous diplomatic overtures (among them his visit to, and patronage of, the Shi'i shrine of al-Muhassin) in order to do so. Thus, this shrine's earliest patron was perhaps an example of a wealthy urban notable – possibly a merchant or some other figure who travelled frequently – who saw an opportunity to make a personal contribution to the wider phenomenon of sanctification of the land for Islam, a phenomenon that reached its apex in this period.

Little did that Qurqubi man know that the shrine would go on to become so important in the creation of that new holy landscape. The shrine receives the usual cursory notice from the pilgrimage guide author 'Ali al-Harawi (d. 1215) at the beginning of the thirteenth century. Al-Harawi called the shrine the tomb of Umm Kulthum.[85] But his contemporary the Spanish pilgrim Ibn Jubayr (d. 1217), who visited Syria in the 1180s, travelled to the site and spent the night there, as he said, to 'receive the *baraka* (blessed emanations) of the saint'. His is a particularly rich and descriptive account, one that clearly demonstrates just how generous the Qurqubi man's endowment must have been, and how successful was his enterprise:

> Among the other monuments of the members of the family of the Prophet is that of Umm Kulthum, daughter of 'Ali b. Abi Talib, who is also known as Zaynab al-Sughra; Umm Kulthum is a *kunya* (nickname) that the Prophet gave to her because of her resemblance to his daughter Umm Kulthum. And God knows best. Her venerated monument is in a village in the south of the city, called Rawiya, at a distance of a *farsakh*. It is covered with a grand oratory and built around with habitations. It is provided with a *waqf*. The people of the area know it by the name of the Tomb (*qabr*) of Umm Kulthum. We (went there) to spend the night and receive the *baraka* of seeing it, may God make it profitable for us![86]

Ibn Jubayr does a number of important things in this description. First, he unambiguously establishes the ancestry of the woman venerated in the shrine: she is the daughter of 'Ali ibn Abi Talib, who is known both by the name Umm Kulthum and as Zaynab al-Sughra, or the Younger. But he takes this assertion a step further by providing a straightforward solution to the riddle of her name, the riddle that had plagued Ibn 'Asakir just a few decades previously. Umm Kulthum, Ibn 'Asakir claims, was a nickname for both the daughter of the Prophet (presumably Zaynab al-Kubra [or the Elder]), and also the nickname of his granddaughter by 'Ali and his Fatima. Ibn Jubayr indicates that this is probably hearsay by appending the phrase *wa'llāhu a'lam* (and God knows [best]).

Ibn Jubayr then continues by giving an important description of the shrine. It was certainly a significant building, 'covered by a magnificent oratory' and 'built around with habitations'. Then, as today, it seems the pilgrimage traffic the shrine brought also worked to the benefit of the town, ensuring that the shrine at its heart was a remarkable structure. Ibn Jubayr does not give any specific information about its architecture or plan, but he provides the important detail that the shrine was endowed with *waqf*s, or charitable endowments, meant to provide for the permanent upkeep and maintenance of the shrine. Although it is impossible to know, these *waqf*s may have been the legacy of the Qurqubi man's initial act of generosity, or they may have been endowments that were given to the shrine in the century that had elapsed following his gesture.

In any case, Ibn Jubayr adds a personal note, saying that he visited the shrine in order to partake of the saintly lady's *baraka* by spending the night in her presence. Clearly, the appeal of the shrine was irresistible even for this devout Sunni, a figure who, as has been noted elsewhere, was otherwise shocked at the evidence of widespread Shi'i 'heresy' and who had cursed the Shi'i distortion of 'true

religion'.[87] The anecdote recounting Ibn Jubayr's visit suggests that
the shrine of Sayyida Zaynab, then as now, was thus an important
locus of shared piety between Muslims of all sectarian leanings.
Given the strong feelings Ibn Jubayr expressed against the Shi'a, he
would probably not have been inclined to visit it if it were regarded
as 'Shi'i space'. The sectarian neutrality of the shrine is especially
notable in light of Zaynab's pivotal role in the Battle of Karbala': she
is often cited as an example of great courage for her role in the battle,
during which she is said to have urged al-Husayn to fight against the
Sunni caliph, even placing the sword into his hands.[88] That a Sunni
would revere a figure so central to the formative narrative of Shi'i
identity speaks strongly of the highly fluid semiotic value of these
shrines: able to transform themselves to suit the needs of believers
from multiple sects.

The topographer and historian Ibn Shaddad (d. 1284) mentions
the shrine, but he simply copies the account of Ibn 'Asakir from the
previous century.[89] Subsequently, the shrine is not mentioned for
nearly a century, until it appears in the work of the Syrian historian
Ibn Shakir al-Kutubi (d. 1363). Ibn Shakir largely repeats the information given by previous scholars; however, he adds a few interesting
details about the shrine's foundation. 'This mosque,' he writes, 'was
built by a man from Aleppo, named Ya'ikh. He pretended to have
found a stone (nasība) upon which was written the name of the
woman who rests in the tomb.'[90] Whether this was part of the original foundation story or whether it reflects the growth of an appropriate mythical foundation story for the shrine's increasing profile as
a site for pilgrimage is not clear. However, with this account, the
Mashhad Sayyida Zaynab joins the company of the Mashhad al-
Naranj, the Mashhad Sayyida al-Ruqayya and many other shrines in
Syria where a stone, in some form or another, served as final proof
of the authenticity of the shrine. Furthermore, the stone that was
found seems to have been a kind of tombstone, meaning that story
conforms to another common *topos*, seen also in the foundation
story for the Mashhad al-Husayn in Aleppo. In this story, a long-lost
burial place was once again found, usually by means of a vision or
dream, in which the seeker was instructed to dig at a certain spot
whereupon the buried tombstone of the forgotten holy person's grave
was miraculously unearthed.[91] By the late fourteenth century, the
Aleppan founder had also acquired an appropriately foreign-sounding
name, Ya'ikh, possibly meant to underscore his status as a Persian
outsider and thereby accentuate the extraordinary character of the
foundation tale.

If so, the story seems to have given the shrine increased credibil-
ity, for a few decades later it was to receive its first official stamp of
legitimacy when it was patronised by one of Damascus's most elite
religious leaders. Thus, 'in the year 768 (1366), the Naqib al-Ashraf
of Damascus, Sayyid Husayn Ibn Shaykh al-Islam al-Sayyid Musa al-

Musawi gave what he possessed of carpets and rugs to the *maqam*, and began renovations of the building'.[92] This account comes from a modern history of the shrine, published by the foundation that administers it today, and because it does not cite the original source, is impossible to verify the claim. If it is correct, however, this would have been a remarkable act, for the Naqib al-Ashraf, the overseer of the descendants of the Family of the Prophet (the *ashrāf*), was among the most important religious and community leaders in medieval Islamic cities. The Naqib al-Ashraf was responsible for the administration of *waqf*s, arbitration of certain legal disputes and maintenance of the purity of the family line of the Prophet's descendants.[93] He could be Sunni or Shi'i, and though he most often was Shi'i and sometimes also served as *de facto* leader of the Shi'i community, he was a figure revered by members of both sects. This act of patronage, then, represented a major intervention in the shrine's history and also an official act of recognition by one of the most revered religious leaders in the city.

Aside from the donation of carpets and rugs, the source does not mention what the renovation of the shrine by the Naqib entailed, nor is it specific about the architectural details of the restored building. The shrine is mentioned next by the traveller Ibn Battuta (d. 1377). He notes that 'upon (her *mashhad*) is a distinguished mosque (*masjid karīm*), and around it is a town (*masākin*)'.[94] Over a century later, the *mashhad* is noted briefly by the topographer Ibn al-Mibrad (d. 1503).[95] At virtually the same time, the *fadā'il* author al-Badri (d. 1503) recorded a longer entry on the shrine. His account is primarily concerned with establishing that the ancestry of the shrine's inhabitant was valid, indicating that in the early sixteenth century, there still remained some uncertainty as to the legitimacy of the site. He presents two lines of evidence. First, he quotes his own shaykh, the *hāfiz* Burhan al-Din al-Naji, who taught that Zaynab the elder was the daughter of 'Ali and Fatima, while claiming Zaynab the younger was a child of 'Ali who was born from another wife, after Fatima had died and 'Ali remarried. Then, al-Badri continues with a story of a miraculous appearance by the saintly Zaynab herself, quoting another shaykh, Abu Bakr al-Mawsali:

> The Shaykh Abu Bakr al-Mawsali said in his book the *Futuh al-Rahman*: 'Sayyida Zaynab the Elder, the daughter of Imam 'Ali, died in the Ghuta of Damascus, following the tragedy that befell her brother, and was interred in a village called Rawiya. Thereafter (the town) was called after her and is today know as the Qabr al-Sitt. I visited her once, with a group of my friends. We did not (dare to) enter openly the area of the tomb, but rather would face her and turn our eyes down in accordance with what the *'ulamā'* have admonished, namely that the visitor (*zā'ir*) should treat the dead with the same respect as if they were living. While I was in

a state of weeping, humility and submissiveness, an image of a lady suddenly appeared before me, displaying (an aspect of) venerable and exalted nobility; a person is not able to fully look at her out of reverence. So, I turned and lowered my head. And she said to me 'Oh my dear son! May God increase your respect and good manners. Did you not know that my grandfather the Messenger of God PBUH, and his Companions used to visit (the grave of) Umm Ayman (the Prophet's nursemaid) since she was an honourable woman. Rejoice . . . that my grandfather the Messenger of God, PBUH and all of his Companions and his *umma* (Islamic community) and his progeny love this bondswoman, except for those who abandoned the road. They loathe her.' I was disquieted by her words, and they caused me to become unconscious. When I came to, I did not find her. This prompted me to visit her down to this day.[96]

This story seems intended to accomplish three things: first, on a personal level, to explain the Shaykh Abu Bakr al-Mawsali's devotion to this particular saint; second, to demonstrate proper etiquette and behaviour for the visitation of holy persons; and third, to provide a religious justification for the act of visitation more generally. The subtext of this passage was undoubtedly the ongoing debate among some pious Sunnis over whether shrine visitation was a legally permissible activity.[97] The miraculous appearance of Sayyida Zaynab, and particularly the story she then tells of the Prophet and his Companions' visits to the tomb of Umm Ayman, are presented to justify and sanction the act of visitation more generally, and encourage the visitation of Zaynab in particular. In fact, from this passage we are clearly meant to understand that not only is visitation permissible, but those who loathe her and neglect to visit her, as she tells the shaykh, have 'abandoned the road'.

Al-Badri was not the last author to use the Shaykh al-Mawsali's story in this way, and, indeed, those who wrote about it in subsequent years anchored their account of the shrine with the tale. Like al-Badri, the pilgrimage guide author Ibn al-Hawrani (d. 1562) seems intent primarily on establishing her genealogy and justifying visitation of the shrine, which he does by once again quoting in full the story of the visit of the Shaykh al-Mawsali and asserting her pure genealogy.[98] Similarly, in the early seventeenth century, another guidebook author, al-'Adawi (d. 1623), repeats the story, once again with testimonials to her genealogy and her death in the Ghuta region outside Damascus. Al-'Adawi, unlike Ibn al-Hawrani, does mention her 'famous *mashhad*, replete with loftiness and nobility' and praises the beautiful building, but gives little specific information about its constitution or structure.[99] However, these accounts, with their repeated assertion of her sacred genealogy and their consistent use of the miracle experienced by the Shaykh al-Mawsali, probably reflect two things: that the legitimacy of the shrine never ceased to be a matter of debate, and that within and around that debate it was nevertheless continuously revered and visited throughout the medieval and into the early modern period. It was, as al-ʿAdawi is at pains to point out, a 'famous *mashhad*', and its strong profile in the medieval sources is an indication of how then, as today, it was among the most frequented sites of visitation in Damascus.

What is missing in these accounts, for the purposes of architectural history, is specific information about the shrine as a physical structure. Several medieval sources indicate it was a striking and beautiful, even a 'lofty' building. But it is difficult to tell whether these are simply literary tropes, or whether they reflect an accurate, eyewitness response to the shrine's architectural presence. Furthermore, aside from the initial act of patronage by the 'Qurqubi man from Aleppo', which must have occurred some time before the early twelfth century (perhaps, as noted above, in the year 1106) and the work of the Naqib al-Ashraf in 1366, there are no patrons mentioned for this building.

Yet it must have been consistently restored and renovated in order to survive, and thrive, on the scale that it appears to have done through the centuries. Some later secondary sources shed light on the appearance of the shrine in the early modern period, and they seem to contradict the accounts of a 'lofty building' presented by medieval authors. In 1840, the caretaker of the shrine, a certain 'Sayyid Musa', said to be an ancestor of the Murtada family, built a '*haram*' or enclosure around the building, surrounding the tomb. A few decades later, in 1884, the shrine caught the attention of the Ottoman Sultan 'ʿAbd al-Aziz Khan'.[100] He is said to have restored the dome, but there is clearly something unlikely about the story since the Sultan Abdülaziz had been deposed, and committed suicide, a decade earlier in 1876. Perhaps it was, once again, the Sultan Abdülhamid, whose regnal dates (1876–1909) correspond to the date of the restoration of the dome, and who was known for his generous contribution to the shrines of the cemetery of Bab al-Saghir (see Chapter 3).

In any case, despite the restoration of the dome, the shrine appears to have been a modest building of brick, clay and stone, as it appears in a photo taken in the middle of the twentieth century (Fig. 4.20). It remained so until 1950, when a local initiative sponsored by the Murtada family set in motion the transformation that, though modestly regional in its beginnings, culminated forty years later in the complete reframing of the site by the Syrian and Iranian governments and its emergence as a major transnational centre for pilgrimage.

Conclusion

How to study these shrines, with their obscure or entirely absent physical remains, their unreliable appearance in the sources, and

مقام السيدة زينب ﻉ. عام
١٩٥٥ - ﻫ١٣٧٤

AL SAYDAH ZEINAB SHRINE
1374 H 1955 A.C.

Figure 4.20 *Shrine of Sayyida Zaynab in 1955. Photo: After Al-Sayedeh Zeinab Centre for Information and Research (publicity materials for the Sayyida Zaynab trust)*

their simultaneous vital role in the religious life of the city of Damascus? Like those of archaeology, the gods of medieval source material are capricious, leaving what they will and obfuscating much; and as in archaeology, one way to approach such buildings is with a classically meticulous method: namely, straightforward textual analysis. The goal of this analysis has been, first, to simply trace the evolution of individual shrines through time by presenting, in chronological order, each known mention of the building. But it has also gone deeper, to analyse individual texts by paying attention to the rhetorical context of the writer in question: his profession, the confines of the genre within which he worked, his sectarian leanings, and how and why he may have presented the information he does. When relevant, this analysis has also noted what information was absent from these writers' accounts.

In the absence of any traces of the original buildings, this analysis aims to reconstitute or re-imagine important nodes of ritual practice within the lost urban and suburban landscape of medieval Damascus. Each of these sites has been transformed almost beyond recognition, a feature, it has been argued here, that is the particular fate – perhaps to some degree the unique fate – of shrines in general, and shrines for the *ahl al-bayt* in particular. Shrines may be ephemeral or enduring, and the cause of one shrine's rise and another's fall may not always be clear from the evidence remaining in the sources. This analysis reveals that, as elsewhere in Damascus, there was often a rich

interaction of political, pious and popular motivations behind their
founding and renewal. At times, as was the case with the *mashhad*
of al-Husayn in the Umayyad mosque, the impetus for the restoration or remaking of a shrine was likely to be primarily political; for
the Mamluk Sultan Baybars would certainly have seen the advantage
of presenting himself as a guardian of popular holy places through
his restoration of the Umayyad mosque and its accessory structures.
At other times, as at the Mashhad al-Naranj south of the city, whose
walls were adorned with gifts of beautiful fabric hangings, popular
affection for a place of visitation may have been the cause behind
the upkeep and perpetuation of a shrine for many centuries. And yet,
even such a beloved shrine as the Mashhad al-Naranj can disappear
from the landscape of piety forever.

Yet sometimes, as has happened in recent years with the Mashhad
s Ruqayya and Zaynab, an entirely new set of interests can converge
in such a way as to make the original building obsolete and provoke
the rebuilding and re-imagining of the importance and meaning of
a place of pilgrimage. This re-imagining is particularly relevant for
the Mashhads Ruqayya and Zaynab, for both these shrines have
a somewhat unstable 'history of identity'. The Mashhad Ruqayya
probably began as a shrine for al-Husayn, although as has been
shown here, by the late thirteenth century Ruqayya was also revered
there. The authenticity of the *mashhad* for Zaynab in Rawiya seems
to have been in question throughout its history, to the degree that
every medieval writer felt the need to either deny it was her burial
place or provide an elaborate justification for why it *was* her burial
place. These examples illustrate, once again, the central characteristic of medieval sites of visitation: their inherent flexibility and
fluidity of meaning, relevance and identity. Furthermore, while this
quality of inherent changeability or adaptability is the very thing
that allows for their survival and success, it could also work the other
way, for a building whose identity is too unclear could also dwindle
in importance. That flexibility was not only confined to the identification of the person revered in such a *mashhad*, but extended to the
sectarian identity of those who visit as well. Shrines for the family
of the Prophet function as a neutral palette, from which Damascus's
many inhabitants and visitors could simultaneously paint an image
of sectarian specificity or of pan-Islamic inclusivism, depending on
the needs and context of those who found them relevant.

From the evidence presented here and in Chapter 3, this lost
landscape of Damascene piety begins to take form. One observation
noted at the beginning of this chapter is that the majority of these
shrines were located outside the city walls. Indeed, of the eighteen
Damascene shrines considered here, only two are found within the
city walls: the Mashhad al-Husayn in the Umayyad mosque, and
the Mashhad Sayyida Ruqayya. Why should this network of sacred
sites have been largely 'exiled' by being created outside the city

itself? Why should these sites, so central to the vivid and living
world of popular piety, have been confined to areas outside the main
life of the city? One might propose that since Damascus was a predominantly Sunni city, the shrines' status as locales of behaviours
rejected by some pious Sunnis caused most of them to be located
far from the main centres of Sunni piety. Such an answer, however,
both underestimates the role and widespread acceptance of pilgrimage activities in medieval Islam by giving too much weight to the
few pious scholars who rejected such practices; and, more importantly, it risks overlooking the physical and topographical realities
of the Damascene cityscape. More likely, shrines were located on
the fringes of the city not because they were 'exiled', but for a very
simple reason: because they were almost always sites of burial, and
burial grounds are nearly always outside the city walls. Furthermore,
cemeteries were not then, nor are they today, 'dead' spaces located
outside the city fabric. On the contrary, as has been shown time
and again, and as can be seen every Friday in cities throughout the
Islamic lands, cemeteries are sites of gathering, of meeting, of interaction among family members and friends, of eating, of sleeping, of
remembering, of worship and devotion and of all those profound and
mundane social interactions that bind humans to each other. These
locales outside the city walls, these cemeteries and shrines, were not
'outside' except in a strictly physical and perhaps artificial sense:
they were vital, living spaces that completed the constellation of
sites that made up the landscape of Damascene devotion. Located as
they were at the critical nexus of sectarian identity, popular practice
and official patronage practices, such sites provide a unique window
onto the social and religious life of the medieval Islamic city.

Notes

1. Dorothée Sack, *Damaskus: Entwicklung und Struktur einer orientalisch-islamischen Stadt* (Mainz am Rhein: P. von Zabern, 1989),
   p. 96, no. 2.7.
2. There was a cemetery of al-Faradis at least by the eleventh century;
   al-Rabaʿi (d. 1052) refers to the *Maqbarat al-faradis*. See ʿAli ibn
   Muhammad al-Rabaʿi, *Fadaʾil al-Sham wa-Fadl Dimashq*, ed. Abi
   ʿAbd al-Rahman ʿAdil ibn Saʿd (Beirut: Dar al-Kutub al-ʿIlmiyya, 2001),
   p. 87.
3. For the contemporary transformation of the site, see Yasser Tabbaa,
   'Invented pieties: The rediscovery and rebuilding of the shrine of
   Sayyida Ruqayya in Damascus, 1975–2006', *Artibus Asiae: Studies
   in Honor of Priscilla Soucek* 66 (2006), 95–113. Some other work has
   been done on the contemporary history of the shrines explored in this
   chapter; see Irene Calzoni, 'Shiite mausoleums in Syria with particular
   reference to Sayyida Zaynab's mausoleum', in *Convegno sul Tema:
   La Shiʿa nell'impero Ottomano* (Rome: Accademia nazionale dei
   Lincei, 1993), pp. 191–201; Sabrina Mervin, 'Sayyida Zaynab: Banlieue
   de Damas ou nouvelle ville sainte chiite?', *Cahiers d'études sur la*

Méditerranée orientale et le monde turco-iranien 22 (1996), 149–62. See also Paul Pinto, 'Pilgrimage, commodities, and religious objectification: The making of a transnational Shiism between Iran and Syria', *Comparative Studies of South Asia, Africa, and the Middle East* 27 (2007), 109–25; Michelle Zimney, 'History in the making: The Sayyida Zaynab shrine in Damascus', *ARAM Periodical* 19 (2007), 695–703; and Aliaa El-Sandouby, 'The places of the Ahl al-Bayt in Bilad al-Sham: The making of a "shrine"', *ARAM Periodical* 19 (2007), 673–93.

4. I was repeatedly told this by scholars and local authorities while doing my fieldwork in Damascus.

5. Akram Hasan Al-ʿUlabi, *Khitat Dimashq: dirasa tarikhiyya shamila ʿala mudda alf ʿam, min sanat 400 H. -hatta sanat 1400 H* (Damascus: Dar al-Tabbaʿ, 1997), pp. 221 and 335.

6. Ibid., p. 335.

7. ʿAli ibn al-Hasan Ibn ʿAsakir, *Taʾrikh Madinat Dimashq*, ed. Salah al-Din al-Munajjid (Damascus: Matbuʿat al-Majmaʿ al-ʿIlmi al-ʿArabi, 1951), vol. 1, p. 73.

8. Ibid., p. 84

9. Janine Sourdel-Thomine, preface to her translation of al-Harawi, *Guide des lieux de pèlerinage* (Damascus: Institut français de Damas, 1957), pp. xx–xxii. Janine Sourdel-Thomine was the first modern scholar to speculate that the shrine of al-Husayn mentioned by al-Harawi is to be identified with the shrine of Sayyida Ruqayya; see p. 35, n. 8. With the exception of Sourdel-Thomine, neither Wulzinger and Watzinger nor Sack, nor numerous other secondary sources consulted, list medieval references for the site. Sack, however, does note that the shrine was Ayyubid and later in its construction, without providing a reference. This is a good index of how little is known about the history of the shrine. See Sack, *Damaskus*, p. 99; Karl Wulzinger and Carl Watzinger, *Damaskus: die islamische Stadt* (Berlin & Leipzig: W. de Gruyter, 1924), p. 56.

10. ʿAli Ibn Abi Bakr Al-Harawi, *Kitab al-Isharat ila Maʿrifat al-Ziyarat*, ed. J. Sourdel-Thomine (Damascus: al-Maʿhad al-Faransi bi-Dimashq, 1953), p. 14. Trans. by Sourdel-Thomine, *Guide*, p. 35. Ed. and trans. by J. Meri, *A Lonely Wayfarer's Guide to Pilgrimage* (Oxford: Oxford University Press, 2004), pp. 30–1. Meri claims (p. 58, n. 156) that this shrine is known today as the Shrine of the Martyrs (*mashhad al-shuhadāʾ*), but I have never heard this term used to refer to the shrine of Sayyida Ruqayya, nor would the plural appellation *shuhadāʾ* be logical since there is only one figure believed to be buried there today. No Mashhad al-Shuhadaʾ appears in an official list of shrines obtained from the Department of Islamic Waqfs in Damascus in 2005, although that does not rule out the name being used on the popular level. In his translation of al-Harawi, Meri writes that the shrine of al-Husayn/Zayn al-ʿAbidin in the Umayyad mosque (see below, note 25), is also called the *mashhad al-shuhadāʾ*: perhaps he has confused these two shrines since they are located quite near each other east of the Umayyad mosque (although the latter, al-Harawi is careful to point out, is attached to the eastern portion of the Umayyad mosque, while the former is near Bab al-Faradis, and they are entirely separate listings).

11. Muhammad ibn ʿAli Ibn Shaddad, *Al-Aʿlaq al-Khatira fi Dhikr ʾUmaraʾ al-Sham wa-l-Jazira*, ed. Yahya ʿAbbara (Damascus: Wizarat al-Thaqafa wa al-Irshad al-Qawmi, 1978), vol. 3, p. 506.

12. Muhammad ibn ʿAli Ibn Shaddad, *Al-Aʿlaq al-Khatira fi Dhikr Umaraʾ al-Sham wa-l-Jazira: Taʾrikh Madinat Dimashq*, ed. Sami al-Dahhan (Damascus: al-Maʿhad al-Faransi lil-Dirasat al-ʿArabiyya, 1956), p. 186. The notation reads: 'in Bab al-Faradis is the Mashhad al-Husayn'. On p. 119 of the same book, Ibn Shaddad also notes a 'Masjid of Bab al-Faradis' located outside the wall and attached (*mulāṣiq*) to it'. This is a word-for-word copy of Ibn ʿAsakir's entry, see note 7.

13. Muhammad Ibn Shakir al-Kutubi, *ʿUyun al-Tawarikh*, ed. and trans. by H. Sauvaire as 'Description de Damas', *Journal Asiatique* (May–June 1896), 386.

14. F. Rosenthal, 'al-Kutubi, Abu ʿAbd Allah Muhammad b. Shakir al-Darani al-Dimashki', *Encyclopaedia of Islam*, 2nd edition, ed. P. Bearman et al. [hereafter *EI2*]. Brill Online http://referenceworks. brillonline.com.ezproxy.lib.utexas.edu/entries/encyclopaedia-of-islam-2/al-kutubi-SIM_4595 (accessed 23 July 2013).

15. Although the interior of this *madrasa* has largely disappeared, the inscription over the lintel is still visible, immediately to the left as one enters Bab al-Faradis. It was also known as the *Masjid* al-Sadat because three of the Prophet's companions known as the Sadat were buried there. One of these is Hujr b. ʿAdi, who agitated against Muʿawiya and was later killed by him. Because of his support for ʿAli and his martyrdom by Muʿawiya he is revered by the Shiʿa. Muhammad Asʿad Talas, 'Dhayl (Postscript)', in Yusuf ibn Hasan Ibn al-Mibrad, *Thimar al-Maqasid fi Dhikr al-Masajid*, ed. M. A. Talas (Beirut: n.p., 1943), pp. 223–46.

16. Ibn ʿAsakir (d. 1176) listed 'the mosque of Bab al-Faradis, inside the door and adjacent (*mulāṣiq*) to the rampart. It has a minaret and a canal.' As with the entry by Ibn Shaddad (see note 11), Ibn Shakir al-Kutubi probably copied the first part of the account of the great Damascene historian Ibn ʿAsakir. Apparently believing Ibn ʿAsakir was referring to the nearby Ruqayya shrine, however, Ibn Shakir seems to have mistakenly conflated the two holy sites. Ibn ʿAsakir does not mention a shrine to al-Husayn at Bab al-Faradis. See Ibn ʿAsakir, *Taʾrikh Madinat Dimashq*, vol. 1, p. 73.

17. The shrine in the Umayyad mosque is today said to be the location of the *burial* of the relic, but probably originally commemorated the place the head was said to have been *hung* for display by the Umayyad Caliph Yazid. This is probably an attempt to link the story to the hagiography of John the Baptist, whose head was also said to have hung outside the gate. See Khalid Sindawi, 'The head of Husayn Ibn ʿAli from decapitation to burial, its various places of burial, and the miracles that it performed', *Ancient Near Eastern Studies* 40 (2003), 246, n. 6. It is not clear why the Bab al-Faradis shrine is no longer revered as a *mashhad* for al-Husayn, but perhaps it was simply overshadowed by the Husayn shrine in the Umayyad mosque nearby. Undoubtedly the incomparable reputation and aesthetic splendour of the great mosque exerted an irresistible gravitational effect on any holy site within its orbit.

18. Gars al-Din Khalil Ibn Shahin al-Zahiri, *Zubdat Kashf al-Mamalik wa-Bayan al-Turuq wa-l-Masalik*, ed. Paul Ravaisse (Paris: E. Leroux, 1894), p. 45.

19. Ibn al-Mibrad, *Thimar al-Maqasid*, p. 165. This rock was probably the same as one originally placed in the *Madrasa* al-Mujahidiyya: al-

Harawi noted an identical rock, also said to be from Hawran, in the *madrasa* near the end of the twelfth century and Ibn Shaddad also listed it. Al-Harawi, *al-Isharat*, ed. Sourdel-Thomine, p. 15, ed. and trans. J. Meri, pp. 31–2; Ibn Shaddad, *al-A'laq al-Khatira*, ed. Sami al-Dahhan, p. 186. For further information about this stone and other relics of the Buyid period, see Jean-Michel Mouton, 'De quelques reliques conservées à Damas au moyen-âge: stratégie politique et religiosité populaire sous les Bourides', *Annales Islamologiques* 27 (1993), 245–54, especially 246.

20. 'Abd al-Qadir ibn Muhammad Al-Nu'aymi, *Al-Daris fi Ta'rikh al-Madaris*, ed. Ja'far al-Hasani (Cairo: Maktabat al-Thaqafa al-Diniyya, 1988), vol. 2, p. 330.

21. Ibid., vol. 1, p. 22 and n. 2.

22. Ibid., vol. 2, p. 331.

23. 'Uthman ibn Ahmad Ibn al-Hawrani, *Kitab al-Isharat ila Amakin al-Ziyarat*, ed. and trans. Josef Meri as 'A late medieval Syrian pilgrimage guide: Ibn al-Hawrani's *Al-Isharat ila amakin al-ziyarat (Guide to Pilgrimage Places)'*, *Medieval Encounters* 7, 1 (2001), p. 27. Meri transliterated Ibn al-Mibrad's name as 'Ibn al-Mabrad'.

24. For example, it is noted in the pilgrimage guide of Al-'Adawi in the mid-seventeenth century. Mahmud ibn Muhammad Al-'Adawi, *Kitab al-Ziyarat bi-Dimashq*, ed. Salah al-Din al-Munajjid (Damascus: Al-Majma' al-'Ilmi al-'Arabi bi-Dimashq, 1956), p. 25.

25. As'ad Talas, '*Dhayl* (Postscript)', in Ibn al-Mibrad, *Thimar al-Maqasid*, p. 229. I am grateful to Dr Samer 'Ali, Associate Professor of Arabic at the University of Texas at Austin, for assistance with the translation of this passage.

26. Tabbaa, 'Invented pieties', 109–12.

27. A plan of this passageway and the buildings on the exterior of the north-east corner of the mosque can be seen in Wulzinger and Watzinger, *Damaskus*, p. 64 (abb. 7).

28. Ibn 'Asakir, *Ta'rikh Madinat Dimashq*, vol. 2, p. 72.

29. Al-Harawi, *Kitab al-Isharat*, ed. Sourdel-Thomine, p. 15, trans. by Sourdel-Thomine, *Guide*, p. 37, ed. and trans. by Meri, *Wayfarer's Guide*, pp. 32–3. In her translation, completed in the late 1950s, Janine Sourdel-Thomine wrote that in her day there was a shrine to 'Ali Zayn al-'Abidin, not 'Ali b. Abi Talib, at that location. Clearly, as Sourdel-Thomine suggests, there was a confusion in the sources about who was actually commemorated there, 'Ali, al-Husayn, or Zayn al-'Abidin. See Sourdel-Thomine, *Guide*, p. 37 n. 4. Although Meri's translation has facing-page Arabic text, he mistranslates this section as 'the shrine of 'Ali ibn Abi Talib and the shrine of al-Husayn *ibn* Zayn 'Abidin'. The Arabic text of both Sourdel-Thomine's edition and Meri's own clearly says '*wa*' (meaning 'and'), not '*ibn*' (meaning 'son of'). This is an important distinction because the error changes the meaning of al-Harawi's text considerably. Meri here adds a footnote (see above, note 9), that seems to collapse their identities into one, saying that the 'Mashhad al-Shuhada', or the Shrine of the Martyrs, today stands on the spot of both these shrines'. Meri, *Wayfarer's Guide*, p. 59, n. 159. I have not seen the shrine called by that name elsewhere.

30. Muhammad ibn Ahmad Ibn Jubayr, *Rihla, or The Travels of Ibn Jubayr*, ed. William Wright (Leiden: Brill, 1907 [reprinted 1973]), p. 238.

31. Ibn Jubayr, *Rihla*, p. 267; trans. and annotated by Maurice Gaudefroy-Demombynes, *Voyages* (Paris: P. Geuthner, 1949), vol. 3, p. 308.
32. Ibid., ed. Wright, p. 269; trans. Gaudefroy-Demombynes, p. 310.
33. Muhammad ibn ʿAli Ibn Shaddad, *Taʾrikh al-Malik al-Zahir*, ed. Ahmad Hutayt (Wiesbaden: Franz Steiner, 1983), p. 355.
34. Ibn Shaddad, *al-Aʿlaq al-Khatira*, ed. Sami al-Dahhan, pp. 79–80. The previous story, about the renovation of the mosque, also appears here.
35. Such stories are still common. In 2001, a similar account circulated in Aleppo's rural hinterland. President Bashar al-Assad's English-born fiancée Asma had, according to local informants, visited the villages of Syria disguised as a foreign aid worker in advance of her official introduction as Assad's wife, in order to assess the needs of the ordinary people.
36. Ibn Shaddad's account of the renovation of the Bab al-Barid in the Umayyad mosque is the first example; it appears in his *al-Aʿlaq al-Khatira*, ed. Sami al-Dahhan, p. 80; while Baybars' repair of the mosque is described on p. 79.
37. The location of these column bases can be seen on the plan by A. Dickie, published in Wulzinger and Watzinger, *Damaskus*, p. 144 (abb. 50). The Mashhad al-Raʾs is mentioned on pp. 66 and 145, and is described in detail on p. 157. There is a thorough description of all the rooms outside the north-east wall of the courtyard of the mosque on pp. 156–7. The water clock was built in Nur al-Din's time and was a great marvel in its day: it may still have existed during Baybars' reign. See Finbarr Barry Flood, *The Great Mosque of Damascus: Studies on the Makings of an Umayyad Visual Culture* (Leiden & Boston, MA: Brill, 2001), pp. 114–18.
38. For example, the shrine of the companion and famous *hadith* transmitter, Abu Hurayra (located in Cesarea), was also commissioned by Baybars. Abu Hurayra is among the most prodigious transmitters and was revered by both Sunnis and Shiʿis. See Yehoshuʿa Frenkel, 'Baybars and the sacred geography of *Bilad al-Sham*: A chapter in the Islamization of Syria's landscape', *Jerusalem Studies in Arabic and Islam* 25 (2001), 153–70.
39. Ibn Shakir al-Kutubi, *ʿUyun al-Tawarikh*, p. 385.
40. Today John the Baptist is commemorated in a separate, freestanding shrine located inside the prayer hall of the Umayyad mosque. Ibn Shakir is the only source to mention a shrine to him outside the eastern door of the mosque.
41. Ahmad ibn ʿAli Al-Qalqashandi, *Al-Subh al-Aʿsha fi Sinaʿat al-Inshaʾ*, trans. by Maurice Gaudefroy-Demombynes as *La Syrie à l'époque des Mamelouks* (Paris: P. Geuthner, 1923), p. 40.
42. See note 34 above.
43. Ibn Battuta, *Rihlat Ibn Battutta al-Musamma Tuhfat al-Nuzzar fi Gharaʾib al-Amsar wa-ʿAjaʾib al-Asfar*, ed. ʿAbd al-Hadi al-Tazi (Rabat: Al-Mamlaka al-Maghribiyya, 1997), vol. 1, p. 311.
44. Ibn Shahin al-Zahiri, *Zubdat Kashf al-Mamalik*, p. 45; Ibn al-Mibrad, *Thimar al-Maqasid*, pp. 86–7.
45. Ibn al-Mibrad, *Thimar al-Maqasid*, pp. 165–6.
46. Ibid, pp. 165–6. The passage reads: 'In the eastern portion of the mosque (*bi-sharqi al-jamiʿ*) is the *masjid* of ʿUmar ibn al-Khattab and the Mashhad ʿAli ibn Abi Talib and the (*waʾl-*) Mashhad al-Husayn and (*wa*) Zayn al-ʿAbidin. Ibn Shaddad (d. 1284) had similarly mentioned

the two *mashhad*s of Ibn 'Urwa (aka 'Ali b. Abi Talib?) and Zayn al-'Abidin separately in the same paragraph. See Ibn Shaddad, *al-A'laq al-Khatira*, ed. Sami al-Dahhan, p. 81.

47. Al-Nu'aymi, *Daris*, where the various shrines in the eastern part of the Umayyad mosque are mentioned in vol. 1, pp. 82–3, 265, 478, and 557–8; and in vol. 2, pp. 330, 397, 399, 403 and 407–8.

48. Ibid., vol. 1, p. 478.

49. Claude Cahen, 'Ibn al-Djawzī, Shams al-Dīn Abu'l-Muzaffar Yūsuf b. Kizoghlu, known as Sibṭ', *EI2*. Brill Online, http://referenceworks.bril lonline.com.ezproxy.lib.utexas.edu/entries/encyclopaedia-of-islam-2/ ibn-al-djawzi-shams-al-din-abu-l-muzaffar-yusuf-b-kizoghlu-known-as-sibt-SIM_3140 (accessed 23 July 2013).

50. Al-Nu'aymi, *Daris*, vol. 1, pp. 82–3.

51. This was Fakhr al-Din 'Abd Raḥman ibn 'Asakir Abu Mansur al-Dimashqi (d. 1223), the nephew of the great historian of Damascus 'Ali ibn 'Asakir. Fakhr al-Din taught under the Qubbat al-Nasr in the Umayyad mosque (the main dome and the most revered place of teaching) and at many of the greatest *madrasa*s in Jerusalem and Damascus. Al-Malik al-'Adil wanted him to be a *qāḍī* but he refused. Al-Nu'aymi, *Daris*, vol. 1, p. 85.

52. Ibid., vol. 2, p. 399.

53. Ibid., vol. 2, p. 407.

54. Ibn al-Hawrani, *Kitab al-isharat*, p. 25.

55. The Mashhad al-Husayn/Zayn al-'Abidin was 'rediscovered' in 1857 after the collapse of a wall, and renovated at that time. It seems likely the enclosure for Zayn al-'Abidin dates to that time. Stefan Weber, *Damascus: Ottoman Modernity and Urban Transformation (1808–1918)* (Aarhus: Aarhus University Press, 2009), vol. 2, p. 244.

56. A *naranj* is a bitter orange (the most common variety of which is the Seville orange), as opposed to the *burtuqal*, or sweet orange. Bitter orange is prized in the production of sweets and marmalade and for its essential oil, used as a perfume or flavouring. The sweet orange was brought to Europe from China or India by Portuguese traders (hence its Arabic name, *burtuqal*) only in the fifteenth century, and probably arrived in the Mediterranean before that date, while the bitter orange seems to have arrived earlier. 'Orange.' *Encyclopædia Britannica* Online, www.britannica.com/EBchecked/topic/430873/ orange (accessed 26 September 2007).

57. Ibn 'Asakir, *Ta'rikh Madinat Dimashq*, vol. 2, p. 93. Coincidentally, the shrine was situated somewhere near where Ibn 'Asakir's own grave is located today, at the southern end of the cemetery of Bab al-Saghir.

58. The *musalla* is located on the map 'Damas au milieu du XIIIe siècle' in Jean Sauvaget, 'Esquisse d'une histoire de la ville de Damas', *Revue des Études Islamiques* 8 (1934); but it does not appear on 'Abd al-Qadir Rihawi, *Damascus: its History, Development, and Artistic Heritage* (Damascus: n.p., 1977), plan no. 9. It likely disappeared in the expansion of the city suburbs that occurred in the latter half of the twentieth century.

59. The mosque was completed in 1216. Ibn al-Mibrad, *Thimar al-maqasid*, p. 195. See also Kutayba al-Shihabi, *Ma'adhin Dimashq: ta'rikh wa tiraz* (Damascus: Manshurat Wizarat al-Thaqafah fi al-Jumhuriyah al-'Arabiyah al-Suriyah, 1993), pp. 119–21.

60. Ibid., pp. 119–21.

61. ʿAli al-Harawi, *Kitab al-Isharat*, ed. Sourdel-Thomine, p. 12, trans. Sourdel-Thomine, *Guide*, p. 32, Meri, *Wayfarer's Guide*, p. 30.

62. Ibn Jubayr, *Rihla*, p. 279, trans. Gaudefroy-Demombynes, vol. 3, p. 324.

63. The use of fabric in architectural decoration – indeed, as a form of architecture itself – was a ubiquitous phenomenon in the medieval Islamic lands. For a study of this 'textile obsession', see Lisa Golombek, 'The Draped Universe of Islam' in *Content and Context of Visual Arts in the Islamic World*, ed. Priscilla P. Soucek (University Park, PA & London: Pennsylvania State University Press, 1988), pp. 25–50.

64. Al-Nuʿaymi, *Daris*, vol. 2, p. 211.

65. On this shrine, see al-Harawi, *Kitab al-Isharat*, ed. Sourdel-Thomine, p. 13, trans. Sourdel-Thomine, p. 31, ed. and trans. Meri, *Wayfarer's Guide*, p. 26; Ibn al-Mibrad, *Thimar al-Maqasid*, p. 165; al-Nuʿaymi, *Daris*, vol. 1, p. 385 and vol. 2, p. 302.

66. Ibn Shaddad, *Al-Aʿlaq*, pp. 48–9. For further references, see above, Chapter 3, section on the Mashhad al-Husayn in the Umayyad mosque.

67. Al-Harawi, *Al-Isharat*, ed. Sourdel-Thomine, p. 4, trans. Sourdel-Thomine, *Guide*, p. 4, ed. and trans. Meri, *Wayfarer's Guide*, p. 12; Ibn al-ʿAdim, *Zubdat al-Halab*, vol. 2, pp. 285–6, where he notes the burial of Imad al-Din Zangi at the site; Ibn Shaddad, *Al-Aʿlaq*, ed. D. Sourdel, p. 42; Muhibb al-Din Muhammad ibn Muhammad Ibn al-Shihna, *al-Durr al-Muntakhab fi Taʾrikh Mamlakat Halab*, ed. Yusuf Sarkis (Beirut: Al-Matbaʿa al-Kathulikiyya, 1909), and trans. by Jean Sauvaget as *'Les perles choisies' d'Ibn ash-Shichna* (*Mémoires de l'Institut français de Damas: Matériaux pour servir à l'histoire de la ville d'Alep*, I.) (Beirut: Institut français de Damas, 1933), p. 79.

68. Ibn Shaddad, *Al-Aʿlaq*, ed. Sami al-Dahhan, p. 42.

69. A. J. Wensinck, 'Kaʿba', *EI2*, Brill Online, http://referenceworks.brillonline.com.ezproxy.lib.utexas.edu/entries/encyclopaedia-of-islam-2/kaba-COM_0401 (accessed 23 July 2013).

70. Ibn Shaddad, *Al-Aʿlaq*, ed. Sami al-Dahhan, p. 184; Ibn al-Mibrad, *Thimar al-Maqasid*, p. 165, where the author also notes that Ibn Shaddad copied al-Harawi; Ibn al-Hawrani, *Kitab al-Isharat*, p. 46; Al-ʿAdawi, *Ziyarat*, p. 23.

71. Al-Nuʿaymi, *Daris*, vol. 1, p. 265.

72. Ibid., vol. 2, pp. 365, 419.

73. Sack, *Damaskus*, pp. 25, 81.

74. Several maps present the suburbs of Damascus, see for example 'Damas au milieu du XIIIe siècle', in Sauvaget, 'Esquisse'; and Rihawi, *Damascus*, plan no. 9. More recently, detailed maps of the southern suburbs are presented in Ross Burns, *Damascus: A History* (London & New York: Routledge, 2005), p. 317, map 5.

75. Ibn ʿAsakir, *Taʾrikh Madinat Dimashq*, vol. 2, p. 93.

76. Al-ʿAdawi, *Ziyarat bi Dimashq*, p. 23.

77. Some sources say she was the daughter not of ʿAli but of al-Husayn, making her the great-granddaughter of the Prophet.

78. Pinto, 'Pilgrimage, commodities, and religious objectification', 109–25.

79. Mervin, 'Sayyida Zaynab', 149.

80. Or of Syrian president Bashar al-Assad surrounded by Iranian president Ahmadinejad and Hezbollah leader Hasan Nasrallah. Before

the outbreak of civil war in Syria, this trinity could be seen all over Damascus and was a particular favourite of taxi drivers who pasted the posters in the back window of their taxis. The alliance speaks legions about the success of the propaganda effort undertaken by the Syrian government to portray Iran and Syria as allies united against western influence and control.

81. Sayyida Nafisa was the wife of Ishaq al-Mu'tamin, a son of the sixth Shiʻi Imam Jaʻfar al-Sadiq, according to *Al-Mawsem* 25 (1996), 137. *Al-Mawsem* is an Arabic quarterly on archaeology and culture; this was a special edition entirely devoted to the shrine of Sayyida Zaynab. This report appears in an article on the history of the shrine, but the author does not cite sources and I am so far unable to discover the origin of this claim.

82. Ibn ʻAsakir, *Taʾrikh Madinat Dimashq*, vol. 2, p. 80.

83. *Al-Mawsem* 25 (1996), 137. Once again, the source for this claim is not provided.

84. Georgette Cornu, *Atlas du monde arabo-islamique à l'époque classique (Ixe–Xe siècles)* (Leiden: Brill, 1985), p. 38.

85. Al-Harawi, *Kitab al-Isharat*, ed. Sourdel-Thomine, p. 12.

86. Ibn Jubayr, *Rihla*, pp. 280–1, trans. Gaudefroy-Demombynes, *Voyages*, vol. 3, pp. 325–6.

87. See the beginning of Chapter 2 for the full text describing Ibn Jubayr's dismay at the number of Shiʻis in Syria.

88. I. Calzoni, 'Shiite mausoleums in Syria', 200–1. See also Irene Calzoni, 'Il Mausoleo di Sayyida Zaynab a Damasco'. Unpublished PhD dissertation, University of Venice, 1988.

89. Ibn Shaddad, *al-Aʻlaq*, ed. Sami al-Dahhan, pp. 134, 182.

90. Ibn Shakir al-Kutubi, *ʻUyun al-Tawarikh*, p. 387.

91. For the foundation story of the Mashhad al-Husayn, see Chapter 2.

92. Hani Muhsin Mourtada and Rida Mahdi Mourtada, Untitled pamphlet (Damascus: Al-Sayedeh Zeinab Centre for Information and Research, n.d.), p. 15; *Al-Mawsem* 25 (1996), 137. Unfortunately, neither of these works cite their authors' sources and I am unable to verify the authenticity of this claim.

93. Axel Havemann, 'Naḳīb al-Ashrāf', *EI2*, Brill Online, http://reference-works.brillonline.com.ezproxy.lib.utexas.edu/entries/encyclopaedia-of-islam-2/nakib-al-ashraf-COM_0841 (accessed 23 July 2013). For a study on the spread of the office of the *niqāba* after the ninth century, see Kazuo Morimoto, 'A preliminary study on the diffusion of the *Niqaba al-Talibiyin*: Towards an understanding of the early dispersal of *Sayyids*', in Hidemitsu Kuroki, ed., *The Influence of Human Mobility in Muslim Societies* (London & New York: Kegan Paul, 2003), pp. 3–42.

94. Ibn Battuta, *Rihlat ibn Battuta*, vol. 1, p. 323.

95. Ibn al-Mibrad, *Thimar al-Maqasid*, p. 166.

96. ʻAbdallah ibn Muhammad Al-Badri, *Nuzhat al-Anam fi Mahasin al-Sham*, ed. and trans. Henri Sauvaire as 'Description de Damas', *Journal Asiatique* 9 (May–June 1896), 452.

97. Because Shiʻis have rarely forbidden visitation, this debate was largely a Sunni one, as noted previously (see Introduction, note 9). For a scholarly defence of the Shiʻi position on visitation and an overview of ideas about visitation from medieval to modern times, with copious footnotes to primary sources, see Shaykh Muhammad Mahdi Shams

al-Din, 'Chapter 2: The *Ziyara*', in *The Revolution of al-Husayn [a]: Its Impact on the Consciousness of Muslim Society*, trans. I. K. A. Howard (West Wimbledon: Muhammadi Trust of Great Britain and Northern Ireland, 1985). Online at www.al-islam.org/revolution/2.htm (accessed 9 October 2011).

98. Ibn al-Hawrani, *Al-Isharat*, p. 67.
99. Al-'Adawi, *Ziyarat bi-Dimashq*, p. 21.
100. *Al-Mawsem* 25 (1996), 137; Mourtada and Mourtada, Untitled pamphlet, p. 15.

CHAPTER FIVE

A Landscape of Deeds: ʿAlid Shrines and the Construction of Islamic Sacred Topography

> There is no Muslim to whom, when he makes *ziyāra* on the land
> ... the land will not say: 'Beseech God Almighty on this land, and
> I will bear witness for you on the day when you shall meet Him.'[1]

MEDIEVAL MUSLIMS EXPERIENCED sacred history through the land.
Put differently, for medieval Muslims, sacred history was *emplaced*:
it was situated in space by means of ritual actions and behaviours
that had material consequences. This emphasis on the land occurred
in concert with a textual discourse of historical scholarship disseminated broadly among certain groups within a highly literate medieval
society. And yet, for the majority of ordinary Muslims, the crucial
point of interaction with Islamic history was not literary, but physical: through contact with holy places, by means of *ziyāra*. Beginning
in the eleventh and twelfth centuries, Islamic history, and thus a
distinctly Islamic sense of self, was reified through the production
of a new, conspicuously Islamic topography: a great, interconnected
network of individual shrines that functioned as focal points of holy
power. This network formed a meaningful landscape that confirmed
the place of Islam in sacred history and provided a vital experience
of contact with that history for individual Muslims, by means of the
holy and the miraculous.

Until now in this study, we have focused primarily on the
archaeological and architectural documentation of these sites and an
explanation of their intersectarian social context. Here, we will take
a broader view, locating these ʿAlid shrines as holy centres within a
landscape that had itself long been perceived as holy. We have seen
that medieval Muslims perceived the land of Syria as sacred, and that
they viewed Greater Syria as a concentrated nexus of holy sites that
created a localised landscape of sacrality. But Syria was part of a
more expansive landscape, too, and its relationship to these external
sites was important for the creation of the notion of landscape inter-
nally, within the bounds of *Bilād al-Shām*. This Islamic landscape
was able to account for the historical and religious particularities of
Islam, while also acknowledging connections to previous Greek and
Roman, Jewish and Christian devotional traditions.

Medieval visitors were conscious of these interrelationships. From the eleventh century onwards, ʿAlid sites in Syria were actively reaffirmed as both unique and as part of this wider landscape, by acts of visitation and by acts of visual and textual 'mapping'. Such acts functioned both literally and figuratively. Literally, notions of landscape could be expressed in varied ways: in textual form in works of scholarship, in visual form as actual maps or other representations, or by actions such as architectural construction, expansion and renovation.[2] Figuratively, the sacred was inscribed, and repeatedly reinscribed, by belief and by varied ritual actions and experiences: the initial event linked to the presence of a holy person at the place, and later by the action of supplicants: their belief, visitation, prayer and ritual behaviours. Acts of literal mapping, however, also have a figurative quality, for they are representations linked to the social, political, cultural and economic practices of their production and reception as much as they are to geographical realities, as we have seen in previous chapters. Furthermore, texts, buildings and landscapes are not passive, and they also act to *generate* space, by making visible what is experienced in the realm of the figurative and the conceptual. Acts of figurative mapping, including visitation, ritual practice, dream visions and experiences of healing, miracle and supplication, both generate and reinforce literal actions and allow pilgrims to participate in them.[3]

Towards a material conceptualisation of the sacred in Islamic societies

From the perspective of architectural history, another way of approaching this notion is to say that acts of literal and figurative mapping can be conceived of as social behaviours that produce materiality in certain locations and not others: or, in other words, as actions that literally and figuratively 'take place'.[4] This notion, originated by J. Z. Smith, has been developed over the past few decades in a substantial body of scholarship that aims to account for the social production of sacred space.[5] The object is to move beyond mere description of holy places and, instead, to use material culture to understand process: to understand *how* these initially ordinary places, locations and sites became extraordinary. Such an aim underscores the necessity to improve on the simple designation or assignation of the sacred as the end point of analysis, thus 'highlight[ing] the need for a distinction to be made between the use of the term "sacred" as a descriptor and its employment as an analytical concept'.[6]

This corpus of research that aims towards an analytical notion of the sacred is applicable here, especially because it is directly tied to material culture and to the use of archaeology to gain insight into social history. It creates the means for a more comprehensive integration of Islamic archaeology – a field whose methodologies and critical insights are sometimes lost in the arcane figures of a dig report – into the humanistic disciplines. Likewise, it provides an alternative to the tendency of scholars in Islamic studies to embrace textual primacy at the expense of other sources, or to view material culture as a supplementary source that can only function to confirm information derived from written sources. As Alistair Northedge has pointed out, this 'logocentrism' has limitations that are often ignored, and

> the role of archaeology in Islam, as everywhere in historical archaeology, is to explore the alternative visions of the past that material evidence offers, and to fill out the aspects of that past that authors of the time were unable to see, or thought too familiar to explain.[7]

In other words, the problem is that accounts that rely on textual sources alone tend to privilege a single perception or actor at the expense of many possible others, and because most medieval authors only briefly describe the sites they visited, their descriptions usually fail to account for the material and topographical characteristics of the sacred. It is all too easy to forget that for most medieval Muslims, reading about a sacred site was rarely, if ever, part of their experience. The shrine, however, and the lived experience of that shrine within a broader landscape, was at the centre of it all.

An analytical approach to the sacred also brings us closer to comprehending how, as I have argued in the previous four chapters, the ʿAlid shrines could be so unifying: how they could bring together Muslims of varied allegiances and backgrounds, whether Sunni or Shiʿi, sultan, military elite, merchant, scholar, craftsman or shepherd. For behind the notion of the role of figurative actions in generating space is the idea that it is not only bricks and stones, but also lived ritual practice, that makes a space a place; that transforms an ordinary 'space' into an extraordinary 'place'. Indeed, as has recently been argued, it is ritual, even more than architectural practice, that makes place: that *emplaces* the sacred in the landscape. Further, architectural practice is conceived as being *itself* ritual action, not merely as the container for it.[8] Ritual, in this way of thinking, is not an activity carried out by an individual isolated in time and space, but instead is conceived as a series of interconnected actions, performed over time and repeated again and again, that acts to generate place in the material world. It is this quality of repetition that defines ritual, as one popular dictionary has, as being 'a series of repeated actions performed according to a prescribed order': but it is also this quality of repetition, of repeated action in a particular place, that enables the sacred to become visible in the material world. This points to the reciprocal relationship that develops between ritual, materiality and place-making. If ritual action is by definition repeated action, its characteristic of repetition ensures it is often identifiable by its material traces in the landscape. Reciprocity also tends to occur at such sites because places made by ritual tend to ensure that future ritual practice will occur at the site, and repetitive ritual practice, in turn, then generates place. Ritual practice, it can be argued, is thus material, and the material is of necessity located at a certain place.[9] Thus we find that ritual actions both literally and figuratively create place: that ritual actions are emplaced.

This generation of material traces makes archaeology and architectural history an ideal method of interpretation for ritual practice.[10] Ritual actions are materially visible in the initial creation of sites of pilgrimage and, later, in their expansion and elaboration into larger complexes, but they are also visible in less ostentatious ways. Even actions as simple as the addition of an oven for bread making in the *mashhad* at Balis (Chapter 1) can be revealing of further ritual investment, in the context of associated evidence. On a larger scale, pathways, burials, relics and inscriptions, for example, are material traces of ritual action that can be read in archaeological context. Thus, literally, ritual actions are visible in the changes that occur over time at a specific place, but they are also visible in the more figurative realm, by the creation of a wider landscape of many such places. Such sites are discrete, but also connected to all of the others, literally by roads, markers and pathways through the landscape, and figuratively by discourses that were enacted in ritual behaviour and in oral and textual sources that linked them to each other. Of course, to create such a landscape is to make claims about the land itself, about its history, about its borders, boundaries, about what belongs and what does not. As we have seen in previous chapters, from the perspective of medieval Muslims, the ʿAlid shrines nearly always belonged, and this belonging to all Muslims was, I have argued, their salient characteristic. But what were the wider boundaries of this landscape, and why, as has been shown here, did this process of ritual emplacement and expansion take such an urgent turn in the eleventh to thirteenth centuries?

To return to the premise with which this chapter opened, it is a particularly Islamic connection between history and the land that is the key to understanding why this landscape was created and expanded during this period. At the same time, this connection was reliant upon the prior Biblical discourse of the holiness of the land to create a notional framework for its implementation. Using both literal and figurative means, medieval Muslims created a sacred landscape that embraced and accommodated both previous and new traditions. In this way, Muslims enacted ritual practices that actively emplaced these histories and created a sacred topography that linked the land to Biblical history as an important marker of antiquity and sanctity, while simultaneously arguing for the primacy of Islamic history.

Among these sites, the most important in the twelfth and thirteenth centuries were those that commemorated figures who played a key role in Islam's early history, particularly the Companions of the Prophet and the ʿAlids.[11] For sites devoted to the ʿAlids, the core area of this wider landscape was the central Islamic lands: an area that reached eastwards beyond Syria to include Iraq and westwards to encompass Egypt. For these ʿAlid shrines, Syria forms the heartland of this wider landscape, situated as it is at the midpoint between the other important centres of ʿAlid commemoration in Iraq and Egypt, and theatre for some of the defining moments of ʿAlid history. The boundaries of this ʿAlid landscape link the land to key events in sacred history and to the memory of formative events experienced by the Muslim community.

Mapping the landscape in twelfth- and thirteenth-century Syria

A key theme explored in this book is the notion that something shifted around the twelfth century: that the twelfth century was a period of expansive architectural construction of mosques, *madrasa*s and also shrines. But why then? From the evidence at hand, it seems that the primary factors were twofold: the recent experience and memory of Crusader claims for the sacrality of the land, alongside a heightened awareness of sectarianism in the period of the Sunni Revival. Both factors, at play in this period, meant devotional sites received particularly dutiful attention. We have explored aspects of sectarian interaction in previous chapters, and with respect to the Crusades, similar proposals have been explored before – over ten years ago, Yehoshuʿa Frenkel noted that the period of the Crusades marked a turning point in the construction of an Islamic sacred landscape. Prior to the Crusader era, Frenkel wrote, early Islamic *fadāʾil* literature had emphasised the prophets and saints of a remote Biblical past, but this changed over time and particularly in the post-Crusader era. Thus, in the tenth and eleventh centuries, sites sacred to Old Testament prophets like Abraham, Noah and Lot, and New Testament figures like Jesus, Mary and John the Baptist, formed the bulk of holy places noted, whereas in the post-Crusader era in the twelfth and thirteenth centuries, sites devoted to specifically Islamic figures began to proliferate, with notably less emphasis on Biblical sites. This was confirmed, in more empirical terms, by Cyrille Jalabert, who meticulously quantified the shift in the twelfth century from Biblical to Islamic saints in a 2002 article.[12] Indeed, according to Jalabert, the eleventh and twelfth centuries marked the decisive period when cities like Damascus became genuinely Islamic cities. It was then that, according to the Arabic sources, sacred traditions multiplied and mosques and *madrasa*s were diffused in the urban fabric, giving Islam an institutional importance and urban visibility it had not previously had. Furthermore, all of this architectural investment happens in the context of massive conversions to Islam that were occurring at the same time.[13]

Following Frenkel and Jalabert, scholars like Paul M. Cobb, Josef Meri and Daniella Talmon-Heller, among others, have enriched and added nuance to our understanding of this process. Cobb, for example, showed that notions of sanctity had been kept alive in the period when Syria was not a political centre, between the downfall of the Umayyads and the Seljuk era, and Meri and Talmon-Heller demonstrated that the expansion of shrines, sites of pilgrimage and other sanctuaries was marked after Syria's reversion to political autonomy in the twelfth century.[14] More recently, Zayde Antrim has shown that Ibn ʿAsakir was the key figure in this literary reorientation of Syria's sacred topography, one that shifted focus from Jerusalem as a sacred centre to Damascus, and thereby laid claim to a more Islamically focused landscape. As Antrim put it:

> The Syria represented in the introduction to the *Taʾrikh madinat Dimashq* was not, therefore, an 'abode of the prophets', as it had been for geographers and *faḍāʾil* authors up to Ibn ʿAsakir's time, a characterisation that implicated Syria in the birth and development of Judaism and Christianity as well as Islam. Instead, Ibn ʿAsakir's Syria was an exclusively Islamic Syria, defined by its importance to the early community of believers under Muhammad.[15]

Put in terms of the argument here, Ibn ʿAsakir was a literal actor whose aim was the emplacement of the sacred within *Bilād al-Shām* and the encouragement of ritual practices that would ensure the generation there of a distinctly Islamic sacred topography.

Despite this recent interest in what the textual sources have to say about notions of sanctity in this era, the stones-and-mortar, archaeological evidence of this growth of holy sites has remained virtually unexamined, and the question of whether Ibn ʿAsakir's literary reorientation was matched by ritual practices like a growth in architectural investment in sites of pilgrimage has remained unanswered. In other words, to what degree can we demonstrate that the land itself reflected this transformation in thinking about the role of Muslim saints? As we have seen in this study, there are indeed numerous indications that beginning in the eleventh and twelfth centuries, the production, expansion and architectural embellishment of new cultic sites flourished in Syria, in concert with their textual proliferation. Thus this period does appear to have witnessed not just a shift in emphasis, but the actual generation of a new and distinctly Islamic landscape of sacred sites, which was given official legitimacy through patronage by members of the courtly and ʿulamāʾ circles. This brings us to the question of how this new notion of landscape differed from previous ones, and also to ask what, precisely, it was that marked the landscape as Islamic? How did these sites function to emplace Islamic history?

Pre-Islamic and Islamic notions of sacred landscape

To answer this question, it is helpful to understand the historical background for the appearance of these Islamic sites, and to grasp how they may have interacted with past landscapes of holiness. In ancient Syria, as elsewhere, Greek and Roman landscapes were, for the most part, topographically grounded, meaning that holiness existed outside of time, and was inherent in natural features of the earth's topography. Thus, many Greek and Roman sacred sites had a quality of inherent sanctity that relied upon, and arose out of, features of the land itself – for example, caves, springs, groves or hills – and less upon historical, mythological or spiritual events. This is not to say that ancient sites that commemorated events in historical or mythological time did not exist; in fact, many such sites were venerated. However, ancient historical or mythological events nearly always occurred at sites that already had a long history of feature-based holiness that was impersonal and inherent in the natural landscape, such that 'certain Roman holy places were thought to possess precisely that "inherent sanctity" ... which did not arise from human action but was merely confirmed by it'.[16] More often than not, rather than being primary sources of holiness themselves, mythological or historical events served to make the long-perceived holiness of topographical and natural features explicable and, thus, to augment an already holy site. The city of Rome itself, for example, which would later become the site of countless historically grounded holy locales, was originally, according to Vergil, a sacred grove 'dark with forest undergrowth. Even then a fearful dread of the place pressed on the timid country folk, even then they trembled at the forest and the rock.'[17] Clearly there is an aspect of pagan belief in the power of nature spirits at work in such accounts, and, indeed, a key aspect of the holiness of ancient sites was that they derived their ultimate legitimacy from naturally occurring phenomena and characteristics.

Within the monotheistic faiths, features of the land were also often venerated, but with a different emphasis, one that always included a reference to, and the clear precedence of, sacred history, as an attempt to differentiate monotheistic practice from polytheistic worship. A residual reliance on inherent topographical features remained in some locations, but Judaism and Christianity, with their dependence on the reifying power of holy texts, relied more fully on human intervention to mark the land and to locate historically grounded Biblical events, particularly graves, tombs and shrines for Biblical figures. In cases where natural topography was invoked it was often a secondary feature, for example the tombs of

prophets and saints located in grottoes or near holy springs, mountains or trees that played a role in Biblical events. And much more
than in Roman times, holy places with no nature-based association
became the dominant form of pilgrimage site. Over time, a distinction arose between Christian holy places in the Biblical holy land,
where events from Biblical history formed the backbone of the
sacred landscape, and Western Europe, where holiness came to be
focused almost exclusively on the saintly presence of a holy figure
in a tomb. But at Christian sites, some antique themes remained: for
example, churches, tombs and shrines were envisaged as they were
in antiquity – as the 'home' of the deceased.

As it developed, a notion of Islamic sacred topography continued
the already established progression away from the natural world as
locus of sacred power towards an even more abstract, historically
based landscape commemorating Biblical and Qurʾanic events. In
doing so, Islamic topography created what I shall term, building on
the framework of emplacement described previously, a 'landscape
of deeds'. In such a landscape, holiness was infrequently or only
incidentally inherent in features of the land itself, and instead was
primarily reliant on actions and events in historical time. Although
natural features like springs or mountains were still occasionally
found at such sites, they usually served in a purely verificatory role
– as proof of the miraculous at sites that were in actual fact made
holy by *events* in historical or eschatological time, as we saw, for
example, in Aleppo, where a spring arose from under the goat's feet
marking the place where al-Husayn's head had rested (Chapter 2).
Thus, holiness was generated not by natural features of the land,
but by specific ritual actions *on* the land – by deeds – at various
points in pre-Islamic or Islamic history, serving to emplace a specifically Islamic notion of sacredness. This is of crucial relevance
because Islam has a weighty sense of itself as a historical faith, and
particularly as the culmination, in historical time, of the two great
monotheistic faiths of Judaism and Christianity. Though Ernest
Renan's observation that Islam was 'born in the full light of history'
is a notion whose factual basis has been thoroughly challenged in
recent years, Islam's self-perception was, nevertheless, as such a
faith.[18] Thus, even more than in Judaism or Christianity before
it, in Islam, holy deeds performed in historical time, at particular
locations within the landscape, created, marked, reinforced and
mediated history; and history, in turn, created the sacred landscape, lent it legitimacy, generated it psychologically, spiritually
and physically. This reciprocal, perpetually renewing relationship
between history and space is a notable feature of the Islamic sacred
landscape. While previous monotheistic religions had also been
concerned, to varying degrees, with the emplacement of sacred
history, for Islam, it was paramount. Christianity and Judaism
were faiths founded as counter-narratives within a dominantly

polytheistic milieu, and they therefore had to justify themselves in the context of notions of sacred topography that had, for many millennia, prized features of the natural landscape. Muslim claims to the land, however, evolved in a dominantly monotheistic context in which precedence in sacred history was the primary reifying force. For a patron, to claim such holy spaces was, quite literally, to map yourself into history.

The Mashahid Husayn as framework for 'Alid topography

Perhaps the clearest example of this sort of emplaced Islamic landscape, particularly for how it was both characteristically Islamic and yet linked to prior Biblical discourses, is an 'Alid one – the network of shrines that marked the journey of the head of al-Husayn from Karbala' in Iraq to its eventual resting place in Cairo. The story of the death of al-Husayn is one of the key narratives of early Islamic history and perhaps the most pivotal sacred event in the formation of Shi'i memory and identity, and it was a narrative that actively and systematically strove to 'take place': that generated sites that marked key events and thus created a reciprocal relationship between history and place. Also, as we have seen in previous chapters, the Husayn shrines epitomise the twelfth- and thirteenth-century trend towards inclusive piety and the generation of a landscape of sites that were shared among all Muslims. Despite their critical role in Shi'i pious practice, like many other locales discussed in this book, nearly all of the Husayn shrines were built and maintained by Sunnis, and they were spaces that were visited and revered by all.

Al-Husayn, grandson of the Prophet Muhammad and third Imam of the Shi'a, was martyred at the battle of Karbala' on the banks of the Euphrates on the tenth day of Muharram ('Ashura' day) in year 61 of the *hijra* (AD 680). He died after being decapitated by Shimr b. Dhi al-Jawshan, commander of the army of Umayyad Caliph Yazid b. Mu'awiya. When the battle was over, Shimr placed al-Husayn's head on his lance and gave it to his deputy to carry from Karbala' to Kufa, to be presented at the house of the governor. In Kufa, the head was exposed and paraded around the city, along with prisoners from the battle, including many of al-Husayn's wives and family members who had been taken prisoner during the battle.[19] Following this, the governor ordered that the head and the prisoners be taken to Damascus and presented to the Caliph Yazid. Along the way, he directed that the head be ritually exposed in a public procession in each city and town, demonstrating the caliph's triumph and underscoring the fate of those who sought to challenge Umayyad authority.

The sources list the Iraqi and Syrian towns that celebrated the passage of Husayn's head, and also enumerate those for whom the event provoked shock and grief – six in celebration and five in

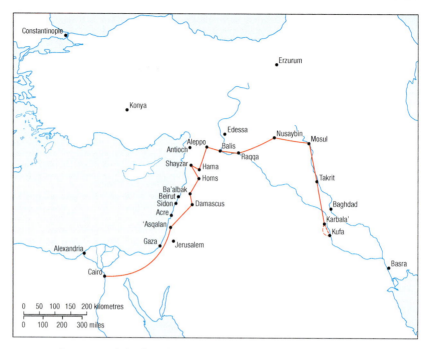

Map 5 *The route of the head of al-Husayn, delineating its passage from Karbalaʾ to Cairo, as chronicled in the medieval Arabic sources.*

mourning, perhaps a gesture intended to indicate the population expressed roughly equal support for and condemnation of Yazid's action, but also one that suggests that even at this early period, there was a nascent topography linking cities and locations that valued the Prophet's descendants (Map 5).[20] Using the accounts of both Arab chroniclers and pilgrimage guide authors, we can reconstruct its passage to the caliph's palace in Damascus, a passage that forms a verifiable sacred route. The head seems to have begun its journey, interestingly, by following the riverine path – going north up the Tigris to Takrit and Mosul, and then crossing over into northern Syria via Nisibin.[21] It then followed the Euphrates west, beginning at Raqqa and resting briefly at Balis, and then, leaving the river, moving over land to Aleppo, after which it was brought southwards into central Syria, to Hama, Shayzar and Homs.[22] It was then carried further south to Baʿalbak and, finally, eastwards to Damascus. Upon its arrival at the Caliph Yazid's palace in Damascus, the head of the martyr was presented to the caliph, resting inside a golden bowl.

It is here that things get even more interesting, for this detail about how the head was presented to the caliph is one of many that consciously connected the story of al-Husayn to that of John the Baptist. It is an example of the pattern described above, by which

Muslim authors, religious leaders and pilgrims both literally and figuratively strove to connect Islamic holy places to those of the Jewish and Christian past, by mimicking and appropriating aspects of their hagiographies. However, in doing so, they were transforming and expanding an already extant notion of the land's holiness and appropriating it in favour of Islam. Shi'i authors writing about al-Husayn were directly influenced by the biography of John, and many key episodes of his life were replicated in their accounts, including their conception and birth, their nursing, the process by which they were named, the light emanating from their faces and the fact that both their heads spoke after their decapitations.[23] But Sunnis also clearly saw the parallels – associating the decapitated martyr John with the similarly martyred al-Husayn, and, in the ultimate act of assimilation, directly emplacing this association by burying part of al-Husayn's head in the Umayyad mosque.[24] Today, as we have seen in Chapter 4, it is housed in a special Mamluk- and Ottoman-era shrine on the eastern wall of the courtyard. The Shrine of the Head of al-Husayn thus rests just steps away from the Shrine of the Head of John the Baptist inside the prayer hall of the mosque, the relics of their martyrdom forever intimately linked, creating a muti-layered holy space beloved and visited by pilgrims of various religions and confessions.

But, as we know, the head had a further afterlife. The sacred route created by its initial passage did not end in Damascus. At some point, for reasons we do not understand, the head, or the remainder of the head, was transferred further west to the coastal city of 'Asqalan. Some traditions say it was brought there after Yazid commanded his men to continue their march through the Syrian towns to expose the head, and the city's governor then buried the head.[25] But for the most part, they are silent on this unusual choice of location. Several medieval authors, including Ibn Taymiyya, speculated about why the head came to 'Asqalan and when it was taken there.[26] In any case, although no trace remains today, several sources mention the presence of a shrine there throughout the early Islamic era. At some point just before 1154, as Maqrizi says, because of the threat it would be desecrated by the advancing Crusader armies, the head was transferred to Cairo by the Fatimid vizier al-Salih Tala'i, and, after being sanctified in the Emerald Palace in Cairo, was enshrined in the famous Fatimid-era mausoleum north of the al-Azhar mosque, where it rests today.[27]

The sacred route formed by the passage of the head of al-Husayn gave rise to multiple sites of devotion, marking within its bounds the range and extent of the primary 'Alid shrines. It emplaces a key narrative from early Islamic history by ritually inscribing the memory of past action on the land, and by connecting it, via literal and figurative associations with the Christian saint John the Baptist, to past narratives of holiness in Bilad al-Sham.

Emplacing a landscape of deeds

How did such discrete early Islamic narratives become a comprehensive medieval-era landscape of deeds? In the twelfth century, during the period of the most rapid expansion of these sites, the need for the emplacement of sacred history was most often met by adducing the presence of graves, historical events or sites of miracle long forgotten and rediscovered through divine revelation or miraculous events, as we have seen at sites like the Mashhad al-Husayn and Mashhad al-Muhassin in Aleppo (Chapter 2). In the Arabic sources, this becomes a sort of literary *topos*: an example is recounted by the medieval historian Ibn al-'Adim, who tells of the recent construction of a mausoleum on the newly rediscovered ancient tombs of righteous men, or by 'Ali al-Harawi, the author of the twelfth-century pilgrimage guide, who writes that in Damascus the graves of seventy of the *ṣaḥāba* or Companions of the Prophet were rediscovered in the cemetery, which until then had been ploughed and sown for a hundred years and their graves forgotten.[28] Such stories are common in the medieval sources, and in this period, Islamic history was linked to the landscape in an ever-increasing variety of ways, evident in the development of a diverse range of new types of sites: places of the witnessing of significant events, or *mashhad*s, places of remembrance of holy figures, or *maqām*s, sites of battle, sites of miracle, sites of healing, sites of divine intervention in the affairs of human beings. On the popular level, Islamic history is unimaginable without these sites. The visitation of shrines and the historical and religious knowledge conveyed there was a primary means by which ordinary Muslims understood their place in history – and in this sense, it was Islam itself that was literally emplaced.

For Muslims concerned with the Islamisation of sacred topography, certain categories of sites obviously had more clout than others. Accordingly, the sites most prolifically rediscovered were those related to the early history of Islam, especially tombs and shrines for Companions of the Prophet.[29] And among those shrines, holy sites devoted to the 'Alids had a particular place, particularly in the tenth and eleventh centuries in the period of Fatimid and Seljuk friction. Somewhat later, by the twelfth and thirteenth centuries, as the land was being reclaimed for Islam after a period of Crusader occupation, the 'Alid shrines also served a key, and more sectarian-neutral, role as holy sites for exemplary Muslim saints.

In many cases, acts of repossession were explicitly noted and commented upon by historians and topographers. Indeed, acts of reclamation appear in the sources with some frequency. For example, in his description of the coastal city of Acre, written some time in the early twelfth century, the pilgrimage guide author al-Harawi reported on a miraculous vision that quickly led to the transformation of a formerly Christian site:

'Akka ... contains 'Ayn al-Baqar (The Spring of the Ox), from which it is said that the ox came out to Adam, and he used it to cultivate his lands. Over this spring was a shrine (*mashhad*) ascribed to 'Ali ibn Abi Talib. This is the one the Franks made into a church, and they (had) appointed an overseer for its building and care. (One morning) the overseer awakened and said, 'I saw a person who said, "I am 'Ali ibn Abi Talib. Tell them to revert this place to a mosque (*masjid*), otherwise whoever lives here will perish!"' (The Franks) did not believe him, however, and appointed another, but when they awakened the next morning they found (the new caretaker) dead. After that they allowed it to return to a mosque, and thus it remains today. God knows best.[30]

This wonderful anecdote is rich with several intersecting threads of meaning. On the simplest level, the story of the Mashhad 'Ali in Acre functions as a kind of cautionary tale, an illustration of the potential fate of anyone so presumptuous as to ignore dream-missives of the sort described here. In this case, it provided not only a positive incentive for the foundation of the site, but also a serious proscription – imminent death for those who might disregard the holy person's instructions. As the story illustrates, this threat was not mere empty posturing, and the original overseer's dream-message was vindicated in the unfortunate demise of the Crusaders' second appointee.

Looking more closely, this account is another example of that ubiquitous phenomenon by which holy sites were created in response to a miraculous dream or vision, and by which figurative mapping served to create literal sites of *ziyāra*. A similar story – and its unpleasant sectarian consequences – opened this study and was discussed in the Introduction. As we have seen, particularly in Chapter 2, such dream-stories became essential literary *topoi* in this era, for they played a crucial role in the creation and legitimation of new sites of pilgrimage. Thus, the story can also be read as one small victory in the deeper, ongoing literal and figurative effort to create a new landscape of holy sites. In this case, the story reinforces a notion of the pre-existing Islamic character of the land, for it reports on the reversion of an 'occupied' holy site to Islamic purview during a period when Acre was still firmly in Christian hands.[31] On the literal level, it re-emplaces an Islamic notion of the sacred and reinscribes it on the land by transforming one type of architecture, a church, into another type, a mosque. On a more figurative level, it would be difficult to discover more convincing evidence for the extraordinary power of such tales, and their associated claims to the holiness of the land, to alter the behaviour and belief of medieval Muslims, and, apparently, sometimes even that of contemporary Christians. Dream-visions resulting in the foundation or reclamation of shrines serve as a primary example of the kind of figurative mapping discussed previously, and indeed such visions were a critical force shaping the course of architectural patronage and sectarian relations in the medieval period and a key means by which Muslims achieved the expansion of the boundaries of the Holy Land.

In the context of the Crusades, the growth and increasing frequency of such phenomena make sense. Following the capture of the holy city of Jerusalem – a shocking loss for medieval Muslims, for whom Jerusalem had been the 'first *qibla*' – the Crusaders embarked on a building campaign that filled their small seaside fiefdom with a remarkable number of Christian holy sites. Although several scholars have pointed to the influence of the Frankish conquest as a reason for the intensification of saint veneration by Muslims, research has focused on the city of Jerusalem and its hinterland, or on the transfer of relics from Palestine to Syria, instead of on the broader architectural impact of the conquest, and the evidence for the Christian building campaign as an impetus for Muslim construction has, so far, remained unexamined.[32] In fact, until recently the most comprehensive survey of Crusader architecture dated to the 1920s: Camille Enlart's *Les Monuments des croisés dans le royaume de Jérusalem*, a work that described only about sixty structures. This has meant that until now, our understanding has been that Crusader building activities were quite limited and therefore, by implication, unlikely to have had a significant effect on Islamic building practices outside of the immediate environs of Jerusalem.

In the past decade, however, the publication of Denys Pringle's monumental four-volume study on the churches of the Crusader kingdom of Jerusalem has provided an enlightening new corpus of evidence.[33] According to his catalogue, no fewer than 400 churches, chapels, cathedrals and other holy places were built during the period of the Latin Kingdom, and there were undoubtedly more.[34] This is an astonishing number of new architectural constructions. Given that the Crusader kingdom lasted just under 200 years (and a mere eighty-eight years as a regional power before the loss of Jerusalem in 1187 ushered in the relentless regaining of territory for Islam), even the most conservative estimate, then, indicates an architectural campaign of incredible energy: the Crusaders were building churches and other sacred sites at a rate of at least twenty, perhaps even forty, per decade. Pringle's corpus demonstrates that the emplacement of Christian history by means of the architectural marking of the landscape was of critical concern for the Crusaders. The study has overturned prior conceptions of Crusader church and shrine-building activities, and it also opens up a new context for understanding Muslim architectural construction during and after the Crusades.

Faced with such a rapid transformation of the land in favour of Christianity, a concomitant shift in Muslim attitudes toward this territory and its landscape seems easily explicable, even inevitable.

Indeed, one can directly trace this transformation. As noted briefly in the Introduction, the earliest Islamic sources, while concerned with establishing the holiness of the land of 'al-Sham', did so primarily in terms that any Christian would have found acceptable. These sources, such as Ibn al-Faqih (who died at the end of the ninth century) and al-Raba'i (d. 1052), list sites such as the birthplace of Jesus, the grave of Maryam or the tombs of Biblical prophets such as Hud or Musa as commonly as they do Islamic sites.[35] Furthermore, the Holy Land is understood as primarily the area around Jerusalem, which only occasionally extended to the surrounding territories. As time went on, however, the boundaries of this definition expanded. A hundred years later, the great historian of Damascus Ibn 'Asakir (d. 1176) would speak of the 'Holy Land' (ard al-muqaddasa) in definitively expanded terms: stretching from the coastal plain to the Euphrates. By the Mamluk period, Ibn Shaddad's (d. 1284) description clearly included the entire area known in modern times as the Levant.[36] Along with this expansion of territory, there was a corresponding growth of shrines having a specifically Islamic identification at the expense of the old Biblical and Christian sites. And it was this need for a more clearly defined Islamic landscape that probably accounts most simply for the appearance of so many new shrines and the contemporary expansion of the literature that described them, their locations, and their merits and efficaciousness.

Among such a large number of newly generated sites, devoted to a dizzying array of Islamic saints, Prophetic companions and heroes, the shrines of the 'Alids occupied a very particular place. For perhaps no other Islamic shrine type had such a broad appeal, no other type is so easily infused with specifically Islamic meaning, as these 'Alid holy sites. Unlike so many other holy sites and figures in this sacred territory, the 'Alid shrines were visited primarily by Muslims. And even among sites that were identified as specifically 'Islamic' in this newly generated landscape, only the shrines of the 'Alids could evoke affection and sympathy across the wide and diverse spectrum of Islam's varied sectarian milieu. These 'Alid sites were unifying, to a degree that can be attributed to no other Islamic holy place: for the 'Alids were revered by all Muslims. Thus, they were ideal as objects of patronage by those elite figures who wished to use their symbolic capital to promote or coopt various ideological or political agendas. They were also ideal for patrons of lesser means and influence, for it was rare that devotion to a shrine for the 'Alids would be read as a controversial gesture. In patronising these 'Alid holy places, their benefactors knew they could gain only benefit.

And they certainly patronised them, in numbers that are probably difficult to pin down with certainty. In 2004–5, as part of this research, I carried out an architectural survey of 'Alid shrines that aimed to ascertain the present state of this landscape, following the

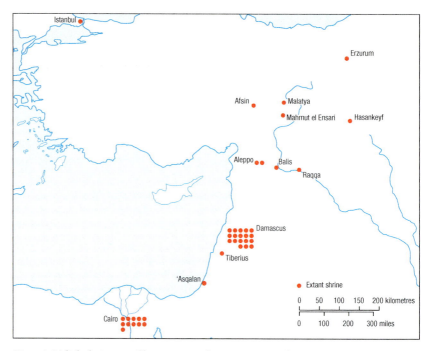

Map 6 *ʿAlid shrines still extant in the eastern Mediterranean.*

itinerary laid out by medieval authors such as al-Harawi. The survey, stretching from eastern Turkey in the north, southwards through Syria from Aleppo to Damascus and ending in Cairo, encompassed much of the medieval region of *Bilād al-Shām* and directly recorded some thirty-seven ʿAlid shrines via photography and GIS technology (Map 6). The survey revealed that a significant number of these medieval-era ʿAlid sites of veneration are still extant. Many retain at least a portion of their medieval architectural fabric intact, and a surprising number are still functional as sites of pilgrimage and devotion. In support of the testimony of later medieval authors, the vast majority of these shrines are located not in the vicinity of Jerusalem, but rather in the area of modern Syria: a full twenty-four of the thirty-seven shrines mentioned by them, and confirmed by the survey, are located in Aleppo or its hinterland, Raqqa or Damascus. Damascus, with fourteen shrines, has by far the highest concentration of ʿAlid holy sites. Their long survival into the contemporary period, in which Shiʿism has become a minority sect, stands as further testimony to the intersectarian quality of devotion to the ʿAlids.

Thus, the generation of an Islamic sacred topography quite literally 'took place' in the form of an increasing number of architectural constructions, and this emplacement of key actions and events in Islamic history appears to be at least in part a response to the rapid Christian sanctification of the land that occurred during the Crusader occupation. There were undoubtedly other influences as well – we have discussed at length here the heightened awareness of sectarianism in the period of Sunni Revival, but there was also the rise of Sufism and the expansion of popular religion during what Daniella Talmon-Heller has called a 'pious age'.[37] Furthermore, Zangid, Ayyubid and Mamluk investment in shrines and holy places was part of a larger building boom that led to the construction of an unprecedented number of madrasas, khanqas and dār al-ḥadīths, in addition to shrines. According to Stephen Humphreys, in Damascus alone there were 241 acts of construction in the sixty-seven years between 1193 and 1260.[38] And, as we have seen, Christian holy places were transformed and reappropriated, as churches became mosques and shrines lost their Christian tenants to be reclaimed for Muslim holy figures. Frankish churches in cities like Ramla, Hebron, Gaza and Tarsus were transformed into mosques, and cathedrals like that of St John the Baptist in Beirut or the Byzantine Cathedral of St Helena in Aleppo were reinvented as mosques or madrasas.[39] It is clear that the land was mapped by Muslims both figuratively, by means of ritual practices such as dream-visions, rediscovered relics, miraculous events and rituals associated with ziyāra, and literally, by means of architectural construction.

If, as argued above, such acts of architectural construction are ritual practice, the creation of a broader landscape of such sites is, in essence, a kind of meta-ritual act. Meta-rituals are rituals that affect the ritual sphere as such: rituals that by virtue of their enactment change or alter the practice of other rituals.[40] This is why the expansion of an Islamic sacred landscape in this period was to have a far-reaching effect on ordinary Muslims' understanding of history, and of their place in its unfolding: because it enabled a notion of connection between otherwise individual shrines marking the actions that comprised history. For as we have seen, this was not primarily a feature-based landscape, it was – more decidedly than had been Christian and Jewish holy topography before it – a 'landscape of deeds', in which the actions of holy figures at specific locations in the landscape, and the ritual behaviours of the countless Muslims who came after them, were the defining and consolidating generative forces. It was a landscape made up of varied but related types of holy sites, each of which marked an event in historical or eschatological time. These types included turbas, qubbas and qabrs, all created to mark the action of burial of a holy figure, mashhads, or places of the witnessing of significant events, maqams, places of remembrance of holy figures who perhaps stopped at the site, sites of battle and victory, sites of miracle, sites of healing, sites of martyrdom and 'predictive' sites that marked the location of future events that would unfold in Islamic eschatology, such as the location of Jesus's future descent upon the south-east minaret of the Umayyad mosque in Damascus.[41] These sites are the locations at which the individual acts that made up sacred history unfolded, at which holy figures stopped to preach, to pray, to fight or to die, and these initial acts were the generative forces for the initial transformation of sites from ordinary to extraordinary. But its sustaining force was the reciprocal one brought into play by popular ritual practice, the actions of generations of pious visitants, scholars, religious leaders, sultans and shaykhs whose behaviours included visitation, prayer and remembrance, but also building, renovation and expansion of the site itself, which, in turn, encouraged and supported further visitation and veneration. The creation of a broader landscape of such sites can be conceived of as a meta-ritual because this more comprehensive notion of landscape influenced the perception of each of its localised component sites of devotion. The meta-ritual of constructing landscape by linking sites in textual sources, by architectural construction, and the marking of pathways by visitation and devotional practice, contextualised, linked and connected each discrete ritual site and aligned them as individuals within a shared, unified field of pious ritual locales: a new, Islamic sacred landscape that could indeed – as Ibn ʿAsakir observed at the opening of this chapter – serve as intercessor for pious Muslims of all sectarian allegiances on the Day of Judgment.

Notes

1. ʿAli ibn al-Hasan Ibn ʿAsakir, *Taʾrikh Madinat Dimashq*, ed. Salah al-Din al-Munajjid (Damascus: Matbuʿat al-Majmaʿ al-ʿIlmi al-ʿArabi, 1951), vol. 2, p. 96.
2. Although not explored here, Islamic cartography was well developed by the ninth century. See S. Maqbul Ahmad, 'Kharīṭa (or Khārīṭa)', *Encyclopaedia of Islam*, 2nd edition, ed. P. Bearman et al. Brill Online, http://referenceworks.brillonline.com.ezproxy.lib.utexas.edu/entries/encyclopaedia-of-islam-2/kharita-or-kharita-COM_0498 (accessed 24 July 2013); J. B. Harley and David Woodward, eds, *The History of Cartography, Volume 2, Book 1: Cartography in the Traditional Islamic and South Asian Societies* (Chicago, IL: University of Chicago Press, 1992).
3. I borrow the literal/figurative dichotomy from Dorothea French, but the definition of the terms here is my own. See Dorothea French, 'Mapping sacred centers: Pilgrimage and the creation of Christian topographies in Roman Palestine', in *Jahrbuch für Antike und Christentum. Ergänzungsband* (Münster: Aschendorff, 1995), p. 792.
4. J.Z. Smith, *To Take Place: Toward Theory in Ritual* (Chicago, IL: University of Chicago Press, 1987).
5. Catherine Bell was the first to define ritual as being situated in the body and as being a non-habitual, repetitive practice, thus paving the way for the relationship between the body, its action in space and its role in the creation of place. She laid out her theory of ritual in two books: *Ritual Theory, Ritual Practice* (New York: Oxford University Press, 1992) and *Ritual: Perspectives and Dimensions* (New York: Oxford University

Press, 1997). J. Z. Smith's *To Take Place* built upon this notion by arguing for the 'emplacement' of ritual practice. Theorisations of space and place have grown rapidly in fields such as anthropology and geography in the past few decades; for a summary see Erica Carter et al., eds, *Space and Place: Theories of Identity and Location*, (London: Lawrence and Wishart, 1993); and, more recently, Paul C. Adams et al., eds, *Textures of Place: Exploring Humanist Geographies* (Minneapolis, MN: University of Minnesota Press, 2001). Authors who have engaged ritual and its traces in the material record via archaeology include Colin Renfrew, *Archaeology of Cult: The Sanctuary at Phylakopi* (London: British School at Athens and Thames & Hudson, 1985); Timothy Insoll, *Archaeology, Ritual, Religion* (London and New York: Routledge, 2004); and Anna Lucia D'Agata et al., *Archaeologies of Cult: Essays on Ritual and Cult in Crete* (Princeton, NJ: American School of Classical Studies at Athens, 2009).

6. Ian Straughn, 'An aptitude for sacred space', in Cecelia Feldman Weiss and Claudia Moser, eds, *Locating the Sacred: Theoretical Approaches to the Emplacement of Religion*, Joukowsky Institute Press series, no. 3 (Oxford: Oxbow Books, forthcoming 2014). My sincere thanks to Cecelia Feldman Weiss for sharing an advance copy of several articles from this volume.

7. Alastair Northedge, 'Archaeology and Islam', in Graeme Barker, ed., *Companion Encyclopedia of Archaeology* (London & New York: Routledge, 1999), vol. 2, 1077–107.

8. Smith, *To Take Place*, p. 104; Straughn, 'Aptitude', 282.

9. Paraphrasing Straughn, 'Aptitude', 282.

10. Weiss and Moser, eds, *Locating the Sacred*, p. 10.

11. Cyrille Jalabert, 'Comment Damas est devenue une métropole Islamique', *Bulletin d'Études Orientales* 53–4 (2001–2), 18.

12. Ibid., 14–41.

13. Ibid., 32–3.

14. Paul M. Cobb, 'Virtual sacrality: Making Muslim Syria sacred before the Crusades', *Medieval Encounters* 8, 1 (2002), 35–55; Josef Meri, *The Cult of Saints Among Muslims and Jews in Medieval Syria* (Oxford: Oxford University Press, 2002), p. 31; Daniella Talmon-Heller, *Islamic Piety in Medieval Syria: Mosques, Cemeteries and Sermons under the Zangids and Ayyubids (1146–1260)* (Leiden: Brill, 2007), pp. 190–209.

15. Zayde Antrim, 'Ibn Asakir's representations of Syria and Damascus in the introduction to the *Tarikh madinat dimashq*', *International Journal of Middle East Studies* 38 (2006), 115.

16. Sabine MacCormack, 'Loca sancta: The organization of sacred topography in late antiquity', in Robert Ousterhout, ed., *The Blessings of Pilgrimage* (Urbana, IL and Chicago, IL: University of Illinois Press, 1990), p. 9.

17. Vergil, *Aeneid*, 8:347–54.

18. Chase Robinson, *Islamic Historiography* (Cambridge: Cambridge University Press, 2003). For more on the role of history writing in Islamic society, see especially Chapter 6, 'Historiography and Society'.

19. 'Alid figures who eventually died and were buried in the cemetery of Bab al-Saghir in Damascus (see Chapter 3).

20. Khalid Sindawi, 'The head of Husayn Ibn 'Ali from decapitation to burial, its various places of burial, and the miracles that it performed', *Journal of Ancient Near Eastern Studies* 40 (2003), 246.

21. Nisibin, today in Turkey on the Syrian border, is located opposite the Syrian town of Qamishli. Sindawi, 'Head', 246; ʿAli Ibn Abi Bakr Al-Harawi, *Kitab al-Isharat ila Maʿrifat al-Ziyarat*, ed. and trans. Josef Meri as *A Lonely Wayfarer's Guide to Pilgrimage* (Oxford: Oxford University Press, 2004), p. 164.

22. Several other, less well-known cities and towns are also mentioned. Sindawi, 'Head', 246; Al-Harawi, *al-Isharat*, ed. Meri, p. 295.

23. Sindawi, 'Head', 246–7. For more on this phenomenon, see Khalid Sindawi, 'Al-Husain Ibn ʿAli and Yahya Ibn Zakariyya in the Shiʿite sources: A comparative study', *Islamic Culture* 78 (2004), 37–54.

24. Al-Harawi, *al-Isharat*, ed. Meri, p. 32. As noted in Chapter 4, Meri's translation is inaccurate here; it reads 'The shrine of al-Husayn *ibn* Zayn al-ʿAbidin', but on the facing page the Arabic text clearly reads 'The shrine of al-Husayn *and* Zayn al-ʿAbidin': these two shrines are present today.

25. Sindawi, 'Head', 249.

26. Meri, *Cult of Saints*, p. 193.

27. Ibid., pp. 193–4.

28. Talmon-Heller, *Islamic Piety*, p. 191.

29. Jalabert, 'Damas', 14–15.

30. Meri, *Wayfarer's Guide*, pp. 43–5.

31. Acre would be famously taken by the Mamluk armies only in 1291, in a decisive rout that drove the Crusaders from the Holy Land. Since the account appears in the narrative of al-Harawi, who died in 1215, the reversion of this shrine must have take place no sooner than the early thirteenth century, when the Crusaders were still in control of the city.

32. Examples include Emmanuel Sivan, 'Le caractère sacré de Jérusalem dans l'Islam aux XXIIe–XXIIIe siècles', *Studia Islamica* 27 (1967), 149–82; Elchanan Reiner, 'A Jewish response to the Crusades. The dispute over sacred places in the Holy Land', in *Juden und Christen zur Zeit der Kreuzzüge*, ed. A. Haverkamp (Sigmaringen: Jan Thorbecke Verlag, 1999), pp. 202–31; Joseph Sadan, 'Le Tombeau de Moïse à Jéricho et à Damas. Une Compétition entre deux lieux saints principalement à l'époque ottomane', *Revue des Études Islamiques* 49 (1981), 59–100.

33. Denys Pringle, *The Churches of the Crusader Kingdom of Jerusalem, A Corpus*, 4 vols (Cambridge: Cambridge University Press, 1993–2009).

34. Ibid., vol. 1, p. 1.

35. ʿAli ibn Muhammad al-Rabaʿi, *Fadaʾil al-Sham wa-Dimashq*, ed. Salah al-Din al-Munajjid (Damascus: Matbaʿat al-Turqi, 1950), p. 19; Antrim, *Place and Belonging*, pp. 85–8.

36. Antrim, *Place and Belonging*, pp. 267, 287.

37. Talmon-Heller, *Islamic Piety*, p. 207.

38. R. Stephen Humphreys, 'Politics and architectural patronage in Ayyubid Damascus', in C. E. Bosworth et al., *The Islamic World from Classical to Modern Times* (Princeton, NJ: Darwin Press, 1989), 169–71.

39. Carole Hillenbrand, *The Crusades: Islamic Perspectives* (Edinburgh: Edinburgh University Press, 1999), pp. 374–5.

40. For a brief discussion of this concept, see Paul Töbelmann, 'Excommunication in the Middle Ages: A meta-ritual and the many faces of its efficacy', in William Sturman Sax, Johannes Quack and Jan Weinhold, eds, *The Problem of Ritual Efficacy* (Oxford: Oxford University Press, 2010), pp. 106–10.

41. Josef Meri defines various shrine types; see *Cult of Saints*, pp. 262–72.

CONCLUSION

A Time of Miracles

While I was in a state of weeping, humility and submissiveness, an image of a respectable and important woman suddenly appeared before me, venerable ... and she said to me, 'Oh my dear son! May God increase your respect and good manners. Did you not know that my grandfather the Messenger of God MPBUH and his Companions used to visit Umm Ayman ...?' I was disquieted by her words, which caused me to become unconscious. When I came to, I did not find her. This prompted me to visit her down to this day.[1]

THE WORLD DESCRIBED in this book was one where miracles like this were commonplace. It was a world where divine lights frequently descended to earth from the heavens, where poor shepherds could become visionaries and inspire grand building projects, and where preachers filled mosques much in the way that pop stars fill stadiums today. It was, as noted in the Introduction, a time of great religious excitement, generating a vibrant and transformative climate of revivalism. The generation of this 'Alid landscape of deeds, the pragmatically ecumenical attitudes of the shrines' patrons and the broader emplacement of Islamic history that occurred in the eleventh to thirteenth centuries in Syria were both the result of this climate and potent forces for its perpetuation, creating new places for the remembrance and preservation of the Islamic past and assuring the shrines' future survival, in many cases up until the present.

In the time I have been completing this manuscript between 2011 and 2013, the Syria I knew – where I lived and carried out research over the previous decade – has joined the Arab uprising, fallen into armed conflict and experienced a devastating loss of life and cultural patrimony. In late July 2012, the shrine of Sayyida Zaynab sustained damage from suicide bombing, and it was attacked again with mortar shells in July 2013 as fighting raged between Shi'i militias charged with protecting the shrine and Syrian army forces. Entire neighbourhoods in Damascus and Aleppo were largely destroyed, and in Aleppo, one of the great monuments of Islamic architecture, the eleventh-century minaret of the Umayyad mosque, has been reduced to a great pile of rubble in a corner of its vast courtyard. In Aleppo's ancient *sūq* – for centuries the beating heart of the city with its seemingly endless winding alleyways lined with goods of every description – medieval caravanserais, religious schools and mosques lie burned and abandoned. The conflict is now clearly sectarian in nature, with profound consequences for neighbouring countries like Lebanon and Iraq.[2] This reality has made writing about the unifying force of Syria's landscape of ʿAlid shrines a poignant enterprise, leaving me to wonder at times whether the past I have written of here is relevant for Syria's present. And yet, that past beckons, with its evidence of coexistence even in times of contestation. This is not to say that Syria's past was free of controversy, sectarian or otherwise; far from it. But it is clear that the history of relations between Syria's richly varied population of Muslims, not to mention its Christians and Jews, is far more nuanced than can be accounted for by direct dichotomies of sect or political allegiance. Just as today, Syria's past was one in which such boundaries were fluid and continuously-negotiated, and one in which the symbolic appropriation, creation and renewal of holy sites played a role in creating places of cooperation and pragmatic coexistence.[3]

As we have seen in this study, Syria's sectarian history is little known. 'The study of Shiites in the Ayyubid epoch is confronted with a major problem of sources,' writes Anne-Marie Eddé in her monumental study on the Ayyubids of Aleppo.[4] Few Shiʿi sources seem to have survived the Sunni reaction of the Zangid, Ayyubid and Mamluk periods. Sunni authors, she continues, give only limited notice of the activities of prominent Shiʿis, a fact that has led many scholars of the Ayyubid period to conclude that Shiʿism was indeed eliminated, or at least greatly curtailed, following the arrival of Nur al-Din. Yet Eddé herself is able to write nearly twenty large-format pages on the subject of the survival of Shiʿism in north Syria. 'Aleppan Shiʿism is not dead in the thirteenth century, far from it,' she declares. Indeed, twelfth- and thirteenth-century Syrian Shiʿism seems to have been more durable and adaptable than is often supposed. The previous pages have aimed to lend a material dimension to this sometimes inconsistent textual evidence, endeavouring also to illustrate the utility of a fruitful marriage between disciplines. Here we have seen that architecture, and the broader landscape created by the collective presence of individual works of architecture, can speak as eloquently as texts about the intentions and aims of patrons, visitors and pilgrims. As we have seen at a myriad of ʿAlid shrines examined in previous chapters, both Sunni and Shiʿi actors were committed to their perpetuation and sustenance. Furthermore, this sort of materially grounded approach can add dimension and depth to the sometimes limited textual sources by demonstrating the strength and relevance of Shiʿi communities over long periods of Syria's history. This research directly builds on Eddé's claim by demonstrating that not only was Shi'ism not dead, but in some parts of Syria, it was a force to be reckoned with well into the Mamluk era. It was a force that demanded, and generated, an alternating politics of both dissent and cooptation but, ultimately, some form of conciliation.

As noted in the Introduction and alluded to in the previous paragraph, another goal of this research has been to develop a methodology for the study of buildings that, despite their demonstrable social, pious or political importance, do not fit into traditional aesthetic categories. While we carefully investigated the architecture and social histories of these buildings in the first four chapters, there are some further questions to be raised about their more purely formal properties, questions that have implications for Islamic architecture as a whole. The buildings discussed here all, in one way or another, raise interesting new issues about patronage and the aesthetic impulse. Why, for example, are the shrines for al-Husayn and al-Muhassin in Aleppo (see Chapter 2) so aesthetically refined? They were each, in their way, landmark buildings. The *mashhad* for al-Muhassin was one of the first buildings to employ, in stone, a brilliant new method of typically Islamic architectural decoration: an interlocking *muqarnas* hood over the portal – an architectural form imported from Mesopotamia, which had no precedent in Christian art whatsoever, and which was given a distinctly Syrian character when it was transformed from plaster into stone. Meanwhile the nearby shrine to al-Husayn stands as one of the great medieval Islamic buildings, its complex formal plan and stunning entrance portal employed in the service of one Sunni sultan's desire to promote sectarian conciliation in the largely Shi'i area over which he ruled. In the service of that impulse, he created a rich iconographic and epigraphic manifesto in stone, and deployed it on the building's exquisite portal, where every entrant to that holy place could easily interpret for himself the main points of the sultan's programme.

And yet, it is puzzling that despite their aesthetic brilliance, these buildings are devoted to a figure, and an event, that were by no means central in Islamic history. While the actual martyrdom of al-Husayn was undoubtedly one of the pre-eminent events of Islamic history, as we have seen in Chapter 5, his head rested at numerous locales along the way. Thus there seems to be no inherent reason why this shrine should be monumentalised more than any other. And al-Muhassin, as noted in Chapter 2, was hardly an important figure in Islamic history; indeed he was so obscure that a fictitious and highly specious genealogy seems to have been concocted, ad hoc and on the spot, to explain the revelatory dream of the shrine's founder, the Hamdanid Sayf al-Dawla.

In Damascus, on the other hand, nearly the reverse is true. The shrines of the cemetery of Bab al-Saghir (discussed in Chapter 3) and four other 'Alid shrines in the city (discussed in Chapter 4), often commemorated far better known figures, such as 'Ali ibn Abi Talib, Sayyida Ruqayya bt. al-Husayn and Sayyida Zaynab bt. 'Ali. And yet, until very recently, their shrines were modest structures which, though they had been continuously visited since the medieval period, were not transformed into large or beautiful buildings. Indeed, the shrines in the cemetery appear never to have been more than simple, one-room, dome-on-square structures, although, as in the case of the shrine for Sayyida Sukayna (Chapter 3), they might have been decorated very beautifully.

Two explanations of this very different manifestation of the aesthetic quality of these shrines present themselves. One is utilitarian, and was discussed in Chapter 3. Namely, it proposed that such shrines were constrained by the fact that they were located in cemeteries, where strong sanctions against moving the graves of the dead and the building of places of prayer over tombs would have prevented their expansion. Yet, such an explanation is only partially satisfactory, and can only begin to account for the vast gulf between the greatly differing aesthetic impacts of these diverse places of pilgrimage. Furthermore, as was shown in Chapter 1, when necessary, such impediments of location seem hardly to have troubled those who desired to expand and beautify shrines, for the Balis *mashhad* showed evidence that its expanded walls cut directly into previous graves.

Additionally, this incredible diversity raises another, even more basic question: namely, how can we know a shrine is, well, a shrine at all? And is there such a thing as an architecture that can be associated with one sect or the other in the medieval period? To take the example provided in the opening chapter, we might ask what clues led the Princeton-Syrian team to identify the small, multi-room structure they excavated at Balis as a shrine? Could it not easily have been a small mosque, a *madrasa* or even a Sufi lodge (*khanqa*)? These are questions that play into a larger observation about Islamic architecture more generally, which I can only touch on briefly here: namely its remarkably 'modular' quality. Students of Islamic architecture have often noted that, absent of clues such as inscriptions and decoration, a visitor to a traditional medieval Islamic building would often be hard-pressed to identify it as a mosque, a school, a shrine or, in some cases, even a palace.[5] This formal similarity amongst various building types is a characteristic that seems to have emerged and been solidified first in the Seljuk era, when a kind of 'toolkit' of forms derived from Sasanian and late Antique architecture were gathered together and redeployed by the Seljuks and their ideological successors, the Zangids and Ayyubids, in what would re-emerge as a specifically Islamic configuration. This 'kit' included formal elements such as the *iwān* (barrel-vaulted hall), a very ancient form dating to at least the Parthian era, monumental domes as markers of sacred space (and their smaller cousins that borrowed the sacred association), the use of towers for both commemorative purposes and as markers of religious space, and certain decorative elements such as changes in writing style and the adoption of decorative and structural *muqarnas*. With the exception of the last two, none of these elements is distinctly Islamic, but combined in certain configurations, they become clearly and undeniably so. And yet, despite this innovative combination of inherited and original elements, there is a certain standardised and recognisable aspect to the way these forms are deployed.

Robert Hillenbrand has addressed the issue of the variation of forms that have traditionally characterised the Islamic mausoleum.[6] While there is a seemingly infinite range of possibilities for how to commemorate the dead in Islamic architecture, there is a simultaneous unifying and conservative thread that runs throughout the formal choices made for all of these buildings, namely a remarkable fidelity to some variation on the simplest possible plan: a domed square.[7] While there are certainly exceptions to this rule, it remains a valid observation, one that has certainly characterised nearly all of the buildings addressed in this study. Except, of course, for two: the Mashhad al-Husayn in Aleppo and the Balis *mashhad*, which was possibly, as I have argued in Chapter 1, devoted to 'Ali. It is interesting to note that these two shrines share a characteristic that is not repeated elsewhere in any of the shrines described in this study: namely, they are not 'tombs'. They are commemorative structures, each devoted not to a burial but to an event – the presence (perhaps only in a dream) of a holy figure or their relics there at some point in the past – but not to the entombment of a holy figure. They most precisely fit the type described in Chapter 5: they are religio-historical events that are distinctively emplaced by means of a highly visible architectural form. This distinctive form was clearly intentional and meant to set these buildings apart from other, more ordinary shrine types. Thus, it seems reasonable to build upon Hillenbrand's observation about the typical form of tombs and mausolea with another type: the *mashhad* type, a commemorative structure which appears to have a much broader range of formal possibilities.

And yet, these formal possibilities nevertheless all share an overlapping set of characteristics with many other Islamic building types. How, then – to return to our question – could the Syrian-Princeton team be sure they had discovered a *mashhad*? And how, to broaden the question, can we find unifying aesthetic and formal characteristics for any of the buildings we have studied here? For they range from forms so grand as to evoke comparison with the greatest buildings of Islamic history to those so humble that they have not, until now, been considered as even worthy of the art historian's notice.

The answer, I believe, lies not in the realm of form, but in that of practice, the kind of ritual practice that generates materiality and that thereby generated the landscape of deeds discussed in Chapter 5. The Balis *mashhad* was identified as a shrine because of several features that fall more comfortably within the realm of social praxis and ritual behaviour than under the rubric of any specific architectural element or formal quality. Indeed, in form, the Balis shrine is a simple, multi-room building with a prayer hall, built around a columned central space, and as such, its form could have encompassed any small mosque or religious school. But several aspects of its siting and use argue otherwise.

First, it was built within a cemetery. In the canonical collections of *hadīth*, congregational mosques are generally prohibited from being built in cemeteries, an interdiction that is generally observed.[8] While many *madrasa*s are known to have been built at the graves of famous scholars, it is rare that tombs were incorporated into the plans of mosques.[9] Furthermore, as noted in Chapter 4, ʿAlid shrines are often located near, yet outside of, cities. It is not entirely clear why this should be, but of the seventeen shrines examined in detail here, this is true of all but two. This habit perhaps arose from a desire to divert the large number of pilgrims inevitably attracted to such sites and to confine ritual practices and behaviours to a locale where large numbers of people would be more easily managed and accommodated. As extremely beloved sites of popular devotion, these shrines' urban liminality played an important, and largely overlooked, role in the urban and suburban development of Islamic cities. It is also another means by which a shrine can be differentiated from other types of Islamic architecture, despite the seemingly endless creativity invested in their medieval form, decoration and spatial configuration. And it is precisely this quality of social praxis, rather than merely their formal elements, which makes shrines such a rich source, not only for architectural history, but also for the social history of the medieval central Islamic lands.

Scholars of medieval social history have long commented, with frustration, on the limitations of their sources. Most medieval historians are primarily textualists, and because of comparatively high rates of literacy in the medieval Islamic world, Islamic studies has always benefited from a marvellous surfeit of texts. However, these texts, sponsored as they were by the court and emerging from the circles of the *ʿulamāʾ* or religious scholars, have been criticised for perpetuating a view of medieval Islamic history that is perhaps unduly focused on the interests and worldview of the court and the religious scholars, and which is limited in terms of its ability to reveal wider aspects of the medieval social world: the lives of peasants or women, for example, or of political or religious opponents of the ruling class, the sources for which were often suppressed or destroyed. The historian Roy Mottahedeh once declared 'Ulamology is a noble science – at least we have to think so, because it is almost all the Islamic social history we will ever have.'[10] This research suggests otherwise, and argues that architecture and material culture can be the very source material that fills the perplexing lacunae of these textual sources.

Here, we have situated ourselves where the shrines themselves did: at the critical juncture between materiality and textuality, between belief, politics and social praxis. Indeed, this research has argued that material culture, in this case an architectural manifestation in the form of the shrines of the ʿAlids, is a greatly underutilised source for the sectarian history of the central Islamic lands. While these shrines have long been associated primarily with Shiʿi practice, the ʿAlid shrines of the Levant were revered by virtually all Muslims and, as such, were locales that generated and embraced multifaceted and polysemous meanings – and meaning-making – at a particularly charged moment in Islamic history: the period of the revival of Sunnism. Thus, though at first glance many of these shrines appear rather insignificant architecturally, close analysis and investigation can yield new information about the relationships between various Islamic groups in the medieval era, groups that have sometimes been marginalised and neglected because of the scattered nature of the source material. Indeed, perhaps more than any other building type, buildings like the shrines of the ʿAlids are ideally suited for 'making the silent masses speak'.[11] In our study of them, we gain much: in understanding not only how Syria's sectarian landscape expressed itself architecturally in the past, but also how Syria's past has already emplaced a model for a rich and diverse coexistence in the present.

Notes

1. As quoted in Ibn al-Hawrani, *Kitab al-Isharat ila Amakin al-Ziyarat*, ed. and trans. Josef W. Meri. *Medieval Encounters* 7, 1 (2001), p. 67; the full text can be found in Chapter 4. The story appears in several sources, see also Yusuf ibn Hasan Ibn al-Mibrad, *Thimar al-Maqasid fi Dhikr al-Masajid*, ed. Muhammad Asʿad Talas. Beirut: n.p., 1943), p. 166.
2. 'UN observers enter Syrian town after bombing damages shrine', *CBC News*, 14 June 2012. Online at www.cbc.ca/news/world/ story/2012/06/14/syria-shrine-bombing.html, (accessed 31 July 2012).
3. Pouzet speaks eloquently of the complexity of sectarian relations in medieval Damascus; see *Damas au VIIe–XIIIe siècle: vie et structures religieuses d'une métropole Islamique* (Beirut: Dar al-Machreq, 1988), pp. 245–6, 260–3.
4. Anne-Marie Eddé, *La principauté ayyoubide d'Alep* (Stuttgart: Steiner, 1999), p. 436.
5. I thank Oleg Grabar for bringing this characteristic of Islamic architecture to my attention.
6. Robert Hillenbrand, *Islamic Architecture* (New York: Columbia University Press, 1994), pp. 268–330.
7. Ibid., p. 270.
8. The reason for this separation of places of prayer from gravesites has to do with a desire to prevent perceived 'pagan' practices that were reminiscent of idolatry, such as the worship of ancestors. See

Muhammad ibn Ismaʿil al-Bukhari, *Kitab Jamiʿal-Sahih*, ed. Ludolf Krel (Leiden: Brill, 1862–8), vol. 1, p. 20; Ahmad ibn Muhammad Ibn Hanbal, *Musnad al-Imam Ahmad ibn Hanbal*, ed. ʿAli ibn Malik Muttaqi (Beirut: Al-Maktab al-Islami lil-Tabaʿah waʾl-Nashr, 1398/1978), vol. 1, pp. 229, 287; Abu ʿAbd al-Rahman Ahmad Al-Nasaʾi, *Sunan*, ed. Muhammad ibn ʿAbd al-Hadi Sindi (Cairo: Al-Matbaʿa al-Maymaniyya, 1894), vol. 1, p. 287. Some Shiʿi *hadīth* scholars also recorded this prohibition; see Muhammad b. al-Hasan Hurr al-ʿAmili, *Wasaʾil al-Shiʿa ila Tahsil Masaʾil al-Shariʿa*, ed. ʿAbd al-Rahman Rabbani and Muhammad Razi (Tehran: Al- (?)Maktaba al-Islamiyya, 1977–8), vol. 4, p. 127.

9. A famous example may be found at the grave of the Imam al-Shafʿi in Cairo, where Saladin built an expansive *madrasa* in the late twelfth century. See Stephennie Mulder, 'The mausoleum of Imam al-Shafʿi', *Muqarnas* 23 (2006), 15–46.

10. Rizwi Faizer, 'Review of Jonathan Berkey, *Popular Preaching and Religious Authority in the Medieval Islamic Near East*', H-Mideast-Medieval, H-Net Reviews, May 2003. Online at http://www.h-net.org/~midmed (accessed 13 July 2013).

11. Nikki R. Keddie, 'Material culture and geography: Toward a holistic comparative history of the Middle East', *Comparative Studies in Society and History* 26, 4 (October 1984), 734.

Bibliography

Primary sources

Al-ʿAdawi, Mahmud ibn Muhammad. *Kitab al-Ziyarat bi-Dimashq*, ed. Salah al-Din al-Munajjid. Damascus, Al-Majmaʿ al-ʿIlmi al-ʿArabi bi-Dimashq, 1956.

Al-Badri, ʿAbdallah ibn Muhammad. *Nuzhat al-Anam fi Mahasin al-Sham*, ed. and trans. Henri Sauvaire as 'Description de Damas', *Journal Asiatique* 9 (May–June 1896), 369–459.

Benjamin of Tudela, *The Itinerary of Benjamin of Tudela*, ed. M. N. Adler. New York: P. Feldheim, 1907.

Al-Bukhari, Muhammad ibn Ismaʿil, *Kitab Jamiʿ al-Sahih*, 3 vols, ed. Ludolf Krel. Leiden: Brill, 1862–8.

Al-Ghazzi, al-Kamil ibn Husayn. *Nahr al-Dhahab fi Taʾrikh Halab*, ed. Mahmud Fakhuri and Shawqi Shaʿath. Aleppo: Dar al-Qalam al-ʿArabi, 1991.

Al-Harawi, ʿAli Ibn Abi Bakr. *Kitab al-Isharat ila Maʿrifat al-Ziyarat*, ed. Janine Sourdel-Thomine. Damascus: al-Maʿhad al-Faransi bi-Dimashq, 1953.

——. *A Lonely Wayfarer's Guide to Pilgrimage*, ed. and trans. Josef Meri. Oxford: Oxford University Press, 2004.

——. *Guide des lieux de pèlerinage*, ed. and trans. Janine Sourdel-Thomine. Damascus: Institut français de Damas, 1957.

Hurr al-ʿAmili, Muhammad b. al-Hasan. *Wasaʾil al-Shiʿa ila Tahsil Masaʾil al-Shariʿa*, 20 vols, ed. ʿAbd al-Rahman Rabbani and Muhammad Razi. Tehran: Al-Maktaba al-Islamiyya, 1977–8.

Ibn al-ʿAdim, Kamal al-Din ʿUmar. *Bughyat al-Talab fi Taʾrikh Halab*, 12 vols, ed. Suhayl Zakkar. Damascus: S. Zakkar, 1988–9.

——. *Zubdat al-Halab min Taʾrikh Halab*, 3 vols, ed. Sami al-Dahhan. Damascus: Al-Maʿhad al-Faransi bi-Dimashq lil-Dirasat al-ʿArabiyya, 1951–68.

Ibn ʿAsakir, ʿAli ibn al-Hasan. *Taʾrikh Madinat Dimashq*, ed. Salah al-Din al-Munajjid. Damascus: Matbuʿat al-Majmaʿ al-ʿIlmi al-ʿArabi, 1951.

Ibn al-Athir, Diyaʾ al-Din. *Rasaʾil Ibn al-Athir*, ed. Anis al-Maqdisi. Beirut: Dar al-ʿIlm lil-Malayin, 1959.

Ibn al-Athir, ʿIzz al-Din. *Al-Kamil fi-l-Taʾrikh*, 13 vols, ed. C. J. Tornberg. Beirut: Dar Sadr and Dar Beirut, 1965–7.

Ibn Battuta. *Rihlat Ibn Battuta al-Musamma Tuhfat al-Nuzzar fi Gharaʾib al-Amsar wa-ʿAjaʾib al-Asfar*, ed. ʿAbd al-Hadi al-Tazi. Rabat: Al-Mamlaka al-Maghribiyya, 1997.

Ibn Hanbal, Ahmad ibn Muhammad. *Musnad al-Imam Ahmad ibn Hanbal*, 6 vols, ed. 'Ali ibn Malik Muttaqi. Beirut: Al-Maktab al-Islami lil-Taba'ah wa'l-Nashr, 1978.

Ibn al-Hawrani, 'Uthman ibn Ahmad. *Kitab al-Isharat ila Amakin al-Ziyarat*, ed. and trans. Josef W. Meri as 'A late medieval Syrian pilgrimage guide: Ibn al-Hawrani's Al-Isharat ila amakin al-ziyarat (Guide to Pilgrimage Places)', *Medieval Encounters* 7, 1 (2001), 3–78.

Ibn Jubayr, Muhammad ibn Ahmad. *Rihla, or The Travels of Ibn Jubayr*, ed. William Wright. Leiden: Brill, 1907 (reprinted 1973).

——. *Voyages*, trans. and annotated Maurice Gaudefroy-Demombynes. Paris: P. Geuthner, 1949.

Ibn al-Mibrad, Yusuf ibn Hasan. *Thimar al-Maqasid fi Dhikr al-Masajid*, ed. Muhammad As'ad Talas. Beirut: n.p., 1943.

Ibn Shaddad, Muhammad ibn 'Ali. *Al-A'laq al-Khatira fi Dhikr 'Umara' al-Sham wa-l-Jazira*, ed. Y. 'Abbara, vol. 3, parts 1–2. Damascus: Wizarat al-Thaqafa wa al-Irshad al-Qawmi, 1978.

——. *Al-A'laq al-Khatira fi Dhikr Umara' al-Sham wa-l-Jazira: Ta'rikh Madinat Dimashq* (Damascus), ed. Sami al-Dahhan. Damascus: Al-Ma'had al-Faransi lil-Dirasat al-'Arabiyya, 1956.

——. *Al-A'laq al-Khatira fi Dhikr 'Umara' al-Sham wa-l-Jazira* (Aleppo), ed. Dominique Sourdel. Damascus: Al-Ma'had al-Faransi bi-Dimashq, 1953.

——. *Al-A'laq al-Khatira, Wasf li-Shamal Suriyya* (Northern Syria), ed. Anne-Marie Eddé. *Bulletin d'Études Orientales* 32–3 (1981–2).

——. *Déscription de la Syrie du Nord*, ed. and trans. Anne-Marie Eddé-Terrasse. Damascus: Institut français de Damas, 1984.

——. *Ta'rikh al-Malik al-Zahir*, ed. Ahmad Hutayt. Wiesbaden: Franz Steiner, 1983.

Ibn Shahin al-Zahiri, Gars al-Din Khalil. *Zubdat Kashf al-Mamalik wa-Bayan al-Turuq wa-l-Masalik*, ed. Paul Ravaisse. Paris: E. Leroux, 1894.

Ibn Shahrashub, Muhammad ibn 'Ali. *Manaqib Al Abi Talib*, 3 vols, ed. Muhammad Kazim al-Kutubi. Najaf: Al-Matba'a al-Haydariyya, 1956.

Ibn Shakir al-Kutubi, Muhammad. *'Uyun al-Tawarikh*, ed. and trans. H. Sauvaire as 'Description de Damas', *Journal Asiatique* (May–June 1896), 369–424.

Ibn al-Shihna, Muhibb al-Din Muhammad ibn Muhammad. *Al-Durr al-Muntakhab fi Ta'rikh Mamlakat Halab*, ed. Yusuf Sarkis. Beirut: Al-Matba'a al-Kathulikiyya, 1909.

——. *'Les perles choisies' d'Ibn ash-Shichna*, trans. Jean Sauvaget (Mémoires de l'Institut français de Damas: Matériaux pour servir à l'histoire de la ville d'Alep, I.). Beirut: Institut français de Damas, 1933, pp. 85–8.

Ibn Tulun, Shams al-Din Muhammad ibn 'Ali. *Qurrat al-'Uyun fi Akhbar Bab Jayrun*, ed. Salah al-Din al-Munajjid. Damascus: Matbu'at al-Majma' al-'Ilmi al-'Arabi bi-Dimashq, 1964.

Kahhala, Rida. *A'lam al-Nisa' fi 'Alamay al-Arab wa'l-Islam*, 5 vols. Damascus: al-Matba'a al-Hashimiyya, 1358/1959.

Al-Muqaddasi, Muhammad ibn Ahmad. *Ahsan al-Taqasim fi Ma'rifat al-Aqalim*, ed. de Goeje (vol. 3 of *Bibliotheca Geographorum Arabicorum*). Leiden: Brill, 1967.

——. *The Best Divisions for Knowledge of the Regions: A Translation of Ahsan al-taqasim fi ma'rifat al-aqalim*, ed. and trans. Basil A.

Collins. Reading: Centre for Muslim Contribution to Civilization/Garnet Publishing, 1994.

Al-Nasa'i, Abu 'Abd al-Rahman Ahmad. *Sunan*, 2 vols, ed. Muhammad ibn 'Abd al-Hadi Sindi. Cairo: Al-Matba'a al-Maymaniyya, 1894.

Nasir-i Khusrau, *Safarnama*, ed. Mahmud Ghanizada. Berlin: Chapkhana Kaviyani, 1922.

Al-Nu'aymi, 'Abd al-Qadir ibn Muhammad. *Al-Daris fi Ta'rikh al-Madaris*, ed. Ja'far al-Hasani. Cairo: Maktabat al-Thaqafa al-Diniyya, 1988 [1948].

Al-Qalqashandi, Ahmad ibn 'Ali. *Al-Subh al-A'sha fi Sina'at al-Insha'*, selections trans. Maurice Gaudefroy-Demombynes as *La Syrie à l'époque des Mamelouks*. Paris: P. Geuthner, 1923.

Al-Raba'i, 'Ali ibn Muhammad. *Fada'il al-Sham wa-Fadl Dimashq*, ed. Abi 'Abd al-Rahman 'Adil ibn Sa'd. Beirut: Dar al-Kutub al-'Ilmiyya, 2001.

Al-Shaybi, Kamil Mustafa. *Al-Sila bayn al-Tasawwuf wa-l-Tashayyu'*. Cairo: Dar al-Ma'arif, 1969.

Al-Subki, Taj al-Din. *Tabaqat al-Shafa'iyya al-Kubra*, 10 vols, ed. A. al-Hilu and M. al-Tanahi. Cairo: 'Isa al-Bab al-Halabi, 1964–76.

Al-Tabari, Abu Ja'far Muhammad ibn Jarir. *Ta'rikh al-Rusul wa-l-Muluk*, ed. M. J. de Goeje. Leiden: Brill, 1879–1901.

Tabari, Muhammad Ibn Jarir Ibn Rustam. *Dala'il al-Imama*. Najaf: Al-Matba'a al-Haydariyya, 1949.

Yaqut ibn 'Abdallah al-Hamawi, *Mu'jam al-Buldan*, 10 vols, ed. Muhammad Amin Khanaji. Cairo: Matba'a al-Sa'ada, 1906.

Al-Yunini, Musa ibn Muhammad. *Dhayl Mir'at al-Zaman*, 4 vols. Hyderabad: Matba'at Majlis Dayrat al-Ma'arif al-'Urthmaniyya, 1954–61.

Secondary sources

Adams, Paul C., Steven Hoelscher and Karen E. Till, eds, *Textures of Place: Exploring Humanist Geographies*. Minneapolis, MN: University of Minnesota Press, 2001.

Afsaruddin, Asma. *Excellence and Precedence: Medieval Islamic Discourse on Legitimate Leadership*. Leiden & Boston, MA: Brill, 2002.

Allen, Terry. *Ayyubid Architecture*, 7th edition. Occidental, CA: Solipsist Press, 2003. Online at www.sonic.net/~tallen/palmtree/ayyarch/index. htm.

Antrim, Zayde. 'Place and belonging in Medieval Syria, 6th/12th to 8th/14th centuries'. PhD dissertation, Harvard University, 2004.

——. 'Ibn Asakir's representations of Syria and Damascus in the introduction to the *Tarikh madinat dimashq*', *International Journal of Middle East Studies* 38 (2006), 109–29.

——. *Routes and Realms: The Power of Place in the Early Islamic World*. New York: Oxford University Press, 2012.

Ashmore, Wendy and A. Bernard Knapp. *Archaeologies of Landscape: Contemporary Perspectives*. Oxford: Blackwell, 1999.

Bahnassi, A. 'La sauvetage des vestiges de la zone de submersion du barrage de Tabqa sur l'Euphrate', *Monumentum. International Council on Monuments and Sites* 17 (1978), 63–6.

Bar-Asher, Meir Mikhael. *Scripture and Exegesis in Early Imami-Shiism*. Boston, MA: Brill, 1999.

Bausani, Alessandro. 'Religion under the Mongols', in J. A. Boyle, ed., *The Cambridge History of Iran*, 7 vols. Cambridge: Cambridge University Press, 1968, vol. 5, pp. 538–49.

Bell, Catherine. *Ritual: Perspectives and Dimensions*. New York: Oxford University Press, 1997.
——. *Ritual Theory, Ritual Practice*. New York: Oxford University Press, 1992.
Berkey, Jonathan. *The Formation of Islam*. New York: Cambridge University Press, 2003.
Bernheimer, Teresa. *The ʿAlids: First Family of Islam*. Edinburgh: Edinburgh University Press, 2013.
——. 'Shared sanctity: Some notes on ahl al-bayt shrines in the early Talibid genealogies', *Studia Islamica* 108 (2013), 1–15.
Bianquis, Thierry. *Damas et la Syrie sous la domination Fatimide (359–468/969–1076)*. Damascus: Institut français de Damas, 1986.
Bloom, Jonathan. 'The Mosque of the Qarafa in Cairo', *Muqarnas* 4 (1987), 7–20.
Bosworth, Clifford Edmund. *The New Islamic Dynasties*. New York: Columbia University Press, 1996.
Burns, Ross. *Damascus: A History*. London & New York: Routledge, 2005.
——. *Monuments of Syria*. London & New York: I. B. Tauris, 1999.
Caetani, Leone. *Chronographia Islamica: Ossia Riassunto cronologico della storia di tutti i popoli musulmani dall'anno 1 all'anno 922 della higrah (622–1517 dell'èra volgare) corredato della bibliografia di tutte le principali fonti stampate e manoscritte*, 5 vols. Paris: P. Geuthner, 1912.
Cahen, Claude. 'Un chronique chiʿite au temps des Croisades', *Comptes rendus des Séances de l'Académie des Inscriptions et des Belles-Lettres* (1935), 258–69.
Calzoni, Irene. 'Il Mausoleo di Sayyida Zaynab a Damasco'. Unpublished PhD dissertation, University of Venice, 1988.
——. 'Shiite mausoleums in Syria with particular reference to Sayyida Zaynab's Mausoleum', in *Convegno sul tema: La Shiʿa nell'impero Ottomano*. Rome: Accademia nazionale dei Lincei, 1993, pp. 191–201.
Canaan, Tewfik. *Muhammedan Saints and Sanctuaries in Palestine*. London: Luzac and Co., 1927.
Carey, Moya and Margaret S. Graves, 'Islamic art historiography', *Journal of Art Historiography* 6 (June 2012).
Carter, Erica, James Donald and Judith Squires, eds, *Space and Place: Theories of Identity and Location*. London: Lawrence and Wishart, 1993.
Chamberlain, Michael. 'The Crusader era and the Ayyubid dynasty', in Carl Petry, ed., *The Cambridge History of Egypt*, 2 vols. Cambridge: Cambridge University Press, 1998, vol. 1.
Cobb, Paul M. 'Virtual sacrality: Making Muslim Syria sacred before the Crusades', *Medieval Encounters* 8, 1 (2002), 35–55.
Conteneau, G. 'Deuxième mission archéologique à Sidon', *Syria* 5 (1924), 9–23.
Cornu, Georgette. *Atlas du monde arabo-islamique à l'époque classique (IXe–Xe siècles)*. Leiden: Brill, 1985.
D'Agata, Anna Lucia, M. B. Richardson and Aleydis van de Moortel, *Archaeologies of Cult: Essays on Ritual and Cult in Crete*. Princeton, NJ: American School of Classical Studies at Athens, 2009.
De Lorey, Eustache and Gaston Wiet, 'Cénotaphes de deux dames musulmanes à Damas', *Syria* 2 (1921), 221–5.
Diem, Werner and Marco Schöller, *The Living and the Dead in Islam: Epitaphs in Context*. Wiesbaden: Otto Harrassowitz, 2004.

Dodd, Erica Cruikshank and Shereen Khairallah. *The Image of the Word*, 2 vols. Beirut: American University of Beirut, 1981.

Dussaud, René. *Topographie historique de la Syrie antique et médiévale.* Paris: P. Geuthner, 1927.

Dussaud, René, Paul Deschamps and Henri Seyrig, *La Syrie antique et médiévale illustrée.* Paris: P. Geuthner, 1931.

Eddé, Anne-Marie. 'Notes sur la fiscalité de l'État ayyoubide d'Alep au XXXIe siècle', in Philippe Contamine, Thierry Dutour and Bertrand Schnerb, eds, *Commerce, finances et société (XIe–XVIe s.). Recueil de travaux d'histoire médiévale offert à M. le Profeseur Henri Dubois* (Cultures et Civilisations Médiévales, 9). Paris: Presses de l'Université de Paris-Sorbonne, 1993.

——. 'Hérésie et pouvoir politique en Syrie au XIIe siècle: l'exécution d'al-Suhrawardi en 1191', in André Vauchez, ed., *La religion civique à l'époque médiévale et moderne (chrétienté et islam).* Rome: École française de Rome, 1995, pp. 235–44.

——. *La principauté ayyoubide d'Alep.* Stuttgart: Steiner, 1999.

Elisséeff, Nikita. 'Les monuments de Nur ad-Din', *Bulletin d'études orientales* 13 (1951), 5–49.

El-Sandouby, Aliaa. 'The places of the Ahl al-Bayt in Bilad al-Sham: The making of a "shrine"', *ARAM Periodical* 19 (2007), 673–93.

Fakhry, Majid. *A History of Islamic Philosophy.* New York: Columbia University Press, 2004.

Faizer, Rizwi. 'Review of Jonathan Berkey, *Popular Preaching and Religious Authority in the Medieval Islamic Near East*', H-Mideast-Medieval, H-Net Reviews, May 2003. Online at www.h-net.org/~midmed

Farhat, May. *Islamic Piety and Dynastic Legitimacy: The Case of the Shrine of 'Ali ibn Musa al-Rida in Mashhad (10th–17th century).* Unpublished PhD dissertation, Harvard University, 2002.

Finkbeiner, Uwe and Thomas Leisten. 'Emar and Balis 1996 and 1998: A preliminary report of the joint Syrian-German excavations in collaboration with Princeton University', *Berytus* 44 (1999–2000), 5–57.

Flood, Finbarr Barry. *The Great Mosque of Damascus: Studies on the Makings of an Umayyad Visual Culture.* Leiden & Boston, MA: Brill, 2001.

——. *Objects of Translation: Material Culture and Medieval 'Hindu-Muslim' Encounter.* Princeton, NJ: Princeton University Press, 2009.

French, Dorothea. 'Mapping sacred centers: Pilgrimage and the creation of Christian topographies in Roman Palestine', in *Jahrbuch für Antike und Christentum. Ergänzungsband* (Münster: Aschendorff, 1995), pp. 792–7.

Frenkel, Yehoshu'a. 'Baybars and the sacred geography of *Bilad al-Sham*: A chapter in the Islamization of Syria's landscape', *Jerusalem Studies in Arabic and Islam* 25 (2001), 153–70.

Gaube, Heinz. *Arabische Inschriften aus Syrien (Beiruter Texte und Studien*, vol. 17). Beirut: Orient-Institut der Deutschen Morgenländischen Gesellschaft, 1978.

Gaube, Heinz and Eugen Wirth. *Aleppo: Historische und geographische Beiträge zur baulichen Gestaltung, zur sozialen Organisation und zur wirtschaftlischen Dynamik einer vorderasiatischen Fernhandelsmetropole.* Wiesbaden: Ludwig Reichert, 1984.

Gelvin, James L. 'The other Arab nationalism: Syrian/Arab populism in its historical and international contexts', in Israel Gershoni and James Jankowski, eds, *Rethinking Nationalism in the Arab Middle East.* New York: Columbia University Press, 1997, pp. 231–48.

Glassen, Erika. *Der mittlere Weg: Studien zur Religionspolitik und Religiosität der späteren Abbasiden-Zeit*. Wiesbaden: Steiner, 1981.

Golombek, Lisa. 'The draped universe of Islam', in Priscilla P. Soucek, ed., *Content and Context of Visual Arts in the Islamic World*. University Park, PA & London: Pennsylvania State University Press, 1988, pp. 25–50.

Golvin, Lucien and André Raymond. 'Meskene/Balis', *Antiquités de l'Euphrate. Exposition des découvertes de la campagne international de sauvegarde des antiquités de l'Euphrate*. Aleppo: Direction Générale des antiquités et des musées de la République Arabe Syrienne, 1974.

Grabar, Oleg. 'The earliest Islamic commemorative structures, notes and documents', *Ars Orientalis* 6 (1966), 7–46.

Halevi, Leor. *Muhammad's Grave: Death Rites and the Making of Islamic Society*. New York: Columbia University Press, 2007.

Harley, J. B. and David Woodward, eds, *The History of Cartography, Volume 2, Book 1: Cartography in the Traditional Islamic and South Asian Societies*. Chicago, IL: University of Chicago Press, 1992.

Hartmann, Angelika. *An-Nasir li-Din Allah*. Berlin & New York: Walter de Gruyter, 1975.

——. 'Al-Nasir li Din Allah', *Encyclopaedia of Islam*, 2nd edition, 1960–2005. BrillOnline, http://referenceworks.brillonline.com.ezproxy.lib.utexas.edu/entries/encyclopaedia-of-islam-2/al-nasir-li-din-allah-COM_0854

Herzfeld, Ernst. 'Mashhad ʿAli, ein Bau Zeng's II AH 589', *Der Islam* 5 (1914), 358–69.

——. *Die Ausgrabungen von Samarra*, 5 vols. Berlin: D. Reimer, 1921–48.

——. 'Balis', in M. Th. Houtsma, T. W. Arnold, R. Basset and R. Hartmann, eds, *Encyclopaedia of Islam*, 1st edition. Leiden: Brill, 1913–38, p. 634.

——. 'Damascus: Studies in Architecture I, II, III, and IV', *Ars Islamica* 9 (1942), 1–53; 10 (1943), 13–70; 11–12 (1946), 1–71; 13–14 (1948), 118–38.

——. *Matériaux pour un Corpus Inscriptionum Arabicarum. Pt. 2, Syrie du Nord. Inscriptions et monuments d'Alep (MCIA Alep)*, 3 vols. Cairo: Institut français d'archéologie orientale, 1954–6.

Hillenbrand, Carole. *The Crusades: Islamic Perspectives*. Edinburgh: Edinburgh University Press, 1999.

——. 'The Shiʿis of Aleppo in the Zengid Period: Some unexploited textual and epigraphic evidence', in Hinrich Biesterfeldt and Verena Klemm, eds, *Difference and Dynamism in Islam. Festschrift for Heinz Halm on his 70th Birthday* (Würzburg: Ergon-Verlag, 2012), pp. 163–79.

Hillenbrand, Robert. *Islamic Architecture*. New York: Columbia University Press, 1994.

——. 'Qurʾanic epigraphy in medieval Islamic architecture', *Revue des Études Islamiques* 54 (1986), 171–87.

Hodgson, Marshall G. S. *The Order of Assassins. A Struggle of the Early Nizari Ismaʿilis Against the Islamic World*. 's Gravenhage (The Hague): Mouton & Co., 1955.

——. *The Venture of Islam*, 3 vols. Chicago, IL: University of Chicago Press, 1974.

Hoffman-Ladd, Valerie. 'Devotion to the Prophet and his family in Egyptian Sufism', *International Journal of Middle Eastern Studies* 24 (1992), 615–37.

Humphreys, R. Stephen. 'Politics and architectural patronage in Ayyubid Damascus', in C. E. Bosworth, Charles Issawi, Roger Savory and A. L. Udovitch, eds, *The Islamic World from Classical to Modern Times*. Princeton, NJ: Darwin Press, 1989, 169–71.

Insoll, Timothy. *Archaeology, Ritual, Religion*. London & New York: Routledge, 2004.

Jalabert, Cyrille. 'Comment Damas est devenue une métropole Islamique', *Bulletin d' Études Orientales* 53–4 (2001–2), 13–42.

Al-Jamil, Tariq. 'Cooperation and contestation in medieval Baghdad'. Unpublished PhD dissertation, Princeton University, 2004.

Keddie, Nikki R. 'Material culture and geography: Toward a holistic comparative history of the Middle East', *Comparative Studies in Society and History* 26, 4 (October 1984), 709–35.

Khayat, H. M. 'The Si'ite rebellions in Aleppo in the 6th A. H./12th A. D. century', *Revista degli Studi Orientali* 46 (1971), 167–95.

Kohlberg, Etan. 'Some Imami Shi'i views on the Sahaba', *Jerusalem Studies in Arabic and Islam* 5 (1984), 143–75.

Korn, Lorenz. *Ayyubidische Architektur in Ägypten und Syrien: Bautätigkeit im Kontext von Politik und Gesellschaft 564–658/1169–1258*, 2 vols. Heidelberg: Heidelberger Orientverlag, 2004.

Lapidus, Ira. 'Ayyubid religious policy and the development of the schools of law in Cairo', *Colloque international sur l'histoire du Caire*. Cairo: Böhlau, 1969, pp. 279–86.

Leiser, Gary. *The Restoration of Sunnism in Egypt: Madrasas and Mudarrisun, 495–647/1101–1249*. Unpublished PhD dissertation, University of Pennsylvania, 1976.

Leisten, Thomas. 'Between orthodoxy and exegesis: Some aspects of attitudes in the Shari'a toward funerary architecture', *Muqarnas* 7 (1990), 12–22.

———. *Architektur für Tote: Bestattung in architektonischem Kontext in den Kernländern der islamischen Welt zwischen 3./9. und 6./12. Jahrhundert*. Berlin: D. Reimer, 1998.

———. 'For prince and country(side) – The Marwanid Mansion at Balis on the Euphrates'. Paper delivered at the Colloquium on Late Antique and Early Islamic Archaeology in Bilad al-Sham, Deutsches Archäologisches Institut, under the aegis of the Ministry of Culture – Directorate General of Antiquities and Museums in Syria. Damascus, 5–9 November 2006.

MacCormack, Sabina. 'Loca sancta: The organization of sacred topography in late antiquity', in Robert Ousterhout, ed., *The Blessings of Pilgrimage*. Urbana, IL and Chicago: University of Illinois Press, 1990, pp. 7–40.

Makdisi, George. 'The Sunni Revival', in D. S. Richards, ed., *Islamic Civilization 950–1150*. Oxford: Oxford University Press, 1973, pp. 155–7.

Margueron, Jean. 'Les fouilles françaises de Meskéné-Emar (Syrie)', *Comptes rendus de l'Académie des Inscriptions et Belles-Lettres* (April–June 1975), pp. 202–3.

Massignon, Louis. 'Les sept dormants d'Éphèse en Islam et en chrétienté', *Revue des Études Islamiques* 22–5 (1955–7), 61–112.

Mazzaoui, Michel M. *The Origins of the Safawids: Shi'ism, Sufism, and the Ghulat*. Wiesbaden: F. Steiner, 1972.

McGregor, Richard J. A. *Sanctity and Mysticism in Medieval Egypt: The Wafa Sufi Order and the Legacy of Ibn 'Arabi*. Albany, NY: State University of New York Press, 2004.

Meri, Josef. 'Re-appropriating sacred space: Medieval Jews and Muslims seeking Elijah and al-Khadir', *Medieval Encounters* 5 (1999), 237–64.

———. 'A late medieval Syrian pilgrimage guide: Ibn al-Hawrani's *Al-Isharat ila amakin al-ziyarat* (Guide to Pilgrimage Places)', *Medieval Encounters* 7 (2001), 3–78.

——. *The Cult of Saints Among Muslims and Jews in Medieval Syria*. Oxford: Oxford University Press, 2002.

Mervin, Sabrina. 'Sayyida Zaynab: Banlieue de Damas ou nouvelle ville sainte chiite?', *Cahiers d'études sur la Méditerranée orientale et le monde turco-iranien* 22 (1996), 149–62.

Migeon, Gaston. *Manuel d'art musulman: arts plastiques et industriels*, 2 vols. Paris: Picard, 1927.

Mirza, Nasseh Ahmed. *Syrian Ismailism*. Richmond: Curzon, 1997.

Moaz, Khalid and Solange Ory. *Inscriptions arabes de Damas: les stèles funéraires, I. Cimetière d'al-Bab al-Saghir*. Damascus: Institut français de Damas, 1977.

Momen, Moojan. *An Introduction to Shi'i Islam*. New Haven, CT: Yale University Press, 1985.

Morimoto, Kazuo. 'A preliminary study on the diffusion of the *Niqaba al-Talibiyin*: Towards an understanding of the early dispersal of *Sayyids*', in Hidemitsu Kuroki, ed., *The Influence of Human Mobility in Muslim Societies*. London & New York: Kegan Paul, 2003, pp. 3–42.

Mourad, Suleiman and James E. Lindsay, 'Rescuing Syria from the infidels: The contribution of Ibn 'Asakir to the Jihad campaign of Sultan Nur al-Din', *Crusades* 6 (2007), 37–55.

Mourtada, Hani Muhsin and Rida Mahdi Mourtada, Untitled pamphlet. Damascus: Al-Sayedeh Zeinab Centre for Information and Research, n.d.

Mouton, Jean-Michel. 'De quelques reliques conservées à Damas au moyen-âge: stratégie politique et religiosité populaire sous les Bourides', *Annales Islamologiques* 27 (1993), 245–54.

Mulder, Stephennie. 'The Mausoleum of Imam al-Shafi'i', *Muqarnas* 23 (2006), 15–46.

——. 'Seeing the light: Enacting the divine at three medieval Syrian shrines', in David J. Roxburgh, ed., *Envisioning Islamic Art and Architecture: Essays in Honor of Renata Holod*. Leiden: Brill, 2013.

——. 'Abdülhamid and the 'Alids: Ottoman patronage of "Shi'i" shrines in the Cemetery of Bab al-Saghir in Damascus', *Studia Islamica* 108 (2013), 16–47.

——. 'Shrines in the central Islamic lands', in Richard A. Etlin, ed., *The Cambridge World History of Religious Architecture*. New York and Cambridge: Cambridge University Press, forthcoming 2014.

Musil, Alois. *The Middle Euphrates, a Topographical Itinerary*. New York: American Geographical Society of New York, 1927.

Nasr, Sayyid Hossein. 'Shi'ism and Sufism', in Seyyed Hossein Nasr, Hamid Dabashi and Seyyed Vali Reza Nasr, eds. *Shi'ism: Doctrines, Thought, and Spirituality*. Albany, NY: State University of New York Press, 1988, pp. 104–20.

Northedge, Alastair. 'Archaeology and Islam', in Graeme Barker, ed., *Companion Encyclopedia of Archaeology* (London & New York: Routledge, 1999), vol. 2, pp. 1077–107.

Pinto, Paul. 'Pilgrimage, commodities, and religious objectification: The making of a transnational Shiism between Iran and Syria', *Comparative Studies of South Asia, Africa, and the Middle East* 27 (2007), 109–25.

Pouzet, Louis. *Damas au VIIe–XIIIe siècle: vie et structures religieuses d'une métropole Islamique*. Beirut: Dar al-Machreq, 1988.

Powers, David S. *Muhammad is not the Father of Any of Your Men: The Making of the Last Prophet*. Philadelphia, PA: University of Pennsylvania Press, 2009.

Pringle, Denys. *The Churches of the Crusader Kingdom of Jerusalem, A Corpus*, 4 vols. Cambridge: Cambridge University Press, 2007.

Raghib, Yusuf. 'Les premiers monuments funéraires de l'Islam', *Annales Islamologiques* 9 (1970), 21–36.

——. 'Essai d'inventaire chronologique des guides à l'usage des pèlerins du Caire', *Revue des Études Islamiques* 41 (1973), 259–80.

Raymond, André. *Le Caire*. Paris: Fayard, 1993.

Raymond, André and J. L. Paillet. *Balis II: histoire de Balis et fouilles des îlots I et II*. Damascus: Institut français de Damas, 1995.

Reiner, Elchanan. 'A Jewish response to the Crusades. The dispute over sacred places in the Holy Land', in *Juden und Christen zur Zeit der Kreuzzüge*, ed. A. Haverkamp. Sigmaringen: Jan Thorbecke Verlag, 1999, pp. 202–31.

Renard, John. 'Khadir/Khidr', *Encyclopaedia of the Qur'an*, ed. Jane Dammen McAuliffe, Brill Online, http://referenceworks.brillonline.com.ezproxy.lib.utexas.edu/entries/encyclopaedia-of-the-quran/khadir-khidr-SIM_00248

Renfrew, Colin. *Archaeology of Cult: The Sanctuary at Phylakopi*. London: British School at Athens and Thames & Hudson, 1985.

Répertoire chronologique d'épigraphie arabe. Cairo: Publications de l'Institut français d'archéologie orientale du Caire, 1931–.

Rihawi, 'Abd al-Qadir. *Damascus: its History, Development, and Artistic Heritage*. Damascus: n.p., 1977.

Sack, Dorothée. *Damaskus: Entwicklung und Struktur einer orientalisch-islamischen Stadt*. Mainz am Rein: P. von Zabern, 1989.

Sadan, Joseph. 'Le tombeau de Moïse à Jéricho et à Damas. Une compétition entre deux lieux saints principalement à l'époque ottomane', *Revue des Études Islamiques* 49 (1981), 59–100.

Salles, George. Notice listed under 'Nouvelles Archéologiques: Les fouilles et recherches archéologiques en 1931, en Liban et Syrie', *Syria* 13 (1932), 112.

——. Notice listed under 'Les Missions archéologiques en Syrie en 1929', *Syria* 10 (1929), 370.

——. 'Les décors en stuc de Balis', in *IIIe congrès international d'art et d'archéologie iraniens: mémoires, Leningrad, septembre 1935*. Moscow & Leningrad: Académie des sciences de l'URSS, 1939, pp. 221–6 and plates 99–102.

Sarre, Friedrich. 'Makam Ali am Euphrat, ein islamisches Baudenkmal des X. Jahrhundertts. I. Baubeschreibung. II. Kunstwissenschafltiche Untgersuchung', *Jahrbuch der königlichen Preuszischen Kunstsammlungen* 29 (1908), 63–76.

Sarre, Friedrich and Ernst Herzfeld. *Archäologische Reise im Euphrat- und Tigris-gebiet*, 4 vols. Berlin: D. Reimer, 1911–20.

Sauvaget, Jean. 'Deux sanctuaires chiites d'Alep', *Syria* 9 (1928), 319–27.

——. 'Inventaire des monuments musulmans de la ville d'Alep', *Revue des Études Islamiques* 5 (1931), 59–114.

——. 'Esquisse d'une histoire de la ville de Damas,' *Revue des Études Islamiques* 8 (1934), 421–80.

——. 'Glanes épigraphiques,' *Revue des Études Islamiques*, 6 (1941–6), 17–29.

'Sayyida Zaynab', *Al-Mawsem* 25 (1996), special edition devoted entirely to the shrine.

Shams al-Din, Muhammad Mahdi. *The Revolution of al-Husayn [a]: Its Impact on the Consciousness of Muslim Society*, trans. I. K. A. Howard.

West Wimbledon: Muhammadi Trust of Great Britain and Northern Ireland, 1985. Online at www.al-islam.org/revolution/2.htm

Al-Shihabi, Kutayba. *Maʾadhin Dimashq: taʾrikh wa tiraz*. Damascus: Manshurat Wizarat al-Thaqafah fi al-Jumhuriyah al-ʿArabiyah al-Suriyah, 1993.

Sindawi, Khalid. 'The head of Husayn Ibn ʿAli from decapitation to burial, its various places of burial, and the miracles that it performed', *Journal of Ancient Near Eastern Studies* 40 (2003), 245–58.

——. 'Al-Husain Ibn ʿAli and Yahya Ibn Zakariyya in the Shiʿite sources: A comparative study', *Islamic Culture* 78 (2004), 37–54.

Sivan, Emanuel. 'Le caractère sacré de Jérusalem dans l'Islam aux XXIIe–XXIIIe siècles', *Studia Islamica* 27 (1967), 149–82.

Sobernheim, Moritz. 'Das Heiligtum Shaikh Muhassin in Aleppo', *Mélanges Hartwig Derenbourg (1844–1908)*. Paris: Ernest Leroux, 1909, pp. 379–90.

Sourdel, Dominique and Janine Sourdel-Thomine, 'Épitaphes coufiques de Bâb Saghîr', in Jean Sauvaget, *Les Monuments Ayyoubides de Damas*, 4 vols. Paris: E. de Boccard, 1938–48, pp. 147–67.

——. 'La date de construction du minaret de Bâlis', *Les Annales Archéologiques de Syrie* 3 (1953), 103–5.

——. 'Un sanctuaire chiite de l'ancienne Balis', in P. Salmon, ed., *Mélanges d'Islamologie*. Leiden: Brill, 1974, pp. 247–53.

Sourdel-Thomine, Janine. 'Balis', in P. J. Bearman, Th. Bianquis, C. E. Bosworth, E. van Donzel and W. P. Heinrichs, eds, *Encyclopaedia of Islam*, 2nd edition, 1960–2005. Brill Online, http://referenceworks.brillonline.com.ezproxy.lib.utexas.edu/entries/encyclopaedia-of-islam-2/balis-SIM_1147

——. 'Les anciens lieux de pèlerinage damascaines d'après les sources arabes', *Bulletin des Études Orientales* 14 (1952–4), 65–85.

Straughn, Ian. 'Materializing Islam: An archaeology of landscape in early Islamic period Syria'. Unpublished PhD dissertation, University of Chicago, 2006.

——. 'An aptitude for sacred space', in Cecelia Feldman Weiss and Claudia Moser, eds, *Locating the Sacred: Theoretical Approaches to the Emplacement of Religion*, Joukowsky Institute Press series, no. 3. Oxford: Oxbow Books, forthcoming 2014.

Stewart, Devin J., *Islamic Legal Orthodoxy: Twelver Shiʿi Responses to the Sunni Legal System*. Salt Lake City, UT: University of Utah Press, 1991.

——. 'Popular Shiʿism in medieval Egypt, vestiges of Islamic sectarian polemics in Egyptian Arabic', *Studia Islamica* 84 (1996), 35–66.

Tabbaa, Yasser. 'Monuments with a message: Propagation of Jihad under Nur al-Din', in V. Goss and C. Vézar-Bornstein, eds, *The Meeting of Two Worlds: Cultural Exchange between East and West during the Period of the Crusades*. Kalamazoo, MI: Medieval Institute Publications, Western Michigan University, 1986, pp. 223–40.

——. *Constructions of Power and Piety in Medieval Aleppo*. University Park, PA: Pennsylvania State University Press, 1997.

——. *The Transformation of Islamic Art During the Sunni Revival*. Seattle, WA & London: University of Washington Press, 2001.

——. 'Invented pieties: The rediscovery and rebuilding of the shrine of Sayyida Ruqayya in Damascus, 1975–2006', *Artibus Asiae: Studies in Honor of Priscilla Soucek* 66 (2006), 95–113.

Talmon-Heller, Daniella. *Islamic Piety in Medieval Syria: Mosques, Cemeteries and Sermons under the Zangids and Ayyubids (1146–1260).* Leiden: Brill, 2007.

——. 'Graves, relics and sanctuaries, the evolution of Syrian sacred topography', *ARAM Periodical* 19 (2007), 601–20.

Taragan, Hana. 'The tomb of Sayyidna ʿAli in Ar[sdotu]uf: The story of a holy place', *Journal of the Royal Asiatic Society* 14 (2004), 83–102.

Taylor, Christopher. 'Reevaluating the Shiʿi role in the development of monumental Islamic funerary architecture: The case of Egypt', *Muqarnas* 9 (1992), 1–10.

——. *In the Vicinity of the Righteous: Ziyara and the Veneration of Muslim Saints in Late Medieval Egypt.* Leiden: Brill, 1999.

Tezcan, Baki. 'Dispelling the darkness: The politics of "race" in the early seventeenth-century Ottoman Empire in the light of the life and work of Mullah Ali', in Baki Tezcan and Karl K. Barbir, eds, *Identity and Identity Formation in the Ottoman World: A Volume of Essays in Honor of Norman Itzkowitz.* Madison, WI: University of Wisconsin Press, 2007, pp. 73–95.

Töbelmann, Paul. 'Excommunication in the Middle Ages: A meta-ritual and the many faces of its efficacy', in William Sturman Sax, Johannes Quack and Jan Weinhold, eds, *The Problem of Ritual Efficacy.* Oxford: Oxford University Press, 2010, pp. 93–113.

Tonghini, Christina. 'Recent excavation at Qalʿat Jaʿbar: New data for classifying Syrian fritware', in K. Bartl, *Continuity and Change in Northern Mesopotamia.* Berlin: Dietrich Reimer, 1996.

Al-ʿUlabi, Akram Hasan. *Khitat Dimashq: dirasa tarikhiyya shamila ʿala mada alf ʿam, min sanat 400 H. -hatta sanat 1400 H.* Damascus: Dar al-Tabbaʿ, 1997.

Al-ʿUsh, Abuʾl Faraj. 'Les bois de l'ancien cénotaphe de Khalid ibn al-Walid à Hims', *Ars Orientalis* 5 (1963), 11–39.

Al-ʿUsh, Abuʾl Faraj, Adnan Joundi and Bachir Zouhdi, *Catalogue du musée national de Damas, publié à l'occasion de son cinquantenaire.* Damascus: Direction générale des antiquités et des musées, 1969.

Van Berchem, Max. 'Arabische Inschriften', in Friedrich Sarre and Ernst Herzfeld, *Archäologische Reise im Euphrat- und Tigrisgebiet,* 4 vols. Berlin: D. Reimer, 1911–20, vol. 1.

Weber, Stefan. *Damascus: Ottoman Modernity and Urban Transformation (1808–1918),* 2 vols. Aarhus: Aarhus University Press, 2009.

Wensinck, A. J. *The Muslim Creed: Its Genesis and Development.* London: Frank Cass, 1965 [1932].

Williams, Caroline. 'The cult of ʿAlid saints in the Fatimid mosques of Cairo. Part I: The Mosque of al-Aqmar', *Muqarnas* 1 (1983), 37–52.

——. *Islamic Monuments in Cairo.* Cairo & New York: American University in Cairo Press, 2002.

Wulzinger Karl and Carl Watzinger. *Damaskus: die islamische Stadt.* Berlin & Leipzig: W. de Gruyter, 1924.

——. *Damaskus, die antike stadt.* Berlin; Leipzig, W. De Gruyter, 1921.

Zimney, Michelle. 'History in the making: The Sayyida Zaynab shrine in Damascus', *ARAM Periodical* 19 (2007), 695–703.

Illustration Acknowledgements

Smithsonian Institution

Fig. 2.2 Aleppo, Mashhad al-Muhassin (Mashhad al-Dikka), plan. FSA A .6 05.0016. Aleppo: Mashhad al-Dikka: Ground Plan Displaying Various Architectural Periods and Locations of Arabic Inscriptions, 1908. Ink and pencil on paper: 51 x 50.5 cm. The Ernst Herzfeld papers. Freer Gallery of Art and Arthur M. Sackler Gallery Archives. Smithsonian Institution, Washington, D.C.

Fig. 2.5 Aleppo, Mashhad al-Muhassin, portal, elevation and section. FSA A.6 05.0026. Aleppo: Mashhad al-Dikka: Entrance Portal of lbn Tarira: Plan, Elevation and Section. 1908. Ink on paper: 55.5 x 39 cm. The Ernst Herzfeld papers. Freer Gallery of Art and Arthur M. Sackler Gallery Archives. Smithsonian Institution, Washington, D.C.

Fig. 2.14 Aleppo, Mashhad al-Husayn, plan. FSA A.6 05.0839. Aleppo: Mashhad al-Husayn: Ground Plan. 1908. Ink on paper: 67.8 cm x 100 cm. The Ernst Herzfeld papers. Freer Gallery of Art and Arthur M. Sackler Gallery Archives. Smithsonian Institution, Washington, D.C.

Fig. 2.18 Portal of al-Husayn, elevation and section drawing. FSA A.6 05.0001. Aleppo: Mashhad al-Husayn: Elevation of Portal. 1908. Ink and pencil on paper: 76 x 55.5cm. The Ernst Herzfeld papers. Freer Gallery of Art and Arthur M. Sackler Gallery Archives. Smithsonian Institution, Washington, D.C.

Fig. 2.26 View of the Caliph al-Nasir li-Din Allah's inscription on the gate of the *serdab* (cave) of the shrine of Imam al-Mahdi. FSA A.6 04.23.005. Excavation of Samarra: Shiite Shrine Complex: View of Caliph Al-Nasir li-Din Allah's Inscription in the Serdab of the Shrine of Imam Al-Mahdi. 1911. Collodion photographic print: 11.8 x 16.9 cm. The Ernst Herzfeld papers. Freer Gallery of Art and Arthur M. Sackler Gallery Archives. Smithsonian Institution, Washington, D.C.

Fig. 3.3 Herzfeld's drawing of the Ayyubid arch that once formed the entrance to the tomb of Bilal al-Habashi. FSA A .6 05.0192. Damascus: Maqbarat al-Bab al-Saghir (outside of Bab al-Hadid): Arch over Door and Architectural Ornaments. 1903. Ink on paper: 19.7 x 28 cm. The Ernst Herzfeld papers. Freer Gallery of Art and Arthur M. Sackler Gallery Archives. Smithsonian Institution, Washington, D.C.

Cresswell Archives

Fig. 2.10 Mashhad al-Muhassin, view east from under main dome of prayer hall. Creswell Archive, Ashmolean Museum, Oxford, neg. EA.CA.5718. Image courtesy of Fine Arts Library, Harvard College Library.

Fig. 2.11 Mashhad al-Muhassin, north wall of courtyard. Creswell Archive, Ashmolean Museum, Oxford, neg. EA.CA.5716. Image courtesy of Fine Arts Library, Harvard College Library.

Fig. 2.20 Mashhad al-Husayn, view into main portal. Creswell Archive, Ashmolean Museum, Oxford. Image courtesy of Fine Arts Library, Harvard College Library.

Moaz and Ory

Permission to reproduce figures 3.4, 3.5, 3.6, 3.7, 3.24, 3.43 3.44 and map 4, from Moaz, Khalid and Solange Ory. *Inscriptions arabes de Damas: les steles funéraires, I. Cimetière d'al-Bab al-Saghir.* Damascus: Institut français de Damas, 1977, was kindly authorised by Institut français du Proche-Orient

Fig. 3.4 Inscriptions for Ibn 'Aqil and al-Sharazuri in south-east corner of the mausoleum of Bilal al-Habashi.
Fig. 3.5 Inscription for al-Sharazuri.
Fig. 3.6 Mausoleum of Bilal al-Habashi, inscription at foot of his grave.
Fig. 3.7 Inscription on lintel of west-facing entrance to mausoleum of Bilal al-Habashi.
Fig. 3.24 East and south faces of stone sarcophagus in mausoleum of Fatima al-Sughra.
Fig. 3.43 Cenotaph, mausoleum of Aban ibn Ruqayya.
Fig. 3.44 Stela, mausoleum of Aban ibn Ruqayya.
Map 4 Damascus, plan of cemetery of Bab al-Saghir, showing locations of 'Alid shrines.

Index

Figures are indicated by page numbers in *italics*; 'n' following a page number indicates an endnote; 't' following a page number indicates a table.

Aban ibn Ruqayya bint Muhammad
  see Damascus: Bab
  al-Saghir cemetery,
  Mausoleum of Aban ibn
  Ruqayya bint Muhammad
'Abdallah ibn Umm Maktum,
  shrine to, 185n97
Abdülhamid II, Sultan, 89, 145, 146,
  150–1, 159, 161, 175, 176,
  235
al-'Abidin, 'Abdallah b. Zayn *see*
  Damascus: Bab al-Saghir
  cemetery, Mausoleum
  of 'Abdallah b. Zayn al-
  'Abidin
al-'Abidin, Zayn ('Ali b. al-Husayn),
  11, 155, 158, 217
shrine to *see* Damascus: Mashhad
  'Ali Zayn al-'Abidin/
  Mashhad al-Husayn
Abu Bakr, Caliph, 97
Abu Hurayra, 242n38
Abu Shama, 1, 182n60
Acre, 258, 259
al-'Adawi, Mahmud ibn
  Muhammad, 183n75, 226,
  234–5
al-'Adil Sayf al-Din, Sultan, 27, 28,
  100, 222
Afsaruddin, Asma, 142
'Aisha, 167, 207
Aleppo, 5, 10–11, 63–105
  Bab Antakya (Antioch Gate), 63
  cathedral, 74
  damage to (2012–), 267–8
  Jabal Jawshan, 63, 68, 82
  Mashhad al-Dikka *see* Mashhad
    al-Muhassin

Mashhad al-Husayn, 63, 64,
  269, 271; cenotaph, 80–1;
  Crusaders' pillaging of, 5;
  east façade, *83*; exterior
  courtyard, *85*; foundation
  story, 83, 85, 87, 232;
  inscriptions, 87, 90, 92,
  92, 93, 94, 95, *95*; interior
  courtyard, *88*; patronage,
  11, 87–9; pilgrims, 110n67;
  portal, *86*, 87, 89–90,
  91, *92*, *93*, *94*, 95–9, *95*,
  96; restoration, 110n67;
  stone relic, 224; as storage
  facility, 110n67
Mashhad al-Muhassin (Mashhad
  al-Dikka), 56, 58–9, 63,
  118; cenotaph, 80–1;
  cistern, 75; courtyard,
  77; Crusaders' pillaging
  of, 74; foundation story,
  72–3, 224; inscriptions,
  69, 73, 75, 76, 77, 78–80,
  78, 82; latrines, 75;
  Mongols' plundering of,
  80, 89; *muqarnas* dome,
  76; patronage, 11, 81–2;
  portal, *68*, 69, 71, 72, 75,
  269; prayer hall, 76, *78*;
  reservoir, 75; sanctuary,
  76, 77; tomb chamber, 70,
  75, 77
Mashhad 'Ali, 224
mosques, 74, 267–8
representations of, 4
siege of, 74
Shi'is in, 28, 66–8, 82,
  230

'Ali, *see* Ibn Abi Talib, 'Ali
'Alid identity, 2
Allen, Terry, 68, 75, 89, 108n33,
    109n49
al-Amin, Muhsin, 193
Antrim, Zayde, 4
archaeological investigation of
    shrines, 21–2
archaeology, Islamic, 249
architectural survey of shrines,
    261–2
al-Asghar, 'Ali, 183n76
Ash'aris, 139
al-Ashraf Barsabay, Sultan *see*
    Barsabay, Sultan
al-'Askari, Hasan, 103
Asma' bint Umays, mausoleum,
    167–71, *168, 170, 171*
'Asqalan, 257
al-Assad, Asma, 242n35
al-Assad, President Hafez, 193, 200
Assassins *see* Nizari Isma'ilis
Aswan, 136
authenticity of shrines, 2–3,
    229–30
Ayyubids, 6, 28, 220
al-'Aziz, Sultan, 78, 80, 82

Bacchus, St, 25, 26
al-Badri, 'Abdallah ibn Muhammad,
    130, 132, 233–4
Baghdad, 98, 103, 144–5
Balis, 9, 10
    archaeological investigation, 30–2
    Byzantines in, 25
    canal, 27
    city ruins, 22, *23*
    Crusaders in, 28
    Greeks in, 25
    Islamic era, 26–9
    mashhad, 18–22, *18, 20, 21,* 32–5,
        40; courtyard, 19, *20, 40,*
        46, 46, 47, 48–9; cistern,
        19, *46*–7, *46, 47,* 49, 52, 57;
        doorway, 49–50, *50, 51,* 52;
        oven, *48,* 52, 250; east-
        central room, *20, 21,* 42,
        43, 44, *46*; exterior wall,
        42; foundation walls, 51;
        graves, 50–1; hallway, *44,*
        51–2; identity of, 55–7, 58,
        272; latrines, 44, *45, 46,*
        50, 51; main entrance, 47,
        48, 49; modifications to,
        51–3; north-central room,
        49; north-east room, *40,*

        44–6, *45*; origins, 19–21;
        painted decoration, 53, *53*;
        pit feature, *49*; pottery,
        46–7, 57; prayer hall, 19,
        34, *34,* 39, 41, *43, 46, 47,*
        54; prayer niches, 19, 34,
        42, *43,* 45, 47, 53; stucco
        decorations, 19, 20, 54–5,
        54
Mashhad al-Hajar, 55, 56, 271
Mashhad al-Khidr, 35, 37–8, 54,
    55
Mashhad al-Tirh, 38, 39, 55
Mashhad 'Ali ibn Abi Talib, 12,
    25, 38, 55–6, 58, 207, 208,
    271
minaret, 28–9, *29,* 30
Ottoman fort, 29
Qasr (palace), 30–2, *31*
Romans in, 25
Sasanians in, 25
scholarship, 27
shrines, 38, 55–6
strategic importance, 22
trade, 26–7, 28
al-Balisi, Abu Bakr, 27
al-Balisi, Safi al-Din Tariq b. 'Ali b.
    Muhammad (Ibn Turayra),
    35, 58–9, 75, 87
al-Balkhi, Muhammad, 141, 143,
    145
Barsabay, Sultan, 217, 219, 220
Baybars, Sultan, 80, 141–3, 146,
    208–12, 217, 219, 220, 224,
    237
Benjamin of Tudela, 27
Berkey, Jonathan, 16n16
Bilad al-Sham, 3, 186, 230, 247, 252,
    257, 261, 262
Buriha bt. al-Husayn, 131

Cairo, 184n87, 257, 274n9
calligraphy, 36–7, 80
cartography, 264n2
cathedrals, 263
cemeteries 238, 270, 271; *see also*
    Damascus: Bab al-Faradis
    cemetery; Damascus: Bab
    al-Saghir cemetery
Chamberlain, Michael, 16n16
Christianity, 253–4, 254–5
Companions of the Prophet, 97,
    101, 114, 119, 251, 258
Crusades/Crusaders, 3, 4–5, 13, 28,
    74, 177, 259, 260
cuneiform tablets, 22, 59n1

damage to shrines (2012/13), 267–8
Damascus, 11
    Arab seige of (635–6), 114
    Bab al-Faradis (Paradise Gate),
        188
    Madrasa al-Mujahidiyya, 194,
        196, 197
    Bab al-Faradis cemetery
        (Cemetery of Dahdah), 188
    Bab al-Saghir cemetery, 11, 37,
        265n19, 269–70
    Bilal al-Habashi mausoleum,
        119, *120*; Ayyubid arch,
        120–1, *121*, 126, 129;
        cenotaph, 120, 121, *122*,
        123, *125*; inscriptions, 121,
        122, 123, *124*, 125–6, *126*,
        127, *127*, 128; patrons,
        127–9; restorations, 120,
        126, 128
    Ibn ʿAsakir's grave, 243n57
    location, 180n38
    Masjid Maqam Ruʾus al-
        Shuhadaʾ Karbalaʾ, 151–7,
        151, *152*, *153*; basalt basin,
        153, 155–6, *155*, *156*;
        courtyard, 154–5, *154*;
        inscriptions, 156–7, *157*;
        Ottoman mausoleum,
        152–3, 156–7, *157*;
        patronage, 161; stone
        upright, 153, 155, *155*;
        well, *154*, 155
    Mausoleum of Aban ibn
        Ruqayya bint Muhammad,
        162–7, *163*, *164*; cenotaph,
        165, *166*, 167; dome, 163,
        164, *165*; inscriptions, *164*,
        165, *165*, *166*, 167; interior
        decoration, 163; patronage,
        167; renovations, 167;
        stela, 165, *166*
    Mausoleum of ʿAbdallah b.
        Zayn al-ʿAbidin, 157–62,
        158, *159*; dome 159, *160*;
        inscriptions, *158*, 160, *161*;
        palm tree motif, 159, *161*
    Mausoleum of ʿAbdallah ibn
        Jaʿfar al-Sadiq, 171–3, *172*,
        173
    Mausoleum of Asmaʾ,
        Maymuna and Hamida,
        167–71, *168*; cenotaph,
        168, *169*; inscriptions, 168,
        171–2, *172*, *173*; patronage,
        168

Mausoleum of Fatima al-
    Sughra, 146–51, *147*,
    148; cenotaph, 146,
    148; crypt, 148–9, *148*;
    inscriptions, 149–51;
    patronage, 150–1, 161;
    provenance, 162; stone
    sarcophagus, 148–50, *149*
Mausoleum of Sayyida
    Fidda, 174–6, *174*,
    175; inscription,
    175–6, *176*; patronage,
    175–6; stone upright, 175,
    176
Mausoleum of Sukayna bt.
    al-Husayn, 129, 130, *130*,
    131, 145, 177; cenotaph,
    37, 130, 133, 134, *134*, 136,
    137, *137*, 141; crypt, 133,
    134, 135–6; inscriptions,
    37, 137–41; patronage, 141,
    146, 161, 224; provenance,
    162
Mausoleum of the
    Qalandariyya, 130, 131,
    132, *132*, 142, *143*, 144,
    210; inscriptions, 141,
    142; patronage, 142–3, 145,
    146
Mausoleum of Umm Kulthum,
    129, 130–2, *130*, *131*, 136,
    145; cenotaph, 134, 145–6;
    crypt, 133, *134*, 135–6, *135*;
    patronage, 117, 127–9, 145,
    177; shrine to ʿAbdallah ibn
    Umm Maktum, 185n97;
    textual/architectural
    evidence, 117–18; tomb of
    Caliph ʿUmar b. ʿAbd al-
    ʿAziz, 136
Bab al-Saghir gate, 114
Bab Jayrun, 201, 208, *211*, 213–14,
    221; mosque, 212; shrine of
    Malika, 1–2
Buyid relics, 241n19
Cemetery of Dahdah *see*
    Damascus: Bab al-
    Faradis
city walls, 114
damage to (2012/13), 267
Dar al-Hadith al-ʿUrwiyya *see*
    Damascus, Umayyad
    Mosque: Mashhad ʿAli ibn
    Abi Talib
Hammam Nur al-Din, 221
Khan Asʿad Pasha portal, 221

Madrasa al-Atabakiyya, 129
Madrasa al-Jaqmaqiyya (now
    Museum of Arabic
    Calligraphy), 201
Madrasa al-Mujahidiyya, 194
Maristan (hospital) al-Qaymari,
    129
Mashhad al-Naranj (Shrine of the
    Orange [Grove]), 221–2
Mashhad al-Qadam (Masjid al-
    Aqdam), 224
Mashhad Ra's al-Husayn, 193,
    195–7, 257
Mashhad Sayyida Ruqayya bt.
    al-Husayn, 12, 186, 188,
    189–93, 196–7, 198–201;
    arch, 197; authenticity of,
    237; courtyard, 189–90;
    dome, 189, 191, 192;
    portal, 190, 191; tomb
    enclosure, 192; western
    wall, 190; mosques, 193–5,
    197–200
mosques: Mashhad Ra's, 193,
    Bab al-Faradis, 193–4;
    Mausoleum of the
    Qalandariyya, 141, 142;
    Jami' al-Musalla, 222, 226;
    Mashhad al-Naranj (Shrine
    of the Orange [Grove]),
    221–2; Masjid Khan al-Sabil
    (Maydan al-Hasa), 225–6;
    Umayyad mosque, 185n98,
    217, 219, 220, 223
National Museum: stucco
    panels, 32–3, 32, 33–7, 38,
    54; inscriptions, 32, 35–7,
    38
representations of, 4
    Mashhad al-Husayn/
    Mashhad 'Ali b. al-Husayn
    (Imam Zayn al-'Abidin),
    12, 203, 204, 205, 212, 214,
    221, 232, 257; courtyard,
    201, 202; dome, 206, 210,
    212, 213; inscriptions,
    203; patronage, 220; as a
    pilgrimage site, 215–16;
    portico, 201; prayer halls,
    202, 203, 204; restoration,
    208–10, 219; Roman
    propylaeum, 210; shrine
    entrance, 203; tomb
    enclosure, 206
    Mashhad 'Ali ibn Abi Talib,
    215, 216–17, 218t

Mashhad 'Umar ibn al-
    Khattab, 211, 217, 218t,
    219–20
Shrine of the Head of John
    the Baptist, 213, 218t, 219,
    242n40, 257
Umayyad mosque, 185n98,
    201, 212, 212, 213–14, 217,
    263–4; water clock, 210,
    214
al-Dawla Aq Sunqur, Qasim, 74
de Lorey, Eustache see Lorey,
    Eustache de
al-Din, Jawhar Muhammad Burhan,
    Sultan, 157
dreams, 68, 70, 121, 224–5, 259
Druze, 65

Eddé, Anne-Marie, 268
Egypt, 16n16; see also Aswan; Cairo
Emar, 22, 25, 25
Enlart, Camille: Les Monuments
    des croisés dans le
    royaume de Jérusalem, 260
Euphrates river, 10, 22, 26, 28, 256

Farhat, Mary, 17n20
Fatima al-Kubra, 73, 141
Fatima bt. al-Husayn ('al-Sughra'),
    mausoleum see Damascus:
    Bab al-Saghir cemetery,
    Mausoleum of Fatima al-
    Sughra
Fatimids, 5, 177; see also Isma'ilis
Franks, 28
futuwwa, 99–100, 103–4

al-Ghazali, 139
ghulāt, 6
Ghurabiyyah, 65
Glassen, Erika, 16n16
Golvin, Lucien, 30
graves, 19, 50–1; see also cemeteries
Greeks, 253

al-Habashi, Bilal see Damascus: Bab
    al-Saghir cemetery, Bilal
    al-Habashi mausoleum
al-Hadi, 'Ali, tomb of, 103
hadith, 27
Hafsa, shrine to, 167
Hagen, Gottfried, 184n87
al-Hakim, Caliph, 65
al-Halabi, Ab'ul-Makarim Hamza
    ibn 'Ali (Ibn Zuhra) see Ibn
    Zuhra

Hamdanids, 27, 66
Hamida bint Muslim ibn ʿAqil *see*
    Damascus: Bab al-Saghir
    cemetery, Mausoleum
    of Asmaʿ, Maymuna and
    Hamida
al-Harawi, ʿAli Ibn Abi Bakr, 7,
    38–9, 55, 102, 130, 152,
    175, 195, 207, 219, 222,
    225, 230, 241n19, 258–9
Hasan III of Alamut, 101–2
Herzfeld, Ernst, 28, 68, 75, 92, 95,
    96, 126, 129
  'Damascus: Studies in
    Architecture – III', 120–1
Hillenbrand, Robert, 181n53, 271
Holy Land
  boundaries of, 260, 261
  Christian sites in, 13, 254
  Syria as, 4, 177, 230
  see also sacred landscape
Hülegü (Mongol leader), 195
Humphreys, Stephen, 263
al-Husayn
  death of, 7, 117, 255
  head of, 183n76, 196–7, 200, 204,
    207, 213, 224, 255–7, 269;
  and light, 81
  memorialisation of martyrdom,
    178n4
  sacred landscape of, 56, 87, 117,
    151–2, 196–7, 254, 255–7,
    269
  shrines to: Aleppo, 5, 11, 63, 64,
    68, 70, 82–3, *83*, *84*, 85, *85*,
    86, 87–9, *88*, 89–90, *91*, 92,
    92, *93*, *94*, 95–9, *95*, *96*,
    110n67, 224, 232, 269, 271;
    ʿAsqalan, 257; Balis, 38, 55;
    Cairo, 257; Damascus, 11,
    12, 201, *202*, 203, *203*, *204*,
    205, *206*, 208–10, *212*, *213*,
    214, 215–16, 219, 220, 221,
    232, 257

Ibn Abi Talib, ʿAli, shrines to
  Acre, 259
  Aleppo, 63
  Balis, 55–6, 58, 271
  Damascus, 12, 38, 186, 207, 215,
    221–6, 237
Ibn Abi Tayyiʾ, 67, 72, 73, 107n25
Ibn al-ʿAdim, Kamal al-Din ʿUmar,
    28, 29, 67, 70–1, 74, 75, 82,
    258
Ibn al-Athir, Diyaʾ al-Din, 100

Ibn al-Faqih, 261
Ibn al-Hawrani, ʿUthman ibn
    Ahmad, 126–7, 132, 178n8,
    198–9, 200, 234
  quoted, 267
Ibn al-Jawzi, Shaykh (Shams al-Din
    Sibt Ibn al-Jawzi,) 15n11,
    215–16
Ibn al-Khashshab, Abu al Fadl, 74,
    89, 101, 111, 111n75
Ibn al-Mibrad, Yusuf ibn Hasan,
    130, 132, 197, 199, 215,
    217, 233
Ibn al-Rajjaj, al-Safi Abu Saʿd, 55,
    56–7, 58
Ibn al-Walid, Khalid, tomb of, 80
Ibn ʿAli, Qahir, 108n39
Ibn ʿAli, Wali al-Din Abu al-Qasim,
    75
Ibn ʿAqil (Diyaʾ al-Din Abi al-Hasan
    ʿAli b. ʿAqil b. ʿAli b. Hibat
    Allah al-Shafiʿi), 125, 167,
    274n9
Ibn ʿAsakir, ʿAli ibn al-Hasan, 27,
    121, 129, 130–1, 133, 152,
    178n9, 194–5, 197, 203,
    207, 225, 229, 261
  grave of, 243n57
  quoted, 247
Ibn Battuta, 81, 215, 233
Ibn Haritha, Zayd, 140
Ibn Jubayr, Muhammad ibn Ahmad,
    65, 102–3, 130, 207–8, 217,
    219, 222–3, 230–2
Ibn Kathir, ʿImad al-Din, 216
Ibn Shaddad, Ibrahim, 87
Ibn Shaddad, Muhammad ibn ʿAli,
    28, 55–6, 68, 70, 72–3,
    75, 78, 80, 87, 88, 195,
    197, 208–9, 217, 225, 232,
    241n19, 261
Ibn Shahin al-Zahiri, Gars al-Din
    Khalil, 175, 197, 215
Ibn Shahrashub, Muhammad ibn
    ʿAli, 67
Ibn Shahrashub, Rashid al-Din,
    109n62
Ibn Shakir al-Kutubi, Muhammad,
    114, 196, 197, 212–13, 232
Ibn Shaqwayq, Abu Ghanaʾm, 87
Ibn Taymiyya, 81, 257
Ibn Tulun, Muhammad, 1–2
Ibn Turayra *see* al-Balisi, Safi al-Din
    Tariq b. ʿAli b. Muhammad
    (Ibn Turayra)
Ibn Tutush, Ridwan, 66

Ibn 'Urwa al-Mawsali, Sharaf al-Din
    Muhammad, mausoleum
    of, 216–17, 218t, 219
Ibn Zuhra 67
identity of shrines, 133, 270–1
Imams 81, 97, 139, 161
    tombs of (Samarra), 104
Institut Français d'Études Arabes de
    Damas, 30
Iran, 178n9
Iraq, 136, 227; see also Baghdad;
    Mosul
Isma'ilis, 65, 98, 101–2

al-Jawshan, Shimr b. Dhi, 255
Jerusalem, 4, 260
Jesus, 263–4
Jews, 27
John the Baptist, 256–7
    shrine to, 213, 218t, 219, 242n40,
    257
Joscelin I, Count of Edessa 74
Judaism, 253, 254–5
Justinian, emperor, 25

al-Kamil al-Ayyubi, Sultan, 193,
    195, 198, 199
Karbala', Battle of (680), 7, 11, 223,
    232, 255
Karbala' martyrs, 151–2, 155, 156–7,
    181n51
al-Khidr, 35–6
    Mashhad al-Khidr, Balis, 35, 37–8,
    54, 55
Khoury, Nuha 81
Koran see Qur'an
Korn, Lorenz, 108n44
Kufa, 255
al-Kurdi, Barzan ibn Yamin, Amir,
    194
al-Kurdu, Mujahid al-Din, 194

Lake Assad, 10, 30, 33, 33
landscape
    Islamic notion, of 247, 248
    Romans and, 114, 253
    sacred, 13, 253–5, 260–1, 263–4;
    see also Holy Land
Leiser, Gary, 16n16
Leisten, Thomas, 9, 10, 17n19, 39
light: iconography/imagery of, 81,
    139–40
Lineberry, David, 39
literature of shrines, 261
Lorey, Eustache de, 30, 34–5, 54,
    55

Madelung, Wilferd, 107n31
madrasas, 129, 194, 196, 197, 201,
    271
al-Mahdi, Muhammad 35–6
    shrine to, 104
    tomb of, 103
Malika, shrine to, 1–2
Mamluks, 29, 80, 220, 266n31
mapping, 248
al-Maqdisi, 65
Marwanids, 27
Mashhad (Iran): shrine of Imam 'Ali
    b. Musa al-Rida, 145
Maslama Ibn 'Abd al-Malik, 26
Massouh, Jamil, 39
al-Mawsali, Abu Bakr, Shaykh, 233,
    244
Maymuna bint al-Husayn see
    Damascus: Bab al-Saghir
    cemetery, Mausoleum
    of Asma', Maymuna and
    Hamida
al-Mazandarani, Muhammad ibn
    'Ali al-Sarawi see Ibn
    Shahrashub, Muhammad
    ibn 'Ali
Mecca: Ka'ba, 224, 225
Meri, Joseph 16n15, 107n31, 177
mihrab images, 81
miracles, 14n1, 68, 70, 85, 102, 232,
    233, 234–5, 247, 248, 254,
    258–9, 263, 265, 267
Mirdasids, 27–8, 66
Miscarried Foetus, shrines to see
    Aleppo: Mashhad al-
    Muhassin; Balis: Mashhad
    al-Tirh;
    Mosul: Mashhad al-Muhassin
Moaz, Khalid, 121, 132–3, 154,
    183n71, 185n96
Mongols, 29, 57, 80, 89
Moses, 224
Mosul: Mashhad al-Muhassin,
    107n31
Mottahedeh, Roy, 272
Muhammad, Prophet
    Companions of, 97, 101, 114,
    119
    destruction of Masjid al-Dirar,
    1
    family, 7–8, 37, 38, 140–1
    footprint, 199, 200, 224
    mission, 37
    role, 139, 140
Muhammad b. Ahmad b. 'Abd
    Allah, 138

al-Muhassin, shrines to *see* Aleppo:
Mashhad al-Muhassin;
Balis: Mashhad al-Tirh;
Mosul: Mashhad al-
Muhassin
Mulder, Stephennie, 16n16
al-Muqaddasi, Muhammad ibn
Ahmad, 27
muqarnas, 269, 271
Aleppo, 68, *71*, *73*, *75*, *76*, *76*, 82,
83, *90*, *92*, *93*, *94*, *95*, *96*,
96, 269
Balis, *50*, *59*
Damascus, 221
Iraq, 136
al-Murtada, 'Izz al-Din, 101
Murtada, Muhammad Rida,
228–9
Murtada, Muhammad Salim Ibn
Rida, 157, 160, 162
Murtada, Muhsin 'Abbas,
228–9
Murtada, Selim Effendi ibn al-
Sayyid Husayn, 145, 157,
160,161, 176
Murtada,Wa'el Salim, 145, 184n81
Musa, Sayyid, 235
al-Musawi, Sayyid Husayn Ibn
Shaykh al-Islam al-Sayyid
Musa, 232–3
Mu'tazila, 139

al-Naji, Burhan al-Din, 233
Nasir-i Khusrau, 64–5
al-Nasir li-Din Allah, Caliph, 11,
98–104
grave of, 103
al-Nasir Yusuf, 76, 80, 129
Nisibin, 256
Nizari Isma'lis (Assassins), 101–2
Northedge, Alistair, 249
al-Nu'aymi, 'Abd al-Qadir ibn
Muhammad, 130, 132, 141,
152, 197–8, 215
Nur al-Din, 11, 66–7, 75, 96, 230
Nusayris, 65

O'Kane, Bernard, 184n87
Ory, Solange, 121, 132–3, 154,
183n71, 185n96
Osman Agha *see* 'Uthman (Osman)
Agha

patronage, 2, 5, 6, 7, 8, 10, 11, 21,
35, 53, 56–7, 58, 104–5,
261–2, 269

Abdülhamid II, Sultan, 89, 145,
146, 150–1, 159, 161, 162,
175, 176, 235
Aleppo, 63, 64, 75; Mashhad al-
Husayn, 87, 87–9; Mashhad
al-Muhassin, 81–2
Damascus
Bab al-Faradis (Cemetery of
Paradise), Mashhad Ra's
al-Husayn, 200
Bab al-Saghir cemetery,
117, 127–9, 145, 177;
Mausoleum of Asma',
Maymuna and Hamida,
168; Mausoleum of
Fatima al-Sughra, 150–1;
Mausoleum of Sayyida
Fidda, 175–6; Mausoleum
of Sukayna bt. al-Husayn,
141, 224; Mausoleum of
the Qalandariyya, 142–3,
145; Umayyad mosque,
217, 219, 220, 223
al-Nasir li-Din Allah, Caliph,
98–9, 103
Rawiya, Mashhad Sayyida Zaynab
bt. 'Ali, 230, 232–3, 235
Sunnis, 74
al-Zahir, Sultan, 68, 98–9
pilgrims/pilgrimage, 102, 110n67,
125, 178n9
Damascus: Bilal al-Habashi
mausoleum, 128; Mashhad
'Ali b. al-Husayn (Imam
Zayn al-'Abidin), 215–16,
217; Mashhad Sayyida
Ruqayya bt. al-Husayn/
Mashhad Ra's al-Husayn,
188, 189–91, 198–9;
Shahrazuri's grave, 121
Mecca, 224
Rawiya: Mashhad Sayyida
Zaynab bt. 'Ali (or al-
Husayn), 227
Shi'is, 117
veneration of shrines, 6–7
visitation of shrines, 3, 7, 21, 52,
53, 234–5, 237, 248
porcelain, Chinese, 27
Pouzet, Louis, 141, 178n7, 268
Princeton University: Balis
excavation, 30, 33, 39, 54,
55, 271
Pringle, Denis: *The Churches of
the Crusader Kingdom of
Jerusalem, A Corpus*, 260

Qabr al-Sitt *see* Rawiya
Qalandariyya
    fraternity of, 141
    Mausoleum *see* Damascus:
        Bab al-Saghir cemetery,
        Mausoleum of the
        Qalandariyya
Qalʿat Jaʿbar, 59n8
Qaytbay, al-Ashraf, Sultan, 1
Qurʾan, 36–7, 38, 137–41, 165,
    172
Quwayq river, 63

al-Rabaʾi, ʿAli ibn Muhammad, 123,
    130, 261
Rawiya (Qabr al-Sitt)
    Mashhad ʿAli/Mashhad al-Naranj,
        186, 222–6, 237
    Mashhad Sayyida Zaynab bt. ʿAli
        (or al-Husayn), 12, 186,
        220, 227–35, *228*, 236;
        authenticity of, 229–30,
        233–5; damage to (2012/13),
        267; foundation legend,
        229, 232; patronage, 230,
        232–3, 235; renovations,
        227, 228–9
Raymond, André, 28, 30
rebuilding of shrines, 8–9
'rediscovery' of shrines, 1, 4, 5
re-imagining of shrines, 237
relics
    Bacchus, 25
    Buyid, 241n19
    Damascus, Bab al-Faradis, 197
    martyrs', 257
    Mashhad ʿAli, 56
    rediscovery of, 263
    and ritual, 250
    shrines and, 271
    transfer of, 260
        stone, 224–5
Renan, Ernest, 254
restoration of shrines, 186–7, 237
al-Rida, ʿAli b. Musa, shrine to, 145
rituals, 13, 249–50, 263, 264
Romans: and landscape, 114, 253
Rome, 253
Ruqayya bt. al-Husayn, 162
    shrine to, Damascus: 12, 186,
        188, 189–93, *189, 190, 191,
        192*, 196–7, 198–201

Sack, Dorothée, 239n9
sacred history, Islamic, 13, 247, 250,
    254–7, 258
sacred landscape, 2, 13, 20, 57, 103,
    105, 195, 248, 250, 251–5,
    260–1, 263–4
    of al-Husayn, 56, 87, 117,
        151–2, 196–7, 254, 255–7,
        269
    Greek, 253
    Roman, 114, 253
    see also Holy Land
al-Sadiq, ʿAbdallah ibn Jaʿfar,
    mausoleum, 171–3, *173*
al-Sadiq, Jaʿfar, 119
Safiye (mother of Mehmed III),
    127
saints, 2, 16n15
Salah al-Din (Saladin), Sultan, 6, 11,
    87–8, 101, 274n9
al-Salih Ismaʿilis, 67
Salles, Georges, 30, 32, 34–5, 37, 38,
    54, 55
Samarra: Ghaybat al-Mahdi, 103,
    104
El-Sandouby, Aliaa, 16n15
Sarre, Friedrich, 28
Sauvaget, Jean, 68, 80, 110n67,
    111n78
Sayf al-Dawla, 27, 68, 73, 81–2
Sayyida Fidda: mausoleum *see*
    Damascus: Bab al-Saghir
    cemetery, Mausoleum of
    Sayyida Fidda
Sayyida Nafisa, 229
Sayyida Sukayna *see* Damascus:
    Bab al-Saghir cemetery,
    Mausoleum of Sukayna bt.
    al-Husayn
Sayyida Zaynab bt. ʿAli (or al-
    Husayn), shrines to *see*
    Rawiya: Mashhad Sayyida
    Zaynab bt. ʿAli (or al-
    Husayn)
sectarian architecture, 14
sectarianism, 1–2, 3, 268
Seljuks, 3, 6, 66
Sergius, St, 25, 26
Seven Sleepers, 155
al-Shafiʿi, Diyaʾ al-Din Abi al-Hasan
    ʿAli b. ʿAqil b. ʿAli b. Hibat
    Allah (Ibn ʿAqil) *see* Ibn
    ʿAqil
al-Shahrazuri, Muhammad b. ʿAqil
    b. Zayd, 121, 123
al-Sham *see* Bilad al-Sham
Shams al-Din Sibt Ibn al-Jawzi,
    Shaykh *see* Ibn al-Jawzi,
    Shaykh

Shi'is
    Aleppo, 28, 64–5, 66–8
    Balis, 27, 28, 35, 36, 58
    Damascus, 114, 117, 129, 141
    dynasties 66
    flagellants, 202
    identity, 7, 8
    Imami *see* Shi'is, Twelver
    patronage, 58, 177, 220
    Qur'anic interpretation, 139
    sects, 65
    shrine practice, 6, 7, 187–8
    sources for study of, 268–9
    Sufism, conciliation with, 63,
        98–9, 100–2, 142–3
    Sunnis, conflict with, 1–2, 67, 95,
        97, 177
    Twelver, 5, 65, 101
    visitation of shrines, 245n98
    see also Hamdanids; Marwanids;
        Mirdasids; 'Uqaylids
Shuhada' *see* Karbala' martyrs
Sidi Ghawth, 63
Smith, J. Z., 248
social history, Islamic, 272–3
Sourdel, Dominique, 35
Sourdel-Thomine, Janine, 35, 130,
    239n9
Stewart, Devin, J., 97
stones as relics, 224–5
Subki family, 149–50
al-Subki, Taj al-Din, 27, 150
Sufism
    growth/spread of, 5
    and Shi'ism, 142–3
    and Sunnism, 144
al-Suhrawardi, Abu Hafs 'Umar,
    Shaykh, 100
al-Suhrawardi, Shihab al-Din Yahya,
    101
Sukayna bt. al-Husayn *see*
        Damascus: Bab al-Saghir
        cemetery, Mausoleum of
        Sukayna bt. al-Husayn
Sulayman Pasha, 128
Summaqiya, 'Ali, 110n67
Sunnis
    Aleppo, 74
    Damascus, 65, 129
    patronage, 58, 145–6, 177, 220
    religious practice, 6–7, 8
    and Shi'is: conciliation with, 63,
        98–9, 100–2; conflict with,
        1–2, 67, 95, 97, 177
    and Sufism, 142
    and visitation, 245n98

Sunni Revival, 3, 5–6, 11, 28, 54,
    74, 82, 146, 177, 251, 263,
    273
Syria
    conflict (2012–), 268
    as a holy land, 4; *see also* sacred
        landscape
    Islamic conception of (Bilad al-
        Sham), 3, 186, 230, 247,
        252, 257, 261, 262
Syrian Antiquities Authority, 30

al-Tabari, 140
Tabbaa, Yasser, 83, 87, 96–7,
    107n27, 110n67, 184n87,
    200
Tabqa dam, 22, 30
Talas, Muhammad As'ad, 150, 155,
    179n11, 179n22, 180n32,
    199, 200
Talmon-Heller, Daniella, 16n15,
    263
Tamerlane, 217
Taylor, Christopher, 16n15
al-Tayyar, Abdallah b. Ja'far, 119,
    120, 121, 125
textiles, 223–4
textual sources, 272–3
Tigris river, 256
topography *see* Holy Land; sacred
    landscape

al-'Ulabi, Akram, 193
ulamology, 272
'Umar b. 'Abd al-'Aziz, Caliph,
    tomb of, 136
'Umar ibn al-Khattab, Caliph, 97,
    225
    mosque of, 215
    shrine to, 208–9, 218t, 219, 220
Umayyads, 31
Umm Ayman, shrine to, 234
Umm Habiba, shrine to, 185n97
Umm Kulthum (daughter of 'Ali b.
        Abi Talib; also known as
        Zaynab al-Sughra)
    confusion about name 229–30,
        231
        shrines: Damascus, Bab al-
            Saghir cemetery, 129,
            130–1, *130, 131, 132, 133;*
            Rawiya (Qabr al-Sitt),
            Mashhad Sayyida Zaynab
            bt. 'Ali (or al-Husayn), 12,
            186, 220, 227–35, *228, 236;*
            267

Umm Salama, shrine to, 185n97
ʿUqaylids, 27, 66
ʿUthman, Caliph, 97
ʿUthman (Osman) Agha, 127–8, 129

veneration of shrines, 6–7
Vergil, 253
visions see dreams
visitation of shrines, 3, 7, 21, 52, 53, 234–5, 237, 248

Xenophon, 25

al-Yaʿqubi, 28
Yaqut, 28
Yazid ibn Abi Sufyan, Caliph, 114, 117, 255
Yenisehirlioglu, Feliz, 184n87

al-Zahir Baybars al-Salihi, Sultan, see Baybars, Sultan
al-Zahir Ghazi, Sultan, 11, 68, 75–6, 88–9, 97, 98–9, 100, 101
Zangi, 75
Zangids, 6, 28, 220
Zaydis, 65
Zaynab al-Sughra, 132
Zaynab bt. ʿAli (or al-Husayn), 132, 231
    shrines to see Damascus: Bab al-Saghir cemetery, Mausoleum of Sukayna bt. al-Husayn; Rawiya: Mashhad Sayyida Zaynab bt. ʿAli (or al-Husayn)
Zaynab bt. Zayn al-ʿAbidin, 132–3, 141